James M. Peebles

Seers of the Ages

Embracing spiritualism, past and present: doctrines stated and moral tendencies

defined

James M. Peebles

Seers of the Ages

Embracing spiritualism, past and present: doctrines stated and moral tendencies defined

ISBN/EAN: 9783337427771

Printed in Europe, USA, Canada, Australia, Japan

Cover: Foto ©Lupo / pixelio.de

More available books at **www.hansebooks.com**

SEERS OF THE AGES:

EMBRACING

SPIRITUALISM,

PAST AND PRESENT.

DOCTRINES STATED AND MORAL TENDENCIES DEFINED.

By J. M. PEEBLES.

> I have stolen the golden keys of the Egyptians; I will indulge my sacred fury.—KEPLER.
>
> Old and new make the warp and woof of every moment. The highest statement of new philosophy complacently caps itself with some prophetic maxim from the oldest learning. There is something mortifying in this perpetual circle.—EMERSON.
>
> Master mind and you master the universe.—PERASEE LENDANTA.
>
> It doth not yet appear what we shall be.—APOSTLE JOHN.

SECOND EDITION.

BOSTON:
WILLIAM WHITE AND COMPANY,
BANNER OF LIGHT OFFICE,
158 Washington Street.
NEW-YORK AGENTS—THE AMERICAN NEWS COMPANY,
119 NASSAU STREET.
1869.

Greeting

TO THE

Pure Spirit of Aaron Nite.

Love is immortal. Golden is the chain that unites the past with the present. More beautiful is the spirit-blossom for the sweet love-budding of earth. Precious in spirit-history is Yorkshire, England—not so much for thy noble descent and clerical culture, as for thy happy home there, whose first memories of incarnate life, maternally pure, cling to thy soul as lingering melodies from inspired minstrels. Passing early through the pale-curtained doorway of death, to thy "Pear Grove Cottage," in the upper kingdoms of immortality, rapid and rythmic has been thy march of progress.

Though gathering pearls of knowledge from the risen seers of India, Syria and Greece, storing thy receptive nature with those heavenly truths and divine experiences that abound so full and free for all in the ever-green gardens of the Infinite—thou hast not forgotten thy mortal brothers and sisters, who feel their way in comparative darkness, and, like children, continually cry for light and wise spirit guidance.

Oft as hearts have ached, tears fallen, or martyred feet, on missions of mercy, have crimsoned the soil, thou hast turned thy calm presence earthward, laden with balms, baptisms and benedictions.

To me hast thou come in lone evening hours, bringing the dewy freshness of a foreshadowed morning, pearling the veiled moments of despair, diffusing inner sunshine and gladness; in wintry seasons of discontent, scattering delicious blooms, laden with love's incense, and speaking words of tenderness starry with promise—words so aglow with heavenly instruction as to make music in the blissful homes of the glorified. How oft hast thou come with "Celestia," "Morning Star" and "Queen of Morn"—Sisters of Purity—who prelude thy philosophy with the harmonizing melodies of the harp, the lute and the lyre! How indebted am I to thee for thy symbolic illustrations, logical acumen, originality of thought, and messages warm with sympathy from an overflowing heart!

Spirit Brother! as a feeble token of appreciation and soul-felt gratitude, for thy watch-care and many favors, permit me to dedicate this volume to thee, as one of my immortal Teachers.

J. M. PEEBLES.

The Horoscope.

O soul, O hungering, thirsting soul! for thee the fountains of the great deep are breaking up, and sweet life-waves, long obscured in the *debris* of ages, are flowing love at thy feet, "Whosoever will, let him take of the waters of life freely."

Truth is immortal, and long after the lips that spoke it have mingled their dust with the Lethean stream, traceable afterwards by the freed spirit, it echoes through the arches of heaven, the choral base of angel song that celebrates the eras of progress. What, then, cares "Brother James," for praise or blame, approbation or censure? "I testify of myself!" is the language that speaks from his heart, beating along the sun-mantled shores of time "to seek and to save that which was lost."

This brother has subpœnaed me, under solemn oath, to write this preface—actually ordered it as a "Thus saith Perasee Lendanta!" "Well," I said, "tell Perasee, the Italian prince of gods, so majestically calm and commanding, that neither he nor you shall change "one jot or tittle" of my testimony; nor shall either of you know what is written about you and your work, until the same is stereotyped. This proviso being very meekly accepted, I would like your eyes, dear reader, for a deep insight into the ocean mind of "St. James." Earnest, determined, full of innocent sarcasm which no man can tame; toned to sympathy, sparkling with wit and lofty thought; beloved throughout America; himself impressed upon the present age; a confiding companion of his loving brother, John, the disciple of Jesus, it is not too much to prophesy, that his book, here offered the world, will be as a sun in myriad homes on the Western and Eastern continents. Let me snatch from oblivion one of his manuscripts, indexing the man himself, bringing us nearer his soul, so buoyant and free, so childlike and parental:

"Pythagoras lives in sacred memory, as well as in Jamblichus' classic prose. Jesus lives, though the mould is deep over the gardens and olive groves that once felt the pressure of his bleeding feet. Demosthenes lives in that oration upon the crown. Mozart lives in those undying melodies that inspired with diviner ideals the courtly and the sceptered of Europe. The dewdrop writes its history on the plant; the stream its on the mountain side; the fossil its in the rock; the flower its on the passing breeze; you, *yours*, dear reader, on the sensorial faculties and future organisms of a world-wide brotherhood, and you will live, too, on earth forever in the forces you put in motion, the work you accomplish, the *good* you do. I shall live when this parchment will have been smothered under the rubbish of such viewless waste-winds as swept over those fearful midnights that gloomed in darkness the mediæval ages. Inspiration over-swept and over-arched all the past generations. There were paradises lost and gained, scores of centuries since; and, during their growth, or decline, Spiritualism, in some form, was a star of promise in their midst. It is to-day a light, a voice, a power from heaven—a divine power acknowledged by millions, rolling the "stone" of doubt away from the door of a long entombed humanity. It is not only the "second coming," but virtually a *continuous* coming in the clouds of heaven with attending angels, the hope and the pledge of universal redemption."

THE PASTOPHORA is the production of years of close and severe searching, amid other pressing claims upon his attention. With indefatigable labor, James has gathered rich lore where others saw only alloy. A band of spirits, some of them very ancient, and all lovers of antiquity, desirous of blossoming into life "things new and old," has directed his mind and his steps adown the sombre walks of the past, amid the brooding silence of buried civilizations. The pyramids had voices for him; the obelisks glared forth a hidden mystery in their inscriptions; rocks and tombs, scepters and swords, dust and ashes, all bore traces of oracles that once built kingdoms and empires, all were prints of events readable under the spirit-vision of his guides, aflash with the truth that ministering angels have ever been the arbiters of human destinies. THE PASTOPHORA is the faithful record of this pilgrimage of study offered now to the world as a beautiful repository of "Ancient and Modern Spiritualism." It is doubtless the first and only work ever published that has placed the past wave-eras, with their representative spiritual chieftains, in chronological and systematic order. As such, in construction at least, it is "something new under the sun." A book of biographical and spiritual reference, it is of inestimable value. Its literary and philosophical qualities are obviously of a high tone, both in style and sentiment, all throbbing through with a pure love of truth, and a deep reverence for whatever ennobles humanity and lifts it up to divine life.

The greatest difficulty he has had to encounter, amid such a profusion of spiritual evidences, was to do justice to the great multitude of witnesses rising on every side, demanding a hearing. In his descent into the ocean of the past, he found so vast a plain of precious pearls, there is not room to enshrine them all in this beautiful cabinet; but enough are gleaned to show that our heavenly philosophy, like silver veins, branches in all possible directions—a vast and inexhaustible mine of immortal wealth, exhuming for incorporation into the spiritual temple we build. A complete analysis of the spiritual phenomena, variegated with eclectic beauties, sweet with the love of truth, it may be properly styled—" Paradise Regained."

Another attractive feature is its spiritual symbolism—which is the language exalted angels use—conveying to the senses, as well as understanding, truth set as diamonds in gold—a speculum of the spiritual philosophy reflecting the "soul of things." Even the title of the book is peculiarly significant.

PASTOPHORA is lexicographically related with pastor—shepherd—indicative of ministerial office for the protection of the religious flock. It is originally rooted in the Sanscrit—the oldest language in the world; and, used in the plural, Pastophoræ, literally means *dwellers in the temples*. It is, therefore, a most beautiful title, euphonious in pronunciation, symbolizing the inner life, burning as a Shekinah watch-light to the worshiping soul in its own "holy of holies.'

The interested reader will also inquire into the meaning of the symbols on the back of the book—the *cross*, *triangle*, and *circle*. As he carefully peruses these pages, he will discover that the data of the world's progress in civilizations center in India, whose religious symbol, providential as it seems, is the *circle*, representing God, the Universal Soul.

All things are trinal—body, soul and spirit; man is this perfect trinity—the cross, the triangle, the circle. Geologically our world started from the circle. It extended then to the broadness of its orbit in a gaseous condition incipient to crystalization. Contracting, the elements were angularized—divided, sharp-pointed, battling, volcanic, developing latent force, crystalizing into extreme individuality—the cross of crucifixion—when the law of reaction obtained, tending to centrality again—the leveling down of mountains—the leveling up of valleys, encircling all in harmony.

Religion is but the laws of nature spiritualized—love married to science—the angel of heaven acting in practical life. Religion dates in the golden circle—in the tropics—the India of love. Have you noticed that civilization began there, and veered northward to be crystalized into sparkling intellectuality by a colder climate; spreading itself over Europe, thence westward in parallels to America, across the Pacific to Asia, and gradually settling back, laden with mental riches, to the tropics again? All things move in circles. India is the birth-place of religion—the Eden—the conjugal circle of soul. How appropriate, then, is the circle to represent her parental relations with all races, governments, and improvements! The embryonic religion of mankind,

India is seen in the spirit world by the sign of the circle—full-orbed and golden.

Egypt is the child of India, less affectional in faith, but more astronomical, philosophical, and practical—the daughter, whose name is *Science*. The Ganges and the Himalayas are so vast, clouded, mystic, they inspire awe, and, in so sunny a clime, unfold an exuberant contemplation of soul—a poetic religious idealism that enchants every sense and imparadises every thought. Egypt is tamer, not so melancholy, not so vast and spiring, not so cloudy and luxurious, not so mellow and musical. The Nile, mysterious as the Ganges, alluvial and inundating, is not so sweetly imbosomed in the shadows of great mountains and protective banyan forests. Egypt has more burning sands, more raging sea from the north vexed with storms, more poison in her desert winds. Hence, her inhabitants have more angularity of character. She is spiritually tropical; but nature's battles make her contentious, intellectual, fiercely just, the manufacturer of an implacable hell, and of a delightful Elysium across the stormy lake of death. She is, therefore, the circle geometrically changed into a right-angle-triangle. She is three-sided, pyramidal, with stars for heart-beats. Egypt courting science from very love, her horoscopic sign in the spirit world is the right-angle-triangle.

But there must be body to this trinity; the perfect individuality of principle. Palestine, whose people were born and disciplined in the slaveries of Egypt, is a little colder, variegated, and on a smaller scale. The Mediterranean, dashing with awful roar against her shores, is the warning voice of the great Jehovah, angry at the sins of his chosen children. The Jordan is swift and acrid. The valleys and brooks are contracted. Horeb and Sinai and Lebanon are wrapt in jealous solitudes. The Egyptio-codes of Moses, intensified to rigorous penalty, enforce order and racial nationality. What, then, is the Jewish character? Selfish, arrogant, narrow, jealous, and arbitrary. Judaism, spiritualized, is Pauline Christianity—the aggressive sword—the Protestantism of India—the *body* in the triune development—the religious body for the soul of Egypt and the spirit of India. What, then, is the sign of Christianity in the immortal horoscope? The cross, indicative of doctrine, of individuality, of progress *towards* the circle of the Harmonial Philosophy.

So religion, like every other law of life, repeats itself; moves in circles; inversely from circles in incarnations to angles and crosses, and from these back to the circle, spirally climbing round and round in infinite progression. Nothing, then, is lost. All that India gives, or Egypt, or Judea, or America, are translated into newness of life, as the inheritance of the ages to come.

The Pastophora, thus set in prism, is this beautiful trinity expressed —all religions essentially comprised in its circle of philosophy, dividing and sparkling with angular points of electric thought, and blending again in rainbowed drops for oceanic love.

Read then, O world searching for light, carefully read these breathing pages, redolent with words that burn; and then rank the book where it belongs, with the standards of Spiritualism, and, with gratitude, thank God and take courage under the glory that flashes from all inspired pens, and throbs in all honest bosoms, bared so freely to the arrows of persecution as a bulwark of defence to more spiritual and angelic generations coming.

If this volume severs a mental chain, frees a creed-crushed soul, plucks a thorn from a human pathway, planting a rose there, sheds a kindling ray of light upon a pilgrim's path, or causes even a tremulous smile to brighten the brow of sorrow and suffering, then is the author satisfied— aye, richly blessed, for he finds his highest happiness and sweetest blessing in blessing others.

J. O. BARRETT.

New Year's Day, 1869.

Lecture I.

Spirit of the Present Age.

CHAPTER I.

SPIRIT OF THE AGE

> "All grim and soiled, and brown with tan,
> I saw a Strong One, in his wrath,
> Smiting the godless shrines of man
> Along his path."

> "My soul is not a palace of the past,
> Where priest-worn creeds, like Rome's gray Senate, quake,
> Hearing afar the vandal's trumpet hoarse.
> The time is ripe and rotten ripe for *change;*
> Then let it come!"

Progress is God's right hand angel! It is the Christ in our midst, working by methods mystic as the pictured symbols in the Patmos Visions. Its laws diverse, inverse, and often unfathomable, ever act to the same divine purpose of physical refinement and spiritual unfoldment.

Causation is infinite. Change is a necessity of nature. Essential Spirit—that all-interfusing force-presence, filling immensity, and being causative, *does* and eternally *will* act upon matter.

Something from nothing, a self-evident absurdity, there are no absolute creations in the universe, only new and higher formations. Spirit and matter both eternal; spiritual substance in connection with physical substance in its various gradations, constitute one co-eternal duality.

Spirit is independent of matter relative to mere existence; yet dependent upon it for its manifestations.

The God-principle or Divine Energy immanent in, and connected with, the dual forms of matter and spirit, must ever produce motion, disintegration, evolution and pulsations towards perfection. The old dies that the new may sing of birth, maturity, victory.

The past with its lengthened shadows and suns, its defeats and triumphs, was well; so were frightful explosions, during the old Plutonian period. Fossils in silurian rocks were deeply significant as treasured histories of primeval life, bespeaking higher organized existence; and so even the possible of man, as prince of immortal nature, during coming geologic epochs.

> "All bloom is fruit of death;
> Creation's soul thrives from decay,
> And nature feeds on ruin; the big earth
> Summers in rot; and harvests through the frost,
> To fructify the world; the mortal *now*
> Is pregnant with spring-flowers to come;
> And death is seed-time of eternity!"

It is folly, maddened by bigotry, to ask the thinkers of the nineteenth century to hold the flag-staffs of the ancients. Parchments are fixtures. While neither constitutions nor creeds grow, *souls do*. As well strive to fill our arteries with the crimson blood that coursed the veins of Jewish patriarchs and priests, as to appropriate their thoughts, commandments, or religious experiences, forgetful of the living present, hoping thereby to have our spiritual life vitalized. Shall we

> "Load our young thought with the iron shirt,
> By bigots raked from some Judean grave-yard's dirt?"

The yesterdays are gone; let them go! The good of the past preserved and reconstructed, Americans have to do with the to-days, and a brightening future stretching in mellowed radiance, deepening in significance, gorgeous with hope, and prophetic of a coming Eden, whose crowning glories shall be harmonial men and women, being laws unto themselves. True, the present strikes its roots back into the past. It is our legacy; and, so far as it speaks truth to the soul, let us do homage at its shrine.

All those brave souls, Pythagoras, Plato, Anaxagoras, Confucius, Jesus, John, and others, martyred for principle, greatly advantaged and beautifully enriched the succeeding ages by wise utterances that have streamed in golden splendors down to the present. They were helps, having helped humanity; and yet, they are not our masters—not infallible guides. Wisdom did not die with them, and therefore they must not talk to us authoritatively.

Each should be his own authority. God speaks to *us* just as frequently and fatherly as he did to Jewish seers. Seeing in every valley a Jordan, in every sectarian church a "dead sea," in every aspirational heart an altar of worship, in every woodland eminence a mount of ascension, and in every child an embryo angel, what *special* need of Hebrew bounty, styled "*Revelation?*"

Those must indeed be "babes and sucklings," who will persist in partaking of manna—the *history* of bread nearly two thousand years booked—and dried fruit generally, when spiritual vineyards are clustering with grapes, and orchards are bending under a ripened luxuriance, and inspirations, like benedictions, are coming each day from heavenly realms.

It is difficult to Jerusalemize Anglo Saxons. If the soul-lamp would burn brightly, illumining the living *now*, it must be lit from such inspirational fire-fountains as the wants of this age have kindled. Robes may have been well for Aaron, fox-chasing for Sampson, grazing for Nebuchadnazzar, tent-making for Paul, locusts for the Judean Baptists, and manna for Israelitish wanderers; but "give us this day our daily bread;" that is, daily truths and principles, all alive with love from the many-mansioned homes of the angels. The waster should be the builder; and the hand that carries the "torch for the burning," should also carry the hammer for building better. Sectarian churches, doubtless, are partial necessities, and for the time being, *well;* as were baptismal waters for John's disciples; but give *us* the baptism of the Holy Spirit;

or the descending divine afflatus from celestial hosts, submerging and suffusing our natures in a measureless ocean of purity and wisdom.

The revengeful, repenting, personal God of Judaism satisfied the demands of the Hebrews. They could grasp no higher conception of the infinite incarnate life-principle of the universe. It still satisfies millions of conscientious churchmen, with more *zeal* than knowledge, who strive to fill themselves upon the mouldy crumbs that fall from the oily lips of ordained Rip Van Winkles, who "say" their prayers instead of doing them, and "*profess*" instead of *possess* the divine principles of the absolute religion.

What pining! what leanness and lankness even in liberal churches! what moanings from the pulpits over "bleeding Zion!" what quiet slumberings in the pews! what efforts to make special engagements with God during winter-seasons for "revivals!" Oh what a thin, dry, fleshless, marvelously lifeless, soulless "*Skeleton,*" is Orthodoxy! Numbers bitterly feel it to be thus, yet cling from fear, or motives of policy, to its bleached bones and encrusted symbols. Others, good at heart, yet timid, fearing the loss of position, continue to preserve their ecclesiastical connections, faithfully hugging their theologically "dead mother's breast!"

The wisdom of importing all our religion from Asia-Minor is more than questionable, since God is as present with us as with the Asiatics, inspiration being a universal in-breathing from the Infinite.

"He sends his teachers unto every age,
To every clime, and every race of men."

The remembrance of corn that yellowed in Kedron's valleys, the milk and honey that flowed in the lands of Canaan, and the figs and pomgranates that reddened around Olive's mountain, gladdening the disciples of the Nazarene, can not satisfy spiritual hunger; nor can the Jewish crude notions of retrogressive demons and sacrifices offered a personal, local, jealous God, satisfy the growing desires of our inmost nature. Church doctrines are but husks to spiritual consciousness. John Wesley, in an inspired moment, said: "I am sick of opinions; give us good works and the faith of practical benevolence." Scaffoldings are necessary only during the processes of building; and chaff, after the ripening of the grain, is but sport for the winds! Why, old theology appears about as pitiable as would the ancient Hebrew method of treading out corn beneath the hoofs of lazy oxen, to a spirited western farmer in charge of a modern threshing machine.

When human bodies die, sectarists have good sense enough to bury them from sight; but when their creeds perish, becoming as offal to investigators, they strive to embalm and preserve them beneath gothic piles and costly cathedrals, to the merriment of metaphysicians and the almost infinite sorrow of angels. As well strive to bind the waters of the ocean with a rope of sand, or hush the winds fresh from Æolus hand, as to bid the currents of free thought cease circulating among inquiring masses that dare to assert their independence. Popes and priests have measurably been shorn of their power. Century-mossed systems have lost their vitalizing force, and creedal ceremonies have become dull and irksome.

The great throbbing heart of humanity calls for living inspirations, and greater, grander truths fresh from the Father and the angels that do the divine will. Emerson, in an address to the Senior Theological class at Cambridge, said:

"It is my duty to say to you, that the need was never greater of a new revelation than now. From the views I have already expressed, you will infer the sad conviction which I have, I believe with numbers, of the universal decay and now almost death of faith in society. The Soul is not preached. The Church seems to totter to its fall—almost all life is extinct. I think no man can go with his thoughts about him into one of our churches, without feeling, that what hold the public worship once had on man—is gone, or going. It has lost its grasp on the affections of the good, and the fears of the bad. The prayers and even the dogmas of our church are wholly isolated from anything now extant in the *life* and *business* of the people."

A perfectly vigorous and original life, founded upon the science of the soul, is what seems fit and admirably adapted to the genius of this country, now freed from the blight of oppressive institutions; and this life-status is to be supreme, sure as physical landscapes are reflected in individual character, as climate affects religion.

"Light! *more light!*" relative to immortality, the soul's capacities and to the glories of an infinite future, is the demand of our growing humanity. In answer thereto the church offers us "faith" and clerical leading strings, sanctified by custom, telling us to be good, submissive, quiet "babes in Christ;" and then, just over Jordan, we shall find the jasper city paved with gold, and musical with saints serenading "the Holy One of Israel!" But this faith imparts no free, spontaneous energy. It soon degenerates into a languishing formality, a dry cant, a narrowing nondescript, an inexpressible churchianic hybrid between life and death, as "revival" confessions demonstrate. Faith *is* elemental in the human mind, but this *ecclesiastic* faith, devoid of reason, and "without works," is dead! The eccentric Carlyle says, that, "just in the ratio that knowledge increases, faith diminishes; consequently, those that know the most always believe the least."

The age demands, not aping shadows, gloved gentry, nor cowled clergymen fashioned to order in "Theological Seminaries," bewailing the sins of Greeks and Jews, and aiming arrows of rebuke at the poor Hittites and Moabites—not sluggish conservatives infected with stagnant, deathly torpor, staying on earth as do oysters in their bed, praying for the Millennium, because they then hope to "sit"—sit under "ambrosial" vines—fearing to brush down cobwebs in their temples lest the roof fall in, and piously opposing the "new moon," out of a profound respect for the old, forgetting the Carlylean maxim, that the "old skin never falls from the serpent till a new one is formed;" but it demands men and women enthusiastic and full-orbed, who see in every soul a possible Christ, in every life a symbol-thought of God, in every well-timed bath a baptism, in every day a Sabbath, in every house a living temple, and in every heart an altar of worship whereon the fires of love and devotion are kept as incense continually burning, making all life's hours precious like the Eastern fig-tree that bears in its bosom at once the beauty of the early bloom and the matured glory of most delicious fruitage—who are full of warm blood, deep sympathies, and great moral independence, whose arguments against home-sins hit, whose shots tell, eyes flash, words convince, lips persuade, and inspirations touch the heart's best affections, calling down sweet love-baptisms from on high—who will speak the whole truth, as they see it, and actualize it in lives consecrated to divine uses, though the fire, the faggot, and cross are in full view—who, holy and rapt and mystic at times, as John of Patmos filled with ode, rhapsody and lyric, uttering from the depths of the inner consciousness divine principles, as with tongues of fire, causing them to sing through the corridors of the soul's memory-chambers, awakening to resurrectional beatitude all those finer impulses of kindness, forgiveness, and devotion to the right, the just, the true, and the beautiful, that slumber in the sacred heart of our common brotherhood. Then will the kingdom of God, so long the burden of prophecy and prayer, become as practical an institution as it is progressive on earth—the ideal *then* being realized *now*—all to the glory of our divine humanity.

"The new is old, the old is new,
The cycle of a change sublime,
Still sweeping through!"

CHAPTER II.

SPIRITUAL RATIOS.

"All matter is God's tongue,
And from its *motion* God's thoughts are sung.
The realms of space are the octave bars,
And the music notes are the sun and stars."

The Infinite Spirit is the infinite substance of the universe, the only absolute *reality*, and Nature, as a garment, is the manifestation of this reality to the senses. The conscious human spirit, as the innermost of man, is an essential portion of the Infinite, pure and eternal—a divine center—a celestial compass with an infinitude of points, bearing fixed relations, when in conjunction with grosser matter, to time past, present, and future. Time is not a thing *per se*, but only the record of a series of impressions made upon the spiritual sensorium.

"All are but parts of one stupendous whole,
Whose body Nature is, and God the soul."

Each thus connected with all, and human nature the same in all ages, the present generation has much to do in turning to good account the gathered experiences of the past, in finding the "lost arts," and measuring the folly and wisdom of those ancient eras, though grayed with countless decades.

Waves of progress, moving in cycles, continually overlap—the highest reaching the shores, and there writing their thoughts on crystal reams and defiant rocks. The past, then, with its long shadows—symbols, hieroglyphics, poetry, paintings, proverbs and rabbinical lore—converges in the present. Aye, the grand old *past!*—it reaches down its multitudinous hands to us from the Atlantis, from India and Egypt, from Syria, Greece and Rome; from bannered cities long sanded from sight; from ancient temples whose golden gates dazzled like suns; from old Gothic cathedrals and Norman castles magnificent even in ruins.

Unto us, from all surrounding zones, worlds and realms, have poured the streams of eternal life. Rock and ocean, storm and stars, light and darkness, saint and savage, god and demon, with the boundless and fathomless deeps of undying love, have all contributed to make up our physical, mental and spiritual organizations. To every point of the compass in the infinite domain of space, may souls send out their feelers and meet a glad response.

Our particled bodies may exchange with the minerals, the soils, the fruits; our spiritual structures, with the fine etherealized essences and ultimates that infill the surrounding regions; while the deific within, through aspiration and effort, may continually come into diviner rapport with the great, beating, throbbing, loving heart—the Infinite Soul of the universe—God.

This true, the past, with its deep rich veins of experience, its half-buried yet glittering treasures, and its inexhaustible tomes of classic riches, is to us in value above what human speech can express, painter transfer to canvas, or author describe. The legitimate work of the historian is to unveil and present to the people of to-day a speaking panorama of the extinguished ages. This measureless period termed the *past*, when organized and comprehended in its broadest sense, rounds up as the great drama of humanity—as the living epic of human progress—the forecourt of a more transcendent futurity.

The historian, however, is not the bare fact-gatherer. Mere facts may be as devoid of scientific value as fictions. To reach truth there must be a selection of well-attested facts, with their just moral value affixed. These, put into the crucible of reason, systematized, grouped in order, and organized in accordance with the best methods of philosophic research, must also be critically weighed with reference to their producing causes. This done, they naturally crystalize into, harmonize with, and help constitute truth.

While many spirit ripples have danced upon the sea of progress, three mighty waves have loomed up on the ocean of the ages—ancient, mediæval and modern Spiritualism. The first, shedding its kindling glories in India, Egypt, China and adjoining nations, threw such an effulgence of baptismal beauty over the more cultured of those earlier civilizations, that all the subsequent declining eras were illuminated even down to the birth of the Nazarene. Mediæval Spiritualism, dating from the advent of Jesus, that eminent Judean Spiritualist, enriched the Platonic thinkers of Alexandria, ennobled the statesmen of Greece, quickened the orators of Rome, encircled in light the footsteps of seers and martyrs, pierced with scattered sunbeams the gloom of the dark ages, inspired those old reformers, and tinged with a divine brightness the progressive movements that marked nearly twenty centuries preceding the "Rochester Rappings!" This last spiritual wave is familiar to us all.

LECTURE II.

ANCIENT HISTORIC SPIRITUALISM.

CHAPTER III.

INDIAN.

"Searching ancient records lately
In a dusky nook we found
An old volume grand stately,
Iron clasped and parchment bound.

"The five hundred million Brahminic and Buddhist believers hold all the gods, men, demons, and various grades of animated life occupying this innumerable array of worlds compose one cosmic family."

India! author of races—birth-place of art, science, sculpture, fragrant with the lotus—dreamy with emotions and aspirations kindled by the warmth of tropic suns! Mother of religions, India abounded with the poetic, the visionary, the spiritual.

Multiform are the evidences of a conscious communion between mortals and the inhabitants of the spirit world, blossoming along the borders of Time's earlier mornings. All things, from atoms to astral worlds, move in spirals—cycles being the subjects of law.

"A spiral winds from the worlds to the suns,
And every star that shines
In the path of degrees forever runs,
And the spiral octave climbs."

Nations, as men, are born, grow, mature, and die; or they ascend and descend, as sea waves rise and fall. There were golden ages with heroes, poets and scholars, thousands upon thousands of years before the reputed Adam ate the "forbidden fruit" that mellowed along the banks af the Euphrates. Plato, in the Timmæus, speaks of a vast island, larger than Lybia and Asia combined, that, nine thousand years before his time, had its kings, priests, soldiers, arts, guardian gods and goddesses. This thickly-peopled isle, or, more properly, continent, owing to a fearful earthquake or some other violent concussion of nature, sank in a single night into the ocean and disappeared forever.

Le Can, an eminent Mongolian scholar, personally assured us that the Chinese measure time by dynasties; that their sacred historical works, extending back in a line forty-four thousand years, contain many accounts of commerce ceasing, because of the sinking of large islands and the rising of immense continents from the ocean's depths. Among the most prominent of the great nations of old whose footprints were encircled in the light of spiritual phenomena and inspirational truths, uttered by seers, secresses and oracles, we mention Egypt, China, India, Syria and Persia. These either carved their gospels in symbols and hieroglyphics, or penned them on scrolls—Vedas and Avestas.

That profound linguist, Müller, of All Souls' College, Oxford, says, "Every learned man knows that the *Hebrew* was not, as Jerome and other Church Fathers taught, the oldest or primitive language of mankind." The Sanscrit of the old Hindoos was a much more ancient and a far more perfect language. This was in its full flush of glory more than five thousand years ago.

Even Sir William Jones awards to some books, now extant in Sanscrit, an antiquity of four and five thousand years. Rev. Mr. Maurice, as quoted by Higgins, thinks the Bhagavat Gita, so marvellously rich in thought relating to the immortality of the soul and pre-existence, was written over four thousand years since. That fine Scotch scholar, Lord Monboddo, wrote in 1792, that the "language of the ancient Brahmins of India was a richer and in every respect a finer language than even the Greek of Homer." Another European scholar of great renown says the Sanscrit was a written and spoken language hundreds of years before Abraham appeared on the plains of Shinar, and long before the Hebrew language had an existence.

M. Ernest Renan, in his history of the "Shemitic languages," says: "The birth-place of *philosophy* is India, amidst an inquisitive race, deeply pre-occupied by the search after the secret of all things; but the psalm and the prophecy, the wisdom concealed in riddles and symbols, the pure hymn, the revealed book, are the inheritance of the theocratic race of the Shemites—Assyrians, Chaldees, Arabians, Hebrews and cognate tribes." He further adds: "The Shemite race has neither the *elevation of Spiritualism*, known only to India, nor the feeling for measure and perfect beauty bequeathed by Greece to the Neo-Latin nations."

It is generally conceded by all learned Orientals that a large portion of the writings of the Brahmins is anterior to any part of our Bible. In style and spirit they are eminently superior, abounding in the grandest conceptions of Deity, and in communications from the *gods, demi-gods, manes and spirits*. The Vedas, Puranas, Upanishads, Rig-Veda Sanhita, Bhagavat-Gita, Ramayanna, etc., are full of myths inlaid with spiritual thoughts and sublime spiritual ideas, such as "Spirit moving upon chaos and fashioning forms"—the "girdles and spheres" encircling the earth—the "power of the gods to clothe themselves in a luminous ether" and appear to mortals—"the celestial state of eighty-eight thousand saints," the holiest of the Brahmins, and their descent to guard cities and guide the young. The Puranas also describe the oblations offered and the methods devised to dispossess "malignant spirits and enemies of the deities." (Vishnu Purana, p. 329).

Long before the patriarchs pitched their tents under Syrian skies, long before Moses saw the tables of stone on the Mount, long before the oldest Hebrew prophets were inspired to sound the alarm in Judean mountains, there were millions of Spiritualists, prophets, yogees, sages, seers and mediums, in India. What is more, Abraham himself was, without the least doubt, a *Brahmin*. The scholarly Higgins proves this beyond a cavil in his very labored work, the "Anacalypsis."

Terah, the father of *Abraham*, came from an Eastern country called Ur. Higgins clearly proves that this Ur of the Chaldees was in India, that portion of the country lying on the river Jumna and now called Uri, or Ur. Abbe Dubois states that the Hindoos in their earliest times had no images. They worshipped the *one God* as Divinity in duality, positive and negative—father and mother. Abraham refused to worship the female principle in the Godhead. He became a Protestant Hindoo, a wandering pilgrim, and accordingly emigrated from Ur in India to Haran in Assyria; from thence to Phœnicia, and finally into Egypt, nearly 2,000 B. C., in consequence of a terrible famine; and in all his journeyings he took with him the belief in and practice of the mysteries and spirit communion he had been taught in India. Therefore we read in the Old Testament that "the Lord (a spiritual being) appeared to him on the plains of Mamre." Also when he sat in the door of his tent, he lifted up his eyes and looked, and lo, *three men* stood before him; and when he saw them—that is, these *three spirits*—"he bowed himself towards the ground."

The history of the Phœnicians and the Assyrians (Assurians or Assoors from India) has reached us only in fragments, and these through that voluminous author Sanchoniathan, that lived long prior to Moses; and Berosus, the Babylonian historian. Porphyry says, Sanchoniathan received much of his information from Hierombalus, a priest of Iao, that is, Jehovah; accordingly, with deep insight, the sect of learned Gnostics taught, that this Iao, or *Jehovah* of the Jews, was the "*name of an angel.*" This shows that Sanchoniathan was a mystic and medium, as well as historian. It is clear from both Sanchoniathan and Berosus, that the Phœnicians, full five thousand years since, engaged in an extensive commerce. Modern exhumations and discoveries in Peru, Mexico and other portions of the American continent, obviously demonstrate, as shown by symbols of sun-worship carved upon rocks, that they pushed their shipping all along our western sea-coasts. Wherever they anchored they left their ideas of magic and spirit intercourse.

"Light
"Sprung from the deep, and from her native East,
To journey thro' the airy gloom began."

In Pococke's "India in Greece," the author, from a translation of documents existing in the Sanscrit, proves conclusively that,

"In the great conflict between Brahminical and Buddhistic sects in India, the latter being defeated, emigrated in large bands, and colonized other countries. It is demonstrated in this work that the principal locality from which this emigration took place was Affghanistan and North-western India; that the Indian tribes proceeding thence colonized Greece, Egypt, Palestine and Italy; that they also produced the great Scandinavian families, the early Britons inclusive; and that they carried with them to their new settlements the evidences of their civilization, their arts, institutions and religion."

Herodotus informs us that, in the lofty tower of Belus in Babylon, there was a consecrated room upon the summit in which was an oracular gold table; and here a woman of priestly office stayed each night to obtain information from the presiding deity. A similar apartment adorned the Temple of Jove at Thebes, in Egypt, and other Nilotic cities. These media, virtuous in habit, accustomed to fasting and bathing, and other purifications, before divining or conversing with the gods, to give information, were required, in accordance with the laws of the country, to occupy those temples the night previous to the entrancement. This more thoroughly magnetized them. The teachings then brought from the world of spirits were considered sacred.

"I have seen," said Apollonius, "the Brahmins of India, dwelling on the earth and not on the earth, living fortified without fortifications, possessing nothing and yet everything." This he spoke somewhat enigmatically; but Damis (the companion of his journey in India) says they sleep upon the ground, but that the earth furnishes them with a grassy couch of whatever plants they desire. That he himself had seen them, elevated two cubits above the surface of the earth, walk in the air! not for the purpose of display, which was quite foreign to the character of the men; but because whatever they did, elevated, in common with the sun, above the earth, would be more acceptable to that deity. * * * Having bathed, they formed a choral circle, having Iarchas for their coryphæus, and striking the earth with their divining rods, *it rose up*, no otherwise than does the sea under the power of the wind, and caused them to ascend into the air. Meanwhile they continued to chant a hymn not unlike the pæan of Sophocles, which is sung at Athens in honor of Æsculapius." (Philostrat. Vita Apollon. Tyanens. Lib. iii. c. 15, 17.)

Without the light of Spiritualism, the above statements can be regarded in no other sense than chimeras of heated imagination in an age of superstition; but now they appear as embodied facts traceable to causes which our philosophy analyzes. As a common magnet will lift up a piece of steel, so by spirit attraction did Jesus walk upon the sea; and as a table, or other object by invisible hands, under the same law, is carried above the heads of the spiritual circle, so were the Brahmins of India floated in the air, which many a medium to-day can testify is true. How beautiful is history under the light of Spiritualism! We seem now to feel the very breath and heart-beats of those olden seers!

CHAPTER IV.

EGYPTIAN.

"The Egyptian soul sailed o'er the skyey sea
In ark of crystal, manned by beamy gods,
To drag the deeps of space and net the stars,
Where, in their nebulous shoals, they share the void,
And through old Night's Typhonian blindness shine."

"Old sphinxes lift their countenances bland,
Athwart the river-sea and sea of sand."

"Those mystic, stony volumes on the walls long writ,
Whose sense is late revealed to searching modern wit."

If there is a charmed country beneath the bending skies, it is Egypt—land of the Nile and the Pyramids, of the Pharaohs and the Ptolemies—land where art and science gloried in splendid achievements before our historic records, and whose powerful dynasties held sway for long generations over fertile valleys and mighty cities. Thebes, the hundred gated, Heliopolis with its magnificent temples, Memphis with its shining palaces and evergreen gardens, left memorials so wondrous that the men of to-day are attracted thither—to Luxor and Carnak, to the avenues of sphinxes and the summits of the pyramids.

Egypt, whose mystic hierophants vied with the gymnosophists of India—whose "lost arts" have never yet been discovered—whose learning

"Uttered its oracles sublime
Before the Olympiads, in the dew
And dusk of early time,"

had a civilization more than five thousand years ago, which, in some respects, was in advance of ours to-day. In this remote time none were admitted to judicial offices save men of integrity and great erudition. The bench consisted of thirty judges, ten chosen from each of the three greater cities, Thebes, Memphis and Heliopolis. Being duly elected, they were paid by the State. Counsel was employed and justice dispensed gratuitously to all. Thus rights were as accessible to the poor as to the rich. In judicial administration, what a lesson this to Americans so given to boasting and blundering in their selection of officers! "The very spirit of their laws," says Wilkinson, "was to give protection and assistance to the oppressed; and everything that tended to promote an unbiassed judgment was peculiarly commended by the Egyptian sages." Is it strange, then, that Abraham, the Patriarch, journeyed down into Egypt; that Pythagoras spent twenty-two years among her priests and seers; that Moses was learned in the "wisdom of the Egyptians," and Solon, the great lawgiver of Greece, was taught that the Greeks of his time were in philosophy but children?

Through all the palmy days of Egypt's grandeur, Spiritualism, in some form, was the universal belief. The more wise and profound had it under their special supervision. One of her most ancient seers stated, that "this earth was surrounded by aerial circles of ether, and that in these ether regions the souls of the dead lived and guarded mortals." Hermes taught "that this visible is but a picture of the *invisible* world, wherein, as in a portrait, things are not truly seen."

Herodotus mentions a celebrated Egyptian king who descended to the mansions of the dead, and, after some stay in those spirit realms, returned to light. The anniversary of this return was held as a sacred festal day by the ancient Egyptians, as Christians hold feasts and fasts.

Strabo states that in the temple of Serapis at Canopus, "great worship was performed; many miraculous works were wrought, which the most eminent men believed and practiced, while others devoted themselves to the *sacred sleep*"—that is, the unconscious trance. The consecrated temple at Alexandria was still more famous for its oracles, "sacred sleep," and the healing of invalids.

In memory of Memnon, sometimes called by the Egyptians Amenophis, a great ruler, whose mother was Cissiene, and who laid the foundation of Susa, there was erected a famous statue at Thebes that gave melodious sounds when first struck by the sun's morning rays. Both spirit voices and spirit music were heard issuing from this Theban statue for hundreds of years. Greek travelers affirm positively that they heard this music even as late as their own day. It was evidently produced upon the same principle of voices heard in haunted houses. Strabo, Ælius Gallus, Demetrius, and other distinguished characters, testify to having listened to those melodious sounds in the early hours of morning. Those electric sun-flashes produced just the requisite conditions in the statue for musical manifestations. Upon a colossal column of Memnon, rashly broken by Cambyses, carved in Greek and Latin, testifying that the writers heard the heavenly voice at the first dawn of day, are two inscriptions, one of which reads as follows: " *I, Publius Balbisues, heard the divine voice of Memnon or Phamenoph. I came in company with the Empress Sabina, at the first hour of the sun's course, the 15th year of the reign of Hadrian, the 24th day of Athyr, the 25th of the month of November.*"

Hermes, who said, "creation is not a generation of life, but a production of things to sense, and making them manifest," thoroughly understood the philosophy of magnetic sleep and trance. While the winged staff had a symbolic signification, the *magic staff* was most in use in his time. In the fifth book of the Odyssey, we have these lines:

"Forth sped Hermes, and under his feet he bound his ambrosial sandals,
 Then taking his staff, with which he the eyelids of mortals
 Closes at will, and the sleeper's will re-awakens."

Montfaucon and M. Denin, describing the temples of the Upper Egypt, clearly demonstrates that psychology, mesmeric control, and clairvoyance were well understood by Egypt's scholars and priests, and that through these methods, with spirit intercourse, they received their knowledge of the unseen world and the art of healing, which they deemed prudent to withhold from the masses. On those time-defying paintings discovered among the ruins that fringe the Nile, are the figures of priests in the very act of operating by making magnetic passes; and others are seen in the process of being thrown into mesmeric sleep. Anubis is represented in those sacred pictures as tenderly bending over the bed and putting his hands upon the sick, as do the healers of this age.

Emmanuel Rebold, M. D., President of the Academy of Industrial Sciences, France, speaking of that occult science, animal magnetism, says: "It is a science that for more than three thousand years was the peculiar possession of the Egyptian priesthood, into the knowledge of which Moses was initiated at Heliopolis, where he was educated." This accounts for much of Moses' wisdom, and also for his mediumship, equaling in some respects that of Egyptian seers and hierophants. The light of this age clearly proves that the Jehovah with whom he so familiarly conversed was his spirit-guide, and was not very exalted in the sweet graces of charity and love; and that the "word of the Lord" that came to him, "saying" was merely the voice of this attending spirit heard clairaudiently, as Socrates heard the admonishing voice of his good demon. We have authority for saying that this *Jehovah* of the Mosaic age, when on earth, was an Egyptian priest, by the name of *Gee-ho-ka* but neither of the noblest nor purest of the priesthood.

The famed philologist, Kircher, in his "Odipus Egyptiacus," gives the following accounts of gods, demi-gods, and genii of Egypt: "The Egyptians always held in great veneration certain temples and statues—these latter they called serapes; and over provinces, cities, temples, serapes, private houses, and especially men, *gods, demons,* and *genii* presided and watched as familiars, to guard from danger and give advice." Some of these were eventually worshiped by the less wise as private deities, having been ancestors departed from the earth to become gods.

"The signs of those that are inspired are multiform. For the inspiration is indicated by the motions of the (whole) body, and of certain parts of it, by the perfect rest of the body, by harmonious orders and dances, and by elegant sounds, or the contraries of these. Either the body, likewise, is seen to be elevated or increased in bulk, or to be borne along sublimely in the air. An equability also of voice according to magnitude; or a great variety of voice after intervals of silence, may be observed. And again, sometimes the sounds have a musical intention and remission." (Jamblichus de Mysteriis.)

This is nothing at all remarkable, for bodies these days are not only borne aloft, but there are spirit-sounds, dances, and other phases of influence, exactly like the above descriptions of ancient Media.

"The image of the god (Jupiter Ammon) is composed of emeralds and other precious stones, and gives oracles in a way quite peculiar. It is borne about in a golden ship by eighty priests; who, bearing it upon their shoulders, go whithersoever the god (image) by nodding his head, directs them." (Diodor. Sicul. Lib. 17.) This is not much, even though Jupiter did it. About equivalent to tipping a light-stand, or moving some other small furniture."

Within thirty-five years ancient Egypt has become better known to us than it was to the learned men of the Roman Empire; for we not only read its theology and philosophy in its hieroglyphics, but interpret more accurately by their aid, and that of the cuniform inscriptions, the ancient narratives of Herodotus and Diodorus Siculus. Her temples, towers, relics, hieroglyphs and paintings, all unite their testimony with that of the Grecian historians in confirmation of the universal prevalence, in some form, of what is now denominated Spiritualism. It was God's living witness in remotest ages. It is his witness to-day by the mediation of **angels**, voicing the eternal truth of a conscious immortality.

Chapter V.

CHINESE.

> "The awful shadow of some unseen Power
> Floats, though unseen, among us, visiting
> This various world with a constant wing,
> As summer winds that creep from flower to flower,"
>
> "Meanwhile prophetic harps
> In every grove were ringing."

Old as the rocks, gigantic in mental structure, sternly moral, China—circling coronal round the brow of nations—looms up before us an interminable panorama, unrolling religious scenery that enraptures every sense. The Chinese, through cycles of weary ages, have held conscious communion with the inhabitants of the heavens.

After a voyage among the South Sea isles and along the Pacific coast, we were, in 1861, at Placerville, introduced to Le Can, a learned Mandarin, who graduated from a Chinese University, and was then employed as interpreter in the courts of California. Highly intelligent, he was proud of his national literature. The following conversation with him will never fade from our memory:

"Have your people a Bible, or sacred books?"

"Certainly, sir; the sacred books of the kings, and the divine teachings of Lao-tse, and Confucius."

"Do they give any account of a flood occuring several thousand years since?"

"Most assuredly, sir; and not only one, but many floods, also of the sinking of islands, and the rising of continents from the ocean. Physical convulsions were very frequent fifteen, twenty and thirty thousand years ago!"

"How far back does the history of your sacred books extend?"

"Full forty-four thousand years!"

"Why, our historians give no account of your nation reaching into the distance so many thousand years!"

"*Your* historians! When America was inhabited by Indians and Europe by barbarians, we were an old and matured nation. Civilizations, like individuals, have their mornings, noontides and declinations."

"What do your sacred books teach?"

"Ours, with all other oriental scriptures, teach the existence of God, the necessity of morality, and the immortality of the human soul."

"Do your people believe in any intercourse between the living and the dead?"

"They have always believed it; and what now surprises you under the phenomena of Spirit Rappings is as ancient as our national records."

Dr. McGowan, long a missionary in China and Japan, in a lecture delivered a few years since before the Young Men's Christian Association of Chicago, Ill., speaking of the arts, sciences, and wonderful ingenuity of the more ancient Asiatics, said:

"The Chinese were well acquainted with the modes of table tipping now occurring in America, and have been for a great lapse of time. Their great teachers also many thousand years ago offered sacrifices and professed to hold actual converse with the departed of the future world."

Gutzlaff affirms that they sacrificed on high mountains, considered themselves surrounded by hosts of spirits, demons, gods, angels and invisible powers, and that spirits met them at their altars and presided over their temples.

At a grand banquet given to Mr. Burlingame and his associates of the Chinese Embassy, in New York, the dailies reporting the speeches gave this Christian country some new ideas relative to China. Who are the *heathen*, American Christians, or the Confucian Chinese? Mr. Burlingame said·

"The East which men have sought since the days of Alexander, now itself seeks the West. China, emerging from the mists of time, but yesterday suddenly entered your western gates, and confronts you by its representatives here to-night. What have you to say to her? She comes with no menace on her lips; she comes with the great doctrine of Confucius, uttered two thousand and three years ago, 'do not unto others what you would not have others do unto you.' * * I say that the Chinese are a great and noble people. They have all the elements of a splendid nationality. They are the most numerous people on the face of the globe; the most homogeneous people in the world; their language spoken by more human beings than any other in the world, and it is written in the rock; it is a country where there is a greater unification of thought than any other in the world; it is a country where the maxims of the great sages, coming down memorized, have permeated the whole people, until their knowledge is rather an instinct than an acquirement. They are a people loyal while living, and whose last prayer when dying is to sleep in the sacred soil of their fathers. It is a land of scholars and of schools; a land of books, from the smallest pamphlet up to encyclopedias of five thousand volumes. It is a land where the priviliges are common; it is a land without caste, for they destroyed their feudal system two thousand and one hundred years ago, and they built up their great structure of civilization on the great idea that the *people* are the source of power. That idea was uttered by Menchius two thousand and three hundred years ago, and it was old when he uttered it."

An Oxford Professor, England, lecturing upon Orientalism, said: "Buddhist missionaries reached China from India, as early as the third century before Christ." The "language which the Chinese pilgrims went to India to study, as the key to the sacred literature of Buddhism, was Sanscrit."

The Britannica Encyclopedia avers that "Sir William Jones and others attribute to some of the works extant in Sanscrit, an antiquity of four and five thousand years." Speaking of the immense wealth and beauty of this language, Sir William further says: "The Sanscrit is of a wonderful structure, more perfect than the Greek, more copious than the Latin, and more exquisitely refined than either." One of the profoundest thinkers of Chinese antiquity appeared in the person of Lao-tse, between six and seven hundred years,

B. C. He was a great spiritual reformer, and, living a life of self-denial and contemplation, professed frequently to ascend into the immortal realms, and there live during brief seasons with the *genii* and *seën-spirits* and *angels*. Then he would return freighted with new ideas, teaching his countrymen a purer faith and diviner doctrines. His life was calm and beautiful. He taught alchemy and magic; also maxims and morals so exalted that they called him a "doctor of reason;" and yet he strenuously insisted that all great religious and spiritual truths had been brought down to men from such of their honored ancestors as had become gods in celestial climes.

The eminent Chinese sage, Confucius, was born the 19th of June, 551, B. C., at Shanping in the kingdom of Lu. The real name of Confucius was Kong, but his disciples called him Kong-futse, that is, Kong the Master, or Teacher, which the Jesuit missionaries Latanized into Confucius. Remarkable dreams and omens are said to have preceded his birth, and his origin, traced back by his disciples, was derived from Hoang-ti, a powerful monarch, of China, who flourished more than 2000, B. C. In the introduction to the "Chinese Classics," part 1st, Rev. Dr. Legge says: "Confucius, in his frequent references to *heaven*, followed the phraseology of the older sages, giving occasion to many of his followers to identify God with a principal of reason and the course of nature. * * * Along with the worship of God there existed in China, from the earliest historical times, the worship of other *spiritual beings* specially, and to every individual the worship of departed ancestors." In the Confucian Analects, (p. 57), Ke Loo asked about serving the *spirits of the dead*. The master said, "While you are not able to serve men, how can you serve *their* spirits?" Ke Loo added, "I ventured to ask about death." * * The master said, "How abundantly do *spiritual beings* display the power that belongs to them! They cause all the people in the empire to fast and purify themselves; then, like over-flowing

water, they seem to be over the heads, and on the right and left of their worshipers "—that is, admirers.   *   *   *
" He who attains the sovereignty of the empire, having these three important things, shall effect few errors under his government. His presenting himself with his institutions before *spiritual beings*, without any doubts about them arising, shows that he knows *heaven*."

Chapter VI.

PERSIAN.

> "I am of that impious race,
> Those slaves of fire, who, morn and even,
> Hail their Creator's dwelling place
> Among the living lights of heaven!"

> "Such are the parables of Zartusht address'd
> To Iran's faith, in the ancient Zend-Avest."

Persia is the region of bloom, of flowers, of fire-altars, of sun-worshipers—where the tamirand, the date, the cassia, and the silken plantains of the valley mingle their loveliness in rich contrast with the fan-like foliage of palms, graceful as those that fleck "Araby's green sunny highlands."

The Persians neighbored commercially with the Egyptians, and the "Jews came up out of Egypt." This accounts for the similarity traceable everywhere between the teachings of the Zend-Avesta and the Kabbala of the Jews. The Rabbins contend that the more philosophical portions of this latter work originated in heaven—that the angel Raziel instructed Adam in it; the angel Japhiel, Shem; and the angel Zedekiel, Abraham. Abounding in angelic ministrations, miraculous works, and profound mystical truths, the more erudite Jews considered the Kabbala as embodying the principles of all genuine science, and the true interpreter of the Hebrew Scriptures.

The Persians were naturally a worshipful people. Their *magi* were their wise men. The Asiatic rendering of the word signifies *consecrated men*, men devoted to the worship of God. Accordingly, the word magic originally signified the practice of worship, and the Magi of the East were those who devoted themselves to science and worship.

Says Alger: Zoroaster prays, "When I shall die, let Aban and Bahman carry me to the bosom of joy." It was a common belief among the Persians, that souls were at seasons permitted to leave the under world, and the upper regions and visit their relatives on earth.

The confusion relative to the time and teachings of Zoroaster, has arisen from overlooking the well established fact, that there were certainly two, probably three, distinguished personages bearing the name. Zoroaster occurs as a royal name in the Chaldean lists of Berosus. Pliny, following the positive affirmation of Aristotle, declares that Zoroaster the first, flourished six thousand years before Plato. Hermippus, a man of great erudition, places him five thousand years before the Trojan war. Meoyle, Rhode, Volney, Gibbon, and other reliable scholars, concur in throwing him back into this vast antiquity.

The *great* religious chieftain of Persia, called by the Greeks Zoroaster, and by the Orientals, Zendust, was born according to Herodotus, about the year 1250, and, according to other historic writers, full 1,400 B. C., in Aderbijan, ancient Media. Suidas terms him a Perso-Mede. His birth was announced to his mother in a wonderful dream. She also saw in vision a brilliant angel hurling a book at evil demons, and a youth rising up and becoming a mighty person in the lands of the Orient. Zoroaster was often warned in dreams; saw celestial spirits; entered by trance into the heavenly world, and, being ushered into the presence of Ormuzd. conversed with him and his hosts of angels. The historian informs us that he obtained the commandments of the Avestan rolls from Ormuzd on a mountain, amid awful flames of light, as did Moses on Mt. Sinai.

After a quiet retreat of "twenty years duration," according to Pliny, as a work of preparation by fasting and communing with heaven, he commenced the public propagation of his doctrines, at the age of thirty, in the capital of the kingdom of the Bactrians. His system was eminently spiritual, abounding in revelations, prophecies and miracles—in visions, attending angels, good and evil spirits. Scarcely is a man dead, say the Zend books, "before demons good, or demons evil, come to possess him, and bear him to their own state of life."

Richardson informs us "that, among other religious ceremonies, the Magi used to place upon the tops of high towers various kinds of rich viands, upon which it was supposed the Peris and the spirits of their departed heroes regaled themselves." This corresponds with the scriptural account of Jesus' partaking of "broiled fish and an honey comb," after his resurrection. During the rise, the reign and fall of the Persian kingdom, the *Magi*, or media, were held in great repute, sitting often as counselors in the courts of kings.

Magic was but another name for wisdom. The magic of the Persians and Chaldeans, says the scholarly Brucker, "is not to be confounded with witchcraft, or a supposed intercourse with evil spirits only; it consisted in the performance of certain religious ceremonies or incantations, which were supposed, through the interposition of *good demons*, to have supernatural effects." Magic and miracle, dream and vision, prophecy and angel intercourse, blending with the Persian philosophy and theology as rainbow hues, were among the prevailing religious ideas of this powerful empire. From these the later Hebrew prophets, of Old Testament memory, borrowed largely.

Chapter VII.

HEBRAIC.

"Who is he that cometh from Edom? with dyed garments from Bozrah? traveling in the greatness of his strength." * * *
"I have trodden the wine-press alone. Who hath believed our report?"

O Israel! how beautiful upon the mountains thy patriarchs, prophets, apostles! What a lyrical sweetness, richness of expression, moral grandeur of thought, flame through their language, bridging and brightening the historic passage of full four thousand years! Abraham, girded with faith—David, poetic—Isaiah, inspirational—Ezekiel, psychologic—Daniel, prophetic—Jeremiah, sympathetic—Jesus, spiritualistic—James, practical—John, pictorial and affectionate;—all these starred the highway of their "Lord" with heavenly truths, voiced the word of angels from the Dead Sea to Gennesaret, shed upon their "promise land" a light that lingers now in vesper beauty there, but re-lit to blaze with loftier inspirations—a sun rising in the West.

No scholars versed in Shemitic tongues, or well read in antiquity, will deny that the Hebrew scriptures are made up principally from religious records, superstitious relics, and the sacred books that long preceded them. Hence, Godfrey Higgins (F. R. Asiatic Society, Ana., p. 272) says, in referring to Wilson's discoveries, "*It is now certain that all the first three books of Genesis must have come from India.*"

The dogmas, laws, rites, and ceremonies that characterized the Mosaic dispensation, were taken almost bodily from the mythic codes of Egypt's priests and subordinate castes. The deciphered hieroglyphs demonstrate this. The writings of the lesser Jewish prophets, booked in the Bible, are largely drawn from the symbols, wonders, night visions, and general religious literature of the older Persian Magi. To this end the author of the English Penny Cyclopedia informs us that "some of those prophecies recorded in the Bible were extant in books written long before the events took place to which they refer."

Few historic facts are better established than that India colonized Egypt. After giving many sound reasons for this, Higgins states with emphasis, that "India was the parent of Egypt." Manetho, a man of great wisdom, Egyptian by birth, residing at Heliopolis in the time of the Ptolemies, yet writing his history in Greek, considered the Hebrews as low in caste, a loose, war-like, wandering people, given to heinous vices. He further contends that this nomadic "nation, called shepherds, were likewise called captives in their sacred books." After "being driven out of Egypt," as the great Jewish historian Josephus admits, they journeyed through the "wilderness of Syria, and finally built a city in Judea, which they called Jerusalem." Professor Morton, an eminent scientist, giving us the representation of a mummied cranium, taken from one of the oldest Egyptian sepulchres, remarks: "This head possesses a great interest on account of its decided Hebrew features, of which many examples are extant on the monuments." The Egyptians being originally from India, and the Hebrews residing in, and then ultimately driven out from Egypt, it is perfectly natural that the customs, and particularly the theological ideas of the Jews, relating to this and the future life, should in a great measure coincide with those of the riper and superior nations.

The Pentateuch of Moses was nearly all made up from the Brahminical Vedas and Phœnician manuscripts. "In

Sanchoniathon," says Higgins, " we have, in substance, the same cosmogony for the Phœnicians as is found in Genesis. On this account the genuineness of his books has been doubted, but I think without sufficient reason." (Anac. B. 8, C. 2, p. 391). Father Georgius, who was master of the Tibetian language, quotes the story of Anobret from Sanchoniathon, and shows that the Jeud of this forerunner of Moses, is the Jid of the Tibetians. Both Alexander Polyhistor and Abydene, the one a learned compiler in Scylla's time, the other referred to for his wisdom by Eusebius, agree to Sanchoniathon's ante-dating Moses, and to the account of the deluge, and other portions of Genesis, being purely Chaldean, taken from "manuscripts of an almost infinitely remote period of time."

The philosopher, Porphyry, student of Origen and Longinus, writes (Lib. iv, Adv. Christianos), that Sanchoniathon and Moses gave the like accounts of persons and places, and that Sanchoniathon extracts his account partly out of the annals of the cities, and partly out the book reserved in the temple, which he received from Jerombalus, Priest of the God Jeud, who is Jao or Jehovah."

Though the Jews were ever less spiritual than the inhabitants of the sunny clime of India, less learned than the Egytians, less poetic than the Persians, they ever had among them rare spiritual gifts; and all through that collection of books called the Old Testament, Spiritualism stands out prominent. Among the many, note the following passages:

"And there came two angels to Sodom at even, and Lot, seeing them, rose up to meet them."—*Gen.* xix : 1.

" And the Lord appeared to him (Abraham) in the plains. * * * And he lifted up his eyes and looked, and lo! three men stood beside him; and when he saw them he ran to meet them from the tent door, and bowed himself toward the ground."—*Gen.* xviii : 1-2.

When Jacob was traveling to meet Esau, he beheld the angel of God, and said "This is God's host."—*Gen.* xxxii.

" The angel of the Lord appeared to Moses in a flame of fire out of the midst of the bush : the bush burned, but was not consumed. He said, 'I am the God of thy father, the God of Abraham, Isaac, and Jacob;' and Moses hid his face."—*Ex.* iii.

" And the angel of the Lord found her (Hagar) by a fountain of water in the wilderness, * * * and said, ' Whence camest thou?' "—*Gen.* xvi: 7.

" This Moses, whom they refused, * * * did God send to be a ruler and a deliverer by the hand of the angel which appeared to him in the bush."—*Acts* vii: 35.

" And Jacob went on his way, and the angels of God met him."— *Gen.* xxxii: 1.

" And as he (Elijah) lay and slept under a juniper tree, behold, then, an angel touched him and said unto him' 'Arise and eat.'"—1 *Kings* xix: 5.

" Then the Lord opened the eyes of Balaam, and he saw the angel of the Lord standing in the way,"—*Num.* xxii: 31.

Saul consulted a medium at Endor.

"And she said, ' An old man cometh up; and he is covered with a mantle.' And Saul perceived that it was Samuel, and he stooped with his face to the ground, and bowed himself."—1 *Sam.* xxviii: 14.

" Fear came upon me and trembling, which made all my bones to shake. Then a *spirit* passed before my face. * * * It stood still; but I could not discern the form thereof. * * * I heard a voice saying, 'Shall mortal man be more just than God?' "— *Job*, iv: 14-17

" While I was speaking in prayer, even the man Gabriel, whom I had seen in the vision at the beginning, * * * touched me about the time of the evening oblation."—*Dan.* ix: 21.

" Then Nebuchednezzar spake and said, ' Blessed be the God of Shadrach, Meshach and Abednego, who hath sent his angel and delivered his servants that trusted in him, and have changed the King's word.'" *Dan.* x: 9-10. " Yet heard I the voice of his words, and behold a hand touched me." * * * " Then there came again and touched me one like the appearance of a man, and he strengthened me."—*Dan.* x: 18.

" And it came to pass, when I, even I, Daniel, had seen the vision, and sought for the meaning, then, behold, there stood before me as the appearance of a man. And I heard a man's voice between the banks of Ulai, which called and said, Gabriel, make this man to understand the vision."—*Dan.* viii: 15-16.

" Yea, while I was speaking in prayer, even the man Gabriel, whom I had seen at the beginning, being caused to fly swiftly, touched me about the time of the evening oblation."—*Dan.* ix: 21.

A most interesting case of the return of spirits to mortals, is related of Ezekiel. On one occasion the " Lord," that is the ruling spirit of the Jewish nation, appeared to the prophet, and by the hair of his head floated him away to Jerusalem.

"And he put forth the form of a hand, and took me by a lock of mine head; and the spirit lifted me up between the earth and the heavens and brought me in the vision of God to Jerusalem to the door of the inner gate that looketh toward the north."—*Ezekiel* viii : 3.

Arriving at the temple after this ærial voyage, he entered, and there stood before him seventy spirits, who appeared as men; men who had lived many centuries before his time:

"And there stood before them seventy men of the ancients of the house of Israel, and in the midst of them stood Jaazaniah, the son of Shaphan, with every man his censer in hand."—*Ezekiel* viii : 11

At another time, being in vision, having been carried thither as before, he saw five and twenty men, or spirits, some of whose names were given, who were known as conspicuous actors in the ancient days of Israel:

"Moreover the spirit lifted me up, and brought me unto the east gate of the Lord's house, which looked eastward : and behold at the door of the gate five and twenty men ; among whom I saw Jaazaniah the son of Azur, and Pelatiah, the son of Benaiah, princes of the people."—*Ezekiel* xi : 1.

About 3260, B. C., a powerful Mede, visiting Sardanapalus, reproved him for the luxuriousness of his court, and conspired with Belesis, of Babylonia, to overthrow him. Diodorus Siculus informs us, that when Sardanapalus heard of it, he laughed the whole thing to contempt, saying, an ancient prophecy, since confirmed by the voices of the 'gods,' had promised that Nineveh should never be taken by force. This exhibits the faith those old Assyrians had in omens and oracles from the immortals.

Berosus states that the winds, aided by the gods, angels, or spirits, destroying the towers of Babel, introduced the confusion of tongues; and that their wise men, in dreams and visions, frequently foretold the ruin of nations.

ANCIENT HISTORIC SPIRITUALISM — HEBRAIC.

The terms *gods, lords, angels, demons, spirits*, were used interchangeably by Egyptian, Phœnician, Persian, and the more ancient Grecian writers. This understood, much of the mysticism connected with God and Jehovah, Lord and Angel, as used by theologians, is cleared away. In the Old Testament we read: "In the beginning Gods, (Elohim, plural) created the heaven and the earth." Hesiod has a poem entitled Theogonia, giving the "generation of the gods." "In the book of Moses," says that learned church authority, Calmet, "the name of God is often given to the *angels*. * * * Princes, magistrates, and great men are called gods. If a slave is desirous to continue with his master, he shall be brought to the gods. The Lord (an exalted angel) is seated amidst the gods, and judges with them."

The testimony of the truly eminent Philo Judæus, relative to the identity of *god, lord, angel, spirit, etc.*, is exceedingly important. We quote from Yonge's translation: "Those (referring to gods) of the most divine nature are utterly regardless of any situation on earth, but are raised to a greater height, and placed in the ether itself, being of the purest possible character, which those among the Greeks that have studied philosophy, call heroes and demons, and which Moses, giving them a most felicitous appellation, calls angels, acting, as they do, the part of ambassadors and messengers. Therefore, if you look upon souls and demons and angels as things differing indeed in name, but as meaning in reality one and the same thing, you will thus get rid of the heaviest of all evils—superstition. For as people speak of good demons and bad demons, so do they speak of good and bad souls; and also of some angels as being by their title worthy ambassadors * * * from God to men, being sacred and inviolable guardians; others as being unholy and unworthy. Hence, the Psalmist David speaks of the 'operation of evil angels.'"

In harmony with the above, from a different source, yet in confirmation of the same general idea, we quote from the third volume of Plato, by Burges, Trinity College, Cambridge: "They are demons, because prudent and learned. * * * * Hence, poets say well, who say that when a good man shall have reached his end, he receives a mighty destiny and honor, and becomes a demon according to the appellation of prudence."

Concurring with the general belief of those ages, the Grecian poet Hesiod, in his "Works and Days," says:

"But when concealed had destiny this race,
Demons there were, called holy upon earth,
Good, ill-averters, and of men the guard."

Also, this significant line occurs:

" Holy demons by great Jove designed."

Earnest Renan, one of the most eminent Shemitic scholars living, speaking, in his "Life of Jesus," of the group that assembled upon the banks of Lake Tiberias to listen to Jesus says: " They believed in spectres and in spirits."

These citations from Hesiod, Plato, and especially Philo Judæus, a few years the senior of the Galilean, clearly demonstrate the fact of the identity of gods, spirits, demons and angels, that there were good, learned, and holy demons, and those denominated unholy; and that these demons, or spirits and angels, held intercourse with, and were the guardians of mortals.

As a general thing, the magi, magicians, or media of Egypt, excelled Moses in the production of wonders manifest in the different phases of phenomenal Spiritualism. Taking *their* account, they were doubtless always the victors. They certainly had several trials for the mastery. Accepting the scriptural rendering, it is evident that the wonderful works wrought by Moses were also accomplished, with hardly an exception, through the "enchantments" of Pharaoh's "wise men and magicians." This enchantment was the mesmeric will-force—a part of the very "*wisdom*" that Moses had learned in Egypt. Psychologists are always aided more or less by their spirit guides.

Referring to the so-called miracles recorded in the 7th chapter of Exodus, we find that the magicians turned their rods into serpents (psychologically, of course); water into blood; and produced the frogs also, with seemingly the same ease and celerity that Moses and Aaron did, and by the *same* psychologic law. But when the Lord, through Moses, commanded Aaron to "stretch out his rod" and go to manufacturing "*lice*," the magicians begged to be excused; it was too small business—utterly beneath the magi, or media of old, proud and classic Egypt! They would not thus degrade their psychologic knowledge—a portion of their sacred mysteries. To be sure Moses says they "*could not.*" This is Moses' version of the matter, however, (if indeed, he ever wrote the Pentateuch); and Moses, holding himself in high estimation, wrote in his own interest; and, what is more, a man, courting fame, that could write an account of his own death and burial, is entitled, write what he may, to little credit.

Never charmed with Moses' characteristics, we do not deny his mediumship, nor the truth of his frequent conversations with the "Lord God, face to face;" that is, his *familiar spirit*, but we rate it second to the mediumistic powers of the seers of Egypt and Persia, and immeasurably inferior to that of the Judean prophets. See the power of the *gods* when the Syrians came to seize Elisha: "When the servant had risen early and gone forth, behold an host encompassed the city, both with horses and chariots. And his servant said unto him, 'Alas! my master! what shall we do?' * * * "And Elisha prayed, and said, 'Lord, I pray thee open his eyes (clairvoyant eyes) that he may see.'" And the Lord, angel or spiritual being, opened the eyes, that is, the interior or *spiritual eyes*, of the young man, and he saw—saw because the inner vision was unsealed—and "behold, the mountain was full of horses and chariots of fire round about Elisha.—2 *Kings* iv.

Titus, in his address to his soldiers before Jerusalem, said, "For what man of virtue is there that does not know that those souls which are severed from their fleshy bodies in battles by the sword, are received by the ether, that purest of elements, and joined to that company which are placed among the stars; that they become *good demons*, and propitious heroes, and *show themselves as such to their posterity afterward?*"—*Josephus*, B. vi : chap. 1., § 5.

The Hebrew scriptures, Talmud, and Kabbala, all abound in dreams, omens, prophecies, angelic interpositions and spirit communications, often beautiful, and sometimes absolutely grand; all of which bear a close resemblance in form and purpose to those more marked manifestations of spirit power, that threw such a transcendent glory over the older nations of Central and Southern Asia. "The most usual form," said the learned and Orthodox Calmet, "in which good angels appear, both in the Old Testament and New, is the human form." It was in that shape they showed themselves to Abraham, Lot, Jacob, Moses, Joshua, Manoah the father of Samson, to David, Tobit, and the Prophets. The one that appeared to Joshua on the plain of Jericho, appeared apparently in the guise of a warrior, since Joshua asked him—"Art thou for us or for our adversaries?"

But enough has been adduced to prove that the Hebrew government, in all its religious and secular interests, was regulated by spirit oracles, and that these constitute the chief beauty of its administration.

> "There was a time when *all* mankind
> Did listen to a faith sincere,
> To tuneful tongues in mystery verse."

But alas, how infidel now is the church that practically scorns the voice of faith! Let Tertullian speak to such; "Thou canst not call that madness of which thou art proved to know nothing."

CHAPTER VIII.

GRECIAN.

> "Go on, spotless mortal, in the path of virtue;
> It is the way to the stars;
> Offspring of the gods thyself—
> So shalt thou become the father of gods."

> "Then side by side along the dreary coast,
> Advanced Achilles and Patroclus' ghost,
> A friendly pair."

Enchanted is olden Greece! Pre-eminently the land of poetry, painting and music, of art and witching song, her republics voiced the heaven-winged words of freedom long before the "Son of Man" said, "whom the truth maketh free is free indeed." Her classic mind drank deep of inspirations that gushed, fountain-like, from mountain, hill and vale, haunted by nymphs and sylphs—from sun-kissed seas peppered with ever-green isles embossed with rainbows under gorgeous skies, deific in guardianship. All things conspired to engender mental vivacity, genial heart, and aptitude for spiritual impression and culture. Incidental to these influences, the literature, attributed to the poets, historians, tragedians, philosophers, statesmen and moral heroes of Greece, abounds in brilliant thoughts and the most sublime ideas, touching the invisible realities of the spirit-world.

As Americans look to English universities for samples of highest culture—as Northern Europe once looked to Rome—

Rome, in her palmiest periods, to Greece, and Egypt to India, so the literati and philosophers among the Greeks looked up and bowed in profound reverence before the authors, poets and long-treasured wisdom of Egyptian savans. Thither flocked the wisest of the Grecians to perfect their education both scientific and religious. The learned Jacob Bryant says: "The whole theology of Greece was derived from the East." Josephus wrote in his day: "All that concerns the Greeks, we may say is of yesterday only." He further assures us that the Greeks "acknowledged that it was not they, but the Phœnicians, Egyptians and other nations of antiquity, who preserved the most memorials and arts of mankind, and that from Egypt they *themselves* imported them; and that to those who introduced philosophy and the knowledge of things celestial and divine among them, such as Pherecydes the Syrian, Pythagoras and Thales, they were greatly indebted. All with one consent agreed that they learned what they knew of the Egyptians and Chaldeans, and wrote but little." Though tinged and tinctured more or less with the older philosophers of Egypt and India, Spiritualism was, for a long period, the universal religion of Greece. Hesiod flourished about 1000 B. C., and in his Theogony gave a faithful account of the gods (spirits) of antiquity. He himself consulted oracles, as to the future, and at a certain time the Pythia—priestess of Apollo—(that is, the female medium controlled by Apollo—an ascended mortal termed *god*) directed him to shun the grove of Nemean Jupiter, which he did, saving his life. He declares, himself prophetically inspired by the gods and goddesses, saying of the daughters of Jove:

>"They gave into my hand
>A rod of marvelous growth; a laurel bough
>Of blooming verdure; and within me breathed
>A heavenly voice, that I might utter forth
>All past and future things, and bade me praise
>The blessed of ever-living God."

Hesiod frequently breathes his firm belief in the tender watch-care of guardian spirits, as well as those that take cognizance of vice:

> "Invisible, the gods are ever nigh,
> Pass through our midst, and bend the all-seeing eye;
> The men who grind the poor, who wrest the right,
> Aweless of heaven's revenge, stand naked to their sight;
> For thrice ten thousand holy demons rove
> This breathing world, the delegates of Jove.
> *Guardians of man*, their glance alike surveys
> The upright judgments and the unrighteous ways."

Writing of the seers and sages of a past golden age, the spirits of which became the guardians of men, he says in his Works, Elton's translation:

> "When earth's dark womb had closed this race around,
> High Jove as demons raised them from the ground
> Earth-wandering spirits that their charge began,
> The ministers of good, the guards of man.
> Mantled with mist of darkling air they glide
> And compass earth, and pass on every side;
> Kingly their state, and delegate of Heaven;
> By their vicarious hands prosperity is given."

The Arundelian marbles place Homer 907 B. C. Born at Bethsia, a village of Egypt, nearer the Red Sea than the Nile, he became a medium and seer at eight years of age, spirits appearing visible to him with harps and songs, indicating his future greatness. His earthly Egyptian teacher was Helecate, and his Grecian tutor, Myrah. Hesiod was his direct controlling or guardian spirit. In these breathing numbers, immortal utterances and matchless poetical combinations, Hesiod prompted him in the Greek, and Lucitan in the Egyptian, while intellectually and spiritually above them both, was one of those grand old Indian seers that had long summered in the heavens. This accounts for the striking resemblances between the Iliad of Homer and that great Brahminical poem of Valmike, entitled the Ramayana. All, versed in the Iliad and Odyssey, know they are all aglow with oracles, prophecies, dreams—the descriptions of gods, goddesses and demons, and the interest they ever take in human affairs. The very warp and woof of the Grecian poetry and philosophy were spiritual, and hence their beauty and freshness to-day.

Herodotus writes (Euterpe, 53)—"I consider Hesiod and Homer older than myself, by four hundred years. * * * They were the poets who framed the Hellenic theogony; gave distinctive names to the gods; distributed amongst them honors and professions, and pointed out their receptive forms." Diodorus Siculus, in the seventh chapter of his first book, "asserts the same; that is, these historians mean to state that these poets did not invent, but arranged and detailed the *knowledge* of the gods," brought from India into Egypt; then from Egypt and Syria into their country by Orpheus, Danaus and Cadmus. Pherecydes, the early teacher of Pythagoras, flourishing some 600 B. C., taught the immortality of the soul, the guardian care of holy gods and demons, and is considered the first who wrote concerning the nature of the gods in *prose*.

Plato in the Timœus says: "That between God and man are the *daimones* or spirits, who are always near us, though commonly invisible to us, and know all our thoughts. They are intermediate between gods and men, and their function is to interpret and convey to the gods what comes from men, and to men what comes from the gods."

In Plato's Apology and Republic (p. 31, 40, b. x.), that great master Grecian says: "The demons often direct man in the quality of guardian spirits, in all his actions, as witness the demon of Socrates." * * * * "There are two kinds of men. One of these, through aptitude, will receive the illuminations of divinity, and the other, through inaptitude, will subject himself to the power of avenging demons." * * * * They (the poets) do not compose by art, but through a divine power; since, if they knew how to speak by art upon the subject correctly, they would be able to do so upon all others. On this account, a deity has deprived them of their senses, and employs them as his ministers and oracle singers, and divine prophets, in order that, when we hear them, we may know it is not they, to whom sense is not present, who speak what is valuable, but the *god* himself who speaks, and through them addresses us. We are not to doubt about those beautiful poems being not human, but divine, and the work not of men, but of gods; and that the poets are nothing else but interpreters of the gods, (that is, spirits,) possessed by whatever deity they may happen to be.

The dialogue of Plato relative to the conversations of Socrates with his friends, contain the richest veins of spiritual truth. In the Phædon, Cebes says: "Persuade us then not to fear death."

"As for that," says Socrates, "you must employ *spells* and *exorcisms* every day till you be cured."

"But pray, Socrates, where shall we meet an excellent conjurer, since you are going to leave us?"

"Greece is large enough," replies Socrates, "and well stored with learned men. You must likewise look for a conjurer among yourselves; for 'tis possible there may be none found more able to perform those enchantments."

"Do the souls of the dead have a being in the other world or no?"

"It is a very ancient opinion that souls quitting this world repair to the infernal regions, and return after that to live in this world * * * * When a man dies, his mortal and corruptible part suffers dissolution, but the immortal part escapes unhurt and triumphs over death. * * * * The earth we inhabit is properly nothing else but the sediment of the other; that is, that pure earth above, called Ether. In this more perfect earth, everything has a perfection answering to its qualities. The trees, flowers, fruits and mountains are charmingly beautiful; they produce all sorts of precious stones of incomparable perfection of clearness and splendor; those we so much esteem, as jasper, emeralds and sapphire, are not comparable to them. * * They have sacred groves, and temples actually inhabited by the gods, who give (us) evidence of their presence by oracles, divinations, inspirations, and all other sensible signs."

Referring to his eccentricities, Socrates says: "The cause of this is that which you have often and in many places heard me mention; because I am moved by a certain divine and spiritual influence, which also Melitus, through mockery, has set out in the indictment. This began with me from childhood, being a kind of voice which, when present, always diverts me from what I am about to do, but never urges me on. But this duty, as I said, has been enjoined on me by the Deity, by oracles, by dreams, and by every mode by which any other divine decree has ever enjoined anything for man to do."—Cary's Translation.

Reasoning, he asked Miletus, "Do we not take these deities, or demons, for the gods, or the children of gods?"

"Yes, doubtless!"

"Therefore, you acknowledge," said Socrates, "that I believe there are demons, and that these demons are gods. * * * * I have likewise told you that I received my orders from God himself, by oracles, dreams, and all other methods Deity makes use of to make known his pleasure to men."

M. Dacier, in a note, (Apol. of Soc., p. 393) says: "Socrates learned of Pythagoras that demons, or angels and heroes—that is, devout men and saints, are the sons of God, because they derive from him their being, as light owes its origin to a luminous body."

Socrates being inquired of why he busied himself so much in private, and did not appear in the conventions of the people, gives the following reason:

"The thing that hindered me from doing so, Athenians, was this familiar spirit, this divine voice, that you have often heard of, and which Melitus has endeavored so much to ridicule. This spirit has stood by me from my infancy. It is a voice that does not speak but when it means to take me off from some resolution. It never presses me to undertake anything, but it always thwarted me when I meant to meddle in affairs of state." (Apol. Soc. p. 398.)

Turning at a certain time to his friend Simmias, he discoursed thus of virtue and the future immortal life: "What I have said ought to sufficiently show that we should labor all our lives to acquire virtue and wisdom, since we have so great a reward proposed to us, and so bright a prospect before us. As for you, my dear Simmias and Cebes, and all you of this company, you will follow me shortly. My hour is come; and as a tragic poet would say, the surly pilot calls me aboard. It is time I should go to the bath; for I think it better, before I drink the poison, to be washed in order to save the woman the trouble after I am dead."

Crito, inquiring what orders he had to leave with reference to his children and other affairs, further asked: "How will you be buried?" "Just as you please," said Socrates, "if I do not slip from you." At the same time, looking upon them with a gentle smile, said: "I cannot attain my end in persuading Crito that this is Socrates who discourses with you; * * * and still he fancies that Socrates is the thing that shall shortly see death. He confounds *me* with my *corpse;* and in that view asks how I will be buried. And all this after the long discourse I made to you lately in order to show, that, as soon as I shall have taken the poison, I shall stay no longer with you; but I shall part from hence and enjoy the felicity of the blessed." (See Ap. Phedon, p. 247.)

That erudite Platonist, Proclus, writing upon the demon of Socrates, commenced his forty-third chapter on the "Theology of Plato" thus: "Let us speak concerning the demons who allotted the superintendance of mankind * * * The most perfect souls choose a life conformable to their presiding god, and live according to a divine demon. Hence the Egyptian priest admired Plotinus as being controlled (on account of the purity of his life) by a divine demon. And with great propriety also does Socrates call his demon a god, for he belonged to the first and highest demons.

Accordingly, Socrates was most perfect, being governed by such a presiding power, and conducting himself by the *will* of such a leader and guardian of his life."

Remembering, then, that Pythagoras resided for a period of years in Egypt, that Socrates was personally acquainted with some of the disciples of Pythagoras, the anointed Samian, and that Plato was a pupil of Socrates, we perceive the naturalness of the descent from age to age of these spiritualistic teachings relative to the gods and demons— to their gentle guardianship and continuous converse with mortals, and the unspeakable blessedness pertaining to those Elysian fields that gladden with molten glory the homes of the angels.

Jesus, borne in infancy "down into Egypt," early connected with the Essenians, afterwards initiated into the psychologic and mediumistic wisdom of the older Eastern mysteries, as well as conversant with those glittering thoughts that dropped like pearls from the pens of the Persian poets, naturally imbibed, in consonance with his susceptible organism, and taught some of the Platonian doctrines, among which was the "ministry of spirits," preexistence, and the ascent of souls into that Paradisiacal house of "many mansions."

Every scholarly theologian knows that the parables of Jesus, as well as John's Gospel, abound in Platonisms. Accordingly, the orthodox commentator, Dr. Campbell, frankly, yet doubtless unwillingly, confessed that, "Our Lord's descriptions of the abodes of departed spirits were not drawn from the writings of the Old Testament; but have a remarkable affinity to the descriptions which the Grecian poets have given of them."

Nonnus informs us that "there was a statue at Delphi which emitted an inarticulate voice." The spirits were thus experimenting with the solid stone to produce a Memnon in Greece, as they do these days train the muscles which they wish to use in writing or speaking; but doubtless found the material too perverse for their purpose.

Epimenides, a prominent poet, living in Solon's time, possessed the remarkable power with which certain media of our day are gifted, of leaving his body, and, conducted by immortal guides, visiting friends gone before, vast galleries of art, and the magnificent temples of the ascended sages of antiquity. Those trances continued so long, and he revealed so strange truths upon returning into the mortal tenement, that he was held in high repute—almost revered among the Athenians during his life, and at death they gave him a place among their gods. The rarely endowed Hermodorus possessed this same power. Aided by the controlling magnetic influences of spirit-guardians, he frequently quitted the physical frame, and explored the matchless beauties that obtain in the land of souls. So Aristides the Just gives a full account, in the "Orationes Sacræ," of his visits to the healing temples of Æsculapius. Many of his dreams proved to be prophecies, and in his trances he mentioned things as then taking place in distant countries. These were afterwards verified, as in like cases with Swedenborg.

In the night vision, Apollo and Æsculapius came to Epimenides and requested him to compose and sing verses; something which he had never thought of attempting in his normal state. He so did, however, with eminent success. His feelings, while in this inspirational condition, he said, were most delightful. After his sight was more thoroughly opened, he declared that Plato, Demosthenes and Sophocles often stood near the foot of his couch and conversed with him. All through his marked career immortal demons seem to have accompanied him, to whom he owed not only his health, but much of his wisdom. (See Aris., by Canter.)

Thus runs Spiritualism through all Grecian history in converse with gods, angels, demons, spirits, and the appearance of apparitions, symbols and psychological forms, in connection with visions, trances and healings. The mythology of the Greeks, even with all its shadowy vagaries, was infinitely superior to modern theology. The clergy, with few exceptions, have persisted in wickedly misrepresenting the ethical teachings and theological doctrines that prevailed in Greece for many centuries before the Christian era.

Occasionally a clergyman has dared to be just. Such was the Rev. J. B. Gross. In his "Introduction to Heathen Religion," he says: "Perhaps on no subject within the ample range of human knowledge have so many fallacious ideas been propagated as upon that of the gods and the worship of heathen antiquity. Nothing but a shameful ignorance, a pitiable prejudice or the contemptible pride, which denounces all investigations as a useless or a criminal labor, when it must be feared that they will result in the overthrow of pre-established systems of faith or the modification of long-cherished principles of science, can have thus misrepresented the theology of heathenism, and distorted—nay, caricatured—its forms of religious worship. It is time that posterity should raise its voice in vindication of violated truth, and that the present age should learn to recognize in the hoary past, at least, a little of that common sense of which it boasts with as much self-complacency as if the prerogative of reason was the birth-right only of modern times."

The aim of priests, in throwing contempt upon the mythologies of India, Egypt and Greece, was doubtless to enable them longer to continue their hold upon the mind through their superstitions, and the mouldy traditions of church fathers. But the great Newton said, that "ancient mythology was nothing but historical truth in a poetical dress." Bacon said, it "consisted solely of moral and metaphysical allegories." The learned Bryant, as quoted by Sir William Jones, said, that "all the heathen divinities were only different representatives of deceased progenitors." Jamblichus, author of Life of Pythagoras, admits that the "gods and demons of the mythologic ages, were the good and heroic of earth's immortalized, yet giving oracles to the living."

From the facts adduced in Grecian history, we learn what the modern church of Christians dare not recognize, that the images of those ancient gods, some beautiful and others hideous, according to the plane of spiritual perception, were used as oracles, the same as tables, musical instruments and planchetts for spiritual communication, are these days. Theirs were doubtless better media, being forms of the spirits themselves, made by their order for mediumistic purposes. Originally, those "idols," as churchal worshipers scornfully call them, were the channels of sweet and holy communication with presiding angels once inhabiting the earth-sphere.

Beda, treating of the "Seven Wonders of the World," tells us, that, in the capitol at Rome, there were statues (mediumized by spirit magnetism) set up for all the provinces conquered by the Romans. These were images of their gods, on the breasts of which were written the names of the nations. On their necks little bells were hung, and priests were appointed to watch them day and night. When one of these rung by spirit influence, they knew at once what nation was about to rebel against the Romans, of which due notice was immediately given to the civil authorities, who made provision accordingly.

By means of bells the spirits gave many of their communications to the Jewish priests, whose garments were festooned with them, making music, under right conditions, delicious as that we these days hear at the musical entertainments of spiritual circles.

M. de L'Ancre, in his book entitled "The Inconstancy of Demons and Evil Spirits," tells us, "That in the town of Bourdeaux, there was an honest canon of a church who had his house for sometime troubled (haunted) with spirits; and that, among other things, there was heard almost every night a kind of music, like that of the *espirut*, set with little bells, so pleasant, that this partly took from him the fear and apprehension of the spirits."

With the ancient spiritualists communications by sounds were carried to a high state of perfection, showing the delicacy of their spiritual batteries, and the beautiful degree of their musical science blending with their religion. Undoubtedly they discovered a certain mental ratiocination between sound and moral character, and made it practical in the methods above described. Developed by the Spiritual Philosophy, it is already known, that every person, as is every object in the outer world, is ensphered in an atmospheric magnetism exactly of the quality of the inner affection and the co-relative molecular texture of the body. The intonations of every person's voice is a sure index of such qualities—indeed of the very spirit itself. Man is organized on the eternal principles of music, and is keyed to certain grades of love and thought as a musical instrument to sounds which it is intended to produce. This spiritual *keying* of the character determines taste in music. Hence, certain sounds are agreeable to some; to others disagreeable. Deep, solemn psalmody, will stir the soul of the churchal worshiper; such sounds enter into rapport with him interiorly; hence the response. The lute or the guitar will better charm the passional lover or melancholy dreamer.

Gottschalk, the great pianist, speaking of musical philosphy, states that "the flame of the candles oscillates to the quake of the organ. A powerful orchestra near a sheet of water ruffles its surface. * * * The sound of the bassoon is cold; the notes of the French horn, at a distance, and of the harp, are voluptuous. The flute, playing softly in the middle of the register, calms the nerves." Swedenborg discovered the practicability of this musical ratiocination in the spiritual world, when he said, all the speech of the angels, " at the close of every sentence, has its termination in unity of accent, which is merely in consequence of the divine influx into their souls respecting the unity of God."

We see, therefore, a most beautiful truth in Jamblichus' explanation of musical divination by the use of priestly bells. He says in substance: " Various kinds of motions in the world answer to various orders of the gods. Melodies agree according to the principles of their motions (undulatory vibrations), and flow to certain gods to which they are most agreeable, or with which they are most in correspondential harmony. The gods being every where, bestow their gifts where the sounds and melodies chiefly agree to them. Being affected thereby, they insinuate themselves inspirationally into our spirits, and wholly work in us by their musical essence and power."

Pythagoras maintained that a divinity lay hidden in these sacred ringings of bells on the statues, and in the ears they sounded as "the voice of the gods."

Plutarch says, "their sound is only heard by those who keep their minds in a calm and composed state, undisturbed by passions." Then he avers we can hear the holy melodies of "sacred and demoniacal men."

Luther being on an animal plane, coarse and vulgar, yet herculean in will, heard spirit sound answering exactly in quality of melody with this plane of his life; and it was to him "as if a wind went out of his head, the devil driving it!"

Mahomet heard these melodies, whilst in a trance, giving him most heavenly answers to his questions.

The beautiful legend of the ancients is not, therefore, without foundation in psychological law. The bells of their temples were consecrated to divine worship; when, therefore, they were rung "offensive genii" took flight, affrighted at the sounds. When the bell of the soul—the sensorium—is struck with angelic thought, there is a response with the angels, and all evil influences are repelled as darkness before the light of the rising sun. How natural then for those devotees to reverence these oracular images! As they departed from the spiritual senses to the more external, the virtue of that worship dimmed into shadow and gloom, leaving only the bare image, void of soul, like the church to-day, worshiping symbols whose spiritual substance has departed; or, like spirit-rappings, and the other physical phenomena, when wretchedly abused by monopolizing and sensuous Spiritualists. Let us beware how we use the divine oracles, lest our worship be also meaningless idolatry! The readers attention is called to the following facts, culled from the many, exactly parallel:

"There are many oracles among the Greeks, many also among the Egyptians, many in Africa, and many here in Asia. But these give responses neither without priests, nor without interpreters. Here, however, Apollo is self-moved, and performs the prophetic office wholly by himself; and this he does as follows: When he wishes to "communicate," he moves in his place, whereupon the priests forthwith take him up. Or if they neglect to take him up, he sweats, and comes forth into the middle of the room; when, however, others bear him upon their shoulders, he guides them, moving from place to place. At length the chief priest supplicating him, asks him all sorts of questions. If he does not assent, he moves backwards; if he approves, he impels forward those who bear him, like a charioteer. Thus they arrive at responses. They do nothing except by this method. Thus he gives predictions concerning the seasons, foretells storms, &c. I will relate another thing also which he did in my presence. The priests were bearing him upon their shoulders—he left them below upon the ground, while he himself was borne aloft and alone into the air." (Lucian. de Syria Dea.)

"A little before the misfortune of the Lacedæmonians at Leuctra, there was heard the clashing of arms in the temple of Hercules, and the statue of Hercules sweat profusely. At Thebes, at the same time, in the temple of Hercules, the folding doors, which were fastened with bolts, suddenly opened of themselves, and the arms which were hung upon the walls were found thrown upon the ground. There were other signs preceding this calamity. The statue of Lysander at Delphi, which the Lacedæmonians had placed there after his great naval victory over the Athenians, appeared crowned with weeds and bitter herbs, and the two golden stars which had been suspended there as offerings in honor of Castor and Pollux, who had assisted them *visibly* in that battle, fell, and disappeared." (Cicero, de Divinatione i. 94.)

The cultured Greeks, eminently poetic and spiritual, cherished views concerning death quite similar to the spiritualists of this century. Plato was, to them, a central inspiration. Touched and thrilled by his sublime doctrines, they considered this world the only *Hades;* heaven, their native home, and all death an ascent to the higher life.

Avoiding descent for incarnation, and remaining on high, with the gods, was real life, because life in the spirit; while descent into this world was death. Macrobius writes in his "dream of Scipio," "Here, on earth, is the cavern of despair, the infernal region. The river of oblivion is the wandering of the mind, forgetting the majesty of its former life; and a thinking residence in the body the only life." (Lib. i. cap. 9). To the clear vision of those inspired Grecians, dying was ascending to the soul's primal home—the society of the celestial gods in the starry regions of measureless space.

CHAPTER IX.

ROMAN.

"For thrice ten thousand holy demons rove
This breathing world, the delegates of Jove,
Guardians of man, their glance alike surveys
The upright judgments and the unrighteous ways."

"Thus we see how man's prophetic creeds
Made gods of men, when Godlike were their deeds."

Rome! proud, imperial, seven-hilled—Rome! that with nod could crown kings and bury empires—Rome! boastful of her Cicero and her Cæsars—Rome! that humbled Carthage—Rome! with her deep blue skies, southern winds, and ruins rich in ancient legends! she accepted, even in her most famous ages, Greece for her schoolmaster. Her philosophy, religion, science, art, and poetry—her dramas, and even the very laws so long honored in Athens, were brought from Greece and introduced among the Romans more than three hundred years before Christ. Greek art was copied by Roman artists. Greek professors taught the Grecian philosophy to the more promising of the youth of Rome, and all were taught to respect the oracles and reverence the gods and genii that appeared to, guarded, and conversed with mortals.

Sallust, a Platonic philosopher, author of a treatise "On the Gods and the world," says: "But we, when we are good, are conjoined with the gods through similitude; but when evil, we are separated from them through dissimilitude.

And while we live according to virtue, we partake of the gods, but when we become evil, we cause them to become our enemies; not that they are angry, but because guilt prevents us from receiving the illuminations of the gods, and subjects us to the power of avenging demons.   *   *

"Since the providence of the gods is every where extended, a certain latitude, or fitness, is all that is requisite in order to receive their beneficent communications. But since so much providence is displayed in the last things, it is impossible that it should not subsist in such as are first: besides, divinations and the healing of bodies, take place from the beneficent providence of the gods."

Cicero says:—"Now, as far as I know, there is no nation whatever, however polished and learned, or however barbarous and uncivilized, which does not believe it possible that future events may be indicated, understood and predicted by certain persons."—*De Divinatione, lib. 1.*

He further says, "To natural divination, belongs that which does not take place from supposition, observations, or well-known signs; but arises from an inner state and activity of the mind in which men are enabled by an unfettered advance of the soul to foretell future things.   *   *   *   If we turn to ridicule the Babylonians and Caucasians, who believe in celestial signs, and who observe the number and course of the stars; if, as I said, we condemn all these for their superstitions and folly, which, as they maintain, are founded upon the experience of fifty centuries and a half; let us, in that case, call the belief of ages imposture—let us burn *our* records, and say that everything was but imagination. But is the history of Greece a lie, when Apollo foretold the future through the oracles of the Lacedæmonians and Corinthians? I will leave all else as it is, but this I must defend, that the *gods* influence and care for human affairs. The Delphian oracle would never have become so celebrated, nor so overwhelmed by presents from every king and every nation, if every age had not experienced the *truth* of its predictions."

Among the most noted of the ancient oracles were Delphi, Dodona and Trophonius. Delphi was situated at the foot of Mount Parnassus, historic as one of the haunts of the muses. Upon this mountain there was a cave, from which arose electric exhalations intoxicating the brain. It was discovered by a shepherd youth, who, upon experiencing its influences, was caused to pronounce strange words, and foretell future events. Around this cave were erected several temples, one of which was magnificent. To it, all nations flocked for responses. Apollo, a Grecian god, was the spiritual intelligence that gave the oracle. Poets, orators, and generals frequently consulted the Delphian medium, receiving responses and prophecies. This medium, through whom the oracle was delivered, was a priestess called Pythia. Apollo did not always give the communications orally, but impressed the leading ideas upon her mind, and she uttered them in her own language, thus affecting or stamping them with her own peculiarities.

The Pythia prepared herself for the spiritual control of Apollo by purifications and fastings; then, being so charged by him with the electric fluid, that her hair stood upright, eyes wild, and even the foundation of the temple shaking, she uttered strange, mystic words, which were collected by prophets and poets, and woven into verse. Here is a sample, designed to inspire the halting nature of Agesilaus:

> "Sparta, beware, though thou art fierce and proud,
> Lest a lame king thy ancient glories shroud;
> For then 't will be thy fate to undergo
> Tedious turmoil of war and sudden woe."

Plutarch, as translated from the Greek by Philips, gives the reason why the Pythian priestess ceased her oracles in verse. The classical Anthon says, that besides the "Sacred Oaks" at Dodena, "dreams, visions, and preternatural voices also announced the will of the divinities." These oracles continued to speak from the immortal realms, as may be proven from Plutarch and Suetonius, long after the advent of Christianity. Nero and Julian both consulted them and received satisfactory answers. It also appears from the edicts of the Emperors Theodosius, Gratian and Valentinian, that oracles existed and were consulted as late as A. D. 358. These, in fact, have existed in all ages and under all civilizations, as ancient records demonstrate. They were simply phases of mediumship. The utterances of these lords, gods, angels, demons, and spirits, have been termed, in different periods, oracles, scriptures and inspirations.

The Romans, ambitious for fame, not only consulted the prophetic spirits of their own empire, but each year sent authorized individuals, as embassadors extraordinary, to consult with the most noted oracles of Greece. Livy's history of Rome covers a period of time six hundred years from the laying of its foundation to the date of its highest military power as a commonwealth, and that popular English writer, Wm. Howitt, tells us that "in Livy alone he had marked above *fifty* instances of his record of the literal fulfillment of dreams, oracles, prognostics, by soothsayers and astrologers."

The Rev. E. L. Magoon, in his "Grand Drama of Human Progress," writing of Romulus, says:

"We are told by Livy, that soon after his disappearance from among men, the spirit of Romulus visited the distinguished senator, Proculus Julius, and addressed him as follows:—'Go, tell my countrymen it is the decree of heaven, that the city I have founded shall become the mistress of the world. Let her cultivate assiduously the military art. Then let her be assured, and transmit the assurance from age to age, that no mortal power can resist the arms of Rome.' Strict and persevering obedience to this counsel eventually caused that colossal power to extend itself from Siberia to the Great Desert, and from the Ganges to the Atlantic."

When the Roman Emperor Tiberius left the city for Capreæ, the soothsayers—a certain order of mediums gifted with the power of foretelling the future—said, with deep solemnity, he would never again enter the eternal city. This, Tacitus admits, was literally fulfilled. These are his words: "That Tiberius would return no more was, as prophesied, verified by the event." Further illustrating the peculiarities of Tiberius' life, in the sixth book of the Annals, and weighing the testimony as to oracular prophecies, and also to what extent gods and demons exercised guardianship over and came into conscious relations with mortals, he adds:

"That though what is foretold and the events that follow may often vary, the fallacy is not to be imputed to the *ar* itself (that is, the *truth* of mediumship), but to the vanity of pretenders to a science respected by antiquity, and in modern times established by undoubted proof."

The principal events pertaining to the reign of Nero were foretold by the son of Thrassalus, a noted prophetic seer of that time.

Pliny the younger relates marvelous things that occurred within his range of knowledge, as foretold by oracles or predicted in visions and dreams.

The assassination of Caracalla was foreshadowed to him in a dream.

Sylla was apprised of his death by a strange vision the very night before his departure from earth.

Also, on the night that Attila passed to the sunlit shores of immortality, Marius dreamed that Attila's bow was broken; and according to Plutarch, Brutus himself, in a grim twilight hour, was met by Cæsar's spirit, that said, "I shall meet thee at Philippi!" and at Philippi Brutus fell

Presentiments, spirit voices, portents, bodings, visions, dreams and shadowy warnings have frequently preceded individual and almost uniformly national disasters.

Vespasian, probably the most unassuming, and certainly one of the most eminent, of the Roman emperors, was the possessor of several mediumistic gifts, the most prominent of which were seeing and healing. Several instances are recorded of his restoring the sick and causing the blind to see by spirit power. While in Alexandria he restored a paralytic hand by a simple touch. Both Suetonius and Strabo confirm these accounts. The critical Tacitus, writing of Vespasian and his spiritual endowments, relates the fact of his distinctly seeing Basilides clairvoyantly, when many miles distant in body. He also mentions his bringing sight to the rayless eyes of an Alexandrian moving in the humbler walks of life, who came to him by the advice of Serapis, a departed spirit, highly esteemed among the Egyptians. These, and multitudes more of so-called miraculous works, are much better attested by history than those ascribed to the Man of Nazareth. All are entitled to more or less credit. Tacitus further says, that Vespasian concluded that the gods had favored him with supernatural vision, and divine gifts, which gave him confidence that his future reign would be cared for by the gods, and such guardian demons as inhabit the higher elysian lands of heaven.

Based upon research, then, and in the exercise of our best judgment, we accept as *true* most of the wonders, prodigies, visions, trances, spiritual gifts and superhuman works of those elder ages, that (preceded by trials and crosses) ultimately crowned the mediumistic and martyred of India, Egypt, Persia, Greece, Rome and Judea—accept them, whether carved on pyramids, penned on parchment-scrolls, or written in Biblical or Sybilline books—accept them, first, because conformable with the clearest methods of spiritual analysis and humanity's divinest intuitions; and secondly, because reasonable—because corroborated by hosts of eye-witnesses in all ages and countries, and confirmed by thousands of media in the present. The general law is ever the same; the mingling of races in connection with country, civilization and other conditions, have merely modified the manifestations. Jesus declared that "greater works" than his should be done in the future.

But why adduce further testimony? The historic past is comparable to a measureless wilderness, all dotted and gemmed with valleys and mountains, flowers, fruits, and crystal streams, symbolizing immortal truths—*truths* with millions-phased fore-gleams and finger-marks demonstrating an actual converse with those exalted and immortalized souls that traverse the upper kingdom of God! Hence, Sophocles affirmed that—

> "This is not a matter of to-day,
> Or yesterday, but hath been from all time."

And Hesiod, in strains as mellifluous as undying, told of—

> "Ærial spirits designed
> To be on earth the guardians of mankind."

—while the grandly inspired Goethe sang in sweet refrain—

> "The spirit world is not closed—
> Thy *sense* is closed—thy heart is dead."

LECTURE III.

CHRISTIAN SPIRITUALISM.

Chapter X.

THE FORESHADOWING.

> "God has taught but one religion,
> One in every age and land.
> * * * * *
> God has written but one Bible—
> Love—compressed in one quick word."

Religion is natural. The religious sentiment is an essential principle of the human soul. Like the true and the beautiful, like moral consciousness, it is in humanity permanent, *eternal*.

Life's emotional stream from the manger in Nazareth to the "rappings" in Rochester, has been bridged with startling, spiritual phenomena. So devious its windings, the patient student of antiquity often wearies in tracing it among the lights and shadows that alternately dance in brightness, or darken into sullen midnight along its shelving shores.

The genuine historian living in two worlds—the past and the present—is necessarily philosophic and imaginative, painting visible forms, as well as transcribing passing events. Though gathering these, and weighing facts correctly—the hard granitic facts characterizing given epochs—he experiences deeper delights in arranging them in orderly series, and deducing therefrom such great logical conclusions as tally with the mighty march of the ages.

During those fearful mediæval years, when a cultured paganism and Pauline Christianity, brooded by a chrysalis papacy, were struggling for social and political mastery, there were treasured in costly tomes the records of strange psychologic wonders, inner visions, imperial prophecies, and grand demonstrations of immortality. These, exhumed and analyzed under the meridian sun of this century, stand as phenomenal witnesses of spirit intercourse—echoes from the gods flowing in melodious lights, and flaming with promise along the stately steps of humanity.

The nights of those dust-buried centuries had their stars; the angels, their blessed missions; all the old legendary periods, their representative personages. Balanced upon the topmost waves of circling eras, each, in turn, exclaimed: "It is I, be not afraid!" Startling the world, founding new institutions, they disappeared for still greater, to breathe diviner utterances, prophesy of rosier Junes, riper harvests; and bring to a thirsting people fresher draughts from the ever-flowing fountains of inspiration.

Among the eminent leaders that arose under Asian skies, was Joshua—He was so called by his friends and Hebrew countrymen, signifying savior. The Syrian world expected some remarkable leader. " Coming events cast their shadows before." This thought impregnated the national atmosphere. It was truly a propitious period. There was weeping by Babylon's streams; a suspense of spiritual life; a literal reign of ritualism in Judea. The Pharisees corresponded to New England Puritans, being the most prominent of the Jewish sects. In Hillel, disciple of Shammai, and other grave Rabbins, they had interpreters of the law; but the masses and more advanced thinkers of the times, demanded an exposition of the *soul*; its forces, sympathies, capacities and infinite possibilities. Demand brings supply. When India, China, Greece, called, there were born to them, saviors—Chrishna, Confucius, Pythagoras.

The coming of these religious chieftains, as with Jesus, was foretold in dreams and prophecies; foretold, because the *thought* concerning them, and their mediatorial mission on earth, were born and shaped in the Angel Congresses of supernal worlds. The world of spirits is the world of causes; this, of shadows and effects. All broad humanitarian plans, for redemptive purposes, are first conceived in the higher realms of spiritual existence; then inflowed by the natural law of influx to the sensitive of earth, to take form, be enunciated, and ultimately outworked into practical life. Ascended Hebrew prophets, Persian magi, and other sages of the Orient, long in the heavens, planned the birth of a more spiritual organism—a better type of Shemitic manhood, to lift the Jewish nation out of its chronic clannishness and dwarfing formalisms, into the diviner regions of absolute religion—that perpetual gospel destined finally to bless all nations.

Law is infinite. All conceptions, births, deaths, are governed by fixed and established laws; therefore, *natural*. Mary was susceptible to spirit influence. Immortals knowing it, and seeing her to be a future mother, overshadowed her with their piercing, moulding magnetism. To this end the angel Gabriel, through the mediumistic Evangelist, Luke, said to her: "The Holy Spirit shall come upon thee, and the power of the Highest shall overshadow thee." Jesus therefore was precocious and loving; impressional and clairvoyant; a mortal brother of the immortal gods and goddesses who helped fashion him mentally, that he, inspired by them, and a "legion of angels," might aid in fashioning future ages.

Speaking the Syriac dialect, mixed with, if not mostly Hebrew, his better words, dropping like gems from crowns, were gilt-edged, and alive with the logic of love and intuition. His life so rich and suggestive to a spiritual philosopher, so vague and mystical to an external matter-of-fact Jew, was a blended Odyssey and tragedy, with legions of inspiring powers behind the scenes. On Calvary he died a martyr! His principles live forever; while he, a perpetual inspiration to this planet, mediatorially preaches universal love as a redemptive power in all worlds.

Chapter XI.

MYTHIC.

> "Men groped to find the wrecks of primal matter,
>   And wasted long years in putting bone to bone;
> Babel revives where the world's gossips clatter,
>   And fossil words adjust to fossil stone.
> O'er fossil homilies the churches nod
>   Stone heart, stone service, and a stony God!"

Thinkers of the living present will necessarily study the man of Nazareth from three planes of thought:

I. The historic Jesus, copied from the Chrishna of India:

II. The theologic Jesus, a church monster of the "Christian Fathers:"

III. The natural Jesus, an enthusiastic Spiritualist of Judea.

Naturally worshipful, all nations have had their Jehovahs, Chrishnas, Christs, Bibles, and priests to expound them. The oldest of these are traceable to India. Under tropical skies there summered the most ancient civilizations. They had their arts, sciences, ethics, poets, authors, the literature of which, has streamed in such unbroken channels down the intermediate ages, as to overwhelm with astonishment the first scholars of Europe.

Sir William Jones said their "Literature seemed absolutely inexhaustible, reminding him of infinity itself." Johnson wrote: "The Iliad of Homer numbers twenty-four thousand verses; but the Mahabharata of the Hindoos four hundred thousand; and the Puranas comprehending only a small portion of their religious books, extend to two millions of verses. Among the more valued of their religious works, is the Bhagavat-Gita, *Chrishna's revelation.* This is termed by a classical German scholar: "A magnificent Thespesian poem, abounding in metaphysics, ethics, and sublime religious doctrines." The same author classes Jesus among the "first of the Judean poets." Considered as prose or poetry, it has richer veins of thought than the book of Job, and bears certain oriental relations to the gospel of John.

The Bhagavat-Purana, the 18th of the Puranas, is devoted to the history of Chrishna.* Some of the Upanishads dwell largely upon the beauty and purity of his life. He was the eighth Avater of Vishnu, the first person in the adorable "Trinity" of that portion of the Hindoos occupying the more central parts of India. This divine descent, according to the best authority, took place in the beginning of the Kali-Yuga, or "*counted age*"—an "age of vice and iron," about four thousand years since; and was for the purpose of redeeming humanity. Vishnu, thus descending, took upon himself human form, becoming Chrishna incarnate—"God manifest in the flesh." It is the same as the "*verbum caro factum est*"—*the word made flesh*—of St John, who, towards the close of an eventful life, became acquainted, in consequence of his scholarship and high spiritual culture, with the doctrines of the Eastern Magi, a class of philosophers called Gnostics. These Gnostics had derived most of their teachings from the "mysteries" of the Gymnosophists of India.

The close and almost *perfect* parallelism between the Chrishna of the Bhagavat-Gita, and the Christ of the

---

* Sir Wm. Jones invariably spells the name of this celebrated person, *Chrishna;* Dr. Weisse, a distinguished German writer, *Christna.* Orthodox clergy, anxious to make Jesus a purely original character, without the least authority, spell the name differently. An eminent English Divine says: "The churches meanly and pitifully alter the spelling of the name from the original orthography, (Chrishna) which rests on the high authority of Sir Wm. Jones, invariably print it as *Krishna,* or *Kreeshna,* to screen the resemblance of the name to *Christ* from the eye's observance."

Gospels, is of itself sufficient evidence to show that one was borrowed from the other; or that they were both copies from some older myth.

Chrishna is always represented as a savior, the same as Jesus Christ. Considered originally, the Supreme God, he condescended to descend and take upon himself the sinful state of humanity, as Christ is said to have done, by orthodox theologians. Of royal origin, he was born in a lowly condition. Immediately after the birth of Chrishna, he was saluted by divine songs from the Devatas—angels—as was the Nazarene. Surrounded by shepherds, thoroughly impressed with his greatness, he was visited by the Magi, *wise men*, among whom was an Indian prophet, called Nared, who, hearing of his fame, examined the stars, and declared him of celestial descent. His parents "Nanda," the father, and "*Deva Maia*," the divine mother, were compelled to flee by night into a remote country, for fear of a tyrant who had ordered all the male children of those regions to be slain. This story, says the eminent Godfrey Higgins, (Anac. b. iv. s. ii.) "Is the subject of an immense sculpture in the cave at Elephanta, * * * * * * * where the suspicious tyrant is represented destroying the children." The date of this sculpture, Higgins further says: "is lost in the most remote antiquity."

Chrishna was sent to a tutor to be instructed; and instantly astonished him by his profound wisdom, as did Christ, the Jewish doctors, in the temple. Chrishna is called Heri, and Heri, in Sanscrit, means *shepherd*, as well as *savior*. Christ was termed the "shepherd of the sheep. Chrishna had a forerunner in his elder brother, *Rom*, as had Jesus in his cousin, John the Baptist. Rom assisted Chrishna, the "Good Shepherd," in purifying the world from the pollution of evil demons. To show deep humility, Chrishna washed the feet of the Brahmins; so did Jesus the disciples. Upon one occasion a woman poured on Chrishna's head a box of ointment, for which he cured her of an ailment. Matthew's gospel assures us that a woman anointed the head of Jesus in a similar manner. One of Chrishna's first miracles, was the cure of a leper. It was also among the first of Christ's. During the succeeding career of Chrishna, he taught inspirational truths, raised the dead, was crucified, descended into Hades—the under world of spirits—whence he returned, and ascended to Vaicontha, *Heaven*, or the proper Paradise of Vishnu, who is the Father, or first person of the Hindoo Trinity.

There are further similarities in the lives of Chrishna and Christ. Chrishna had a favorite disciple—Arjuna—the third son of Pandu, corresponding to the "disciple that Jesus loved." The first section of the Bhagavat-Gita, is devoted to the grief of the loved Arjuna. The church historians, Eusebius and Athanasius, state, that, when Joseph and Mary arrived in Egypt, they took up their abode in Thebais—in which was a superb temple of Serapis. Entering the temple, miracles were wrought. The full account is recorded in the Evangelium Infantiæ.

The Rev. Mr. Maurice acknowledges that "The Arabic edition of the gospel of the infancy of Jesus, mentions Matarea as the place where the infant savior resided during his absence from Judea, until the death of Herod. Chrishna was born at Mathura. The Evangelium Infantiæ mentions the place where Jesus was born, as filled with light surpassing that of the noonday sun. The moment Chrishna was born the whole room became splendidly illuminated, and the heads of the father and mother were surrounded with rays of glory. These similarities are so striking, that none can fail of perceiving why the "Gospel of the Infancy of Jesus" was voted non-canonical by a council of Christian Bishops. The book was considered inspired, however, by many of the church fathers, and was highly esteemed by St. Irenæus, Bishop of Lyons, who suffered martyrdom, A. D. 202.

Chrishna of India, and Christ of Judea, both born in Asia, were so literally identical in general character, as well as in the minor events and circumstances of their lives, that none can deny their close historic connexion. Which, then, the *original?* which the *copy?*

The Bhagavat-Gita, one of the most sacred of the Puranas, contains an account of Chrishna's life—the Gospels of Christ's life. Both were announced as saviors. Which was, therefore, first, the Bhagavat-Gita, or the New Testament? With profound oriental scholars there can be little, perhaps no difference of opinion.

The sacred Hindoo book—the Bhagavat-Gita—lays claim to nearly the highest antiquity of any of the Brahminical compositions. That very competent judge, Rev. Mr. Maurice admits there is ample proof to show its existence full four thousand years since. Sir Wm. Jones, whose orthodoxy was never questioned, affirms that the name of Chrishna, and the general outline of his history, were long anterior to the birth of our Saviour, and probably to the time of Homer, we know *very certainly.*" This is authority from an unwilling witness.

The celebrated English scholar, Godfrey Higgins, says, (Anac. b. iv. c. i. p. 129,): "The sculptures on the walls of the most ancient temples—temples by no one ever doubted to be long anterior to the Christian Era—as well as written works equally old, prove, beyond a possibility of doubt, the superior antiquity of the history of Chrishna to that of Jesus."

Dr. Prichard admits, (Anal. Egypt. Mythol. p.261,) "That the history of Chrishna is to be found in all the caves of Ellora, Elephanta and others known to be the oldest."

The learned Baldæus observes, (Pref. Uni. Hist. p. 13,) that every "part of the life of Chrishna has a near resemblance to the history of Christ; and that the time when Chrishna's miracles were performed, was during the Duapparajug, which ended thirty-one hundred years before the Christian Era."

In consonance with the above, the Cantab declares: "If there's meaning in *words*, this Christian Missionary admits, (according to Higgins,) that the history of Christ is founded on that of Chrishna." This author further declares, (Anac. b. x. c. ii. p. 593,) "That even the most blind and credulous of devotees must allow that we have the existence of the Chrishna of the Brahmins in Thrace, many hundred years before the birth of Jesus Christ."

Justin assures us, "that the Erythræen Sybil, which foretold the things that should happen to Jesus Christ, also told that, in a neighboring country, between the Indus and Ganges, there was a person, Chrishna, long before Christ's time, to whom were ascribed nearly all the things that were ascribed to Jesus Christ." It is further demonstrated upon the authority of a "passage of *Adrian*, that the worship of Chrishna was practiced in the time of Alexander the Great, (330 B. C.) in the Temple of Mathura, one of the most famous of India." These testimonies settle the matter of time.

Maurice, in his elaborate work, frankly confesses that the Evangelists must have copied from the Bhagavat-Gita and other Puranas; or the Brahmins from the Evangelists. But we have shown from the most incontestable sources, that the sacred Bhagavat-Gita antedated the time of Christ by at least a thousand, and far more probably, *two thousand* years; and that the celebrated Chrishna lived and wrought his marvelous miracles long before the appearance of the Nazarene.

The educated protestant divines of France, and the more erudite of the German theologians, admit the astonishing similarity in the Asiatic saviors, *Chrishna* and *Christ*. This, in a good measure, accounts for the prevalence of German Rationalism. The American clergy, with few exceptions, narrow, conceited and sectarian, prefer reveling in blissful ignorance relative to the antiquity of India, China, Egypt, and the saviors and sacred books of Asia, from which ours have been borrowed, or clandestinely purloined.

From travel, and profound antiquarian research, Rev. Mr. Maurice confesses that the principal incidents in the narrated life of Jesus Christ—the birth at midnight, the chorus of angels, the cradling among shepherds, the child's concealment in a foreign country, from fear of a tyrant; the early wisdom manifest, the curing of the leper, the raisings of the dead, etc., are paralleled in Chrishna—*all* paralleled in the prior life of Chrishna, except the "immaculate conception."

This vacuum is readily supplied in the history of Pythagoras, born nearly six centuries before Jesus, on the Isle of Samos. Of him Jamblichus writes: "No one can doubt that the soul of Pythagoras was sent to mankind from the empire of God, * * * being an attendant on the god, Apollo; or *co-arranged* with him in some other way."

It was the custom of the early Church Fathers to travel for information. This was especially the case with Papias, Hegesippus, Justin and others. These, visiting the most enlightened portions of the East, mingled the teachings there found, concerning Pythagoras, with those relating to the Indian Chrishna, and from the "supernatural" connected with the two, they constructed the mythologic portions of the gospel histories.

When young, Pythagoras went to Tyre and Sidon, to be schooled in their learning. Then he journeyed to Egypt, to be taught in the wisdom of her priests and seers, as did Jesus, according to the testimony of Athanasias and the scholarly M. Denon. After this Pythagoras was borne to Babylon by Cambyses, the restorer of the Jewish temple and religion, and initiated into the divine mysteries of the Persian Magi; and finally, he traveled into India, where he became acquainted with the ethics and occult sciences of the Brahmins. It is not only natural, but very evident that this inspired Samian derived many of his metaphysical doctrines from the Gymnosophic school of philosophy. From extensive travel, this commingling could hardly be avoided.

The method of Pythagoras' *conception* is equally as miraculous as that ascribed to Jesus. They are, in fact, *identical.* In the writings of Jamblichus, who quotes, for authorities, Epimenides, Xenocrates and Olimpiodorus, all living long prior to the birth of Christ, may be found a full account of the immaculate conception and birth of Pythagoras. That truly learned and candid scholar, Godfrey Higgins, writes (Anac. c. iv. p. 150,):

"The first striking circumstance in which the history of Pythagoras agrees with the history of Jesus, is, that they were natives nearly of the *same country;* the former being born at Sidon, the latter at Bethlehem, both in Syria. The father of Pythagoras, as well as the father of Jesus, was prophetically informed that his wife should bring forth a son, who should be a benefactor to mankind. They were both born when their mothers were from home on journeys; Joseph and his wife having gone up to Bethlehem to be taxed, and the father of Pythagoras having traveled from Samos, his residence, to Sidon, about his mercantile concerns. Pythias, the mother of Pythagoras, had a connexion with an Apolloniacal *specter,* or ghost, of the god Apollo, which afterward appeared to her husband, and told him that he must have no connexion with his wife during her pregnancy—a story evidently the same as that relating to Joseph and Mary. From these peculiar circumstances, Pythagoras was known by the same identical title as *Jesus,* namely, *the Son of God,* and was supposed by the multitude to be under the influence of *divine* inspiration.

"When young, he was of a very grave deportment, and was celebrated for his philosophical appearance and wisdom. He wore his hair long, after the manner of the Nazarites, whence he was called the long-haired Samian."

Jamblichus himself says: "The Pythian oracle foretold to Mnesarchus, the father of Pythagoras, that his wife would bring forth a son, surpassing in beauty and wisdom all that ever lived, and who would be of the greatest advantage to the human race, in everything pertaining to the life of man. The infant, upon coming into existence, was called Pythagoras; signifying by this appellation that such an offspring was predicted to him by the Pythian Apollo.

Pythagoras professed to visit the spiritual world, and hold converse with departed spirits, and described the condition of Homer, Hesiod and others there. His pure, holy and divinely wonderful life, makes it impossible to doubt his sincerity. It was said of him, that he "knew every thing, and was right in every thing." It was asserted by many that he was "the Son of God."

Underlying all mythoses are pearls of wisdom and sprinklings of truth. The crucified reformers of to-day become the gods of to-morrow. This applies to the Nazarene. From the lives of Chrishna and Pythagoras, were gathered and woven the principal events connected with the historic Jesus of the Evangelists. He is a *copy* of prior saviors. This was the work of the Church Fathers of the first centuries, and in perfect keeping with their general character! Ambrose, Augustine, St. Jerome, and others, were corrupted with the villainous idea, that "it was right to lie for the sake of religion." Mosheim tells us (Vol. i. p. 130,) the doctrine, "that it was not only lawful, but commendable to deceive and lie for the sake of truth and piety, early spread among the Christians of the second century!" This church historian further admits (Vol. i. p. 155,) "that pious frauds and *impositions* were among the causes of the extension of Christianity!"

CHAPTER XII.

THEOLOGIC.

"The ages sweep around him with their wings,
Like angered eagles cheated of their prey."

"One rosy drop from Jesus' heart
Was worlds of seas to quench God's ire."

The accepted "Savior" of Christian nations to-day, is the *theologic* Christ; a strange Hebraic hybrid; half God, half man—a church monster, shapen by the old ecclesiastic Fathers and Roman Bishops, from the most worthless portion of the cast-off drippings of Pagan traditions.

There is no prophecy of this Christ of the church in the Old Testament Scriptures. Saying nothing of the writings of Colenso, that so completely undermine the Pentateuch, nor of those deep thinking German divines that have shaken the canonical-voted books of the Old Testament to their very foundations, we merely refer to some eminent English divines. Dr. Ekerman and Dr. Geo. S. Clark clearly show that the Old Testament contains no prophecy relating to the person, Jesus Christ. (Class. Jour. vol, xxxiii. p. 47.) Dr. Adam Clark, the annotater of the Bible, contends that the prophecy of Isaiah—"*A Virgin shall conceive and bear a son,*" and "*call his name Immanuel,*" does not mean Christ; but *Isaiah's own son!*" Dr. Clark further observes:

"It is humbly apprehended that the young woman usually called the virgin is the same with the prophetess, and Immanuel is to be named by his mother, the same with the prophet's son, whom he was ordered to name Maher-shalal-hash-baz." (Class. Jour. vol. i. p. 637.)

That there were general and dimly defined prophecies enunciated by the more mediumistic of the Hebrew seers, relating to coming saviors, and looking to the future spiritual illumination of their nation, is evidently true.

The Arian controversy concerning the derivation and deity of Christ, commencing early in the fourth century, between Alexander, Bishop of Alexandria, and Arius, one of his presbyters, finally terminated by the Bishop's asserting: "That the *Son* was not only of the same eminence and dignity, but also of the same *essence* with the *Father*." (Mosh. vol. i.) Accordingly, we have, in the Athanasian creed, received by all evangelical Christians, *this*, concerning Jesus Christ:

"The Son is of the Father alone, not created, but begotten.
"The God-head of the Father, of the Son, and of the Holy Ghost, is all one, the glory equal, the majesty co-eternal. * * *
"Such as the Father is, such is the Son, and such is the Holy Ghost.
"The Father is Almighty, the *Son* is Almighty, and the Holy Ghost Almighty.
"And yet there are not three Almighties, but *one* Almighty. * *
"He, therefore, that would be saved, must thus think of the Trinity."

After God had made the world in "six days," and Adam from the "dust of the ground," he placed him in a garden, and causing a "deep sleep" to fall upon him, "took one of his ribs and made he a *woman*." The Bible says it. This woman "frail," and conversing with, was tempted by the "serpent," which serpent, the Methodist, Dr. Adam Clarke, thinks was an ape, or an orang-outang! (Com. vol. i. c. iii. p. 47.)

Eve yielding to the temptation, and finding the fruit pleasant, "gave to Adam." They fell! And being the federal heads of the race, falling, they involved all their unborn posterity, even universal humanity, subjecting it to the "miseries of this life, death itself, and the pains of Hell forever." So affirms the creed.

It was a fearful crisis. God was exceedingly angry at Adam and Eve for doing just what he knew they would do. The sword of divine justice was raised. The Throne was in danger!

> ——— "'Twas a seat of dreadful wrath,
> And shot devouring flame;
> Our God appeared consuming fire,
> And vengeance was his name."

Deific justice had been wronged. Atonement must be made. The threatened penalty must be inflicted upon the race of man, or some substitute. A "plan" is devised. God, the Son, equal with the Father, stepping in between an offended God and offending man, says: "Spare the guilty race of humanity! open a way! glut thy vengeance upon me! I will take upon myself the penalty! I will die a substitute!" God the Father hears—relents. God the Son, corresponding to incarnations of India, shapes himself in human form; is born of the Virgin Mary; suffers under Pontius Pilot—"dead and buried." Watts versifies the Christian idea thus:

> "Well might the sun in darkness hide,
> And shut his glories in,
> When Christ, the mighty *Maker*, died
> For man, the creature's sin."

Mark the phrase—the "mighty Maker died"—a *dead God!* dying for the purpose of permitting rebellious sinners to go unpunished, to escape the penalty of the law, providing they believe in this "divine mystery"—the atonement. After this sacrificial death of an innocent Son, opening the way for the guilty to escape the demands of justice, God the Father becomes reconciled—pleased. Watts sings it:

> "Rich were the drops of Jesus' blood
>   That calmed his frowning face,
> That sprinkled o'er the burning throne,
>   And turned his wrath to grace."

> ———— ———"He quenched
> His Father's flaming sword
> In his own vital blood."

Another Christian poet says:

> "With one tremendous draught of blood,
> He drank *damnation* dry!"

This prevailing theologic dogma of the atonement, with a mythologic Jesus as principal actor, is termed the "plan of salvation!"

Salvation, in its more philosophic sense, is soul-growth—divine unfoldment from the innermost outward, and a strictly personal matter. My savior is the *Christ* principle. It was born with me—is *in* me—*is* me. It was before the wandering Galilean; before Abraham; before astral worlds commenced their stately march through the siderial heavens—pre-existent—eternal! Neither the merits of Buddha, Chrishna, nor Christ Jesus, are transferable, like bundles of merchandise. Self-salvation, self-sanctification, were the doctrines taught by that eminent Judean Spiritualist, Jesus. Said he—"I testify of myself." Again—"*I sanctify myself.*" Sound and sensible! The "grace of God" is as powerless to save souls, as the grace of colleges to make scholars, independent of earnest effort. "Work out your own salvation," is among the best of the Pauline writings. Personal character, not the sacrificial blood of goats and kids under the law, not Christ's under the gospel, decide individual destiny.

Jesus' merits saved him, none else. Your merits must save you. Each *soul* is a manger, cradling a savior—God in man. The blood of one cannot atone for the sins of another. That hemlock draught poisoned only Socrates. Jesus' prayer in the garden brought angels to *him*, not us. God is just. Compensation is an inflexible law. Justice is sweet as mercy; both, centering in, flow out from an infinite ocean of love. Happiness comes not by imputed, but by *personal* righteousness; that is, right doing. Only by *being* good, can there be good results. Only in a heavenly state of mind can heaven come to any soul. "What wilt thou have, quoth God—pay for it, and take it," writes Emerson. Over the shining portals that open into the city Celestial, are inscribed—"*No forgiveness!—merit entitles to admission!*—love is life!—*harmony is heaven!*"

CHAPTER XIII.

THE NAZARENE.

> "The 'Twelve' in awful circle stand
> Where mortal dare not enter;
> And, blazing like a solar world
> Stands Jesus in the center."

> I testify of myself.—*Jesus.*

Entombed among myths, and buried under the film that flecks the synoptic gospels, there shines a life, gentle, beautiful, divine. The mythologic and theologic savior, copied from Chrishna, of India, aside, then, we come to Jesus the *Spiritualist*—Jesus the natural man, the expected Son of Syria, child of love and wisdom—our ancient brother.

An impassioned theatre-admiring mother gave to England a Byron, who shocked the State Church with his bold, passional thought, and called down angels to hear his strong, loving heart beat in poetry that will live when his persecutors are unknown, save as "pigmies on Alps." A mother, ambitious and daring, rode a dashing steed upon smoking battle-fields in southern Italy; and Napoleon's sword caused Europe to tremble. Mary was calm, loving, aspirational, spiritual. Overshadowed by heavenly influences, and other beautiful and ante-natal conditions, the civilized world throbs in responsive sympathy to the moral power of Jesus of Nazareth. Whether Joseph, or a priest of the temple, sustained the masculine relation to the welcome Nazarene, matters not, so far as the present exegesis is concerned. Suffice it, that he was the natural offspring of human parents; the begotten of love and harmony, under the sweet baptismal magnetisms of angels; all conducing to an impressional, inspirational, harmonial organism—a *medium*—harp admirably fitted for the play of divine powers.

In the gorgeous East, amid the mellow sunbeams, sifted from Syrian skies, Jesus awoke to the outer consciousness of earth-life.

"Galilee," writes Renan, "is a country very green; dense with masses of flowers; full of shade and pleasantness; the true country of the canticle of canticles, and of the songs of the well-beloved. * * * In no place in the world do the mountains spread out with more harmony, or inspire loftier ideas. Jesus seems to have loved them especially. The most important acts of his divine career were performed upon the mountains; there he was best inspired; there he had secret conferences with the ancient prophets, and showed himself to his disciples already transfigured. * * * As often happens in very lofty natures, tenderness of heart was in him transformed into infinite sweetness, vague poetry, universal charm. * * * The group that pressed around him upon the banks of the Lake of Tiberias, * * * believed in spectres and in spirits. * * * Great spiritual manifestations were frequent. All believed themselves to be inspired in different ways. Some were 'prophets,' others 'teachers.'" (Life of Jesus, p. 210.)

Education has much to do in fashioning character. Where was Jesus between the years of twelve and thirty? In what school of ideas was he educated? To these inquiries the New Testament gives not the least clue. Those scheming superstitious Bishops, that collected the scattered manuscripts, often guilty of conduct that would have lastingly disgraced the frailest of the Alexandrian Platonists, voted gospels in and out of the canon, *ad libitum*. Œcumenical councils debated and decided by majorities upon the comparative merits of some thirty or forty gospels, each claiming by interested parties, divine origin. Among them were the gospel of St. Peter, of St. Andrew, of St. Barnabus; the gospel of the infancy of Jesus, &c. They rejected *all*, save Matthew, Mark, Luke and John. The general character of the Christian Bishops composing these councils, is described thus by Dr. Jortin (Bucks. Theol. Dic. p. 99). "They have been too much extolled by Papists, and by some Protestants. They were a collection of men who were frail and fallible. Some of those councils were not assemblies of pious and learned divines, but *cabals*, the majority of which were *quarrelsome*, fanatical, domineering, *dishonest prelates*, who wanted to compel men to approve all their opinions, of which they themselves had no clear conceptions; and to anathamatize and oppress those who would not implicitly submit to their determinations." Upon the authority of this scholar and Christian theologian, with the testimony of many others, in confirmation, at our disposal, it is clear that the New Testament books have reached us through "fanatical," "quarrelsome" and "dishonest prelates." So "dishonest," that they voted every thing un-canonical that related to Jesus' sojourn in Egypt, and initiation into the Essenian brotherhood.

Fortunately, however, a few of the more honest of the Church Fathers, with certain Pythagoric and Platonic authors, whose integrity stands unquestioned, have left sufficient historic data to establish the theory of Jesus' travels in Egypt, and deep schooling in the "mysteries" pertaining to India, China and Greece.

M. Denon, describing a very beautiful temple of the ancient Egyptians at Philoe, says: "I found within it some remains of a domestic scene, which seemed that of Joseph and Mary, and it suggested to me the subject of the flight into Egypt, in a style of the utmost truth and interest. (Eng. Trs. by A. Aiken, vol. ii. p. 169.)

Both Athanasius and Eusebius state that when Joseph and Mary arrived in Egypt, they took up their residence in a city in which was a splendid temple of Serapis. (Eusb. Demon. Ev. Lib. vi. ch. 20.)

The candid Rev. Mr. Maurice assures us that, "The Arabic edition of the Evangelium Infantiæ records Maturea, near Hermopolis, in

Egypt, to have been the place where Jesus resided during his absence from the land of Judea, until the death of Herod." (Maur. Hist. vol. ii. p. 318.)

"In the Maturea (or Matarea) of Egypt, Jesus Christ is said, as we have before shown, to have spent his *youth*, after he took refuge there, from the tyrant Herod." (Anac. vol. i. p. 242.)

Pythagoras, according to Jamblichus, spent twenty-two years in Egypt, among those savans and templed priests. Whether Jesus remained there all the years till the astonishing of the "doctors of the law;" or all the time from twelve to thirty years of age, we have no means of knowing positively. It is more probable that, like other illustrious men of his age, he traveled in search of wisdom. Thales, Solon, Democritus, Orpheus, Plato, Theodosius, Epicurus, Herodotus, Lycurgus, these great philosophers of antiquity, binding their stoutest sandals upon their feet, and taking the Pilgrims' staff in their hands, left their country, and went forth to visit the vast sanctuaries of Egypt, there to be initiated into those mysteries that had been handed down from the older, riper civilizations of India. "I am persuaded," writes Sir Wm. Jones, "that a connection existed between the old nations of India, Egypt, Greece and Italy, long before the time of Moses." (Asiat. Res. vol. i. p. 259.)

That Jesus was an Essenian is susceptible of the clearest historic demonstration.

Who were they?—what their origin, their teachings and customs?

The Essenians among the Jews, the Magi among the Persians, the Hierophants of Egypt, and the Gymnosophists of India, were all co-related by a common system of science, treasured wisdom and profound mystery; all *one*, with such variations as periods of time, change of language and country, would necessarily produce. Clemens Alexandrinus states, upon what he considered the highest authority, that Buddha was the founder of the sect of Gymnosophists, the Indian philosophers. (The Buddha, of which *avatar*, however, is not specified.) Porphyry, at first a student of Origen and

Longinus, afterwards a disciple of Plotinus, says: "There was one tribe of Indians *divinely wise*, whom the Greeks were accustomed to call Gymnosophists; but of these there were two sects, over one of which, Brahmins presided; over the other, the Samanæons." (De Abst. b. iv. Sect. 17.)

Pythagoras, in India, was a student at the feet of those Gymnosophists. As a senior among the mystics, he there graduated. Higgins affirms, that the "school of this great philosopher from the East—India, Carmel, Egypt, Delphi, Delos—was closely connected with the schools of the Essenians, Samanæons, Carmelites, and Gnostic Christians. The Pythagorians were Essenians; and the Rev. R. Taylor, A. M., * * has clearly proved all the hierarchical institutions of the Christians, to be a close copy of those of the Essenians of Egypt." (Anac. b. x. c. vii. p. 787.)

These Essenians were sometimes denominated physicians of the soul, or Theraputæ; and, "residing both in Egypt and Judea, they probably spoke, or had their sacred books in Chaldee. They were Pythagorians to all intents and purposes, as is proven by their forms, ceremonies and doctrines. * * If the Pythagorians, or Cœnobitæ, as they are called by that famous Neo-Platonian philosopher, Jamblichus, were Buddhists, then the Essenians were originally Buddhists. A branch of these Essenians, termed, Koinobii, lived in Egypt, on the shores of lake Parembole, in Monasteries." (Anac. b. x. c. vii.)

These quotations show the intimate relations, if not direct identity of the Gymnosophists, Yogees, Hierophants, Pythagoreans, Essenians, Magi, Sufis and Rashees. Of these latter, Ayeen Akberry, writes: "The most respectable people in this country are the Rashees, who, although they do not suffer themselves to be fettered by traditions, are, doubtless, true worshipers of God. They revile not any other sect, and ask nothing of any one; they plant the road with fruit trees, to furnish the traveler with refreshments. They abstain from flesh, and have no intercourse with the other sex." There are nearly two thousand of this sect in Cashmeer. Higgins adds: "These Reyshees, or Rashees, same as Sofees, are the Essenians, Carmelites, or Nazarites of the temple." Quoting a passage from the learned and eminent Burnet, in confirmation, he further says: "I was not a little gratified to find that the close relation between the Hindoos and the more respectable of all the Jewish sects, the Essenians, of which I have not the slightest doubt that Jesus Christ was a *member*, had been observed by this very learned man, almost a hundred years ago, before the late blaze of light from the East had shone upon us." (Anac. vol. ii. b. ii. p. 50.)

Old India, the mother of civilizations, colonizing Egypt, necessarily bore her sacred mysteries there. Egypt, celebrating them in her pyramidal chambers, transferred them, in a somewhat modified form, to Persia and Greece, and, through Moses, to the more intellectual of the Jewish people; these, joining by initiation, were called Theraputæ, and Essenes.

Father Rebold says: "This religious and philosophic sect, the Essenians, of which Jesus Christ was a member; was composed of learned Jews, who lived in the form of a society similar to that of Pythagoras. If not the same, in substance, they were intimately connected with another sect, called Theraputes, residing in Egpyt, forming the fraternal link between the Egyptians and the Hebrews. * * * That occult science, designated by the ancient priests, under the name of regenerating fire, is that which, at the present day, is known as *animal magnetism*—a science that, for more than three thousand years, was the peculiar possession of the Indian and Egyptian priesthood, into the knowledge of which Moses was initiated at Heliopolis, where he was educated; and Jesus among the Essenian priests of Egypt or Judea; and by which these two great reformers, particularly the latter, wrought many of the miracles mentioned in the Scriptures."

It being evident, then, that Jesus, spending his youth in Egypt, perhaps traveling in other Asiatic countries than Palestine, was connected with the Essenians, the question of their teachings and practices becomes deeply interesting.

Philo, of Alexandria, in two books, written expressly upon the subject of the Essenes, giving a close and critical account of their doctrines and manners, says: "Listening to the instructions of their chiefs, they were taught, as were the

Pythagorians, the existence of one supreme God, the immortality of the soul, rewards and punishments for good and ill-doing, and the guardian care of gods and angels. It was enjoined upon them to show obedience to authority; fidelity to all men; to be lovers of truth; exercising kindness to inferiors; concealing nothing from their own sect; nor discovering any of their doctrines to others than those who had received them with the white stone and the new name; and lastly, to preserve the books belonging to the sect, and the names of the angels."

At the time of the Maccabees, 180 B. C., on the western coast of the Dead Sea, the Essenians made the doctrine of community of goods, and a life in common, a religious and social dogma. Lodged under the same roof, taking meals at the same table, clothed in the same dress, ignoring marriage, they observed celibacy and lived in continence, abjured oaths and all violence, contemned riches, rejected the use of the precious metals, were given wholly to the meditation of moral and religious truths, and subsisted by the labor of their hands, were content with one meal a day, and that of bread and vegetables and fruits.

Philo further informs us, that, "spreading themselves all through Asia Minor, and in the environs of Alexandria, they became, at a later period, more devoted; renouncing all pleasure, ambition, glory, earthly possessions, and their native country, even, to give themselves entirely to the exercise of prayer, contemplation and deeds of charity." To overcome the passions, the spiritual controlling the Adamic, to subjugate the senses, to raise the soul above the influences of the body, to despise the sham of fame and glitter of wealth, to commune with the gods and orders of celestial beings—these, in the estimation of the Essenians, constituted the ideal of human perfection. Who does not see in it the underlying animus that, from the earthly side, inspired the consecration and catholicity of spirit which so eminently distinguished the reformer of Nazareth?

CHRISTIAN SPIRITUALISM — THE NAZARENE.

Jesus being interiorly sweet and harmonial in organization, fellowshiped by the Essenians, schooled in the Asian mysteries, and a medium, how natural the explanation of the genuine teachings, doctrines and wonderful works ascribed to him! Testifying of himself, living the inner life, and speaking from the divine ideal, he rose so high above country and national narrowness, he astonished both scribe and pharisee. The old prophets were essentially Israelitish; many of the ancient philosophers were decidedly Grecian; the sage, Gotama Buddha, was Hindoo, *par excellence;* but this Judean Spiritualist, grounded in the absolute religion, baptized daily from above, attended by a legion of angels, directed the thirsting of his age to a fountain from which all diversities of race might drink—to a tree of life with fruitage fresh and free for all souls; grasping fundamental truths and broad, beautiful ideas, he spoke the deepest intuitions of his inmost being. No poet or moralist ever enunciated fresher or more charming thoughts, adapted to the masses, or voiced a keener, richer dialect of audacious insight, than he, in those seemingly effortless speeches of the "good shepherd," the "true vine," "the lilies," "the birds," the sun rising "on the evil and the good, and the rain falling upon the just and the unjust."

All truth is immortal; our *conceptions* of it only are new. Jesus taught the world no new truths.

The immortality of the soul had been taught by the ancients, preceding Thales, Zeno, Plato, Anaximenes, Empedocles Indian seers and Persian Magi taught it long before the birth of the Pauline " man Christ Jesus."

The universal Fatherhood of God is distinctly taught in the Socrates of Zenophon, in the hymn of Cleanthes, and in the hymn of Avatus; quoted by Paul in his appeal to the Athenians; in Maximus Tyrius and Simplicius; in Manilius, Epictetus, Seneca and Cicero. Almost every Greek or Roman poet, from Hesiod and Homer down, designates Jupiter as the father of gods and men, and draws the inference therefrom of his infinite love and universal care.

Pythagoras is made to say, by the Rev. Dr. Collyer, (Lec. xii. p. 499,) "God is neither the object of sense, nor subject to passion; but invisible, only intelligible, and supremely intelligent. In his body, he is like the light, and, in his soul, he resembles truth. He is the universal spirit that pervades and diffuseth itself through all nature. All beings receive their life from him. There is but one only God, who is not, as some are apt to imagine, seated above the world, beyond the orb of the universe; but, being himself *All* in *All*, he sees all the beings that fill his immensity, the only principle, the light of Heaven, the *Father of all*. He produces everything; he orders and disposes everything; he is the reason, the life, and the motion of all beings." These doctrines, embodying the universal Fatherhood of God, were the teachings of Pythagoras, concerning Deity. Jesus only reiterated them with a pathos peculiarly his own.

Originality cannot be ascribed therefore to Jesus. The doctrine of the Fatherhood of God, is ancient as the teachings of the wise in India, Syria and Greece.

"May the Father of Heaven, who is the Father of Men, be favorable to us."—*Rig Veda.*

"Father of gods and men."—*Hesiod.*

"Zeus, most great and glorious Father."—*Homer.*

"Father and guardian of the human race."—*Horace.*

"He, the glorious Parent, tries the good men and prepares him for himself."—*Seneca.*

"He, who regards the whole universe as his country, feels bound to seek the favor of its Father and framer."—*Philo.*

"They are children of their Father who is Heaven. * * * * Every nation has its special guardian angels."—*Talmud.*

The Alexandrian Philo Judæus, 41 B. C., belonging to an illustrious Jewish family, emphatically declared all men *brothers*, by virtue of the inspiration of the Eternal Word. Intimately acquainted with the philosophy of India and Egypt, the ancient Grecian schools, and the cabalistic doctrines preceding him, his system was a mixture of Chrishna, Zoroaster, Plato, abounding in Jewish phrases, and wearing

Hebrew forms as garments. From him the Nazarene borrowed largely, in the imagery connected with his parables. Among Philo's principal doctrines, were the divine Logos, the universal brotherhood, pre-existence, the descent of souls, and the guardian care of angels.

The humanitarian spirit of brotherhood pervades the older Brahminical theology that once flooded Asia, finding expression in the " law of love for all."

The eloquent Quintilian constantly appealed to the sentiment of brotherly love, as the sweetest in man, and, "as uniting all men by the will of the Common Father."

Cicero frequently affirmed, that men were "*created* for the *purpose* of mutual help, to love and be loved, and for the simple reason, they were *men*."

Epictetus, Aurelius, Seneca, and others, taught the " common citizenship and *brotherhood* of men."

" All men, everywhere, belong to one family."—*Diodorus.*

" No man is a stranger to me, provided he be a good man; for we have all one and the *same* nature."—*Menander.*

" All men are our friends and fellow-citizens. * * * * * Greeks and barbarians drink from one and the same cup of brotherly love."—*Zeno.*

" Will you not bear with your brother? He has his birth from the same Jove as thou, is *His* son, as thou art, born of the same divine seed. * * * Will you enslave those who are your brothers by nature, children of God?"—*Epictetus.*

" I am a man, nothing human can I count foreign to me."—*Terence.*

Denis, in his learned work on the moral theories and teachings of antiquity, shows clearly that the highest moral sentiments of humanity, brotherhood and self-sacrifice, thread the ethical and religious codes of every cultured age. All the wise sayings ascribed by Protestant clergymen to Jesus, were said before his time. This they ought to know, and, knowing, teach.

Saisset well said, that stoicism "anticipated Christ's teachings, in the recognition, that men are brothers and brothers in God." The more honest of the old Church Fathers, concede a superiority of scholarship and wisdom to the heathen over the first Christians. Conscious of this, the orthodox Merivale, says, that "while the apostles preached the commandment of Jesus, that he who loveth God love his brother also, the same instinct and sympathy sprang spontaneously, and without a sanction but that of nature, in many a (heathen) watcher of the wants and miseries of men."

The "golden rule" belongs to Hillel, as well as to Jesus; more to Confucius; Philo, and the son of Sirach, more than to the son of Joseph, because they enunciated the thought before him. Sir Wm. Jones, writing of the antiquity of this precept, says: "Religion has no need of such aids as many are willing to give it, by asserting that the wisest men of this world were ignorant of the two great doctrines, love to God, and love to all humanity. These dogmas run like silver threadings through the systems of the most ancient nations."

The golden rule was a common teaching among Chinese, Syrian and Grecian philosophers, long before the Christian era.

"That which thou blamest in another, do not thyself to thy neighbor."—*Thales.*

"Thou wilt deserve to be honored, if thou doest not thyself what thou blamest in others."—*Isocrates.*

"Do to no man what thou thyself hatest."—*Tobit.*

"Do not to another what thou wouldst not he should do to thee: this is the sum of the law."—*Hillel.*

"What you do not wish done to yourself, do not do to others."—*Confucius.*

But this golden rule of the Chinese philosopher is put in the negative, says the clerical objector. Granted. So are the ten commandments of the Old Testament; but are they any less commandments?

Thus far we have traced, by good authorities, the consecutive relations of religions from one race and country to another, showing their mutual helps, their co-relations, their upward growth into higher altitudes of thought and use. It remains now to analyze the degree of originality that justly belongs to the Spiritualism of Jesus.

Waves of civilization are consecutive; the first is pushed forward by its next succeeding, and so over the measureless ocean of truth. Circling in all directions, they take shape according to the forms of mind into which they flow.

Human nature is the same in all ages and climes, varying only in expression. Nothing good is lost to the world. Like geological strata, the religion of one age lies upon and overshelves that of the preceding; the former incorporating the latter in new forms and uses. A magnificent tree of life, each branch has the nature of all the rest. The Egyptian, Chinese and Persian copy from the Indian; and the Hebraic and Christian, in turn, from all these. Commercially and educationally, then, those of one generation shape those of the next, in successive order, from the ancient into the mediæval, and thence into the sub-dividing Protestant, which belong to the Catholic, as leaves to the same branch—to culminate in the completion of a grand cycle, as they now do, in the flower of *all* religions—a world-wide Spiritualism.

But another influence molds all these changing materials. Developed in the tropics, the religion of India was passional and gorgeous. Religion in Greece and Rome—farther north—was colder, more select, more intellectual and brilliant. On the isothermal line, Palestine lies in higher latitude than India or Egypt, but not under the more electric, and, therefore, intellectual atmosphere of southern Europe.

Primitive Christianity, the positive religion of Palestine, is, therefore, not so passional and imposingly gorgeous as that of India, nor so philosophic and variegated as the Grecian; but is intermediate, sufficiently emotional to attract and warm the heart, and sufficiently intellectual to evolve a correct philosophy of the soul. Beautiful, therefore, is its fruit high on the tree of life, substantial and vital in spiritual character.

In the Nazarene we have this happy blending—a balanced summer-sunned man—a tropical heart, sweet, full of love-flowers, and tempered to an intellectuality that weaves its silvery philosophic filling through the magnetic vesture that clothes our freezing humanity. In this sense is *primitive* Christianity original, the same as can be said of Buddhism, Mahommedanism, or any other religion.

Here shines in again the all-unsealing light of the Spiritual Philosophy. The Jews borrowed of India and Egypt, and other then enlightened nations, in a closer sense than history defines, than the intercourse of commerce can guarantee. The work of mediumistic minds is by no means ended with their departure from this rudimental sphere. Taking with them their peculiar proclivities of thought, their natural characteristics, their purposes to finish what they began here, they impress upon the new races they affiliate with, their politics, science, religion, thus completing the circle of communication internationally and spiritually. Hence, even with races locked in by seas or mountains, or walls, like old China, there is a general resemblance in these particulars, which only the philosophy of angel-ministry can *fully* explain.

In the light then of the Spiritual Philosophy, we are not to look *exclusively* to anterior races for the origin of the Hebrew, Christian, or of any other subsequent religion; for it was in the power of ancient spirits, and natural to their communicative relationship, to re-construct their religious wisdom, to be mainly original to their media.

Eclectic, then, let us here cull some of the beautiful spiritualities of our dear brother, the self-denying Son of Man.

Reading the beatitudes, we feel a sweet throbbing within, as if the heart's chords were swept by an angel's breath. That one sentence is a life-key that opens to calm sunlight the soul of Jesus—" Blessed are the pure in heart, for they shall see God." There is a very enchantment in his precepts, parables, aptitude of illustration, love of the beautiful, moral heroism, tender sympathy for the sorrowing, non-resistance, and martyrdom for a principle. The picture which Renan draws of him is truthful and charming:

" As many of the grand aspects of his character are lost to us by the fault of his disciples, it is probable that many of his faults have been dissembled. But never has any man made the interests of humanity predominate in his life, over the littleness of self-love, so much as he. Devoted, without reserve, to his idea, he subordinated everything to it, to such a degree that, towards the end of his life, the universe no longer existed for him. It was by this flood of heroic deeds he conquered heaven. * * * * His life-deeds of benevolence will grow without ceasing; his legend will call forth tears without end; his sufferings will melt the noblest hearts; all ages will proclaim that, among the sons of men, there is none born greater than Jesus."

Whence his greatness? It was the blossoming out of his inner divinity, under the ministry of angels! String, on the golden chain that draws us higher the heart-spirit pearls of the New Testament. It is the cable to the bridge of Hope that arches the mystic river, on which humanity may pass safe over to the morning lands.

Gabriel, the prophets' angel, hails Mary—"Blessed art thou among women," announcing the advent of the Judean Spiritualist. Repeating the song sung at the birth of Crishna, a host of angels, appearing to the shepherds, sing at *his* birth: "Glory to God in the highest; on earth peace and good-will toward men." In the temple, when a mere lad, under the heavenly ministry, he confounds the Rabbis. At his baptism the spirit descends in form of a dove, and voices his consecration, as it has to other mediums: "This is my beloved son." At his temptation, when famishing with hunger, "angels came and ministered unto him." Under spirit influence, he heals the diseases of the people. Inspired by a Samson, he drives out the "money changers" of the temple. Moved by his mighty guards, indignant at religious corruption, he utters words that call down upon him the anathamas of all the priesthood—a true sign of the faithful iconoclast. A pure lover of nature, catching his best inspirations from the beautiful and the true, he retires with Peter, James and John, to a high mountain, "and is there transfigured before them." Entranced, "his face shining as the sun, his raiment white as the light, there appears unto them Moses and Elias, talking with Jesus." Upheld by spirit-hands, he walks upon the sea of Tiberias. Spiritually clairvoyant, he reads "what is in man," and prophesies. Foreseeing his martyrdom, he is troubled, and, during his prayer, a spirit voice is heard by the listening people, who "said that it thundered; others said an angel spake to him." In Gethsemane, and before Pilate, "an angel appeared, strengthening him" for the ordeal. At his crucifixion, the electro-spirit batteries are strong enough to "rend the rocks," and "the veil of the temple, from top to bottom." So potent the influence, so mediumistic the people, they see the spiritual bodies of ascended saints, walking in their midst; these "went into the holy city, and appeared unto many." An angel rolls away the stone from his sepulchre. The spirit of Jesus appears to Mary, to Peter and John—to the disciples on their way to Emmaus, when he expounded to them his mission; and at last "their eyes were opened, and they knew him; and he vanished out of sight." Jubilant over the stupendous fact, that their divine Teacher is yet alive, they return to Jerusalem, and, finding the eleven chosen disciples gathered together, earnestly listening to their happy report of his appearance to Simon, lo! the risen "Jesus himself stood in the midst of them, and said, 'Peace be unto you!' But they were terrified and affrighted, and supposed they had seen a spirit." Psychologically assuming the form of the crucified, he thus showed them his "hands and feet, and they handled him."

From this data of spiritual perception, deepening in clairvoyance and clairaudience, they saw the real presence. Being substantially a spiritual organism, and measurably dependent upon material substance for sustenance, at his request, they "gave him a piece of broiled fish and an honeycomb, and he took it, and did eat before them;" that is, by imbibation, he mediumistically partook of, and appropriated, their aromal effluence.

The martyrdom of the cross endured, he appeared as the Christ-spirit to the assembled twelve, charging them to go into "all the world and preach the gospel to every creature."

Why thus preach? To induce belief. What then? "These signs should follow believers:" 'They should cast out demons, speak with new tongues, lay hands on the sick, and heal them; make the lame walk, the blind see, and the deaf hear.' Again, said Jesus: "He that believeth on me, the works that I do shall he do also; and *greater works* than these shall he do; because I go unto my Father." The apostles had these gifts when listening to the charge. The promise, therefore, was to future believers. These signs and gifts do not abound in Christian churches, because they have departed from the "faith once delivered to the saints." But they do follow mediums, and prevail every where among Spiritualists. These works they *do*, being genuine believers, baptized with the Christ-baptism. Media are mediators between the winter-lands of earth, and the summer-lands of heaven, and their spiritual "signs" and powers increase in the ratio of approximation to the spiritualized planes of the pure and holy.

He appeared to his apostles on the mount of Ascension, when "he is parted from them;" and to the little assembly of believers on the day of Pentacost, when they are all of "one accord" in a spiritual circle, and the manifestation comes as a "rushing, mighty wind," and "fills all the house," when "cloven tongues, like as fire," rest upon them, and they "speak in other tongues as the spirit gives them utterance." He confers upon them "the gifts of the Spirit," and they heal by the "laying on of hands;" they have visions, trances, inspirations. They are all mediumized, and, under spirit control, endure deprivation, penury, want, suffering, persecution and martyrdom, as others have done—as their brothers and sisters *now* do. John, the beloved disciple "in the Spirit, (entranced) on the Lord's day," saw thrones, altars, crystal seas, rainbows, falling stars, white vestured angels with golden girdles; and was about to fall down and worship the "shining one," who unrolled to his clairvoyant vision these symbols of revelation and the millennial age, when he was admonished: "See thou do it not; for I am thy fellow-servant, and of thy brethren the prophets." Glorified now in the heavens, honored as a star in the congresses of spirits, he is inspired with love so tender, that his heart still beats down all the ages since, at every pulsation, voicing the divinity within—"LITTLE CHILDREN, LOVE ONE ANOTHER!"

Lecture IV.

Mediæval Spiritualism.

CHAPTER XIV.

TRANSITIONAL.

> "God sends his teachers unto every age,
> To every clime, and every race of men,
> With revelations fitted to their growth,
> And shape of mind, nor gives the realm of *Truth*
> Into the selfish rule of one sole race."

Hyphened by erudition, and inspired by unitive purpose, to arch the years with wisdom, there were certain scholarly standard-bearers, who, conserving the good of the past and compounding it with the new, handed the philosophies of the ages down to incoming dispensations. Some of these were the cotemporaries of Jesus. Among them, were Simeon, the mild and the just; Jesus, the promising son of Sirach; the learned Rabbi, Hillel; Schemaia, the wise; the candid Gamaliel, the elder; and the distinguished writer and scholar, the Judaic Egyptian, Philo. These philosophic thinkers, laying great stress upon dreams and visions, believed in the appearance of spirits. Bating the Sadducees, it was a common dogma of the masses. Ernest Renan, the most learned of living Shemitic scholars, writing in his "Life of Jesus," of the group assembled on the banks of Lake Tiberias, to hear the Nazarene, says: "They believed in spectres and spirits."

PHILO JUDÆUS, born in Alexandria, a city next to Athens, the famous resort of the Greek literati, was, in religion, a

Pharasee; in philosophy, tinctured with Platonism; and, in common with the thinkers of his time, given to allegorical interpretations. Mosaic in theology, he taught the existence of one invisible God—immutable, ineffable and incomprehensible—the originator of all things in connection with the Mother of the universe, whom the Greeks termed, *Sophia*, or *Wisdom*. By virtue of this deific marriage, he accounted for all germinal entities and spiritual types of future embodiment; and, as a corollary, taught that man is a trinity compounded of essential spirit, having, in personality, a more materialized spiritual body, and an external or earthly body. A teacher of pre-existence, he maintained that matter, being dark and gross, is the source of evil, and that man therein veiled, assisted by Sophia and the good angels, is enabled to rise out of this temporary degradation, into the holy sunshine of God's light and love. Another feature of his Spiritualism is thus expressed in Youge's translation:

"The Creator of the gods is also the Father of everything else—the world being an imitation visible to the outer senses of an archetypal model. Some souls have descended into bodies, and others have not thought worthy to approach any portion of the earth. * * * * Those whom other philosophers call demons, Moses usually calls angels; but they are spirits flying through the air. * * * * These spirits are wholly immortal and divine. Those who descend into bodies, are often overwhelmed, as in a whirlpool; but, by struggling, emerge, and fly back to their homes in the upper regions. * * * * By considering that angels, demons and souls, are different names for the same beings, you will clear away much superstition from the subject. The etherial regions are like populous cities, filled with immortal spirits, and numerous as stars in the firmament."

Apollonus, an inspired sage of Tyana, born in Asia Minor, about the time of Jesus of Nazareth, was considered, by some, as superior in mediumistic endowments, to the son of Joseph and Mary. Proteus, famous for his prophetic powers, appeared to the mother prior to his birth, illuminating her apartment with divine radiance. In early youth, he wrought many so-called miracles. The celebrated temple of Æsculapius was his favorite resort for recuperation and spiritual communion. "Philostratus informs us, that he could read the thoughts of men, foresee future events, and, withal, was gifted with the wonderful power of working miracles." These are equally as well substantiated as those of Jesus. "He taught," says L. Maria Child, "there is one God, the Father of all, and that the numerous deities, who are objects of popular worship, are intermediate spirits, employed as agents. He invoked these spirits, placed great reliance upon dreams and omens, and believed that he was often divinely guided by spiritual beings of heaven. * * * * The early Christian Fathers, in alluding to him, do not deny the miracles he wrought, but attribute them to the aid of evil spirits, procured by magical arts." The purity of his life, owing to his affiliation with God and angels, was unquestioned, his benevolence almost unparalleled, and his sympathies so tender and touching, that multitudes hung upon his lips, as though charmed and chained by a power divine.

SIMON MAGNUS, the Samarian magician, who greatly troubled the apostles by his so-called heresies, and miracles wrought independent of Christ, (Acts 9,) was a scholarly medium of general note. He taught that "the Source of all good dwells in plenitude of light;" that "Interior Thought," (*Ennoia*) is the primitive feminine emanation therefrom; and that by the assistance of spirits—her children—she created the world, and gave them its supervision. Regarding matter co-eternal with God, and dark and chaotic, he deduced the logical conclusion, that moral and physical disorders are "mere perversities, occasioned by the soul's contact with it." In his enthusiasm and spiritual rapture, like thousands of other media, who, from flattery, magnify their own achievements, he considered himself to be the "Great Power of God," the "Word of God," sent to redeem the world from evil. Jehovah was simply a leader of spirits, and rebellious at that, from whose imperfect laws he was to emancipate mankind. Not a bad proposition by any means. Like a sensible man, he "denied the resurrection of the body." He advocated holy aspirations that the soul "might be reunited to the Source whence all beings proceeded." According to the authentic accounts, he and the Christian Fathers were competitors in miracles. His influence, doctrines and wonders, so annoyed them, they proverbially called all heretics, "disciples and successors of Simon, the Samaritan magician." They did not question the genuineness of his miracles, but were evidently jealous of his success, and attributed it to the agency of evil spirits. All the marvels related of him are philosophically traceable to psychology or real spirit power. "The fathers of the Church, Clemens Romanus and Anastasius Sinaita," says a writer, "have presented us with a detail of the wonders he actually performed." As cases showing his mediumship to be reliable and explainable on the laws of Spiritual Philosophy, occurring in the present, we quote from the historian: "He flew along in the air; bolts and chains were impotent to detain him; he made all the furniture of the house and the table to change places, as required, without a visible mover; he walked through streets attended with a multitude of strange forms, which he affirmed to be the souls of the departed."

CERENTHUS, a highly educated Jew and spiritual reformer, connected with the Alexandrian school, professed to believe in Jesus, but was deeply tinged, in thought, with the oriental ideas in respect to spirit and matter. He rejected the dogma of the incarnation of Jesus, being unwilling to suppose that a Son of God could be born of woman. Like some of our modern thinkers, he considered Christ a spirit who dwelt in the divine presence before the world was made, and that the Jesus of Galilee was a mere man, son of Joseph and Mary. Grounded upon the philosophical basis of personal merit, as the data of redemption, he sensibly concluded that his Christ-angel, descending in the form of a dove, baptized him into the full glory of celestial truth; and that through the culture of the graces—tenderness, justice and wisdom, in union with deep soul sympathy with ministering spirits, he became, in a special sense, a Son of God—a leader of heavenly hosts, and thereby enabled to work miracles. Versed in the allegorical doctrines of Philo, accepting the mediumship of Jesus, "he regarded Jehovah as merely the delegated Creator, ruler of this world—a subaltern spirit, unacquainted with the character and purpose of the Supreme God, and incapable of appreciating Him. He admitted there are many good things in the Hebrew Sacred Books; but considered them revelations of an inferior order of spirits; and that an angel instructed Moses in legislation." Morally modest, he attributed his own miraculous gifts to spirits and angels. Traveling to Ephesus, in the capacity of a teacher, he there met, as the early Fathers state, the apostle John, with whom he conversed upon mind and matter, and "eternal life."

CHAPTER XV.

APOSTOLIC.

> "As pure, white light through colored glass,
> Truth glimmers through the soul,
> And gives a glimpse, in broken parts,
> Of one grand, perfect whole."

POLYCARP, Ignatius, Clement, Apollinaris, and others, privileged with the personal presence of the first spiritualized disciples of Christ, have received the appropriate appellation of Apostolic Fathers. Blessed with direct inspiration from the spirit of Jesus and Syrian seers, summering in the heavens, we instinctively revere the divine utterances that welled from the inner fountains of their souls, and whatever spiritual phenomena they mediumistically evolved for the enlightenment of humanity.

POLYCARP, a Smyrnian bishop of eastern origin, was, in childhood, a slave, and by Calisto, a charitable lady, redeemed from bondage, in consequence of an angelic dream, and educated at her expense. The later Christian Fathers aver that he listened to the preaching of the apostle John, led a blameless life, presided over the Smyrnian church with assiduous fidelity, and was wonderfully empowered with spiritual gifts. During the persecutions under Marcus Aurelius, the infuriated populace demanded his death. Conscious of approaching danger, and occupied in prayer, he saw, in a vision, his "pillow all on fire," and exclaimed—"I shall certainly be burnt alive!" These words were regarded as prophetic. On the way to the stake, amid the jeers and excitements of Jews and Greeks, followed by a few sorrowing friends, the venerable prisoner was calm and serene as sunlight; and when approaching the fatal scene, a loud and distinct voice was heard to exclaim, as from heaven—"*Polycarp, be firm!*"

IGNATIUS, bishop of Antioch, and a loved and prominent disciple of the apostle John, is said to have been one of the little children whom Jesus took in his arms and blessed. The church fathers record the fact, that, in youth, he was "so innocent he could hear the angels sing." This heavenly music so impressed his mind, that, when becoming a bishop, he introduced into liturgical service the practice of singing in responses, just as he had heard, in youthful years, the laughing melodies of immortal choirs. Arrested by Trajan, he was thrown into chains, and sent to Rome, to be exposed to lions in the amphitheater. On the way thither, conscious of attending angels, inflamed with divine ecstacy, he exclaimed, in language worthy the heroic reformer—"Let them rack my limbs, break my bones, bruise my whole body, hang me on the cross, burn me with fire, throw me into the jaws of furious beasts; I care not for all the torments the devil can invent, so that I may have the consciousness of right, and the personal approval of Christ." When he passed through the city of Smyrna, in chains, the people embraced him and wept; kissing his hands, his garments, and his chains, rejoicing in his courage." How beautiful his character! how inspiring his example!

APOLLINARIS, the Ravennian bishop of note, according to the ecclesiastic historians, accompanied Peter, as an assistant, to Rome. Here that apostle laid his hands upon him, and communicated the gifts of the Holy Spirit; that is, a most excellent spirit influence. Preaching on the eastern coast of Italy, he is said to have silenced the oracles in Roman temples, and "caused deceiving spirits to depart therefrom." Attractive in person, bold in enunciation, and miraculously gifted, he psychologized vast multitudes. Historians relate that he once saw a poor boy, born blind, washing his rags outside the city; and, moved with compassion, he made the sign of the cross on his eyes, (spiritual impressibility) and immediately he received his sight." This miracle, so potent for good, as we naturally infer from our own observation, was the means of converting the father, a Roman soldier, and all his household. Among the instances of his healing, may be mentioned that of a distinguished gentleman of Rome, for several years dumb, who, hearing of Apollinaris, sent for him, and was instantly cured. In this family, finding a case of obsession, he cast out a demon. This remarkable achievement converted the family, with five hundred more, to the spiritualistic principles of Jesus.

CHAPTER XVI.

POST-APOSTOLIC.

"Gather up the fragments that nothing be lost."

"Still gathering as they pour along,
The voice more loud, the tide more strong."

Like mile-posts on the panoramic highway of life, burning with many-colored lights, indicating the true line of spiritual progress, loom up in bold relief the church fathers of the succeeding centuries—Irenæus, Justin Martyr, Tatian the Assyrian, Turtullian, Clement of Alexandria, Origen, Cyprian, and others—who officially represent the continuous revelations of heaven.

IRENÆUS, whose name signifies *peaceable*, an admirer of the apostle John, was endowed with prophetic gifts. As quoted by Eusebius, those times were not so potent in spirit influx, as in the palmy days of the apostles; but in cases of necessity, when a whole congregation, by fasting and prayer, adjusted themselves in harmony with the spirit-batteries, the seeming dead have been restored to life. "Some most certainly," says Irenæus, "cast out demons; others have a knowledge of things to come, as also visions and prophetic communications; and others still heal the sick by the imposition of hands. * * * * * We hear of many of the brethren in the church who have prophetic gifts, and who speak in all tongues through the Spirit, (spirit-influences) and who also bring to light the secret things of men for their benefit, and expound the mysteries of God." Eusebius, in referring to the reasons why these spiritual gifts had measurably declined in the church, in his time, asserts that "the churches had become *unworthy of them.*"

Justin Martyr, of Grecian descent, familiar, in his youth, with the doctrines of Zeno and Aristotle, mingled, in after years, the acknowledged dogmas of the church with the Platonic philosophy. This Grecian culture the better prepared him to analyze the laws of mind and its relations with this and the spirit-world. With Philo, he declared that "no man had ever seen God the Father," but that "it was our Christ, or an angel, who spoke to Moses from the bush, in the form of fire, and said, 'Put off thy shoes.'" In a book ascribed to Justin Martyr, it is stated that "demons, spirits of the dead, still speak by those who are called ventriloquists." In his famous Apology, he teaches that, "when God created the world, he committed the superintendence of it to angels." Maintaining the plausible doctrines of obsessions, he affirmed that evil demons "inflamed women, corrupted boys, and spread terrors among those who did not examine things by reason." Not realizing they were a lower order of spirits, "they called them gods, and gave to each the name he claimed for himself; but Socrates endeavored to expose their practices, and by true reason draw men away from their influences, and the demons, by the help of wicked men, caused this Grecian philosopher to be put to death as an atheist and impious person." According to certain phenomena of the present, does not this statement concerning Socrates bear the semblance of truth?

Tertullian, son of a Roman centurion, at Carthage, 160 A. D., distinguished for his great eloquence, and for his familiarity with Grecian and Roman literature, positive and vindictive in nature, and given to controversy, was fearless in his affirmations of spiritual gifts and communications. In his celebrated work, "De Anima," he says: "We had a right to expect, after what was said by St. John, to anticipate prophecies; and we not only acknowledge these spiritual gifts, but we are permitted to enjoy the gifts of a prophetess. There is a sister among us who possesses a faculty of revelation. Commonly, during religious service, she falls into a trance, holding then communion with the angels, beholding Jesus himself, hearing divine mysteries explained, reading the hearts of some persons, and administering to such as require it. When the Scriptures are read, or Psalms sung, spiritual beings minister visions to her. We were speaking of the soul once, when our sister was in the spirit (entranced); and, the people departing, she then communicated to us what she had seen in her ecstacy, which was afterwards closely inquired into and tested. She declared 'she had seen a soul in bodily shape, that appeared to be a spirit, neither empty nor formless, but so real and substantial, that it might be touched. It was tender, shining of the color of the air, but in everything resembling the human form.'"

As an exhibition of Tertullian's ferocity of nature, positiveness of will, and assurance of spiritual ability, as well as faith in angel ministry, he says: "If a man calls himself a Christian, and cannot expel a demon, LET HIM BE PUT TO DEATH ON THE SPOT!" Referring to the controlling intelligences of Æsculapius, Thanatius, and other oracles, he asserts, with fierce authority—"Unless these confess themselves to be demons, not daring to lie unto a Christian, then SHED THE BLOOD OF THAT MOST IMPOTENT CHRISTIAN!" To suit the action to the word, he commanded, "Let some one be brought forward at the foot of your judgment seat, who it is agreed is possessed with a demon. When ordered by any Christian to speak, that spirit shall as truly declare itself a demon, as elsewhere falsely a god." Tertullian, highly susceptible, was evidently controlled by a spirit on a very low plane; but being powerful and electric, he could easily dispossess any negative medium, even of a celestial angel. His success in this psychological art, was, therefore, no criterion of moral or religious superiority, but simply of physical and mental, which, like Milton's fabled Satan, defied the Almighty, and made war against him in heaven!

HERMAS, brother to Pius, a bishop of Rome, wrote his "Pastor" about the middle of the second century. This book is more appropriately known as "*The Shepherd of Hermas.*" Its contents, divided into "Visions, Commands, and Similitudes," remind one of the visions and angelic interviews of Ezekiel. Origen expresses the opinion that his books were divinely inspired. They give an account of the "Visions of Hermas," seen in his superior state, and generally interpreted in a symbolical sense. Evidently, his epistles were too spiritual to be voted *canonical*. In the ninth of his "Similitudes," an ancient white stone of immense magnitude is described, which had a new gate opened in it; and in the "Visions," Hermas relates that he saw six young men, "or rather angels clothed in shining vestures, building a tower of square white stones, symbolic of the church militant." A writer in Appleton's Biographical Cyclopedia, edited by the Rev. Dr. F. L. Hawks, speaking of this book of Hermas, remarks, that "it is further interesting because affording evidence that the early Christians believed in the ministration of angels around them."

MONTANUS, a Phrygian bishop, flourishing in the second century, preached a firm and fervid Spiritualism, attracting immense crowds. He contended that every true believer in Christ received a direct inspiration. This he based upon the prophecy of Joel—"I will pour out my spirit upon all flesh." Judaism was to him the morning-youth; Christianity, the manhood; the post-apostolic, the culmination or diffusiveness of spiritual gifts. Gifted with prophetic power, he maintained that himself, and two leading prophetesses, had received the fulness of the Divine Spirit, through whose agency all holy works are wrought.

ORIGEN, born in Alexandria, 185 A. D., consecrated himself to spiritual development by extreme abstemiousness, through spirits, who thus taught him the purer inspirations of nature. He attended the lectures where Platonism was inculcated, under the tuition of the celebrated Ammonius Saccas, which accounts for much of his peculiar religious structure. Conspicuous among his popular teachings, were summarily these—That God is immanent in all space; that stars have souls, and sang together on the morn of creation; that angelic beings have the government of fruits and seasons; that angels have etherial bodies, and evil spirits have grosser organisms; that all human souls are fellow-spirits who sinned in some previous existence, but, entering human bodies, would finally be restored to holiness and happiness; and that "all the holy men who have departed from this life, retaining their charity toward those whom they left behind, are anxious for their salvation, and assist them by their prayers, and their mediation with God." Origen says: "There are no longer any prophets or miracles among the Jews, but many vestiges of miraculous works among the Christians; namely, in the middle of the third century. Gregory, Origen's pupil, and bishop of Cæsaria in Pontus, was so famous for his miracles, that he was styled Thaumaturgus, the wonder-worker." This Christian Father further believed, that by prayer and the repetition of sacred writings, "demons could be cast out and numberless evils averted."

CYPRIAN, bishop of Carthage, educated in the most refined school of Roman theology, rigorous towards heretics, was gifted in spiritual powers, and, in common with his coadjutors, was an earnest advocate of the then popular Spiritualism of the church. In youth he had a vision, which he himself thus relates: "Whilst quite awake, I saw a young man of more than mortal stature, who showed him himself, led before the pro-consul and condemned to be beheaded, as a martyr to Christianity. Accordingly, when it came to pass, he knew exactly how and when it would take place." In agreement with his cotemporary, he taught that evil spirits obsess mortals, that they lurk around tutelary statues, inspire soothsayers, excite terror in the minds of men, disturb their sleep, destroy their health, etc., and "then either vanish immediately, or go out gradually, according to the faith of the patient, or the grace of him who effects the cure." He declares that "there is no measure or rule in the dispensation of the gifts of heaven, as in the gifts of earth. The spirit is poured forth liberally, without limits or barriers. * * * * * Besides visions of the night, even boys among us are filled with the Holy Spirit, and in fits of ecstacy see, hear and speak things by which the Lord (a leader or angelic being) thinks fit to instruct us."

Either through candid ignorance of the law, or inexcusable bigotry, the bishop of Antioch, Theophilus, avers that it was evil spirits who inspired the prophets of Greece and Rome— "The truth of this is manifestly shown, because those who are possessed by demons, even to this day, are sometimes exorcised by us in the name of God; and the seducing spirits confess themselves to be the same demons who before inspired the gentile poets."

The honest reader will clearly discover the deep and nurtured jealousy existing between the Classics and Christians, and the studied effort at the mastery over each other's oracles; and draw his conclusions, not from apparent victory—because of better battery forces—but according to justice and integrity, crediting Egyptian, Jewish and Grecian Spiritualists with the virtue justly their due.

We have the most abundant proof of the continuance of spiritual gifts and converse with the immortals, both from the of classic and ecclesiastic writers, during the first six centuries the Christian era. Among the church historians who treated directly of this matter, were Eusebius, Socrates, Scholasticus, Sozomen, Theodoret and Evagrius. Hegisippus and Papias, who preceded Eusebius, testify to the prevalence of spiritual dreams, prophecies, trances and seership, in their age.

GREGORY, a Thaumaturgist, and noted disciple of Origen, was famous for the great number of miracles or spiritual manifestations, wrought through his mediatorial organization.

AUGUSTINE, flourishing about the middle of the fifth century, bears multiform testimony to the continuance of the miraculous gifts of Christians. "Besides the restoration of a child to life, he relates twenty miracles performed under his observation within the space of two years."

AMBROSE, living towards the end of the fourth century, is stated to have fallen asleep (entranced) at the altar on a certain Sunday, remaining so for several hours, to the great wonder of the people. Awakening, he declared that he had attended the funeral of St. Martin, and performed the service. The fact noted, it was ascertained that St. Martin had died at the time specified by this seer. He also assures us that "the martyr Agnes was seen one night at her grave, surrounded by a choir of singing maidens."

JEROME, living in the fifth century, relates numerous miracles occurring in his time, such as "the restoration of sight to a woman ten years blind, the instant cure of paralysis, and the casting out of demons. "These miracles are paralleled by what are now denominated "spiritual manifestations."

Mosheim, (vol. i. p. 104) in his ecclesiastical history, says:

"The light of the Gospel was introduced into Iberia, a province of Asia (now called Georgia), in the following manner: a certain woman was carried into that country as a captive, during the reign of Constantine; and by the grandeur of her miracles, and the remarkable sanctity of her life and manners, she made such an impression upon the king and queen, that they abandoned their false gods, embraced the faith of the Gospel, and sent to Constantinople for proper persons to give them and their people a more satisfactory and complete knowledge of the Christian religion."

This was in the fourth century. After maturely considering the whole ground and all the authorities, on the next page he says:

"I am willing to grant, that many events have been rashly deemed miraculous which were the result of the ordinary laws of nature; and, also that pious frauds were sometimes used for the purpose of giving new degrees of weight and dignity to the Christian cause. But I cannot, on the other hand, assent to the opinions of those who maintain that in this century, miracles had entirely ceased; and that, at this period, the Christian Church was not favored with any extraordinary or supernatural mark of a Divine power engaged in its cause."

Constantine's reign infused a sort of pride into the Christianity of that and subsequent centuries. With national ambition and individual worldliness spurred to intense action by reigning rival powers, there commenced about this time a rapid decline of spiritual gifts among nominal christians, forcibly reminding one of the Apostle Paul's prophecy of the "falling away" that should come. Christianity, a shell devoid the spirit-substance, still flounders in this "fallen" condition.

Chapter XVII.

NEO-PLATONIC

> "We lack but open eye and ear
> To find the Orient's marvels here.
> * * * * * *
> For still the new transcends the old
> In signs and tokens manifold."

As Paris to France socially, as Jerusalem to Syria religiously, as Ephesus to the thinkers of Southern Asia ideally, so Alexandria to all nations of the first Christian centuries. Founded by Alexander the Great, on the commercial thoroughfare between Europe and Asia, it was the center of philosophy, the birth-place of symbols, the arena of all new theories, attractive for her unparalleled libraries, numbering, in her palmier period, seven hundred thousand books, and celebrated for accommodating, at one time within her classic precincts, fourteen thousand students! The literary world in miniature, her fountains of truth, flowing over all deserts and ruins and mausoleums and Edens of beauty, have bathed the whole earth in historic and inspirational wisdom. Her eclectic professors, cooling the egotistic ardor of the Church Fathers, plucked their boasted plumes by exhibiting superior art and literature, magic and miracle.

This Alexandrian school of philosophy, based upon the psychological systems of Pythagoras and Plato, drew its primal inspirations from India and Egypt, and, amalgamating with, overshadowed the dogmas of Christianity.

Dion Chrysostom, writing in the time of Trajan, says: "I see among you Alexandrians, not only Greeks and Italians, Syrians, Sybians, Ethiopians and Arabians, but Bactrians, Scythians, Persians, and travelers from India, who flow together into this city, and are always with you."

Gnosticism, (*ginosko, to know*) budding in the first, blossomed more fully among educated classes in the second century. The Gnostics were Inductionists. *Gnosis* was considered a *divine science;* and, wielded by those metaphysical thinkers, successfully contended against Christianity, in the estimation of the literati. It is averred, with great plausibility, that the Asiatic Gnostics were personally acquainted with the Gymnosophists of India and the Magi of Persia. The Christian Fathers, owing to a lack of literary culture, were disinclined to meet them in discussion. Mani, born in Persia, Marcus Tatian, Cerinthus, the father of Gregory, of Nazianzen, were prominent among the Gnostics. These, with others of the same school, held to the oriental philosophical theory, that all spirits emanated from God, and were a part of him; that angels, by divine appointment, exercised a superintendence over the affairs of this world as guardians; that mortals had the high privilege of communion with these celestials; that Christ, as a heavenly spirit, was not invested with a mortal body after his resurrection, or, better, emancipation; that souls, as *œnons*, emanating from the infinite fountain of Deity, by a law of progress, returned purified to the bosom-source whence they came. Clement of Alexandria, says: "Their worship consists in continual attention to their souls; in meditations upon the Divinity, as being inexhaustible love."

Ammonius Saccas, profound, scholarly and eclectic, combining in his rare organism the extremes of conservatism and radicalism, organized this famous school about the year 220 A. D. Plotinus, Porphyry, Proclus, Jamblichus, and others, rejecting the mouldy crumbs of Hebrew revelations, and versed in the elements and principles characterizing the oriental theosophies, were among the eminent disciples of Ammonius. His lofty purpose was to combine the *good* and *beautiful* found in the theologies and philosophies of India, Egypt, China, Persia, Judea, Greece and Rome, in fact, all nations in all times, and out of these vast materials to form a grand eclecticism, alive with all the thought, wisdom and virtue of the ages, like a superb temple compounded of all the kingdoms of life in the universe.

PLOTINUS, eleven years the student of Ammonius Saccas, retaining his Egyptian idiosyncracies, educated at Alexandria, and of immeasurable influence in society, was the inspiring *animus* of Neo-Platonism, and gave to it much of its prestige and fame in the world. His metaphysical doctrines run thus: That there is one God, the perfect, uncreated principle; that Wisdom is the *Logos* of the *good;* that from Wisdom and Love proceeded the souls of all things; that the human soul, an essential portion of the *Divine Soul*, can, in its highest states, penetrate into all worlds' mysteries, and hold communion with the essence of things; that this life is a mere flash of light, which God, in his goodness, grants to souls for a season; that, whilst this earth-life lasts, memory of the prior existence vanishes, but in the next life, the mind beholds the past, present and future, *at one glance;* that poets, lovers, musicians, philosophers, more etherial-winged, can the easier ascend into the superior regions; that miracles are in harmony with fixed principles of the universe; that self-denial of all lusts and passions is inductive to conscious communication with and glory of the gods, or angels. His enthusiastic disciples ascribed to him miraculous gifts. In their writings it is frequently affirmed that he could discern the secret thoughts of men. When Porphyry contemplated suicide, he discovered it without the least outward intimation. When a theft had been committed in the house, he collected the domestics and immediately pointed out the culprit, without asking a question. They requested him to evoke his guardian spirit, which the Grecians called his "*demon.*" He refused for a long time. Finally, yielding to their entreaties, they saw a *god* appear in their midst. He healed the most dangerous diseases, obtained great reputation for foretelling future events, and walked in daily converse with spirits and angels. Emilius, urging him to attend the services of the church, he replied, "The spirits must come to me, not I to the spirits." After his departure to the spirit world, in the sixty-sixth year of his age, his friends inquired of an oracle as to the residence of his soul. The response was given in verse, to the effect, that owing to his gentleness, goodness, elevated ideas, purity of life, his soul had rejoined the just spirits of Minos, Rhadamanthus and Æacus. By virtue of these graces he was permitted to behold, face to face, the more exalted and glorified of the celestial worlds.

PORPHYRY, of Phœnecian descent, was one of the most distinguished disciples of Plotinus, succeeding him in the third century as president of the Alexandrian school. It is as morally impossible for a Roman Church father to speak or write impartially of Porphyry, as for a modern Protestant of the orthodox school, to award Spiritualists their just position. Deeply read in the lore of the past, an ardent admirer of Plato, Porphyry is described by the church historian, Neander, as "a man of noble spirit, united with profound intellectual attainments; a man of the East, in whom the oriental basis of character had been completely fused with the elements of Grecian culture." He devoted much time to the study of magic, called *Theurgy;* to the psychologic and mystic relations of mind to mind; to the necessity of self-abnegation, as preparatory to the highest angelic communion; and, like his predecessors, Ammonius and Plotinus, he sought to establish a universal eclecticism in religion. Nearly all his works against Christianity were burned by Christians—a proof this of their inestimable value. When a sectarian man cannot meet his neighbor with sound reason, he tries force, fire, perjury, theft! They who *know* the truth, love criticism; and rather than burn philosophy, they cherish it as gratefully as flowers do the sunshine.

Porphyry taught that all religions have a divine origin; that a high standard of morals and purity of life are indispensable to happiness; that men are justified in separating from their angular wives to attain greater holiness and more time to devote to philosophy; that it is wrong to obey civil laws when in opposition to higher law written by God in the eternal constitution of the soul; and, quoting Apollonius in favor of silent prayer, that such devotion is alone worthy the Supreme Being. He beautifully says, that "Similarities unite. Shut up in the body, as in a prison, we ought to pray to gods and angels to deliver us from our fetters. They are our true fathers; and we ought to pray to them like children exiled from the paternal mansion." He believed in the controlling intelligences of heaven, and was much "impressed with the power of evil spirits," often referring to them as the cause of disease, personal quarrels, and national wars. He also maintained that the spirit of prophecy could be attained by abstemious living; and that his soul was once so elevated to a complete union with God, he caught golden glimpses of the eternal world.

JAMBLICHUS, Syrian by birth, student of Porphyry, approached, in precept and practice, nearer the Nazarene than any cotemporary Neo-Platonist. He lived in the reign of Constantine, when Indian philosophy and Grecian theosophy were the cherished principles of the erudite. Teaching the oriental doctrine of emanations, he mingled theurgy, magic and philosophy in his crucible of thought, daily inspected by Alexandrian students. His disciples believed him possessed with supernatural power. History affirms, that whilst engaged in prayer, spirits raised him fifteen feet in the air. Accompanied by his pupils to the baths of Gadara, in Syria, he inquired the names of two springs of water. On being informed they were *Eros* and *Anteros*—deities acknowledged by the Greeks—he scarcely touched the water, uttering a few words, when there rose up before them two beautiful children, who clasped their arms around Jamblichus' neck. From this moment none of his adherents doubted his communion with the gods. His biographer, Eunapius, a very learned and conscientious writer, narrates many other miraculous things attributed to him. So wonderful were they, that "neither Edesius, nor his friends, have dared to put them in their works." In order to attain the highest degrees of mediumship—then called *Theurgy*—he and his wise companions, like the Egyptian Hierophants, prepared themselves by fasting, watching, praying, and devout religious reflection. These spiritual conditions introduced into realms of divine exaltation, are thus described by Jamblichus in his "Mysteries:" "The senses are in a sleeping state. The Theurgist has no command of his faculties, no consciousness of what he says or does. * * * Carried by a divine impulse, he goes through impassable places, through fire and water without knowing where he is. A divine illumination takes full possession of the man, absorbs all his faculties, motions, and senses; making him speak what he does not understand, or rather *seem* to speak it; for he is, in fact, merely the minister, or instrument, of the God who possesses him." What a *perfect* description of modern trance, by this ancient Neo-Platonist!

Of prayer, this most devout philosopher says: "Frequent prayer nourishes our superior part, renders the receptacle of the soul more capacious for the gods, discloses divine things to men, accustoms them with the splendors of the world of intelligences, and gradually so perfects our union with pure spirits, as to lead us back to the Supreme God."

JAMBLICHUS was familiar with clairvoyance in all its phases, with healing by spirit influence, with dreams as spirit impressions, and with the beauties and glories of the trance, both from observation and experience. He explains what is said by Porphyry: "That some immediately fall into a trance on hearing music; and he shows an intimate acquaintance with instances of persons hearing most divine music, especially on approaching death."

Well, therefore, did Jamblichus, in his celebrated work on the "Mysteries," assert that admissibility to, and communion with, spiritual beings, "is eternal and cotemporary with the soul."

PROCLUS, "the heir of Plato," the ascetic teacher of Athens, the young prodigy of the Alexandrian philosophy, saw, in his day, the culmination of Neo-Platonism. He commenced his forty-third chapter on the theology of Plato thus: "Let us speak concerning the demons who are allotted the superintendence of mankind. * * * The highest genus of demons, being proximate to the gods, is uniform and divine. The next in order to these demons, possessing a highly intellectual nature, preside over individuals, as well as over the ascent and descent of souls." The Egyptian priests admired Plotinus as being governed (on account of the purity of his life) by a divine demon. And with great propriety, also, does Socrates call his demon a god, for he belonged to the first and highest demons. Proclus further says: "Socrates perceived a certain voice proceeding from his demon. This he asserts in the *Theætetus* and in the *Phædrus*." What the Grecians termed "divine demons," we denominate ministering angel guides, who delight to do the will of the Eternal Father.

Lecture V.

Churchal Spiritualism.

Chapter XVIII.

CHURCHIANIC.

> "Oh, never rudely will I blame their faith
> In the might of gods and angels!"

> "Sometimes there glimpses on my sight
> Through Christian wrongs the eternal right;
> And step by step since time began
> I see the steady gain of man."

Christianity, heretofore spiritually spontaneous as taught by the Nazarene, became sectarized and nationalized—a court-religion under the reign of Constantine.

Not a vestige of similarity is traceable between the nature-teachings and pure, sweet life of the gentle son of Joseph and Mary, and the worldly Christianity of the 19th century. From this fatal Constantinian era, its purity more rapidly paled, until an eclipse of spiritual midnight brooded over its blinded devotees. Fossils neither flash nor flame with vigorous life. Few blossoms of inspiration come from a leafless, sapless, withered trunk. When doctrines, however beautiful, crystalize into creeds, they die and rust away into Lethean forgetfulness.

Roman Catholicism, imitated by her schismatic daughter, Protestantism, adopted, in her externals, a *paganized Judaism*, combining the ceremonials of the Mosaic and *later* classic, with their sacerdotal, hierarchal paraphernalia, the better to seize and appropriate the more cultured religious theses taught in the mystic temples of the orientals, for priestly power and worldly aggrandizement. As every midnight has its stars, and every stormy ocean its pearls, so, under the cold drapery of the royalized church, were genuine silver-glimmerings of the aspirational and spiritual.

GUIZOT, in his recent work entitled, "Meditations upon the Religious Questions of the Day," in which he evidently uses the word *supernatural* for *spiritual*, says: "Belief in the supernatural is a fact natural, primitive, universal and constant in the life and history of the human race. Unbelief in the supernatural begets materialism, materialism sensuality, sensuality social convulsion, amid whose storms man learns again to believe and pray."

CONSTANTINE, having espoused Christianity, and being menaced in consequence by its enemies, was compelled to take up arms for self-defence. Eusebius states that he heard Constantine declare, under oath, that "when he was going to attack the tyrant Maxentius, and was full of doubt, as he was resting in the middle of the day, and his soldiers about him, he and all the soldiers saw a luminous cross in the heavens, attended by a troop of angels, who said, 'O, Constantine! by this go forth to victory!' * * * At night, Christ appeared to him in a dream, having the same cross, which he ordered to have wrought upon his banners, with the words, 'BY THIS conquer!'" Under this inspiring symbol he *did* conquer.

LACTANTIUS corroborates the statement, that the sign of the cross on the shields of the soldiers, was put there in consequence of a vision or dream. Socrates, Philostorgius, Gelasius, Nicephorus, all testify to the appearance of the cross in the sky. It was a most magnificent psychological presentation, produced by ministering spirits.

SOZOMEN, a church historian of the 5th century, informs us "that when Julian was killed in Persia, his death was seen in Asia by one of his officers, at a distance of twenty days' travel; and by Didymus, a blind Christian, in Egypt." He relates an incident of Eutychian, a Bithynian monk, a friend of Constantine, who desired the jailers to remove the fetters from a prisoner sorely tortured; but, on being refused, he went to the prison, attended by Auscanon, a venerable presbyter of the church. At their approach the doors of the prison opened, and the chains fell from the prisoner's limbs.

This finds corroboration in the case of Peter, who was released from prison by an angel, and of the Davenport Brothers, who were helped to make their escape, by angel power, from prison walls, in Oswego, N. Y., thrust therein at the instigation of the church.

AUGUSTINE, a famous Latin Church Father, living in the 4th century, gives some very beautiful expressions of joy respecting angel guardians:

"They watch over and guard us with great care and diligence in all places, and at all hours assisting, providing for our necessities with solicitude; they intervene betwixt us and Thee, O Lord, conveying to Thee our sighs and groans, and bringing down to us the dearest blessings of Thy grace. They walk with us in all our ways; they go in and out with us, attentively observing how we converse with piety in the midst of a perverse generation; with what ardor we seek Thy kingdom and its justice, and with what fear and awe we serve Thee. They assist us in our labors; they protect us in our rest; they encourage us in battle; they crown us in victories; they rejoice in us when we rejoice in Thee; and they compassionately attend us when we suffer or are afflicted for Thee. Great is their care of us, and great is the effect of their charity for us."

JULIAN, Emperor of Rome, nephew of Constantine, famous in history for his effort to re-establish the shrines of oriental worship, and stigmatized "Apostate," because, being a Christian, he patronized the Neo-Platonic Philosophy. When a boy, he was strongly charmed by the sunlight, and considered it an unconscious longing after the God with whom he was related. The sun was to him a beautiful symbol of the God of the universe. Accordingly, "the private chapel in his palace was consecrated to the sun; but his gardens were filled with altars and statues of the gods and angels." He maintained that there were messengers between God and men, and sometimes, for special purposes, resided in earthly temples—haunted houses. No wonder the church called him "*Apostate!*"

"When Julian and his brother Gallus were induced to undertake the labor of erecting a chapel over the tomb of the martyr Mammas, the work went on rapidly under the hands of Gallus, but the stones which Julian laid were constantly overthrown as by some invisible agency. Gregory of Naziangen says that he had this from eye witnesses; and he seems to regard it as a prophetic miracle."

The Greek Church of Russia, receiving her apostolic hierarchy and priesthood from Greece, has carefully maintained the integrity of the primitive Church with less innovations, doubtless, than the Catholic, and is, therefore, more authoritative in respect to what the Apostolic Fathers taught. The doctrine of ministering spirits, working miracles through their patron saints, is plainly set forth in their religious histories.

M. MOURAVIEFF, a church historian, tells us that "his or her 'angel' is the customary phrase in Russia for the patron saint after whom any one is named; but that they also believe in guardian angels appointed to each baptized person. The church counts, as its chief guardians and intercessors, a considerable number of saints. The Russian Church believes firmly in 'the doctrines of the holy Icons (pictures of saints and the Virgin), in relics, the sign of the venerable cross, of tradition, of the mystery of the most pure blood and body of Christ, of the invocation of saints and angels, of the state of souls after death, and of prayers for the departed.'"

Howitt, in his "History of the Supernatural," adverts to the fact, that "in the time of Peter the Great, the Anglican Church made application to be admitted to unity with the Œcumenical Church, and desired the Russian patriarch to transmit their prayer to Constantinople; but the Russian prelates, having consulted, declined, because the Anglican Church had heretically renounced the traditions of the Fathers, the invocations of saints, and the reverencing of Icons—sacred pictures."

St. Bernard, a healing and most benevolent priest, thus alludes to the divine care over us:

"We owe to our guardian angels great reverence, devotion and confidence. Penetrated with awe, walk always with circumspection, remembering the presence of angels, to whom you are given in charge, in all your ways. In every apartment, in every closet, in every corner, pay respect to your angel. Dare you do before him what you dare not commit if I saw you?" * * * * * * * *

"Consider with how great respect, awe, and modesty we ought to behave in the sight of the angels, lest we offend their eyes, and render ourselves unworthy of their company. Woe to us if they who could chase away our enemy, be offended by our negligence, and deprive us of their visits."

Gregory VII., (Hildebrand) of the 11th century, was a noted thaumaturgist or seer. When Rodolph marched against Henry IV., this pope was so certain of success that he ventured to prophesy, both in speech and writing, that his enemy would be conquered and slain in battle, and would transpire before St. Peter's day, which prophecy was literally fulfilled.

Roger Bacon, of the 12th century, a Franciscan Friar, the accredited inventor of the telescope, and a profound scholar, who much disturbed the church by his seership and science, under the controlling intelligences of the spirit-world, penetrated into the mysteries of life, and, piercing the cloudy sun-mists of intervening ages, seized upon the occult forces that bowed as servants to his beck and adapted them by invention to practical uses.

A profound study of magic with the natural sciences, made him liberal and progressive. The clergy prohibited his lectures, and confined the circulation of his writings to the walls of the convent. Finally a council of Sanfranciscans condemned his books and sent him to prison. He was specially gifted with the power to discern future events, being highly mediumistic. Some of his remarkable prophecies, uttered six hundred years ago, relating to modern inventions, were strikingly practical, as the following testifies:

"Bridges, unsupported by arches, will be made to span the foaming current. Man shall descend to the bottom of the ocean, safely breathing, and treading with firm step on the golden sands, never brightened by the light of day. Call but the sacred powers of Sol and Luna into action, and behold a single steersman sitting at the helm, guiding the vessel which divides the waves with greater rapidity than if she had been propelled by a crew of marines toiling at the oars; and the loaded chariot no longer encumbered by the panting steeds, shall dart on its course with resistless force and rapidity. Let the simple elements do the labor; bind the eternal forces and yoke them to the same plow."

The excellent writer, Prof. Brittan, says that "these prophecies of Bacon embrace the Suspension Bridge, the Diving Bell, Steam Navigation, the Railroad, and the Steam Plow, in the same chain of events, all of which are among the accomplished realities of-day."

Infinite Spirit is infinite causation; finite spirit in man is finite causation. Just so far as this finite causation comes into relation with causes outside and independent of himself, is he able to read the future. Exalted spirits standing upon the plane of causes, and, seeing with unsealed vision certain operative forces, are enabled to determine the legitimate effects thence derived. Prophecy, therefore, is just as natural as cause and effect. Angels, spirits, men, possess the power of prevision just in the ratio of exaltation in wisdom.

Peter d'Apono, 1250 A. D., an eminent philosopher, mathematician and astrologer, is said to have been possessed by seven spirits, from whom he received all information he desired relating to the liberal arts and sciences. Tried in ecclesiastic council for practicing magic, he died before his inquisitors, who, to glut their insatiable churchal malignancy, dug up his bones and publicly burned them!

BISHOP GROSSETETE, of the 13th century, a man of most transcendent intellect and superior acquirements, was endowed with spiritual gifts. The poet, Gower, informs us that he constructed a head of brass in such a manner that mediumistically it answered philosophical questions and foretold future events.

"Nicolas, of Basle, and his friends predicted the death of Gregory XI., which took place at the time foretold—namely, in the fourth week in Lent, 1378. They foresaw also the grand schism in the Popedom, which commenced in the following year. So deeply was Nicolas concerned for the shameful corruptions of the church and of the papal court, that in his seventieth year, in the year 1376, taking a trusty 'Friend of God' with him, he went to Rome; and, in a personal interview with Gregory, warned him of the troubles coming, and of his own death, if he did not commence a real and sweeping reform. The pope received this mission kindly but did not profit by it, and died as they had foreshown. Many wonderful spiritual phenomena and revelations are related as attending the meeting of these Friends of God," —a sect of the 4th century, identified with the Catholic Church, that sought to purify it of its gross iniquities through a more spiritual and angelic life.

MARTIN LUTHER, though careful to reject the doctrine of miracles and the continuation of the spiritual gifts—the fatal error of Protestantism—*was* forced to admit in his day of terrible conflict with the Mother Church, that "angels were watching and protecting," and "'all up in arms, putting on their armor, and girding their swords about them'; but he had so bitterly ridiculed and so heartily abused the Catholics for their manufactured miracles, that he was now afraid to have the power of working true ones, lest they should retort."

In this matter we discover in Luther, not only a want of candor, but also of courage—for according to his own experience and confession in his *Table Talk* and otherwise, he was convicted of direct spiritual inspiration and the probable visitation of spirits and angels. This apparent cowardice and most saddening mistake in the Reformation, constitute the tare in the church-field, which has increased till all the wheat is *smutty*. This reaction from the abuse of spiritual gifts in the Catholic Church, has been all along a killing frost, destroying every beautiful flower of Paradise. Reader! have you thought of the painful fact, that all the Protestant Churches date their spiritual decay back three hundred years to this fatal error of the fathers of the Reformation, whilst the Mother Church, assailed on every side, a thousand times menaced with annihilation, lives on amid Protestant decay, fresh and green in her soul—beautiful vines climbing walls in ruin?

The Catholic Church never lost its cynosure star—the probable ministry of angels. As ever her devotees have said, "We believe in communion with the saints," those angels have felt the prayer and kept the estate secure from blast. The Catholics, clinging with loving tenacity to the beautiful belief of "communion with the saints," have, from time immemorial, preserved it in imposing anniversary. The second of October is the Feast of Angel Guardians, in commemoration, as Alban Butler says, of "a communication of spiritual commerce between us on earth and his holy angels, whose companions we hope one day to be in the kingdom of his glory."

But Luther's vacuum was filled with his "roaring devil!" that haunted him in all his travels and labors, as a "familiar spirit." The devil supped with him, slept with him, watched with him, conversed with him, spoke to him in all calamities and misfortunes. On one occasion, when this spirit interfered with his translation, perhaps only for a playful taunt, he threw his inkstand at him. This iconoclast had a great deal of trouble with this spirit, who evidently delighted in a frolic to keep up a healthful condition with his medium. He little realized that his devil, attracted to his sphere of life, was a power that intensified his will and strengthened him in his reformatory work. Give thy devil his due, O Luther! But these days we have learned not to call these health-giving, rough and playful spirits, *devils*, but *fellow-laborers*.

Poor Luther, *so* protestant as to drive away the higher angels, so iconoclastic as to attract destructive spirits to be his companions! We do not wonder that all his church children have been obsessed, and do to this day see only a "devil" in Spiritualism—the angel of God returned to rescue Protestantism from death. "As a man thinketh so is he." Devilish conditions clothe all spirits with demoniac attributes. Look within, O dying Church! and behold thyself entombed with the real GADARENE!—blank skepticism—wintry atheism, "legion" of doubts and bigotries!

PHILIP MELANCTHON, more spiritual in organization than Luther, had a more equably balanced faith in the ministry of spirits, and relates several instances of such interposition in times of peril. He tells us, that he 'had seen *spectres*, (spirits) and that he knew many men, worthy of credit, who not only had seen, but had likewise discoursed with them."

Leckendoye, on the authority of Solomon Glasse, states that Melancthon was recalled from death by Luther's prayers, positively indicating his healing power under the influence of his attending spirits.:

"Luther arrived, and found Philip about to give up the ghost. His eyes were set, his understanding was almost gone, his speech had failed, and also his hearing; his face had fallen; he knew no one, and had ceased to take either solids or liquids. At this spectacle Luther is filled with the utmost consternation—turning away towards the window, he called most devoutly upon God. After this, taking the hand of Philip, and well knowing what was the anxiety of his heart and conscience, he said, 'Be of good courage, Philip; thou shalt not die.' While he utters these things, Philip begins, as it were, to revive and to breathe, and gradually recovering his strength, is at last restored to health." Melancthon, writing to a friend, said, "I should have been a dead man, had I not been recalled from death by the coming of Luther."

JOHN CALVIN, "the iron-clad," the actual murderer of Servetus for heresy, the father of "election, reprobation and Infant Damnation," and of a church still as rigid as his stern self—a man whose sinewy temperament would not originate or indulge in spiritual fancies, as we might naturally suppose, if he believed at all in spirits, accepted the doctrine of the so-called "supernatural" under the "agency of Satan!" He however claimed to have a genuine spirit of prophecy, and to be clairaudient, as Beza shows in his biography of Calvin.

COLUMBUS, toiling seventeen years under the lofty ideal of faith, at length procured the ships that wooed the shores of the western world. He was pronounced a "visionary and fanatic." When wrestling with sorest difficulties, he heard an unknown voice whispering in his ear, "God will cause thy name to be wonderfully resounded through the earth, and give thee the keys to the gates of the ocean which are closed with strong chains."

CICERO gave this remarkable prediction: "Across the ocean, and after many ages, an extensive and rich country will be discovered, and in it will arise a hero, who, by his counsel and arms, shall deliver his country from the slavery by which she was oppressed. This he shall do, under favorable auspicies; and oh! how much more admirable will he be than our Brutus and Camillus!" This prediction was known to Accius, and was embellished in poetry. Thus prophets have been honored and prophecies preserved in all ages of the world.

THE WALDENSES of the fourteenth and fifteenth centuries, resolved to be pure and clear of Catholic idolatry, were pursued by their enemies with the most malignant persecutions to exterminate them from the earth. Among the fastnesses of the Pedmontese Alps, they defended themselves under the miraculous intervention of the spirits, astonishing as that of Israel under the leadership of Joshua, guided by the reputed Jehovah and his retinue of warlike spirits. Leger, their historian, informs us that on one occasion they were " carried off in great numbers from their harvest fields, and cast into different prisons; but their enemies, to their unbounded astonishment, soon found them all at liberty again, equally to the amazement of the captives themselves, who knew nothing of the arrest of their fellows in different places at the same time, and were set free again 'miraculously,' and in a wonderful manner."

Agrippa, fifteenth century, remarkable for his knowledge of the languages, and vast range of scholarship, possessed rare spiritual powers, which he delighted to exhibit in European courts. When at the court of John George, Elector of Saxony, with Erasmus and others, eminent in the republic of letters, he was solicited to call up the spirit of Tully. Arranging the audience, Tully appeared upon the rostrum and reiterated his oration for Roscius " with such astonishing animation, exaltation of spirit, and soul-stirring gestures, that all present, like the Romans of old, were ready to pronounce his client innocent of every charge brought against him."

By means of the vital magnetic effluences from the mediumistic Agrippa, the spirits uniting their own spheral eminations, Tully was enabled to materialize himself and appear upon the rostrum *en persona*, just as the angels, materializing themselves, rolled away the stone from the sepulchre of Jesus, and as they *now* exhibit spirit hands in visible form.

BODIN, a celebrated writer on jurisprudence, informs us of a person who used to pray heartily to God, morning and evening, that He would send him " a *good angel* to guide him in all his actions;" and, in answer to his soul's entreaty, a spirit at last responded; at first in dreams and visions to correct certain bad habits; afterwards, warning him of dangers, and showing him how to overcome difficulties. When his mediumship was better developed, he heard the voice of his angel, saying, "I will save thy soul. It is I that appeared to thee before." This spirit would knock at his door—spirit rappings—direct him in his devotions—guard him in his sickness—prevent his reading anything morally injurious—warn him of evil by touching his left ear, of good results by touching his right ear—map out for him the true path of life by signs, visions and impressions.

TRITHEMIUS, Abbot of Spanheim, flourishing in the fifteenth century, author of many valuable works, and a man of great learning and dignity, gifted with second sight, saw his departed wife and recognized her. His biographer states that after long pondering upon "secrets unknown to men," until ashamed of his seeming folly to discover "*impossibilities*," he was one night visited by a spirit who assured him that his deep thoughts were inspired. The whole mystery was explained, and the result was the secret instrument entitled *Stenographia*, which, doubtless, was nothing more nor less than a scientific revelation of mental telegraphing, kindred with spirit communications.

In his work on "Secret Things and Secret Spirits," he inculcates the old Hindoo virtue of self-denial: "It is fit that we who endeavor to rise to an elevation so sublime, should study first to leave behind carnal affections, the frailty of the senses, and the passions that belong thereto."

TASSO, the first of Italian poets, was a genius beyond the capacity of his age, and so brilliant that popes, cardinals, princes, and the court of Ferrara, where he resided, esteemed themselves honored with his presence. He ranks among the most distinguished Spiritualists of the ages. Daily conversing with inspiring spirits, his poems abound with beautiful picturings of angels and loving demons, who not only peopled the realm of his imagination, but constituted the real of his life.

"He lived the songs he sung."

The plodding inductionists of his time pronounced him "mad"—*mad?*—mad as Socrates—mad as Jesus—mad as John on Patmos—mad as Spiritualists now are mad. Owing to his spiritual exaltation and magical power of communing with spirits, despite his finely molded form and character, and the felicity of his poetic thought, he was contemptuously persecuted by the petty Duke of Ferrara, one of the minions of the church, and thrust into a cold prison at Santa Anna. Here he was visited by spirits, one of whom he calls *Folletto*.

Strange noises and commotions were produced by this influence, when his mind was thus wrought up to deep feeling and anguish on account of bigoted, envious sectarists; "his books were flung down from the shelves, a loaf was snatched out of his own hands, and a plate of fruit, which he was offering to a Polish youth. 'God knows,' he says, 'that I am neither a magician nor a Lutheran, that I never read heretical books, nor those which treat of necromancy, nor any prohibited art; yet I can neither defend myself from thievish men when I am absent, nor demons when I am present.'" To soothe his sufferings, he had a vision of the Virgin Mary. Through spirit power he was healed, and an appreciation of the heavenly intervention, he embodied it in sweet song.

The eminent author, William Howitt, writing of him, says:

"Whether grave or gay, this spirit often came to him, and he often held long discourses with it. Manso endeavored to persuade him that it was a fancy; but Tasso maintained that it was as real as themselves, a Christian spirit, and which Manso admits gave him great comfort and consolation. Tasso, to convince Manso of the reality of this spirit, begged him to be present at an interview. Manso says that he saw Tasso address himself to some invisible object, listen in return, and then reply to what it appeared to have said. He says that the discourses of Tasso 'were so lofty and marvelous, both by the sublimity of their topics and a certain unwonted manner of talking, that, exalted above myself into a certain kind of ecstacy, I did not dare to interrupt them.' Tasso was disappointed, however, that Manso did not see or hear the spirit—which he ought not to have been after what he himself tells us, that to see spirits the human eye must be purified, or the spirits must array themselves in matter. This is the present acknowledged law in such cases of apparitions. They who see them must be mediums—that is, have their spiritual eyes open—or the spirits must envelop themselves in matter obvious to the outer eye. Tasso did not recollect that Manso might not be in the clairvoyant condition in which he himself was; and Manso, wholly ignorant of these psychological laws, could only suppose Tasso dealing with a subjective idea. Yet Manso evidently *felt* the presence of the spirit, for he was raised by it 'into a kind of ecstacy,' and he confesses that Tasso's spiritual interviews 'were more likely to affect his own mind than that he should dissipate Tasso's true or imaginary opinion.'"

THE ENGLISH CHURCH, founded by the voluptuous Henry VIII., contains in its homilies sundry statements of the gifts of the Spirits, of which the following is a sample:

"The Holy Ghost doth always declare Himself, by His fruitful and gracious gifts—namely, by the word of wisdom, by the word of knowledge, which is the understanding of the Scriptures; by faith in doing of miracles, by healing them that are diseased, by prophecy, which is the distribution of God's mysteries; by discerning of spirits, diversities of tongues, and so forth. All which gifts, as they proceed from one Spirit, and are severally given to man according to the measurable distribution of the Holy Ghost; even so do they bring men, and not without good cause, into a wonderful admiration of God's power."

But this only saving element, casually infused into the creed from its scriptural pledges of allegiance to the "Word of God," was stultified by the transmissible, cancerous poison of Lutheran origin—"the non-necessity of further miracles." A writer, understanding its unspiritual condition, its superficial religion, appropriately calls it the "Anglican drying-house, whose looks and words are of the purest dry-as-dust order, *capites-mortuum* men—of the earth, earthy."

All religion turns to brass to rust in sepultures, when its devotees deny the ministry of angels. It degenerates with fashion, grows lecherous with lust, sinks into an ecclesiastic night-mare, a kind of churchal delirium tremens, that sees only devils in all spiritual phenomena, come to raise "the dead in trespasses and sins." This is the trouble—the dead-lock of every church from the Lutheran down to the Universalist!

Archbishop Cranmer, who stood at the foundation of the English Reform Church, did not care to have any warning sunlight from spirits, the bare "Word" of a book was enough; so all the rest have thought until "they are wells without water." He says, when a spirit comes to you saying, "I am the soul of such a one, give no heed, for it is the devil!" He maintains with the general body of starved pseudo-Bible sticklers, that God has shut up the way, "neither doth he suffer any of the dead to come again hither, to tell what is done there, lest by that means he should bring in all his heresies and subtleties."

But even Cranmer found it hard to smother the burning fires within. Despite the Lutheran laboratory that transformed all angels into devils, he too had his private convictions and spiritual evidences of an order of spirits raised above the dominion of his hell. In 1532, being in a contemplative negative condition, a spirit showed him a great blazing star. Writing to King Henry from Austria, he says: "God only knows what these tokens foretell, for they do not lightly appear, but against some great mutation."

Bishop Latimer, cotemporary of Cranmer, honest and warm hearted, fell into the same "Slough of Despond," and covered himself with exsiccating mud—the church method of embalming clerical mummies. We quote from his biographer:

"And peradventure some one will say, 'How happeneth it that there are no miracles done in these days, by such as are preachers of the word of God?' I answer, the word of God is already confirmed by miracles: partly by Christ himself, and partly by the apostles and saints. Therefore, they which now preach the same word need no miracles for the confirmation thereof; for the same is sufficiently confirmed already."

But Latimer believed in "substitution"—a devil for an angel—and, sandwiching him in, gave his "satanic majesty" the credit of working the miracles of his day! Well, the church has always been consistent with its own plane. But even Latimer prophesied correctly on certain occasions.

His biographer says, "if ever England had a prophet, he might seem to be one." He prophesied his own death by martyrdom. So it is; men may as well try to bottle up the sunlight as the heavenly effulgence of angel ministries. When men attribute the spiritual phenomena to evil spirits, or the devil, what do they on their angle of religious incidence, but clinch the truth of spirit communication?

JUDICIOUS HOOKER, also of the English Church, more *judicious* than his famous compeers, more Platonic and Grecianly colossal in thought, jumped over the Lutheran "Slough" at one bound. A moral lion he whose mane the spirits delighted to magnetize. He says:

"The angels resembled God in their unweariable and even insatiable longing to do all manner of good to men by all means." "The paynims," he says, "had arrived at the same knowledge of the nature of angels; Orpheus confessing that the fiery throne of God is surrounded by those most industrious angels, careful how all things are performed amongst men."

"Angels," says Hooker in another place, "are spirits immaterial and intellectual. In number and order they are large, mighty and royal armies, desiring good unto all the creatures of God, but especially unto the children of men; in the countenance of whose nature, looking downward, they behold themselves beneath themselves; besides which, the *angels have with us that communion* which the Apostle to the Hebrews noteth, and in regard whereof they disdain not to profess themselves our fellow-servants. And from hence there springeth up another law, which bindeth them to works of *ministerial employment.*"

BISHOP HALL, of Norwich, the revered poet, had the moral hardihood, like Hooker, to vindicate the use of spiritual gifts in the Protestant Church. He is very explicit in his declarations of spirit communication in tangible forms. His wife was pointed out to him by an "angel of God." His mother, being prostrated with sickness, had a vision, in which a physician appeared and actually healed her; this he confirms. At one time, when journeying to the Netherlands, an angel delivered him from the hands of robbers—"the manifest hand of God."

He wrote a valuable work on "The Invisible World," in which he maintained that "the spiritual gifts" are perpetual. He often invoked the aid of guardian spirits. He felt their continued presence, and so was impressed with high purposes to "walk carefully but confidently." In his spiritual treatise he says:

"So sure as we see men, so sure we are that holy men have seen angels. Have we been raised up," he continues, "from deadly sickness, when all natural helps have given us up? God's angels have been our secret physicians. Have we had intuitive intimations of the death of absent friends, which no human intelligence had bidden us to suspect, who but our angels have wrought it? Have we been preserved from mortal danger, which we could not tell how by our providence to have evaded, our invisible guardians have done it."

ARCHBISHOP TILLOTSON, a great light in the English Church, confirmed the dark as well as light side of Spiritualism—that both evil (undeveloped) and good spirits influence mortals. Speaking of the continual intercourse of angels with men for their protection and advantage, he says "they are God's great ministers here below."

BISHOP BEVERIDGE supports the reality of "ministering angels and ministering devils," and that both kinds perform miracles! He advocated the doctrine of seership "by strong faith spiritually;" and that spirits "assume a bodily shape."

BISHOP BUTLER argued the credibility of "miracular interpositions."

BISHOP SHERLOCK, agreeing with Tillotson respecting the ministry of both evil and good spirits, discarded the doctrine of a stereotyped revelation. He did not believe in thus tying up God's hands. He re-asserts, "that the graces of the Spirit are the arms of the Christian, with which he is to enter the lists against the powers of darkness, and are a certain indication to us that God intends to call us to the proof and exercise of our virtue; why else does He give us this additional strength?"

These extracts from the writings of the Anglican Fathers, are sufficent to indicate that that very fashionable church has not *entirely* smothered the spiritual light under its silks and cushions; but it is also apparent that said church has been shy of it, because it threatened to burn up their formulary that "miracles are needless." Occupying a middle ground between Catholicity, with its hosts of ministering saints, and extreme Protestantism that has sealed God's lips within the lids of the Bible, and made Jesus the monopolizer of all virtue, they were quite willing to have personal *private* seances with the angels as do other good members of "respectable churches" to-day, but were generally careful how they committed themselves before the world. Light under a bushel basket is better than no light; but the basket will catch fire one of these days, set by such spirits as Hooker, who puts the torch of Freedom into the hands of Colenso and Tyng and Bishop Clark.

PARACELSUS, beholding the morning light near Zurich, about the commencement of the fifteenth century, was distinguished as the founder of the modern science of medicine, in connection with the remedial agents of magnetism. He understood the reciprocal life-forces—being mediumistic. Ennemoser, a great admirer, writes of him thus:

"Paracelsus was the first who compared this universal reciprocity of universal life in all creations, in the great as in the small, with the magnet; so that the word *magnetism*, in the sense in which we understand it, originated with Paracelsus."

He was considered an enthusiast and spiritual adventurer, traveling through Germany, Moravia, Hungary, and other European countries. Believing in dreams, forebodings, presentiments, prescience, he distinctly taught the presence and controlling influence of spirits. In the "Strasburg Edition," 1603, Paracelsus writes in the following manner of the power and operation of the Spirit:

"It is possible that my spirit, without the help of the body, and through a fiery will alone, can wound others. It is also possible that I can bring the spirit of my adversary into an image, and then double him up to his displeasure. Will is a great point in the art of medicine. Man can hang disease on man and beast through curses. * * * * Every imagination of man proceeds from the center of his being. This is the sun of the microcosm; and out of the microcosm flows the imagination into the great world. Thus the imagination of man is a seed, which becomes materialized into the outer. * * * * The imagination of another may be able to kill me. Imagination springing out of pleasure and desire, usually acts in concert with the will-power; therefore, envy and hatred follow; for desire is followed by the deed. No armor protects against magical influences, for they injure the inward spirit of life."

GIORDANO BRUNO, that remarkable Italian inquirer, daring, original and spiritualistic, and intimately connected with the Paracelsus school of thinkers, was, by the Roman Inquisition, arrested and retained in prison two years for spiritual heresy, and thence delivered to the Secular Magistrate after the usual disgusting formula—" that he be dealt with as mercifully as possible, and punished without effusion of blood." Bruno exclaimed—" *Your sentence* strikes more terror into your own hearts than mine?" and he died as a brave man ought.

JEROME CARDAMUS, sixteenth century, the companion of Paracelsus, ranking among the first scholars of his age, a favorite at royal courts, divinely illumined, was very reliable in mediumship. When a child, he spiritually saw groves, landscapes, orbs, "without any previous volition or anticipation that such things were about to happen." He could not recollect any event, good or ill, occurring in life, of which he was not previously admonished either in dream or vision. He spoke with great emphasis of having a *genius* or *demon* perpetually attending him, advising as to what would happen, and forewarning him of danger. Studying astrology, he calculated the nativity of King Edward VI., of Jesus Christ, predicted the time of his own death, which took place in the 75th year of his age, fulfilling his prediction.

JOAN D'ARC, the humble shepherd girl of Domremy, was the political savior of France. Bethlehem's shepherds were not more honored by the Church Fathers than this sunny-souled, spiritually illuminated girl by later mystics. No history is better authenticated than that which relates to her visions, prophecies and angelic communings. As if the very leaves of her favorite tree, under which she so often sat, rapt in heavenly reverie, had tongues, she heard angel voices announcing her future mission. Again and again they called with imperative command; and, at length, inspired with the enthusiasm of patriotic fulness, she meekly and trustfully obeyed. Orleans was besieged! England's reigning monarch was expectantly waiting to snatch the crown of France! Spirit-guided, she mounted the war-steed, unfurled her talismanic banner, thrilled the French soldiers with unconquerable daring to gain a glorious victory.

Immortal in history, artists delighted to transfer her form to the canvas; Schiller and Southey honored her in poesy and song; defeating the phlegmatic English, they burned her for a witch!

JACOB BŒHMEN, of the sixteenth century, surnamed Teutonicus, and known in history as the "German Mystic," or "Theosophic Enthusiast," was a native of Old Seidenburgh, near Goritz. When a shoemaker in his master's shop, he was visited by a stranger of a venerable aspect, who, departing from the place, exclaimed with a loud voice—"Jacob! Jacob! come forth!" The lad was astonished to be called by his Christian name. The spirit-guided personage then taking him by the hand, said, "Jacob, thou art little, but shalt be great, and become another man, at whom the world shall wonder. * * * * Thou must endure much misery and poverty, and suffer persecution; but be encouraged, and persevere, for God loves and is gracious to thee."

These words produced a burning impression upon his mind. He felt the power of the commission to unfold the mysteries of the Apocalypse and the inner sense of the "Divine Word." He became a voluminous writer, suffered persecution for his innovating thought, blessed all the world with brighter light, and finally was summoned to Dresden to answer to the charge of heresy. After a tortuous trial, he was honorably dismissed.

Speaking of himself, he says: "After the gates of spiritual knowledge were opened to me, I was compelled to commence working at this (book) like a child that goes to school. In the interim, I certainly saw the truth as it were at a great depth. * * * * From time to time it opened to me like a plant, but it was twelve years before I could bring it out."

Dr. Hamberger says, introductorily to his manuscripts: "The author wrote with divine inspiration from living contemplation; but it cost him hard battles, and it was not always possible to reduce what he saw into words and ideas." Like illiterate clairvoyants and visionists of the present, he found it difficult to classify and develop his revelations to the comprehension of practical thinkers.

Bœhmen passed to the Summer Land, Nov. 18, 1624. Early in the morning he called his loved son to his side, and asked if he heard that excellent music! Receiving a reply in the negative, he directed him to open the door that he might hear it better. Asking, afterward, "what the hour?" he was told "two"—upon which he remarked that his time was "yet three hours hence." When it was near six o'clock, blessing his wife and son, he took leave of them, saying, "Now I go hence into Paradise!" He then bade his son turn him, and with a deep peaceful sigh, his sweet spirit departed.

RAPHAEL, speaking of his paintings, conscious of inspirations, says his "whole work is accomplished as it were in a pleasant dream!"

DANNECKER, the German sculptor, said he "obtained his idea of Christ in a dream—spiritually impressed—after failing to realize it in his waking hours."

LORD BACON, the master thinker, the religious philosopher, whose wisdom flashes in all our literature, was a clear headed, devout Spiritualist. We respectfully ask the *soi-distant* scientists of the clerical orders to reject Lord Bacon from the list of "authorities," or else respect his teachings, of which the following extracts from his works are samples. In his preface to his "*Great Instauration*," he prays that—

"What is human may not clash with what is divine; and that when the ways of the senses are opened, and a greater natural light set up in the mind, nothing of incredulity and blindness towards divine mysteries may arise; but rather that the understanding now cleared up, and purged of all vanity and superstition, may remain entirely subject to the divine oracles, and yield to faith the things that are faith's." (Bohn's Edition, preface, p. 9.)

Again he says:

"As to the nature of spirits and angels, this is neither unsearchable nor forbid, but in a great part level to the human mind, on account of their affinity. We are, indeed, forbid in Scripture to worship angels, or to entertain fantastical opinions of them so as to exalt them above the degree of creatures, or think of them higher than we have reason; but the sober inquiry about them, which either ascends to a knowledge of their nature by the scale of corporeal beings, or views them in the mind, as in a glass, is by no means foolish. The same is to be understood of revolted or unclean spirits; conversation with them, or using their assistance, is unlawful; and much more in any manner to worship or adore them; but the contemplation and knowledge of their nature, power and illusions, appears from Scripture, reason and experience, to be no small part of spiritual wisdom. Thus says the apostle, 'Strategematum ejus non ignari sumus' (2 Cor. ii. 11). And thus it is as lawful in natural theology to investigate the nature of evil spirits, as the nature of poisons in physics, or the nature of vice in morality." ("Advancement of Learning," 121–2).

SIR THOMAS BROWNE, who lived about half a century after Bacon, one of the ablest thinkers of his age, and an open advocate of Spiritualism, says, in his "Religio Medici":

"Those that, to confute their incredulity, desire to see apparitions, shall questionless never behold any. The devil hath them already in a heresy as capital, as witchcraft, and to appear to them were but to convert them."

An admirer of Paracelsus, he adds: "Our good angels reveal many things to those who seek into the works of nature."

Schiller, an inspirational poet, intimates that his ideas were not his own—"that they flowed in upon him so rapidly and powerfully, his only difficulty was to seize them and write them down fast enough."

George Fox, sainted and sable clad, charged with the magnetic lightnings of heaven, caused the church steeples of England to tremble as cedars of Lebanon before Syrian winds. His inspirations have streamed down to the present, giving him, in the estimation of the appreciative, an almost apostolic sanctity. His spiritual experiences, his power to read souls, his prescience, his healing gifts, and his obedience to "the still, small voice," all rank him one of the first in the angelic phalanx of mediumship. In his "Works" we find the following facts. Entering the city of Litchfield, under spirit control, he had the experiences of a genuine prophet:

"Then I was commanded of the Lord to pull off my shoes. I stood still, for it was winter; and the word of the Lord was like a fire unto me.

"Then I walked about a mile, and as soon as I got within the city, the word of the Lord came unto me—'Cry, wo to the bloody city of Litchfield!'

"So I went up and down the streets and into the market-place, and cried, 'Wo to the bloody city of Litchfield!'

"As I went, there seemed to be a channel of blood through the streets.

"When I had declared what was upon me, and felt myself at peace, I went out of the town. Afterward I came to understand that in the Emperor Dioclesian's time a thousand Christians were martyred there.

"So the sense of their blood was upon me, and I obeyed the word of the Lord.

"At Ulverstone, at the home of Margaret Fell, a woman of high repute, when asked to go to a church to speak, he walked in the field and the word came, 'Go to the steeple-house.'"

Though such experiences are common with the media of our day, the conservative followers of George Fox discard them, indicating the unspiritual tendency of that sect.

On another occasion, he said:

"I went to a meeting at Aruside, where Richard Myers was, who had been a long time lame of one arm. I was moved of the Lord to say to him amongst all the people, 'Stand upon thy legs.' And he stood up and stretched out his arm and said, 'Be it known unto you, all people, that this day I am healed.'

"He came soon after to Swartmore meeting and declared how the Lord had healed him.

"The Lord hath given me a spirit of discerning, by which I many times saw the states and conditions of people, and could try their spirits."

Why cannot the declining sect of the Quakers recognize the marvelous beauty of that spiritual power manifest in our midst to-day, as well as that which has flowed in broken currents of inspiration, tinged with the theological idiosyncracies of intervening centuries?

LUCAS JACOBSON DEBES, of Denmark, a personage in his day of religious authority, published a book in 1667, in which he relates an instance of angelic visitation to Jacob Ollusson, being then at Giow. We quote the language of this reliable author: "On the fourteenth day of his illness, as he lay asleep at night, there came one to him with shining clothes on, whereat he awoke, and perceived him (the angel) by him in that figure, the room appearing full of splendor; and it asked the man where his pain was. Whereunto he answered nothing. Afterward the angel stroked him with his hand along his breast, and round about; whereby he was perfectly healed."

This testimony bears the unmistakable marks of truthfulness, beautifully illustrative of the curative agencies of spirits by the manipulations of the hand direct or indirect by mediation.

RICHARD BAXTER, in his "Historical Discourse on Apparitions and Witches," writes an account of an acquaintance of his, "a gentleman of considerable rank," who, addicted to intemperance, was always visited by a spirit immediately after "he had slept himself sober," warning him of his vice by rapping on his head-board, and other visible signs of heavenly guardianship and discipline. Mr. Baxter, having seen the man, and besought him to reform, believing the spirit presence to have been genuine, conscientiously and feelingly asked, "Do good spirits dwell so near us? or, Are they sent on such messages? or, Is it his guardian angel?"

WALTON, the celebrated, in his biography of the learned Dr. Donne, in King James' time, after giving remarkable tests of spirit influences and revelations, illustrates the law of spiritual sympathy, whereby a spirit can impress a mediumistic mind, by the use of musical instruments. Contending that visions and miracles have not ceased, he says: "It is most certain that two lutes, being both strung and tuned to an equal pitch, the one played upon, and the other not touched, but laid upon a table, at a fit distance, will, like an echo to a trumpet, warble a faint, audible harmony in answer to the same tune. Yet many will not believe that there is such a thing as sympathy with souls!"

JOHN AUBREY, a distinguished antiquarian, published, in 1695, a book of "Miscellanies," in which, bringing King James as witness, he speaks of a haunted house whose superintending spirit was a faithful "rough man." He parallels certain phases of modern psychological influences where the spirit, planed to the earthly, caused the "seer" to "swear, tremble and screech." He recommended the ministry always to intervene in cases of spirit control and "exorcise the ghost." Exorcism, philosophically speaking, consists in bringing a stronger magnetic power to bear upon the subject, scattering and dissipating the previously adjusted spirit-forces. The moral peril of such interferences among ignorant, unspiritual clergy, is, that when "the house is swept and garnished," the dispossessed spirit, *forced* away, returns, at the first opportunity, with seven other spirits worse than himself, and "the last state of that man is worse than the first." Force repels force; hate begets hate; but the only subduing, saving power in the universe, is wisely disciplined love.

The Scotch repeatedly aver that infants are seers—a fact demonstrated by our own observation. How beautifully the legend of our Aborigines chimes in with the Highlander's happy gift! The Indians—nature's children—tell us when the innocent babe, cribbed in its willow basket, looks out into seeming vacancy and smiles, its grandmother has come from the " hunting grounds " to greet it.

The rustic people, especially the Highlanders, of Scotland, have ever been celebrated for their gifts of " Second Sight " —clairvoyance. As gardens and flowers tend to the cultivation of the beautiful, so mountainous regions to the development of the spiritual.

The Scotch historians also testify to what is apparent in the modern phenomena, that this so-called " strange gift " does not depend upon moral character, but upon organization. They assert that certain beasts are seers—horses especially. An instance of this kind occurred in the Isle of Skye, where a horse discerned a spirit at the same time with his rider, and was frightened. This statement is not without its historic support. Paracelsus informs us that horses, and even dogs, have their "auguries." Our good churchmen will not surely discredit testimony like this, since they do believe that Balaam's beast " saw the Angel of the Lord standing in the way, with a drawn sword in his hand. * * * And the Lord opened the mouth of the beast, and she said unto Balaam, ' What have I done unto thee, that thou hast smitten me these three times?' " That an angel spoke to Balaam through a beast, is very acceptable in church circles; but that our spirit friends impress, inspire, and speak through human lips, is blasphemous!

John Knox, the fierce reformer of Scotland, who knocked down steeples and popish mummeries, and who, in his sternness, after the pattern of Luther, stripped religion of the beautiful and gay, theoretically denying the perpetuity of revelations fresh from the divine fountain, had an experience with spirits convicting him of their direct ministry, though he studiously avoided any very public avowal of them. Very Protestant, sure. He avows his belief, however, though with precaution, lest his course might be construed by Catholics as inconsistent with his precept. He was a powerful medium, and under the inner light that flamed in his soul, he said:

"I dare not deny, lest I be injurious to the giver, that God hath revealed unto me secrets unknown to the world; yea, certain great revelations of mutations and changes where no such things were feared, nor yet were appearing. Notwithstanding these revelations I did abstain to commit anything to writing, contented only to have obeyed the charge of Him who commanded me to cry."

THE NEW ENGLAND WITCHCRAFT, that, to this day, casts a lurid light over puritanical history, was a species of psychological epidemic, wherein the magnetisms of both worlds, owing to the prevalence of false ideas touching spiritual laws, were inharmoniously adjusted to the development of moral truth. Spirits, not infallible, evidently endeavored at this period to establish an open communication between the inhabitants of this and the spirit-world; but ignorance was too deep, clerical influence too potent. Priests, basing their authority on the Mosaic teaching—"Thou shalt not suffer a witch to live"—were instrumental in murdering the media. The experiment a partial failure, the immortals withdrew their forces, waiting a more auspicious era.

COTTON MATHER, regarded as good authority, furnished a compendium of mediumistic control. In 1662, Anne Cole, "a person of serious piety, living in the house of her godly father, at Hartford, was taken with strange fits"—trances—and caused to express "strange things unknown to herself, her tongue being guided by a demon." Confessing to the "ministers," that she had "familiarity with the devil"—spirit presences—"the woman was executed!"

The "physical phenomena" of those perilous days bore a striking resemblance to those of the present—such as haunted houses, raising of bodies, noises, trances, clairvoyance, clairaudience and prophecies. The case of the unfortunate Anne Cole was but one among hundreds and tens of thousands who, in this country and Europe, were arraigned, tried and executed for witchcraft!

Had the clergy not sought to divorce reason from religion—mental science from religion—common sense from religion—with an eye to the "glory of God," as revealed through Hebrew goggles, this murderous mania, instigated by priestcraft, would not have stained with blood the historic page.

WILLIAM BLAKE—artist, poet, idealist—oh, for adequate words to sing thy praises! Walking among men, men knew thee not; but angels knew thee, and the richest gold of thy soul which shines now the brighter for the ordeals of thy trials! So completely did he live in the ideal world, which he wove around him as a garment of glory—so constantly did he look thro' it into the *inner life*, that external things became as passing dreams. A seer by birth, he discerned the innermost, and reveled enraptured in what cold plodders called "imagination." An English author, criticising Blake's life by Alex. Gilchrist, says:

"The attempt to do more than accept the subjective reality of the visions, rested solely upon the ground of their confidence in Blake's veracity. Thus he would say, 'I saw Socrates to-day; he said to me thus and thus.'

"The visionary (spirit) heads which Blake drew in the company of John Varley furnish an example to the point. The remarkable productions were professedly copies of what Blake at the moment saw. He would see King Edward I., and looking up now and then, with most perfect composure, at his imaginary sitter, would draw his portrait. Varley, who had faith in Blake's power of vision and also in Blake's doctrine that it was a universal gift, sat beside him, and, since he made some profession to a spiritual sight, being an astrologer in his way, looked wistfully in the direction to which Blake's eyes pointed, in earnest hope of seeing the same sight. He was honest and looked as hard as he could, but his honesty compelled him to confess that he saw no king before his eyes. Blake held that he drew what he saw, and inasmuch as he saw angels more distinctly than some artists seem to see men, he drew them boldly, gave them something to exist in, instead of adopting a common trick, and trying to conceal a fearful absence of body by an unmistakable presence of clothing.

* * * * * * * * * *

"There is a subtle element in Blake's poetry, disengaging one from objects of sense and leading the enchanted spirit on a far journey. A similar power in different form appears in certain poems of Coleridge, which was heightened, if we are to believe his cotemporaries, by the recital of the poet. The entranced listeners might float with Coleridge to Xanadu, to get back as they could at the unfortunate end of the poet's vocal journey, while he traveled on by himself, whither no one but himself could tell, and whither, alas! he has failed to tell us. It is related by his biographer, that Blake used to sing his songs to music which he had composed, but which never was written down. What angelic melody it ought to have been!"

This eminent Spiritualist was born in 1757, and lived uninterruptedly in London, except three years in Chichester, to fulfill an engagement with Haley, Cowper's biographer.

We pour over the productions of Blake's genius, wondering, delighted, awed, and inquire of ourselves, Who is this man, that had so little in common with earth?—who paints his pictures?—who sings his songs? Of *himself* he would say:

"I live in a hole here, but God has a beautiful mansion for me elsewhere. * * * * * * *

"I am not ashamed, afraid, or averse to tell you—what ought to be told—that I am under the direction of *messengers* from heaven, daily and nightly. But the nature of such things is not, as some suppose, without trouble or care. Temptations are on the right hand and on the left. Behind, the sea of time, and space roars and follows swiftly. He who keeps not right onward is lost; and if our footsteps slide in clay, what can we do otherwise than fear and tremble! * * * If we fear to do the dictates of our angels, and tremble at the tasks set before us; if we refuse to do spiritual acts because of natural fears or natural desires; who can describe the dismal torments of such a state! I too well remember the threats I heard: 'If you, who are organized by Divine Providence for spiritual communion, refuse, and bury your talent in the earth, even though you should want natural bread—sorrow and desperation pursue you through life, and after death shame and confusion of face. Every one in eternity will leave you, aghast at the man who was crowned with glory and honor by his brethren and betrayed their cause to their enemies. You will be called the base Judas who betrayed his friend!' Such words would make any stout man tremble, and how then could I be at ease? But I am now no longer in that state, and now go on again with my task, fearless, though my path is difficult. I have no fear of stumbling while I keep it."

Louis XVI., benevolent and reformatory, has been styled "noblest of all the reigning Bourbons." "Coming to his own, his own received him not." Arraigned, tried by a boisterous assembly, he was heartlessly condemned to the block. Seeing the courier sent to inform him of his fate, he exclaimed—"I know it all! I know it all! Last night I saw a female form clothed in stainless white, walking these solitary apartments. When the reigning powers of the throne behold a vision of this character, they know that prince or king is to be dethroned and slain. Tell my accusers to prepare to meet me in the land of the just!"

Maria Antoinette—fated child of imperial destiny! Never was mother more proud than Maria Theresa, on the eve of her daughter's marriage. Before her glittered the first throne of Europe, to be shared by a successor of St. Louis. Night resting upon Vienna, the church festival over, the benediction pronounced, the empress retires to her chamber, but not to sleep. Speaking to the waiting-woman, she inquires who is there?

"A stranger; he has been seeking your presence a full hour."

The waiting-woman leaving, soon returned, and ushered in an elderly man dressed in black. This is Dr. Gassner, one of those men who, about the year 1770, were scattered throughout Europe—a Cagliostro, or St. Germain—performing cures by the laying on of hands, seeing visions, indulging in prophecies and inspirations. "His relations to the spiritual world had brought him in conflict with various ecclesiastical princes, until he found refuge at the court of Maria Theresa, for the empress had a love for the mysterious.

She had frequent interviews with the wonderful man; to-day she wished for a grave proof of his higher knowledge."

The Doctor, placing his hand upon the shoulder of the empress, said slowly, in a hollow voice, "Your majesty, the noble shoulders of Maria Antoinette are destined to bear a heavy cross."

Maria Antoinette, spiritually impressed, as the carriage rolled away, exclaimed, "I shall never see Vienna again!" and cried aloud, "Maria Theresa! Maria Theresa!"

During the Revolution, often thinking of the Doctor's prophetic words, she believed herself destined to a tragical fate. Upon the scaffold, with a true womanly bravery, she uttered these words: "Farewell, my children, I go to your father. * * * * We shall return to you as guardian angels. Trust in God!"

MADAME ELIZABETH, sweetest soul of France, sister of Louis XVI., angel of his household during his trials and translation to the Isles of the Blest, shed a silvery radiance over the royal family and the entire kingdom. Full of divine forgiveness and pious enthusiasm, she was intromitted through the gateway of dreams and visions, into the society of spirits. Though a princess and heir apparent to the throne of the Bourbons, she was so guileless and affectional in her nature, that she daily walked and talked with angels.

> "Every sentence, oh, how tender!
> Every line was full of love."

Like Cecilia, the Catholic martyr, doomed also to fall to "low ambition and the pride of kings," so beautiful was she in form, so harmonious and musical in spirit, she drew the angels down to see her, and "eyes were turned to ears."

JOSEPHINE, the arbitress of Napoleon's destiny, who prophesied his star would set when his ambition sundered the love-chord that furnished him with inspirational power from her own heart, not only accepted faith in guardian angels, but actualized it with the beguiling *Houris* in night visions and day-dreams of the spiritual. She gives the following account of an interview with Euphemia, a *magician* of her native isle:

"The old sibyl, on beholding me, uttered a loud exclamation, and almost by force seized my hand. She appeared to be under the greatest agitation. Amused at these absurdities, as I thought them, I allowed her to proceed, saying, 'So you discover something extraordinary in my destiny?' 'Yes.' 'Is happiness or misfortune to be my lot?' Misfortune: ah, stop!—and happiness, too.' 'You take care not to commit yourself, my good dame; your oracles are not the most intelligible.' 'I am not permitted to render them more clear,' said the woman, raising her eyes with a mysterious expression toward heaven. 'But to the point,' replied I, for my curiosity began to be excited; 'what read you concerning me in futurity?' 'What do I see in the future? You will not believe me if I speak.' 'Yes, indeed, I assure you. Come, my good mother, what am I to fear and hope?' 'On your head be it then; listen: you will be married soon; that union will not be happy; you will become a widow, and then—then you will be *Queen of France!* Some happy years will be yours; but you will die in a hospital, amid civil commotions.'"

MOZART, the great musical genius of his age, speaking of his inspirational moments, when melodies fell unbidden upon his soul, said: "All my feelings and composition go on within me only as a lively and delightful dream."

He gave a further account of receiving his masterly productions from the rythmic sphere of spiritual harmonies in the following language:

"When all goes well with me—when I am in a carriage, or walking, or when I cannot sleep at night, the thoughts come streaming in upon me most fluently; whence, or how is more than I can tell. Then follow the counterpoint—and the clang of the different instruments; and, if I am not disturbed, my soul is fixed, and the thing grows greater, and broader, and clearer; and I have it all in my head, even when the piece is a long one; and I *see it* like a beautiful picture—not hearing the different parts in succession, as they must be played, but the *whole at once*. That is the delight! The composing and making is like a beautiful and vivid dream; but this *hearing* of it is the best of all."

These are fine examples of inspirational influx and clairaudience.

When, in his last days, quietly approaching the summer shore of heaven, being composed and calm, some friend of his passing through the room, he exclaimed—" Listen! listen! I hear music!" His friend said, "I hear nothing." Mozart paused with rapture beaming on his sallow face, averring that he heard music, and quoted the testimony of John with a sweet trust that plumed his spirit-wings for a better flight—

"And I heard music in heaven."

Having finished the "Requiem," his soul filled with inspirations of richest melody, and already claiming kindred with immortals, giving it its last touch, the "cygnean strain" which was to consecrate it through all time, and then falling into a gentle slumber, during which his ministering angel enrapt his soul in the glory forecast from the land of song, he awoke at the light footstep of his daughter Emelie, and called her to him—" Come hither, my Emelie—my task is done—the Requiem—*my* Requiem is finished!" At his earnest request she sung it, commencing—

"Spirit! thy labor is o'er!
Thy term of probation is run,
Thy steps are now bound for the untrodden shore,
And the race of immortals begun."

"As she concluded, she dwelt for a moment on the low melancholy notes of the piece, and then turned from the instrument to meet the approving smile of her father. It was the still, passionless smile which the rapt and departed spirit left upon the features."

BEETHOVEN whose soul was toned to musical ecstacy, confessed to an overmastering power, the rythmic harmonies of angels. In his own words, music was to him a higher revelation than all the artificial philosophy of the world. Hear his inspiring language: "I must live with myself alone. I well know that God and angels are nearer to me in my art than the others. I commune with them without dread.

Music is the only unembodied entrance into a higher sphere of knowledge which possesses man." After some of the sweetest utterances, he would exclaim — "I've had a rapture!" Goethe, in speaking of him, terms him a "demon-possessed person," and adds, "it would be mischievous to advise him, because his genius continually inspires him."

Goethe, rare soul of poetry and song, whose ante-natal tendencies were spiritual, and whose physical perfection justly entitled him to a comparison with Apollo, was heralded into earth-life by wierd dreams of future greatness. If it is true that all poets are prophets, it is equally true that *genuine* poets are Spiritualists. To him a friend said, "Thou livest among spirits; they give thee divine wisdom;" and he said of himself, "I should hold myself assured of the gift of prophecy belonging of old to my family." He considered himself born under favorable stars, and is reported to have said to his mother at seven years of age, "The stars will not forget me, but will keep the promise made over my cradle." At the death of a playmate he did not shed a tear, but said "he had gone to dwell in the fairy world before him."

Swedenborg, the mystic and Christian philosopher, of Sweden, flourishing in the seventeenth century, was of noble birth, scholarly in attainments, material in his scientific pursuits, theistic in his religious tendencies, and, up to the fifty-fifth year of his age, was a traveler, extensive author and man of the world, a guest at royal courts, and of high repute in literary circles. About this period of his life, a startling development of mental conditions blossomed out, opening to his inner vision the spirit world. He had impressions, dreams, visions; conversed with spirits — heard them — saw them — walked with them — reasoned with them; and was so conscious of their presence, that the geography of their homes became as familiar as his own native land.

His mediumship has been seldom excelled. In its beginning, as is the general rule, it was exceedingly disorderly, and, in some respects, quite as disgusting as certain phases of "modern manifestations" are to the church. We select the following, as a few among the many facts, corroborative of this statement, extracted from William White's two London volumes of the "Life and Writings of Swedenborg." These are based upon the testimonies of Rev. Aaron Mathesius—a Swedish minister and Chaplain to the Embassy in 1773—Dr. Smith, Brockmer, John Wesley, Rev. Francis Okeley, a Moravian preacher, and others. Though Mathesius and Swedenborg were antipodal in friendship, the testimony of the former is admitted as valid by Mr. Okeley, who, writing of Mathesius' story as published by Wesley, remarks:

"'There is no denying that in the year 1743 (1744), when Swedenborg was first (as he said) introduced into the Spiritual World, he was for a while insane. He then lived with Mr. Brockmer, as Mr. J. Wesley has published in his *Arminian Magazine* for January, 1781. * * * * As I rather suspect J. W.'s narratives, they being always warped to his own inclination, I inquired of Mr. Brockmer concerning it, and found all the main lines of it truth.'

This may be considered conclusive in favor of the truthfulness of Mathesius.

* * * * * * *

"'Many years ago the Baron came over to England, and lodged at one Mr. Brockmer's, who informed me (and the same information was given me by Mr. Mathesius, a very serious Swedish clergyman, both of whom were alive when I left London, and, I suppose, are so still), that while he was in his house he had a violent fever; in the height of which, being totally delirious, he broke from Mr. Brockmer, ran into the street stark naked, proclaimed himself the Messiah, and rolled himself in the mire.

* * * * * * *

"This was about nine in the evening. Leaving his door and going up stairs, he rushed up after me, making a fearful appearance. His hair stood upright, and he foamed round the mouth. He tried to speak, but could not utter his thoughts, stammering long before he could get out a word.

"At last he said, that he had something to confide to me privately, namely, that he was Messiah, that he was come to be crucified for the

Jews, and that I (since he spoke with difficulty) should be spokesman, and go with him to-morrow to the Synagogue, there to preach his words.

* * * * * * *

"Whilst I was with Dr. Smith, Mr. Swedenborg went to the Swedish Envoy, but was not admitted, it being post-day. Departing thence he pulled off his clothes and rolled himself in very deep mud in the gutter. Then he distributed money from his pockets among the crowd which had gathered.

"In this state some of the footmen of the Swedish Envoy chanced to see him, and brought him to me very foul with dirt."

These well substantiated facts indicate the naturalness of those mental and psychological changes, incident to nearly all media in their growth from the grosser material to the more spiritual and harmonial planes of life. Carlyle, speaking of similar experiences, says: "Such transitions are ever full of pain: thus the eagle when he moults is sickly; and, to attain his new beak, must harshly dash off the old one upon the rocks."

In common with all the churches, the present followers of Swedenborg flippantly berate Spiritualists, especially the mediums in their earlier stages of development, on the ground of "demoniac possessions." It is as amusing as pitiable to witness the holy sneer that plays upon the scorn-curled lips of the crystalized Swedenborgian, who, with unwarrantable assumption, shrugs his shoulders and breathes in manner, if not in words—"Stand by, I am holier than thou!"

Looking at him in after years, when chaos had rounded into symmetrical form, and disorderly mediumship had flowed out into beautiful harmony and sweetness of heavenly trust, he challenges our profoundest admiration. The symbol key held in his hand, he opened the mysteries of the heavens —the "Word" being to him a link of correspondential thoughts and ideas imaging eternal things. Gazing as through an angel microscope, and reading the soul of things, all the universe spread itself before him rightly interpreted—the material being the type of the spiritual—its body—and all objects the representations of mental and moral conditions.

Mauger the chronic church notions of his time, his doctrines and experiences agree with those of modern Spiritualists. In his *Spiritual Diary*, 4602, he affirms—

"That there is an influx from the spiritual world into the natural world, and that the natural world thence subsists, as from it it began to exist, is at the present day utterly unknown; because it is not known what the spiritual is, neither do men wish to know anything but what is natural, wherefore they deny anything else, especially the learned. Man was created to be a type of either world; his interiors to be a type of the spiritual world, and his exteriors to be a type of the natural world, to the end that in him both might be conjoined. Hence it is that his natural world, or microcosm, does not live except by influx from the spiritual world, and that there is, with many, a continual *conatus* to the union of both worlds in him."

He taught that the spiritual is the real man, and dwelt largely upon the substantiality of the spirit world as a realm of groves and gardens, seas and mountains, forests and birds, and nationalities of immortal men and women, having habits, affections and aspirations similar to those they cherished in the earth life. There the scholar pursues his studies, the poet courts diviner muses, the geologist probes newly formed orbs, the mathematician calculates immeasurable distances, the orator discourses in lofty strains of eloquence to assembled multitudes, the astronomer counts distant stars and resolves nebulæ into revolving systems of suns and planets, and the reformer who once walked the earth with bleeding feet, now crowned in the heavens, descends to revolutionize and further consummate the world's emancipation.

In a vision he foresaw his transition, and, full of rest, departed at the time, in confirmation of his own prophecy.

THOMAS SAY, member of the Friends' Church, was esteemed for his great piety, blameless life, and sincerity of soul. A compilation of his writings and manuscripts were published in Philadelphia, 1796, by Budd and Bartram. Gifted as a speaker, his mediumship assumed the forms of trance and healing.

His biographer, affirming that he "could cure wens, remove tumors, and other afflictive diseases, by stroking with the hand," says, that "however some might ridicule this, it was a *fact*, in proof of which many living testimonies could be produced." Fastings and secret prayer ever proved efficacious in opening his inner sight, enabling him to behold with rapturous joy the marvelous glories of the heavenly world. We transfer one of his spiritual experiences to these pages.

"On the ninth day, between the hours of four and five, I fell into a trance, and so continued till about the hour of three or four the next morning. After my departure from the body (for I *left* the *body*), my father and mother, Susannah Robinson and others who watched me, shook my body, felt for my pulse, and tried if they could discern the remains of any life or breath in me, but found none. Some may be desirous to know whether I was laid out or not.

"I found myself, when I opened my eyes, lying on my back, as is a corpse on a board; and was told after getting better, that I was not laid on a board, because mother could not find freedom to have it done. They then sent for Dr. Kearsly, who attended me, for his opinion. He found no pulse nor any remains of life; but as he was going away, returned again, and said that something came into his mind to try further. He then asked for a small looking-glass, which Catharine Souder, who lived with my father, procured. The doctor placing it over my mouth, a short time there appeared on it a little moisture. The doctor then said to them, if he is not dead I think he is so far gone he will never open his eyes again; let him lie while he continues warm, and when he begins to grow cold, lay him out.

"This they told me when I returned into the body. Upon hearing me speak, they were all very much surprised; the second time I spoke they all rose from their chairs, and the third time they all came to me. My father and mother inquired how it had been with me? I answered, and said unto them, I thought I had been dead and gone to heaven. After I left my body I heard, as it were, the voices of men, women and children singing songs of praises unto the Lord God, without intermission, which ravished my soul and threw me into transports of joy. My soul was also delighted with most beautiful glades and gardens, which appeared to me on every side, and such as were never seen in this world. Through these I passed, being all clothed in white, and *in my full shape* without the least *diminution of parts*. As I passed along toward a higher state of bliss, I cast my eyes (being perfectly conscious) upon the earth, which I saw plainly, and beheld three men (whom I knew) die. Two of them were white men, one of which entered into immediate rest. There appeared a beautiful transparent gate opened; and as I with the one that entered into rest came up to it, he stepped in; but as I was about to enter, I stepped into the body.

"When recovering from my trance, I mentioned the names of these persons, telling how I saw them die, and which of them entered into rest. I said to my mother, Oh, that I had made one step further, then I should not have come back to earth. After telling them what I had to say, I desired them to say no more, for I still heard the voices and melodious songs of praises, and longed for my final change.

"After I told them of the death of the three men, they sent to see if it was so, and when the messenger returned, he told them they were all dead, and died in their rooms, &c., as I had told them. Upon hearing it, I fell into tears, and said, Oh, Lord, wouldst thou hadst kept me and sent him back that was in pain, (for he seemed one of the lost.) The third was a colored man belonging to the widow Kearney, whom I saw die in the brick kitchen, and while they were laying his corpse on a board, his head fell out of their hands, which I plainly saw, with other circumstances; for remember, the *walls were no hindrance to my sight*. Though the negro's body was black, his soul was clothed in white, which filled me with joy, as it appeared to me a token of his acceptance with God. * * * Yet I was not permitted to see him fully enter into rest; but just as I thought myself entering, I came into the body again.

"Sometime after my recovery, the widow Kearney, the mistress of the colored man, sent for me, and inquired whether I thought departed spirits knew one another? I answered in the affirmative, telling her I saw her negro man die whilst I was lying as a corpse. She then asked me where did he die? I told her in her brick kitchen, between the jamb of the chimney and the wall; and when they took him from the bed to lay him on the board, his head slipped from their hands. She then said, *So it did!* She then asked if I could tell where they laid him. I informed her, between the back door and street door. She said she remembered that *it was so*, and was satisfied, having reason to believe what she had often thought, that departed spirits knew each other in heaven.

"These men, upon inquiring, were found to die at the very time I saw them, and all the circumstances of their death were found to be exactly as I related them. As some may desire to know how or in what shape these that were dead appeared to me, I would say *that they appeared each in a complete body*, which I take to be the spiritual body, separated from the earthly, sinful body. They were also *clothed*—the two that entered into rest, in white, and the other, who was seemingly cast off, had his garment *somewhat* white, *but spotted*. I saw also the bodies in which each of them lived when upon earth, and also how they were laid out; but my own body I did not see. The reason why I neither saw my own body, nor entered fully into rest, I take to be this: *that my soul was not quite separated from my body*, as the others were; though it was so far separated as to permit my seeing those things, and hearing their songs of praise and thanksgiving. Some may think the dead know not each other. These I would refer to the Scriptures—

asking, did not Dives know both Abraham and Lazarus, though afar off?"

Friend Say's journeyings in the spirit-world, while out of the body, are exceedingly valuable, because occurring long previous to the modern spiritual manifestations; and, among the Quakers, a people distinguished for integrity, simplicity, and devotion to religious convictions.

We are privileged with the personal acquaintance of several prominent media, who, becoming entranced, leave (save by sympathetic and magnetic relations) their bodies, and, traveling with their spirit-guides through the heavenly spheres, observe the scenery and listen to celestial music. Such experiences bless the partakers beyond all blessing.

Paul, referring to himself, according to Biblical expositions, says he knew a man who was "caught up to the third heaven," where he "heard unspeakable words," and "whether he was in the body, or out of the body," at the time, he could not determine. With those accustomed to cite apostolic authority, this scriptural language ought, at least, to favorably commend the idea of mortals leaving their bodies. The phraseology of Paul certainly implies that the spiritual man may be temporarily released from its corporeal relations in a degree, that it may ascend to "the third heaven;" that is, the third sphere of spirit-life. The "unspeakable words" were, doubtless, the sublime utterances of an ancient Semitic seer, long summering in the upper kingdoms of glory, the vernacular of which even the scholarly Gentile Apostle was not acquainted. The past re-lives in the present, and the living *now* proffers the mystic key that unlocks and corroborates much of the past.

JOHN WESLEY, high in the coronal region, gifted with full spirituality, and trained under the paternal roof to hear startling accounts of apparitions, clothed in vestures seamless and glittering, confessed to the spiritual as naturally as flowers turn to the sunshine in May mornings. The Rev. Samuel Wesley, father of the celebrated John Wesley, founder of Methodism, while rector of Epworth, England, in 1716, heard noises and rappings several months in his residence, keeping a detailed account of them.

The Rev. Mr. Hoole, of Haxey, visiting Mr. Wesley, wrote thus concerning the mysterious sounds: "After supper and prayers, we all went up stairs, and as we were standing round the fire, in the east chamber, something began knocking just on the other side of the wall, on the chimney-piece, as with a key. Presently the knocking was under our feet. We went down—he with hope, I with fear. As soon as we were in the kitchen, the sound was above us in the room we had left. Mr. Wesley spoke to it. * * * * Soon after it knocked at the window, and changed its sounds into one like planing boards."

As to the proceeding causes of these disturbances, the learned commentator, Dr. Clarke, has the following:—"For a considerable time all the family believed it to be a trick; but at last they were all satisfied it was something supernatural." * * * "Some thought it was a messenger of Satan." * * * "Mrs. Wesley's opinion was different from all the rest, and was probably the most correct. She supposed that these noises and disturbances portended the death of her brother, then abroad in the East India Company's service. This gentleman * * * suddenly disappeared and was never heard from more."

Having had unquestionable evidence of mysterious agencies and spirit manifestations, in the tender years of childhood, and personally blessed with some of the "gifts" promised to believers, John Wesley, all through his evangelizing career, noted and recorded cases of spirit-power and premonition in his Journals and the "Arminian Magazine."

"He healed the sick," writes a distinguished English author, "by prayer and laying on of hands. He and some others joined in prayer over a man who was not expected to live till morning; he was speechless, senseless, and his pulse was gone. Before they ceased, his senses and speech returned. He recovered; and Wesley says they who choose to account for the fact by natural causes have his free leave: *he* says it was the power of God." (Vol. ii. p. 385.)

"Wesley believed with Luther, that devils—demons—produced disease and bodily hurts; that epilepsy and insanity often proceeded from demon influence. He declared that, if he gave up faith in witchcraft, he must give up the Bible. When asked whether he had himself seen a ghost, he replied, 'No; nor have I ever seen a murder; but unfortunately I am compelled to believe that murders take place almost every day, in one place or another.' Warburton attacked Wesley's belief in miraculous cures and expulsion of evil spirits; but Wesley replied that what he had seen with his own eyes, he was bound to believe; the bishop could believe or not, as he pleased."

Rev. Mr. Fletcher, of Wesley's time, records many striking instances of angelic interposition. One related to his own bathing in the Rhine; when sinking, he remained under water twenty minutes, and yet was restored. Some would say, "Why, this is a miracle!" "Undoubtedly," observes Mr. Wesley. "It was not a natural event, but a work wrought above the power of nature, probably by the ministry of angels."

Southey mentions the psychological tendencies and experiences of Rev. Thomas Walsh, a Wesleyan preacher. "He was sometimes found in so deep a reverie, that he appeared to have ceased to breathe; there was something resembling splendor on his countenance, and other circumstances seemed to attest his communion with the spiritual world." This corresponds to the state of many of our trance speakers. During the sermons, and especially in the prayer circles of the Wesleys, the more susceptible became sufficiently spiritually influenced to manifest symptoms of violent spasms and convulsions. Similarly wrought upon in our day, Methodists have "fallen with the power," and seen visions—all phases of Spiritualism.

The first Methodist preachers, threatened, persecuted, were afterwards cursed and stoned for their heresies and zeal in kindling the fading fires of religion. The English Church denouncing them as "disturbers of the peace, and seducers," compelled them, if preaching at all, to hold their services in lanes, streets and groves. They were humble during this period of their history, and spiritually minded. Prophet-mantles rested upon them. Now, becoming popular, proud, sectarian and persecuting, they are suffering an eclipse of faith—a deserved decline. As ye "mete," said Jesus, "it shall be measured to you again." As a denomination, angelic ministers and spiritual gifts have left them. The shell is thickening. The soul-fires of their primitive forces are dying under church formalisms and mocking sanctities.

DR. ADAM CLARKE, the profound linguist and Biblical Methodist annotator, accepted the central thought connected with Spiritualism—a present communion with departed spirits. Commenting upon the woman of Endor, Saul, Samuel and that upper world peopled by "various orders of spirits," he writes, in his Com. p. 299, vol. ii.:

"I believe there is a supernatural and spiritual world, in which human spirits, both good and bad, live in a state of consciousness.

"I believe that any of these spirits may, according to the order of God, in the laws of their place of residence, have intercourse with this world, and become visible to mortals.

"I believe Samuel did actually appear to Saul, and that he was sent by the especial mercy of God, to warn this infatuated king of his approaching death."

These are unequivocal expressions of belief. If, as Dr. Clarke affirms, the risen Samuel "actually appeared to Saul;" if the ascended Moses and Elias "talked with Jesus" in the presence of Peter, John and James; if spiritual beings, denominated "Angels," "Men of God," "Men," held conscious intercourse with earth's inhabitants during several thousand years of Scriptural history—why not now? Is God mutable? Have deific laws changed? Has the "door" John saw opened in heaven been shut and barred? Did Jesus falsify when ye said, "Lo! I am with you alway unto the end of the world?" This beautiful belief in spirit intercourse, cherished by Dr. Clarke, so expanded his nature, that he clearly enunciated the doctrine of progression, and the final restoration of all souls to holiness and happiness. The thought thrilled him with ecstasy. Annotating upon a verse in

Romans, he exclaimed—"Death shall be conquered; hell disappointed; the devil confounded, and sin totally destroyed!" Writing of the passage of the apostle John—"God is love"—he says, "God is an infinite fountain of benevolence and beneficence to every human being. He hates nothing that he has made. He cannot hate because he is love. * * * * He has made no human being for perdition; nor ever rendered it impossible, by any necessitating decree, for any fallen soul to find mercy. * * * Love seems to be the essence of the Divine nature, and all other attributes to be only modifications of this."

ANN LEE, honored by her admirers with the appellations, "Sainted Mother," and "Sister," overshadowed by angels of purity, and enlightened by the descent of celestial influences, received her heavenly commission in 1758, near Manchester, England. Her visions were remarkable; her prophecies, oracles. The physical manifestations, relating to herself and adherents, consisted of dancing, trembling, whirling, and speaking with tongues. These exercises and spiritual gifts called down upon them the hostility of the Church. Priests and magistrates, who have ever sought to gag the truth, dungeon conscience, and impeach the inductions of science, charged them with disorder and Sabbath-breaking. The religious authorities slandered, fined and imprisoned them.

In 1774, inspired by the "Christ of the new order," she received a revelation to emigrate to America. A few pure-purposed, loving souls clustered around her as a central teacher directed by angel ministers.

This new church—the "Shakers"—much resembles the Essenes of Philo's time. The Nazarene had but three hundred followers when martyred upon Calvary. The increase of the Shaker fraternity has not been rapid; but is permanent. Holding that God is dual, eternal, Father and Mother in deific manifestations, they practically teach the strict equality of the sexes. "First *pure*, then peaceable," they profess to live in the "resurrection state," and preach to those "without"—the Gentiles—to raise few and better children. They all believe in spirit manifestations and revelations.

Elder F. W. Evans wrote Robert Owen, in 1856, that, "seven years previous to the advent of Spiritualism, the Shakers had predicted its rise and progress, precisely as they have occurred, and that the Shaker order is the great medium betwixt this world and the world of spirits. * * * Physical manifestations, visions, revelations, prophecies, and gifts of various kinds, of which voluminous records are kept, and, indeed, 'divers operations, but all of the same spirit,' were as common among us as gold in California."

Elder J. S. Prescott, connected with the community near Cleveland, Ohio, made a similar statement to us during the session of the 4th National Convention of Spiritualists. Mr. Dixon, an English writer of considerable note, visiting Elder Evans, of Mount Lebanon, during his American tour, wrote thus of the Shaker doctrines:

"To this dogma of the existence of a world of spirits—unseen by us, visible to them—the disciples of Mother Ann most strictly hold. In this respect, they agree with the Spiritualists; indeed they pride themselves on having foretold the advent of this 'Spiritual *disturbance* in the American mind.' Frederick tells me—from his angels—that the reign of this Spiritualistic movement 'is only in its opening phase! it will sweep through Europe, through the World, as it is now sweeping through America; it is based on facts, representing an active, though an unseen force.'

"These Shaker communities all claim to be of *spiritual* origin!—to have *spiritual* direction!—to receive *spiritual* protection! Hundreds of *spiritual mediums* are developed throughout the eighteen societies. In truth, *all* the members in greater or less degree are mediums.

"*Spiritualism*," he continues, "in its onward progress, will go through the same *three* degrees in the world at large. As yet it is only in the *beginning* of the *first* degree, even in the United States. It will continue until every man and woman upon the earth is convinced that there is a God—an immortality—a spiritual, no less than a natural world; and the possibility of a social, intelligent communication between their inhabitants respectively," &c., &c.

Basing our opinion upon reliable testimony, these Shaker communities constitute a body of the neatest, healthiest, the most pure-minded and kind-hearted souls of earth. Certainly they are the only people on this continent, who have successfully maintained, for more than seventy years, a system of rational living, one of the fundamental principles of which is the apostolic community of property.

JOHN MURRAY, the father of American Universalisms, born in England, persecuted for his beautiful heresy in his native country, was a Spiritualist. The birth of all great religious thoughts have their origin always in some spiritual agency It was so with Murray.

As early evidence of his mediumship and control by spirits, when but two years old, at his baptism, he articulated "*Amen*"—the first word he ever spoke. Clairvoyant, he saw a spirit—his Eliza—in Newgate prison, "irradiating the walls," before whom he, in his sorrow, prostrated himself, and, inspired by her sweet magnetism, found relief. Speaking of this happy visitation in an hour of deep anguish, he said: "My soul became calm, and although every hope from this world was extinct in my bosom, yet I believed I should be the better able to accommodate myself to whatever sufferings the Almighty might think proper to inflict."

When about to leave England for America, having served his time in prison for heresy, and feeling disconsolate over the departure from the scenes and associations of his home, he heard the voice of a guardian spirit, saying, "Be of good cheer. * * * Be not afraid when thou passest through the waters; I will be with thee, fear no evil!" * *

But the most interesting feature of his spiritual experiences, showing how well and wisely the messengers of heaven direct even life's events, for the consummation of divine purposes, is delineated in his interview with Mr. Potter, after his arrival in America.

By angel direction, Mr. Potter was impressed to build a meeting-house in the woods of New Jersey, under the assurance that in due time the true gospel would appear. Believing in the holy voice that appointed him, Mr. Potter faithfully built his house, and there it stood for years a monument of his so-called "folly," in the estimation of his orthodox neighbors, who taunted him about his "forthcoming minister." Are the winds, too, under the command of spirits, as with Jesus on the sea of Tiberias? They tost that vessel into the intended harbor, and Murray was thus brought to the very shore where lived Mr. Potter, of whom he requested a fish for the hungry sailors.

In the meanwhile, the moment that vessel touched the shore, the familiar voice of the angel, who ordered the house to be built, spoke in his ear with thrilling, melting cadence—

"There, Potter, in that vessel, cast away on that shore, is the preacher you have been so long expecting!"

Convicted, believing, nothing wavering, he waited the sequel, his heart serene with the love which the angel-presence inspired. When Mr. Murray came up to the door, asking for the fish, the mystic voice that, in other climes and ages, entranced the faithful to lofty, sublime deeds, was heard again—

"Potter, this is the man, this is the person, whom I have sent to preach in your house!"

Mr. Murray, astonished, bewildered—for he had resolved to abandon the ministry forever—persuaded, entreated, prayed to be absolved from the task; but no, angel voices spoke to him in his nights of reflection; and the strange circumstances thus developed, showing a heavenly providential overruling of tides and seasons, all crowded upon him with the afflatus of prophetic divinity. Yielding at length to the order of powers above, whose forces are law, and whose influences are sunbeams that bud and blossom the flowers of hope under tears of sorrow, he buckled on the armor of the "soldier of the cross," waked up the slumbering people to the action of freer thought and character, led to glorious victory, and, departing, left a trailing light of inspiration that has flooded deeper, higher, broader, till all the land is under the auroral baptism now of angels.

When the heavenly inspirations of the faithful Murray and his self-sacrificing coadjutors, crystalizing into a creed, were chilled by formularies, interpreted by fossiliferous Conventions, stultified by straining after "ecclesiastic respectability," the angels of progress left the denomination to wither, shrivel, die! 'Tis God's voice to every organic body—grow or perish! Universalism was a stepping-stone from a broad Protestant faith to demonstrated immortality. The good it had is blossoming and seeding into Spiritualism.

The tendency of all Christian sectarisms is downward, demanding faith without evidence, and saying to the aspirational soul—"thus far and no farther." The followers of all religious iconoclastic chieftains have, in after years, fallen far below their original standard-bearers. The Lutherans are *per se* sectarians. Methodists, degenerating from Wesley, Whitefield, Fletcher, as a church, virtually now deny all spiritual gifts and communications. Calvinists, condemning the barbarities of Rome, turned inquisitors and persecuted dissenting souls unto death. The Puritans, leaving England, settling at Plymouth, and founding the New England colonies, fled professedly from persecution, seeking a place to worship God according to the dictates of conscience, with the ulterior purpose of christianizing (?) the Indians! Settled, they commenced robbing those Aborigines, enslaving their women and children, and visiting upon them inhuman and self-degrading cruelties. They plundered the towns of the natives; paid bribes to assassinate Indian chiefs; burned hundreds of red men alive—and all in the name of Christ, the "Prince of Peace!"

A prominent New England author bears the following testimony:

"Their ablest and favorite divines declared that the burning of four hundred Indians at once, mostly women and children, seemed a sweet savor to God, while they admitted that it was awful to see their blood running and quenching the violence of the burning wood. * * They turned upon the Quakers. They imposed heavy fines for hearing them speak. They passed blue-laws. * * * They flogged, inhumanly, women and children. They put them in prison and whipped them daily. They cut off their ears. They bored their tongues with red-hot irons. They hung men, women and children as witches, and continued it for fifty years. * * * They banished Roger Williams. They drove women and helpless children, under severest penalties, to seek protection among the savages, (where they were all murdered) because they differed with them on metaphysical divinity. * * As late as 1740, they enacted the most barbarous laws against heretical thinkers, and enforced the Saybrook Platform."

Such *was*—such *is*, though modified by the genius and intelligence of the age, creedal Christianity, devoid of spirituality — formal Christianity, unbaptized of Spiritualism. Chaff without wheat! shell without substance! a swollen body without the spirit that giveth life!

"Far from the golden shores of fate
I gaze across the past;
Forever on life's dial-plate
The shade is backward cast."
* * * * *

"Ere long a fairer morn shall rise,
With purer air and brighter skies,
When force shall lay his scepter down
And strength shall abdicate its crown,
And *truth* incarnate sway the race,
With mildest power and tenderest grace."
* * * * * * *

"Ring out the darkness of the land,
Ring in the *Christ* that is to be."

Lecture VI.

Segmentary Spiritualism.

CHAPTER XIX.

THE PRELUDE.

> "Through the harsh noises of our day
> A low, sweet prelude finds its way;
> Through clouds of doubt and creeds of fear
> A light is breaking calm and clear.
>
> That angel song, now low and far
> Ere long shall sound from star to star!
> That light, the breaking day which tips
> The golden-spired Apocalypse."

Circles are the highest symbols. There are probably no straight-line motions in the universe. Those seeming such are on a scale so vast the curve cannot be perceived. Fragments are all parts of circular bodies, as a piece of granite rock is a part of those primitive formations that encircle the earth. Atoms gyrate upon their axes and follow the line of their strongest attractions. Things move in spirals, and generally with the sun, from left to right. Sea-shells are built up spirally. Vines ascend forest trees spirally. Particles of steel flying toward a magnet move spirally. This law, with few exceptions, applies to atoms, worlds, systems, civilizations, and all those historic cycles of ever-recurring spiritual epochs and eras that distinguish antiquity.

Progress underlies all things, and Spiritualism, though ever majestic in its past windings, may be compared to the ocean waves that rise and fall. It has had its mornings and evenings of decline. Its careers fleck the nights and days of earth's varied revolutions with splendors unspeakable, and its heaven-illumined truths, voiced by angelic inspired chieftains, have rolled in solemn grandeur all along the sunlit periods of the half-buried ages; and its musical echoes add to the glories of the nineteeth century.

Each spiritual wave, in accordance with the laws of accelerated motion, rose above the preceding, bearing the masses higher up the altitudes of wisdom. The impetus was greater; the spray from the wave more glittering; the principles involved, coupled with its holy teachings, were, during each succeeding period, more widely diffused.

Under some name and in some form Spiritualism, as herein demonstrated, has constituted the basic foundation, and been the motive force of all religions in their incipient stages. The Spiritualism of to-day differs from that of five thousand years since only in the better understanding of its philosophy, the general concession of its naturalness and its wider dissemination through the different grades of society. It has been and *is* God's visible seal of love to all climes and ages.

The spirit-world is the world of causes; this of effects. Objective entities are but the projections of etherealized spirit-substances. Inventions relating to industrial activities, or the spiritual exaltation of the races, have their first birth in the inner life. All great projects for the moral redemption of humanity, primarily conceived in the upper deeps of infinity, are inflowed from immortal minds to receptive mortals by the law of influx. These mediumized souls, impressionally catching the shadowy dim-defined plans, fashion them into forms; or perhaps partially constructing, push them out into the sensuous world. As spirit moulds and takes on form, so wisdom ceaselessly descends from the heavens.

Cognizant of a rising spiritual wave, Congresses of Angels devised the noble project of laying the foundation-stone of this new Temple, majestic, cosmopolitan, and strikingly sublime, in America—land of free thought, free speech, free press—land where the people, conscious of their God-given rights, and cringing before no cowled priests, feel themselves sovereigns—" kings and priests unto God."

Premonitions and prophecies are announcing heralds, breathing

> "—— A mystical lore,
> And coming events cast their shadows before."

The record stands undisputed, that Swedenborg, just before his departure to spirit-life, in 1772, prophesied that, in about eighty years, wonderful phenomena of a spiritual nature would occur on the earth. The four score years expired in 1852.

A young man, residing in Western New York, 1836, and other individuals in different localities, examining the merits of Mesmerism, fell into trance conditions, disclosing the fact, that within twelve or fourteen years a remarkable book would be published, the contents of which would not be as startling as the source from whence it originated. In about eleven years, "Nature's Divine Revelations" was dictated by spirits through A. J. Davis, in his clairvoyant state, and issued from the press.

In 1835, and several years thereafter, Wm. Miller and adherents, were impressed with great impending changes, denominated "the end of the world and the second coming of Christ to judgment." They interpreted the "word" of the Scriptures literally, thus confounding the personal with the spiritual coming. The blunder was fatal to the progress of the sect. The end of the theologic world of creeds and popish dogmas was approaching, and Christ was speedily coming as a spirit spiritually in the "clouds of heaven, with all his holy angels with him." These "holy angels" were the ministering spirits with whom many of earth's inhabitants now hold converse.

About this period immortalized spirits, originally from India, China, Persia, European countries, and American Indians, visited the various Shaker communities of the country, and controlling the more mediumistic members, "spoke in tongues," prophesied, and gave remarkable communications relative to the opening of the "seals," and the descent of spiritual powers and gifts to the "world's people." Earth and heaven abounded in signs of an approaching new era.

In 1846, some two or three years before the faintest translatable echo from the summer-land had reached an American ear, A. J. Davis stated, and it stands recorded in his "Divine Revelations," (p. 175,) that the shining intelligences of the second sphere of existence were soon to hold tangible communion with the people of earth. These were his prophetic words—"It is a *truth* that the spirits of the higher spheres commune with persons in the body by influx, although they are unconscious of the fact. This truth will ere long present itself in the form of a living demonstration. * * * * And the world will hail with delight the ushering in of the era!"

> "Why come not spirits from the realms of glory
> To visit earth, as in the days of old—
> The times of ancient writ and sacred story?
> Is heaven more distant? or has earth grown cold?
>
> To Bethlehem's air was their last anthem given
> When other stars before the One grew dim?
> Was their last presence known in Peter's prison,
> Or where exulting martyrs raised the hymn?"

LECTURE VII.

MODERN SPIRITUALISM.

CHAPTER XX.

SPIRIT PHENOMENA.

"He who, outside of pure mathematics, pronounces the word *impossible*, lacks prudence."—*Arago.*

"The Angel of the Lord descended from heaven and rolled back the stone from the door and sat upon it."—*Matthew.*

"Peter, sleeping between two soldiers, bound with chains, the keepers at the door of the prison! the Angel of the Lord came and smote him, and the chains fell from his hands.

"Passing the first and second wards and coming to an iron gate, it opened of its own accord, and they went out.

"When Peter knocked at the door of the gate; a damsel came, who knowing his voice opened the door with gladness, and returning told them Peter stood at the gate.

"They said to her, thou art mad. * * * * It is his angel. But Peter continued knocking.

"When they had opened the door and saw him, they were astonished."—*Acts.*

"The thing that hath been, is that which *shall* be, and that which is done, is that which shall *be* done."—*Ecclesiastes.*

> "Loved ones are rapping to-night!
> Heaven seems not far away!
> Death's sweeping river is bright!
> Soft is the sheen of its spray.
> Oh, bid them welcome in garments of white
> To hearts that are pure and illumined with light."—EMMA TUTTLE.

The rappings!—listen, theologians! The "Rochester knockings!"—sweet æolian-toned echoes from spirit-lands in demonstration of immortality!

"Behold," said Jesus, "I stand at the door and knock." That apostolic "cloud of witnesses"—our sainted loved ones, approaching the doors of our understanding through sounds, dreams, visions, premonitions and inspirations, plead for recognition and admission!

"The love which survives the tomb," says Irving, "is one of the noblest attributes of the soul."

Golden memories are undying. Pure love is immortal. The bud of friendship that begins to bloom on earth, bears precious fruitage in heaven. Holy remembrances call the ascended hither. Death, the silent key that unlocks life's portal to let earth-encoffined spirits up one step higher, severs no sweet attraction. Sympathies between the two worlds, are as natural as between the two continents. The translated mother looks down lovingly upon her weeping child. Delicate the electric table-touch—musical the "rap" —blessed the intelligent response—sacred the message! and happy each glory-bathed soul, who, catching, cherishes the whisper-accents breathed from those angel dwellers upon the shadowless shores of immortality.

Minute the initial steps of all great movements! How pale the thinkers face, standing in that retired mechanic's workshop! He paces the cinder-paved floor crazily, while riveting processes are being adjusted through a succession of little continuous "raps." Rivet after rivet fastened—wheels poised—machinery arranged, and lo! steam engines bidding defiance to winds and waves—crossing continents and whitening oceans—dash the gifts of commerce at our feet. Robert Fulton, inspired by inventors of the better land, is on earth immortal!

Bouchard, digging in 1799, in the fort of St. Julian, discovered the Rosetta stone written over in speaking characters, epistolary, hieroglyphic and symbolic. This, with subsequent discoveries, equally important, led to a full verification of the historic records of Herodotus. These figures and hieroglyphs carved upon Lydian stones, on obelisks and pyramids, permitted ancient Egypt to tell the world, in her own native language, of prior golden ages, putting to shame the boasted civilizations of Greece and Rome.

Newton, on a summer's afternoon, saw an apple drop to the earth. It was an effect. Investigating, studying inductively, the great law of gravitation flashed upon his mind. Arkwright, carefully watching the vibratory motions of a cog in a wheel, was repaid by discovering the principles of a new mechanical law, resulting in the saving of labor and life. Franklin, with kite and string, called subtle electric fire-fluids from the storm-clouds above him, and chaining them to machinery, threw an eternal truth into the face of all the sere-mantled ages. Now telegraphic wires girdle the globe, and words from Americans to Asians, outfly the winds and sunbeams. Joshua, Grecianized into *Jesus*, awoke to outer conscious life in a Judean "manger." Humble and unpropitious the advent! But there lay concealed causes destined to shake kingdoms, and give practical force to a higher civilization. Few attend the birth of genius. All newly-conceived truths are cradled in mangers. No age appreciates the martyr souls that take advanced positions.

The riveting—then the engine whose motive force lies behind the gracefully folding sails that whiten oceans; the kite and silken strings—then telegraphic communications belting the planet with burning thoughts; the vacated manger adjoining Bethlehem—then nations and swarming empires bowing to the "cross of Christ;" the "rappings" near Rochester, the heavens opened—then overjoyed multitudes, shouting—See!—*behold!* a tangible demonstration of a future existence!

This has ever been the divine formula for inaugurating new dispensations. God was not in the whirlwind bending Lebanon's cedars; but in the "still small voice." To inductive plodders, however, the more potent causes employed in the establishment of these tidal eras, pass unnoticed, because spiritual. Scientists deal only with phenomena and forms of substance. They see mountains; but not the hidden volcanic fires that rend them. They discern oaks in the distance; but not the electricity that shivers them to atoms. They behold parlor tables move without visible contact; yet are blind to those potential spirit-forces connected with the motions. Science needs spiritualizing. The gods playing upon the harp-strings of unseen causes, ever conquer. In spirit-life, wisely to plan is to perfect.

The mediative heralds of higher, brighter cycles—the standard-bearers of newly-conceived truths, bathing their pale foreheads in the first pearling sprays from celestial fountains, unappreciated, persecuted, pronounced "mad," banished from aristocratic circles—generally suffer social martyrdom, or are put to slow torturous deaths by the prevailing "respectable" conservatism of the times.

Reformers of all ages, whose mystic words startled the world, and whose inspired thoughts streamed like pearls down the future, unrecognized by Church or State, were branded "infidels!" But the future *did—will do* justice to such, erecting over their lifeless remains splendid monuments, where millions each spring morning shall delight to scatter flowers and evergreens, beautiful emblems of a fadeless immortality.

When the philosophically inclined heard of these phenomena, starting almost simultaneously in different portions of the world, they earnestly sought the producing cause. This, natural to cultured Germans, was especially praiseworthy in Americans. Truly great men are not only critical reasoners, but rigid investigators of newly-announced subjects or sciences. Theologic darkness trembles at every flash of advancing light. Bigots and moss-wreathed clergymen, fearing, heard in those gentle tappings from loved ones, only ghostly mutterings of the devil. Sectarists religiously canned, scaled and creed-encrusted, cried in tones fearful and sepulchral—"*humbug!*" an exclamation distinguishable for ponderous lungs and liliputian mentality. A parrot can assume grave platitudes and *mouth* the word with pious grace!

Progress daily invites to fresh feasts. "Let the church take care," says Carlyle "when God lets loose a great thought." Inspiration, art, science, theories, discoveries, "knockings!" each, *all*, the results of hidden spirit forces, exert their legitimate influences. Nebulæ—then through methods formative and systematic—worlds. Cells, combinations—then orderly systems. Rappings—then acknowledged angel ministries whispered in millions of home-circles—

> "——This is not a matter of to-day
> Or yesterday, but hath been from all time
> And none hath told us whence it comes, or how."

Egypt had its wierd augural staves from which were elicited meaning sounds rhythmic with melodies of immortality. The spirit-pendulum, mysterious to the masses, was employed in the ancient services of Hydromantia. The alphabet was successfully employed by the initiated few in the times of the Emperor Valens. Melancthon mentions rappings occurring in Germany in his day.

Though mysterious sounds and voices of deep import had been heard in the palmier periods of the Orient, and at brightning intervals for hundreds of years, in different European countries, as historic testimonies and the older British reviews abundantly prove; yet it remained for impulsive, inspirational *Americans* to translate (March, 1848) those disturbing forces and noises, into intelligible communications.

The genius of our institutions, tending to the widest individual freedom, had ripened the intellectual soil of the continent for a rich spiritual seeding. Spirits were to be the sowers. John's prophetic angel was already in the overarching heavens, waiting to preach the "everlasting gospel." The seventh trumpet had sounded. The time had come for "loosening of the seals of the book of life," that a future existence might no longer be considered a matter of faith; but of *absolute knowledge*.

As the Maries—"holy women of Syria, mediumistic and intuitive—were first at the Nazarenean tomb to triumphantly announce—"*he is not here, but risen ;*" so women in the initiatory hour of the spiritual dispensation, were the first to construct the key, and devise the method, for understandingly interpreting the fact, that a blissful converse in harmony with natural law, had been established between the two worlds of conscious existence.

> "Tongues broke out in unknown strains
> And sung surprising grace"—

The gates of heavenly courts ajar, angels, white-robed, and baptized in the silvery dews of paradise, re-appeared, opening again the song that anciently thrilled the watching shepherd-souls of Syria—"Peace on earth and good will to men."

Chapter XXI.

MEDIUMSHIP.*

Sunlight through the ether of space—electricity through the telegraphic wire—steamers through the waves of myriad waters—rivers through valleys—blood through veins and arteries—mind through brain! All principles, indeed, all forces, are mediative. Our organs, our senses, our faculties, are media of life, of love, of thought. Mediumship interpermeates and interlines all phases, all attributes, all motions of being. It is universal. What nature is to spirit, what body is to its soul, phenomenon is to Spiritualism the sign and seal, the portal and initiation of this new religion. As substance precedes forms, so spirit, in the divine order, precedes these "modern manifestations." Phenomena, therefore, are necessary to discoveries of spiritual truth, as facts are to inductive science. All *objective* knowledge of a future existence is obtained through the gradations of spiritual mediumship.

Some writers on the Spiritual Philosophy enumerates seven, others twenty-four phases of mediumship; as well

---

* Aside from book references, we are indebted for many of the ideas in this volume, to ancient spirits, or inspiring influences. These, frequently entrancing Dr. E. C. Dunn, our traveling companion for several years, in the capacity of a healer, gave us valuable suggestions and precious truths, coined from the mint of supernal life. The spirit teacher to whom this book is dedicated, though a member of our circle, is the spirit-guide of Bro. Dunn, phases of whose mediumship we have never seen excelled. In the field of progress, he is a successful healer and eloquent speaker.

specify seven hundred and twenty-four thousand. Truth is a unit; but its manifestations are as diverse as the organizations through which it is revealed. Mediumship, therefore, must be as multiform as the diversities of conditions and relations.

Mediumship, like inspiration, is both general and special. As spirits *en rapport* with the surrounding spiritual atmosphere, breathe and envelop themselves with its aura, they are influenced by the aggregated magnetic force of the age, thus comprehending our needs in faithful ministrations by pouring down upon us love-waves of heavenly inspiration, leveling up humanity at large, the same as the sun attracts and unfolds the floral beauties of all landscapes. But spirits in sympathy of purpose may band together, as do earthly corporations, to accomplish special objects through the best adapted media.

Vibrate one chord of a musical instrument, and all the rest of the same tension will vibrate in harmony with it. So the human spirit, sensitive to the gentlest influence from the spiritual spheres, sustains similar relations with spirits that musical chords do to each other. Thus spirit undulates to spirit. The greater the harmony, the more perfect the responsive undulation. As if comprehending this beautiful law, Jesus prayed that his "disciples might be one with him as he was one with the Father."

The manifestations of mediumship are graded *really* according to the constituent structure of the organism. The outer electric sphere surrounding media, and others, also, is composed of emanations, not only from the body, but from each of its organs. Indeed, each brain faculty has its distinctive radiation. By this both spirits and clairvoyants measure our mental states. Man's spiritual sphere, being interior, emanates from the more ethereal and vitalized substances. The predominance of man's electric sphere from the more gross or material—under control of corresponding spirits—is specially adapted to physical manifestations; while the predominance of his spiritual sphere, allies him more intimately with the "inner life," in harmony with the *spiritual* of the spirit world.

As a general division of mediumship, the following is warrantable:

I. Physical.
II. Psychological.
III. Inspirational.

Under the physical is comprehended the rappings, tippings, mechanical writing, spasmodic motions, movements of extraneous bodies, etc. To inductionists, and the masses generally, these are, like letters of the alphabet, important in arresting attention and giving tests of spirit identity and the transfer of intelligence, leading to the more interior and substantial.

Under the second heading may be classed psychological presentations, trance, vision, dream, dependent clairvoyance, spirit painting, discovery of mineral and oil treasures, and poetical musical improvisations, etc.

Under the third may be enumerated impressions, symbolic pictures, inventions, prophecies, illumined perceptions, exalted inspirations, independent seership, communion with superior intelligences from the heavens, etc.

Spiritual circles should be formed upon scientific principles. The voltaic pile, constructed of copper and zinc plates, in alternation, to evolve the galvanic fluid, is highly suggestive of the best method. It is well to seat in these circles male and female, alternately, as positive and negative, with a discriminating eye to temperament and adaptation. Man is not necessarily positive nor woman negative. In the harmonial man or woman, the attractive and repellant are equally balanced. Joining the hands induces a more unitive intermingling of the magnetic forces. Honest skepticism is no hindrance to success, but angularities and jealousies are. The circle once formed in order, there should be no intrusion—no change of conditions. Minds should be passive, the aspirations heavenly, the heart purely centered upon the elucidation of truth with a patient, devotional spirit; and light will surely reveal what the candid soul is seeking—the *demonstration* of angel presence.

When the inquirers have advanced into the real *inner life* of spirituality, there is little or no need for the circle to center the magnetic forces. Through true development such have come into complete rapport with their spirit-guides, rendering the circle no longer a necessity. They virtually become one of the circle, constituting its earthly polarity, receiving by sympathetic inspiration the enlightened unfoldment of angelic life.

CHAPTER XXII.

WITNESSES.

Judge Edmonds, a jurist of unimpeachable integrity and keen discernment, estimates the number of Spiritualists in this country at "eleven millions." If belief in the mere *fact* of conscious spirit converse legitimately entitles to the appellation, Spiritualist, the venerable Judge is evidently quite correct. In the wider, and, we think, better definition, Spiritualism inter-related to the inductive and deductive methods of research, implies *fact* and *philosophy*—science and religion—culture, growth, and a true harmonial life.

In a lecture delivered by this eminent legal gentleman, before the Spiritualists worshiping in Ebbitt Hall, he said:

"I have been addressed upon the subject of Spiritualism by letter, or personally, by persons from Cadiz in Spain, from Corfu and Malta in the Mediterranean, Bengal and Calcutta in Asia, from Venezuela in South America, from Austria, Germany, England, France, Italy, Greece and Poland in Europe, from Algiers and Constantinople, from almost every State in North America; and I have heard of my own publications being found on the Himalaya Mountains in Asia, and in the forecastle of a whale ship in the Northern Ocean; and in many different languages—Latin, Greek, Spanish, French, German, Polish and Indian. Such and so wide-spread has become, within the short period of fifteen years, the knowledge of and the interest in our faith.

"So among the churches have I witnessed its wide-spreading influence. High dignitaries, archbishops and bishops—both Catholic and Protestant; many untitled clergymen, of almost every denomination, and Jewish Rabbis, have alike shown their belief and their interest in the subject."

A foreign correspondent writing from London, for the Boston *Commonwealth*, informed its readers that—

"It had been publicly stated and not denied, that John Stuart Mill had become a convert to Spiritualism. Certainly the Spiritualists have an imposing catalogue of names to present before England: Ruskin, Mill, Wilkinson, Dr. Whately, William and Mary Howitt, Mr. and Mrs. S. C. Hall, and (it is said) Frederick Tennyson. Doubtless, the majority of these have been helped to this conversion by the extreme reaction against Positiveness and Atheism, with a violent yearning to find something beyond the grave other than the 'desolate perhaps.'"

The Roman Catholic *Guardian*, St. Louis, Missouri, published, Sept. 1868, a pastoral letter from Bishop Viviers, relating to the *planchette* and spiritual manifestations. Here follow extracts of confession and warning:

"Doubtless there are relations between the intelligence of men and the supernatural world of spirits. These relations are necessary; they are all sweet and consoling to the poor creature exiled in this valley of tears. But God has not given us the power of communicating with the other world by *any and every way*, which human imprudence might avail itself of. * * *

"To wish to penetrate it in any other manner, (than the church prescribes) to seek to discover by natural means the hidden mysteries of heaven, or the terrible secrets of hell, *is the most foolish and culpable of undertakings;* this is to make an attempt to disturb the order of providence and to make useless efforts to over-step the limits imposed on our present condition. * * *

"What shall we say to them who fear not to address hell itself, in order to call from it the spirit of Satan? For it is that cunning spirit which most ordinarily plays the principal part in these manifestations! Certainly, *we ourselves do not doubt the fatal intervention of the fallen angels in human affairs.* * * *

"All idolatrous worship was but an incessant communication with demons. Socrates conversed with his familiar spirit; Pythagoras believed in the soul of the world, which animates, according to him, the different spheres, as the soul animates the body. The poet Lucan has described the mysteries which were used to enter into relation with the manes of the dead; and, in times yet more remote, souls from the other world were invoked to demand the revelation of hidden things.

"But," continues the vigilant pastor a long time before the multitude of facts which have been developed from so many quarters, and under so many observing eyes, were able to demonstrate to him the extraordinary frequency of the action of these malicious and perfidious invisible beings, "if there is but little belief in the presence of these spirits which they invoke by means of the tables, they should be not less certainly convinced that these experiments are one of the thousand *ruses* of Satan to cause souls to perish."

The following is from the New York *Independent:*

"Spiritualism is holding up its head in London. The Davenport Brothers, by their physical manifestations, are exciting a greater sensation than Mr. Hume did. He conversed with spirits—or, at all events, claimed to have the power of spiritual intercourse. * * * It cannot be denied that Spiritualism has made many converts in this country, and that some of the most estimable of our literary men and women, like the Howitts, Mr. and Mrs. S. C. Hall, and Mr. Robert Bell, are believers in what I suppose one must call this strange delusion. Mary Howitt's last new story—'The Cost of Caergwyn'—which contains some charming sketches of Welsh life and character, is made weird-like and unnatural by all sorts of ghostly incidents. After all, this is better than the other extreme—that sea of unbelief, to which many of our finest intellects are drifting. Everything denotes a period of transition and change, and I suppose all will come out right in the end."

The New York *Leader,* under the caption—"Spiritualism looking up,"—quotes from Robert Bell's able contribution to the *Cornhill Magazine,* and sagely maintaining that the matter of Spiritualism is "deserving of earnest attention," concludes a very fair article with the following remarks:

"The phenomena witnessed by Robert Bell, were witnessed at the same time by Dr. Gully, the eminent physician of Malvern; by the eminent Dr. Collier, of London, and by other persons distinguished for the social positions they have attained by learning, genius, ability, and vigor of mind. William Howitt, the author, has seen and vouches marvels equally startling. Sir Edward Bulwer Lytton, a Minister of State; Newton Crossland, one of our most successful lecturers and acutest annotators; Parker Snow, of the Arctic expedition; Mr. and Mrs. S. C. Hall, celebrated in literature; Sir David Brewster, Dr. Bird, Lord Brougham, and many others of equal note, are all believers in the spiritualistic theory. It is also known that Louis Napoleon is a firm and ardent student of these phenomena, and that he received many messages through Mr. Hume, purporting to emanate, and believed by him to emanate, from the spirit of Napoleon the First."

The New York *Herald,* devoting nearly a column, awhile since, to the influence and prospects of Spiritualism, admits that—

"Ever since the Fox girls, of Rochester fame, commenced those knockings that made so much noise in the world, this subject has occupied at intervals the attention and invited the investigation of many scientific minds all over the world. Such men as Lord Lyndhurst, Lord Brougham, Sir David Brewster, and others, took much interest in it. Some people claimed that these distinguished men were believers; others asserted that they were confirmed skeptics. No matter for that: they thought the subject worth looking into, like a great many other people. * * * It is said that even Queen Victoria consulted the Davenports, and we know that Louis Napoleon has for a long time been pursuing his star in the séances of the American Spiritualist, Home.

"The *movement* is a growing one, strictly democratic, popular in its character, and revolutionary in its nature, and defiant towards the prevailing theology of the age. Its influence is felt in the jury-box, the ballot-box, the bench, the press, the platform, the pulpit, and even our national council halls. It asserts the great Protestant principle of the right of each man to judge for himself, become his own *Evangelist*, and get to heaven his own way. It presents the strange anomaly of meetings without a ministry, worship without churches, conventions without delegates, halls and fluent speakers that they pay for, and yet without church edifices, funded property or real estate—without ordinations, convents, colleges or creeds, written or implied. Spiritualists as a body act together, and even now have become a great power in this country!"

On another occasion it published an account, saying—

"The capital of Peru has been recently (August 7th) thrown into some commotion by a pastoral letter of its Archbishop, addressed to his flock, in reference to magnetism, Spiritualism, rappings and other phenomena, which had lately received a good deal of attention among the Peruvians."

This Church dignitary stoutly affirms, that it is "all the work of the devil."

The *Round Table*, aristocrat among the New York weeklies, and one of the most astute and critical periodicals published in the country, says—

"This question of Spiritualism has been suggested anew to us through reading an account of a 'mysterious disappearance in Cincinnati, Ohio.' * * *

"We take for our point of departure an extract from a letter written in the autumn of 1852, by Mrs. Sarah Helen Whitman, of Providence, R. I., to Horace Greeley. Mr. Greeley heads the extract with a note to this effect: 'The writer has received the following letter from Mrs. Sarah H. Whitman, in reply to one of inquiry from him as to her own experience in Spiritualism, and especially with regard to a remarkable experience, currently reported as having occurred to Hon. James F. Simmons, late United State Senator from Rhode Island, and widely known as one of the keenest and clearest observers, most unlikely to be the dupe of mystery or the slave of hallucination. Mrs. Whitman's social and intellectual eminence are not so widely known; but there are very many who know that her statement needs no confirmation whatever.'

"By the way, Mr. Simmons was in the Senate for another term after that writing, and he was looked up to as one of the ablest, most practical, and most upright of its members. It may be not improper for us to state, in the same connection, that we have examined some correspondence with Mrs. Whitman relative to the knowledge of her manifestations. She states therein that her attention was called to the mystery in the latter part of the year 1849, about three months before, (mark this,) *before* any intelligence had reached her of the singular exhibitions in Rochester. She noticed the sounds (gentle tappings, they were near the hour of midnight, while she was alone in her chamber) for the first time after the death of a friend. This friend was a boy by the name of Albert Helm, about ten years of age. He came to his death by drowning near noon of the day preceding the night on which the raps were heard. But to Mr. Greeley's letter:

'DEAR SIR—I have had no conversation with Mr. Simmons on the subject of your note until to-day. I took an early opportunity of acquainting him with its contents, and this morning he called on me to say that he was perfectly willing to impart to you the particulars of his experience in relation to the mysterious writing *performed under the very eyes, in broad day light, by an invisible agent.*

'In the fall of 1850, several messages were telegraphed to Mrs. Simmons through the electric sounds, purporting to come from her step-son, Jas. D. Simmons, who died some weeks before in California. The messages were calculated to stimulate curiosity and lead to an observation of the phenomena. Mrs. Simmons, having heard that messages in the hand-writing of deceased persons were sometimes written through the same medium, asked if her son would give her this evidence. She was informed (through the sounds) that the attempt should be made, and was directed to place a slip of paper in a certain drawer at the house of the medium, and to lay beside it her own pencil, which had been given her by the deceased. Weeks passed, and although frequent inquiries were made, no writing was found on the paper.

'Mrs. Simmons happening to call at the house one day, accompanied by her husband, made the usual inquiry and received the usual answer. The drawer had been opened not two hours before, and nothing was seen in it but the pencil lying on the blank paper. At the suggestion of Mrs. Simmons, however, another investigation was made, and on the paper were found a few pencil lines, resembling the hand-writing of the deceased, but not so closely as to satisfy the mother's doubts. Mrs.

Simmons handed the paper to her husband; he thought there was a slight resemblance, but would probably not have remarked it had the writing been casually presented to him. Had the *signature* been given him, he should at once have decided on the resemblance. He proposed, if the spirit of his son were indeed present, as alphabetical communications received through the sounds affirmed him to be, that he should, *then* and *there,* affix his signature to the suspicious document.

'In order to facilitate the operation, Mrs. Simmons placed the closed points of a pair of scissors in the hand of the medium and dropped her pencil through one of the rings or bows, the paper being placed beneath. The hand presently began to tremble, and it was with difficulty it could retain its hold of the scissors. Mr. Simmons then took the scissors into his own hand and dropped the pencil through the ring. It could not readily be sustained in this position. After a few moments, however, it stood as if firmly poised and perfectly still. *It then began slowly to move. Mr. Simmons saw the letters traced beneath his eyes— the words, James D. Simmons, were distinctly and deliberately written, and the hand-writing was a fac-simile of his son's signature.*

'But what Mr. Simmons regards as the most astonishing part of this seeming miracle is yet to be told. Bending down to scrutinize the writing more closely, he observed, just as the last word was finished, that the top of the pencil leaned to the right. He thought it was about to slide through the ring; but, to his infinite surprise, *he saw the point slide slowly back along the word ' Simmons,' till it rested over the letter i, when it imprinted a dot.* This was a punctilio utterly unthought of by him—he had not noticed the omission, and was therefore entirely unprepared for the amendment. He suggested the experiment, and he thinks it had kept pace only with his will or desire; but how will those who deny the agency of disembodied spirits in these marvels, ascribing all to the unassisted powers of the human will, or to the blind action of electricity—how will they dispose of this last significant and curious fact?

'The only peculiarity observable in the writing was that the lines seemed sometimes slightly broken, as if the pencil had been lifted, then set down again.

'One other circumstance I am permitted to note, which is not readily to be accounted for on any other than spiritual agency. Mr. Simmons, who received no particulars of his son's death until several months after his decease, proposing to send for his remains, questioned the spirit as to the manner in which the body had been disposed of, and received a very minute and circumstantial account of the means which had been resorted to for its preservation, it being at the time unburied. Improbable as some of these statements seemed, they were, after an interval of four months, confirmed as literally true by a gentleman then recently returned from California, who was with young Simmons at the period of his death. Intending soon to return to California, he called on Mr. Simmons to learn his wishes in relation to the final disposition of his remains. The above particulars I took down in writing, by the permission of Mr. Simmons, during his relation of the facts.'

"This case we have given as a fair representative of a class of cases—as one among a thousand similar ones, which have been testified to by tens of thousands of witnesses whose candor, truthfulness and common sense touching a usual occurrence, would not be disputed for a moment. Then, we may be allowed to offer it as a particular subject for consideration, just as if it embraced the whole matter seeking discussion and decision. We think it better so than otherwise; because any one, more especially any one who is not much in the habit of arguing, can do his cause fuller justice while confining himself to particulars, than he can when going off into generalities—he is apt, in the latter way, to lose himself and his argument.

"Well, what exactly is the pith of the cause before us? It is this: It in effect is affirmed by many thousand witnesses, who ordinarily would be reckoned trustworthy by any court in christendom, that a certain piece of information had been imparted to them in a certain way. There is not the shadow of a reason for supposing that they—the witnesses—were not in full possession of their every-day senses at the time of the phenomena. They had broad day light and every other natural facility for those senses to be normally impressed. The communication was written by no visible hand—by the hand of no one of themselves present. The chirography is that of no one present; but it does bear a full *fac-simile* resemblance to that which they have been familiar with, of a person whom they knew at the time to be away from among them. There was no possibility for the substance of the communication through common means to be known to them at the time it was given. That substance was proved afterward, upon normal evidence, to be the actual substance, both in general and in detail, of an actual event. Then, here is shown, unmistakably, an act, committed by no discoverable natural instrument, and presided over by an intelligence, by mind, which is outside of, apart from, distant from anybody within the neighborhood of the committal.

"And now comes the point which we desire to hold out to view, and upon which, as upon a pivot, all discussion touching the matter ought to turn. It is this: Where and what is that intelligence? Those tens of thousands of witnesses have been led, not hastily, but gradually, after careful sifting and weighing of evidence, to the conclusion that it is no other than the spirit which has dwelt heretofore in the body now departed. They find confirmation of their belief in their Bibles, which tell them distinctly of departed spirits not only, but of the returning of the same to earth. In that conclusion they are fixed firmly, rightly, according to sound law, until such time as their opponents shall array evidence equally strong to sustain their own contrary theory, whatever that may be. If they maintain that intelligence to be, for example, electricity, they are bound to exhibit to the actual eyesight the producing battery and the conducting wires, and to reveal precisely how it happened that the battery came into possession of just those materials out of which to brew electricity, such as should be identical with the knowledge possessed by a particular body before it parted with its spirit. If they hold the intelligence to be mesmerism, it devolves upon them to point out the mesmerizer, to explain how he manages to throw from his own mind into that of another, information which never was in his mind, and *how he handles the pencil.* Hence the burden of the proof is upon the negative. Let her or him who will take the negative bring forth the proof."

The *Scientific American,* a rightly named and widely circulated paper, writes editorially of the *Planchette*:

"You may hold a conversation with planchette, provided your own part in it consists in interrogation. Its replies, so far as we have seen, are sometimes true and sometimes false. So are the replies given by human respondents. It sometimes refuses to write at all, and plays the most fantastic tricks, in apparently wilful disregard of the feelings of those who are anxious that it should do its best. * * * These motions seem to those whose fingers rest upon the board to be entirely independent of their own wills. their only care being to avoid any resistance to its motions. The fact that it is impossible to suppose that the wills of two persons could be, by their own desire, mutually coincident, without previous agreement, forms one of the most puzzling features of the subject, as the nature of the question asked and answered precludes the possibility of collusion."

"The spirit with which scientific men have looked upon these phenomena, (denominated Spiritualism) has been unfortunately such as has retarded their solution. Skepticism as to their reality, although corroborated by evidence that would be convincing upon any other subject, refusal to investigate, except upon their own conditions, and ridicule not only of the phenomena themselves, but of those who believe in them, have marked their course ever since these manifestations have laid claim to public credence. Such a spirit savors of *bigotry.* The phenomena of table-tipping, spirit-rapping (so called), and the various manifestations which many have claimed to be the effect of other wills acting upon and through the medium of their persons, are exerting an immense influence, good or bad, throughout the civilized world. They should, therefore, be candidly examined, and if they are purely physical phenomena, as has been claimed, they should be referred to their true cause. This is due to truth, and the common duty which all owe to their fellow men. Nothing that affects the welfare of mankind should be considered beneath the notice of a true philosopher. What incalculable benefit might have resulted if the same amount of study had been given to the subject of witchcraft, at the time of its occurrence, that has since been bestowed upon it. When such things become matters of history, there are always enough who do not think it derogatory to their dignity to devote their time to speculation upon their causes. How much wiser is it to throw aside prejudice, and to look at the facts themselves in a spirit of candor and earnest desire for truth."

The *Herald and Review*, a religious journal, writes editorially of the progress of the spiritual movement in this style:

"We often hear the remark, 'Spiritualism is dying out.' Whenever we hear one make such a statement, we are led to think at once, Did you know what it is doing, you would take back that saying, and stand aghast at its gigantic strides. He might as well have said, Popery was dying out in the thirteenth century, because very little noise was made about it. The reason was, there were scarcely any left to oppose, hence all was comparatively quiet. Spiritualism has already planted its sentiments so firmly, and generally, in church and state, that the victory is nearly complete. The opposition is now very feeble, like that of a dying man in his last moments.

"We do not say that the great body of the church and state are yet avowed Spiritualists; but that the *sentiments* of Spiritualists, more or less, are being adopted by the masses."

This, though perhaps an unwilling, is a true manly confession.

Thus are these literati, scientists and sectarists forced to concede to Spiritualism a wonderful destiny of use in every department of earth's government. When the ocean moves in unchainable tides, all the bays and coves fill up to overflowing. Every soul is moved by the inflowing tides of inspiration. All are pushed forward. Even opposition reacts into acceleration. "He maketh the wrath of man to praise Him."

CHAPTER XXIII.

CLERICAL AND LITERARY.

"Out of the strong, came forth sweetness."—*Judg.* 14 : 14.

"In the mouth of two or three witnesses every word may be established."— *Matt.* 18 : 16.

"I give you the end of a golden string :
Only wind it into a ball,
It will lead you in at Heaven's gate,
That invitingly ope's for all."

The ideal is the prophetic. It precedes, in orderly series, the objective actual. The finest human types, moulding the present, are but dwarfs of those promised men, yet to crown the ages with ineffable splendor. Out from the evolutions of a life divine and circular, are continually being born leaders and witnesses for the people. The good abounds everywhere. Progress is universal. The rock that one civilization fails to crush, crumbles into soil to nourish the roots of the succeeding. The bee extracts sweets from thistles and thorn-blossoms. At the tolling of church-bells on Sunday mornings, there stream from old barreled sermons many glittering truths. Piercing through the sophistries of speculation, the lifeless skepticism of science, and the corpse-incrustations of creeds, there are living, regenerating forces at work in the most hidden avenues of society. Angels seek and minister to all conditions of mortality. The clergy, overshadowed by an inspiration that stirs the divinity within, often preach better than they believe—wiser than their confessions of faith warrant. As in apostolic times, a "rushing wind," a descending afflatus from circling bands of spirits, sometimes completely overmasters them. They *then* speak as with tongues of fire, and their words touch the heart, the conscience and the reason.

Souls thus kindled from the love-flames of heaven, pulsate in harmony with the infinite Over-Soul. Spirit answers to the spiritual. Partially intromitted, at times, into the realm of that quickening inner life, as was John, of Patmos, "on the Lord's day," the better portion of American preachers often preach *Spiritualism;* admitting the reality of its phenomena, and the truth of much or all of its philosophy.

Rev. H. W. Beecher's testimony:

"Oh, tell me not that the fathers of this Republic are dead—that generous host, that airy army of invincible heroes. They hover as a cloud of witnesses above this nation. Are *they* dead that yet speak louder than we can speak, and a more universal language? Are they dead that yet act? Are they dead that yet move upon society, and inspire the people with nobler motives and more heroic patriotism?"

In one of his practical sermons, delivered on the 8th of Jan., 1867, he says:

"Our field of conflict is different from that on which men oppose each other. It comprises the whole unseen realm. All the secret roads, and paths, and avenues, in which spirits dwell, are filled with a great invisible host. These are our adversaries. And they are all the more dangerous because they are invisible. Subtle are they. We are unconscious of their presence. They come, they go; they assail, they retreat; they plan, they attack, they withdraw; they carry on all the processes by which they mean to suborn or destroy us, without the possibility of our seeing them.

"I confess to you, there is something in my mind of sublimity in the idea that the world is full of spirits, good and evil, who are pursuing their various errands, and that the little that we can see with these bats' eyes of ours, the little that we can decipher with these imperfect senses, is not the whole of the reading of those vast pages of that great volume which God has written. There is in the lore of God more than our philosophy has ever dreamed of.

"An evil spirit may be consummately refined, may be inspired. Our first thought in contemplating this subject is, that an evil spirit must be a vulgar thing. Doubtless there are vulgar spirits; but it does not follow at all that spirits who are most potential, and most to be feared, are vulgar. On the contrary, where spirits are embodied, it is supposed that those who are the most cultured are the most powerful for evil.

"The perversion of moral ideas—the suborning of all things to selfishness—the want of truth and equity—the corruption of religion—these things are inexplicable on any other supposition than that there are mighty powers at work above the agencies of nature, and beyond the will of men; that there are spirits of wickedness that are abroad in the world, and that render life unsafe.

"On the other hand, I believe that there are angels of light, spirits of the blessed, ministers of God. I believe, not only that they are our natural guardians, and friends, and teachers, and influencers, but also that they are natural antagonists of evil spirits. In other words, I believe that the great realm of life goes on without the body very much as it does with the body. And, as here the mother not only is the guardian of her children whom she loves, but foresees that bad associates and evil influences threaten them, and draws them back and shields them from the impending danger; so ministering spirits not only minister to us the divinest tendencies, the purest tastes, the noblest thoughts and feelings, but, perceiving our adversaries, caution us against them, and assail them, and drive them away from us.

"The economy, in detail, of this matter, no man understands. All we can say is, in general, that such antagonism exists; that there are spirits that seek our good, and other spirits that seek our harm; that that there are spirits that seek to take us to glory, and honor, and immortality, and other spirits that seek to take us to degradation."

In another discourse reported in the New York *Independent*, he employed the following unmistakable language. The quotations are introduced without any special view to their logical connection. Mr. Beecher himself is a stranger to the logic of the schools:

"There is an atmosphere of the soul as well as an atmosphere of nature. In the atmosphere of the soul, God sometimes brings down the divine landscape, heavenly truths, so clearly that the soul rests upon them as upon a picture let down.

"Out of the dust and din and mist and observations of life, there come moments when God permits us to see, in a second, further, wider, and easier, than by ordinary methods of logic we can see in a whole life. Do I undervalue logic when I say that it is inferior to intuition? Intuition, when at white heat, teaches a man in a single moment more than logic ever teaches him. Logic constructs the walls of thought, throws up ramparts, and lays out highways; but it never *discovers*. Logic merely builds, fortifies, demarks The discovering power is intuition. There are certain times when parts of the mind lift themselves up with a kind of celestial preparation, and we see and think and feel more in a single hour than ordinarily we do in a whole year. And however useful and needful reasoning may be, as compared with these sudden insights, it is scarcely to be mentioned with respect.

"Ordinarily we are under the influence of the things which are seen. In our lower life we must be under the influence of sense. But now and then, we know not how, we rise into an atmosphere in which spirit-life, God, Christ, the ransomed throng in heaven, virtue, truth, faith and love, become more significant to us, and seem to rest down upon us with more force, than the very things which our physical senses recognize. There have been times, in which I declare to you, heaven was more real than earth; in which my children that were gone spoke more plainly to me than my children that were with me; in which the blessed estate of the spirits of just men made perfect in heaven, seemed more real and near to me than the estate of any just man upon earth. These are experiences that link, one with another and a higher life. They are generally not continuous, but occasional openings through which we look into the other world. * * * * * These glimpses of the future state are a great comfort and consolation to all those who are looking and waiting for that development of perfect manhood."

This clergyman doing an immense work for freedom and religious progress, should not be too severely criticised by such uncompromising progressionists as were fortunate enough to snap their ecclesiastical fetters at a single bound. Though contradictory, though his clerical trumpet often gives an "uncertain sound," he is a grand man with a warm heart and an inspirational brain. Pardon him, then, for occasionally "falling from grace," to flounce, at intervals, in the miry clay of his childhood catechism. The history of mediumship furnishes many similar cases.

REV. E. H. CHAPIN'S testimony:
In a masterly discourse, entitled "the voices of the dead," this eminent pulpit orator breathed these words of cheer. It is Universalism just blooming into Spiritualism—faith smiling at its first glimpse of knowledge:

"Well, then, is it for us at times to listen to the voices of the dead. By so doing we are better fitted for life and for death. From that audience we go purified and strengthened into the varied discipline of our mortal state. We are willing to *stay*, knowing that the dead are so near us, and that our communion with them may be so intimate. We are willing to *go*, seeing that we shall not be wholly separated from those we leave behind. We will toil in our lot while God pleases, and when he summons us we will calmly depart."

Referring to certain moods and "consecrated hours," he adds:

"Then, though dead, they speak to us. It needs not the verbal utterance, nor the living presence, but the mood that transforms the scene, and the hour supplies these. That face that has slept so long in the grave, now bending over us, pale and silent, but affectionate still—the more vivid recollection of every feature, tone, and movement, that brings before the departed just as we knew them, in the full flush of life and health—that soft and consecrating spell which falls upon us, drawing in all our thoughts from the present, arresting, as it were, the current of our being, and turning it back, and holding it still, as the flood of which rushes by us—while in that trance of soul, the beings of the past are shadowed—old friends, old days, old scenes recur, familiar looks beam close upon us, familiar words re-echo in our ears, and we closed up and absorbed with the by-gone, until tears dissolve the film from our eyes, and some shock of the actual wakes us from our reverie;—all these, I say, make the dead commune with us as really as though in bodily form they should come out from their mysterious silence and speak to us. And if life consists in *experience*, and not mere physical contacts—and if love and communion belong to that experience, though they take place in meditation, or dreams, or by actual contact—then, in that hour of remembrance, we have really lived with the departed, and the departed have come back and lived with us."

REV. THEODORE PARKER'S testimony:

This individual, so self-poised and towering in intellect, was the man-colossus among American clergy. Ascended he is living and speaking still, through our media. Assuming that revelation was no green-house exotic, but perpetual as cycling ages, and that inspiration, native to the postures of the soul, is cognate with the races, he propagated a religious philosophy that will stream in increasing beauty through all the future eras of free thought. His grave is a Mecca under the mellow skies of Florence. Considered mentally he was thoroughly self-conscious of his greatness.

"Tend this head well," says Mirabeau, on his death-bed; "it is the greatest head in France." "God gave me great powers," says the expiring Parker, "and I have but half used them." The coincidence was singular, while saying in his last hours—" There are two Theodore Parkers, the one here sick and struggling, the other at work at home." There was a friend reading at the time one of his great sermons in Music Hall. There *were* "two Theodore Parkers"—the shadow and the substance, for man is dual, aye, trinal. The papers thought him "wandering a little." The Jews evidently thought Paul was "wandering" when "caught up to the third heaven," not knowing whether he was *in* the body or *out*.

In thought and speech, relative to the Spiritual Philosophy, he was manly and heroic. In notes made for a sermon we find the following:

"In 1856 it seems more likely that Spiritualism would become the religion of America, than in 156 that Christianity would become the religion of the Roman empire, or in 756 that Mohammedanism would be that of the Arabian populations:

"1. It has more *evidence for its wonders* than any historic form of religion hitherto.

"2. It is *thoroughly democratic*, with no hierarchy; but inspiration is open to all.

"3. It is no *fixed fact*—has no *punctum stans*, but is a *punctum fluens*.

"4. It admits all the truths of religion and morality in all the world-sects."

"Shall we know our friends again? For my own part I cannot doubt it; least of all, when I drop a tear over their recent dust Death does not separate them from us here. Can life in heaven do it?"

The succeeding paragraphs we transcribe from Wm. Howitt's "History of the Supernatural." Who but Theodore Parker could have written thus upon Spiritualism?

"Let others judge the merits and defects of this scheme; it has never organized a church—yet, in all ages, from the earliest, men have more or less freely set forth its doctrines. We find these men amongst the despised and forsaken; the world was not ready to receive them. They have been stoned and spit upon in all the streets of the world. The 'pious' have burned them as haters of God and man; the wicked called them bad names and let them go. They have served to flesh the swords of the Catholic Church, and fed the fires of the Protestants; but flames and steel will not consume them; the seed they have sown is quick in many a heart—their memory blessed by such as live divine. These are men at whom the world opens wide the mouth, and draws out the tongue, and utters its impertinent laugh; but they received the fires of God on their altars, and kept living its sacred flame. They go on, the forlorn hope of the race; but Truth puts a wall of fire about them, and holds the shield over their heads in the day of trouble. The battle of truth seems often lost, but is always won. Her enemies but erect the blood scaffolding where the workmen of God go up and down, and, with divine hands, build wiser than they know. When the scaffolding falls the temple will appear." * *

"This party has an idea wider and deeper than that of the Catholic or Protestant; namely, that GOD *still inspires men as much as ever; that he is imminent in spirit as in space.* For the present purpose, and to avoid circumlocution, this doctrine may be called Spiritualism. This relies on no church tradition, or scripture, as the last ground and infallible rule. It counts these things *teachers*, if they teach—not masters; *helps*, if they help us—not authorities. It relies on the divine presence in the soul of men—the eternal word of God, which is Truth, as it speaks through the faculties he has given. It believes God is near the soul as matter to the sense; thinks the canon of revelation not yet closed, nor God *exhausted*. It sees him in Nature's perfect work; hears him in all true Scriptures, Jewish or Phœnician; feels Him in the inspiration of the heart; stoops at the same fountain with Moses and Jesus, and is filled with living water. It calls God, Father, not King; Christ, brother, not redeemer; Heaven, home; Religion, Nature! It *loves* and TRUSTS, but does not fear. It sees in JESUS a MAN, living, man-like; highly gifted and living with blameless and beautiful fidelity to God—stepping thousands of years before the race of men—the profoundest religious genius that God has raised up; whose words and works help us to form and develop the native idea of a complete religious man. But he lived for himself, died for himself, worked out his *own salvation*, and we must do the same; for one man cannot *live* for another, more than he can eat or sleep for him. It lays down no creed, asks no symbol, reverences exclusively no time nor place, and therefore can use all time and every place. It reckons forms useful to such as *they help*. Its temple is all space, its shrine the good heart, its creed all truth, its ritual *works of love* and utility, its profession of faith a divine life, works without faith, within love of God and man. It takes all the helps it can get; counts no *good word* profane, though a heathen spoke it—no lie sacred, though the greatest prophet had said the word. Its redeemer is *within*, its *salvation within*, its heaven and it oracle of God. It falls back on *perfect religion*—asks no more, is satisfied with no less."

HARRIET BEECHER STOWE's testimony:

While walking among the trees that surrounded the Aberdeen Cathedral, immortals seemed to accompany this truly inspired woman and author. In "Sunny Memories," she wrote:

"I cannot get over the feeling that the souls of the dead do some how connect themselves with the places of their former habitation; and that the hush and thrill of spirit, which we feel in them, may be owing to the overshadowing presence of the invisible. St. Paul says, 'we are compassed about with a *great* cloud of witnesses;' but how can they be witnesses if they cannot see and be cognizant?"

From one of her articles relating to the New Year, we select a few of the more touching paragraphs. As significant of the subject, she commenced with this poetic quotation:

> "It is a beautiful belief,
> That ever round our head
> Are hovering, on viewless wings,
> The spirits of the dead."

"One of the deepest and most imperative cravings of the human heart, as it follows its beloved ones beyond the veil, is for some assurance that they still love and care for us. As a German writer beautifully expresses it, 'Our friend is not wholly gone from us; we see across the river of death, in the blue distance, the smoke of his cottage;' hence the heart, always suggesting what it desires, has ever made the guardianship and ministration of departed spirits a favorite theme of poetic fiction.

"But is it, then, fiction? Does revelation, which gives so many hopes which nature had not, give none here? Is there no sober certainty to correspond to the inborn and passionate craving of the soul? Do departed spirits in verity retain any knowledge of what transpires in this world, and take any part in its scenes? All that revelation says of a spiritual state is more intimation than assertion; it has no distinct treatise, and teaches nothing apparently of set purpose, but gives vague, glorious images, while now and then some accidental ray of intelligence looks out—

> 'Like eyes of cherubs shining
> From out the veil that hid the ark.'

"But out of all the different hints and assertions of the Bible, we think a better inferential argument might be constructed to prove the ministration of departed spirits, than for many a doctrine which has passed in its day for the height of orthodoxy.

"What then? May we look among the band of ministering spirits for our own departed ones? Whom would God be more likely to send us? Have we in heaven a friend who knew us to the heart's core? a friend to whom we have confessed our weaknesses and deplored our griefs? If we are to have a ministering spirit, who better adapted? Have we not memories which correspond to such a belief? When our soul has been cast down, has never an invisible voice whispered, 'There is lifting up?' Have not gales and breezes of sweet healing thought been wafted over us, as if an angel had shaken from his wings the odors of paradise? Many a one, we are confident, can remember such things. And whence come they?

"But again—there are some spirits (and those of earth's choicest) to whom, so far as enjoyment to themselves or others is concerned, this life seems to have been a total failure. A hard hand from the first, and all the way through life, seems to have been laid upon them; they seem to live only to be chastened and crushed, and we lay them in the grave at last in mournful silence. To such, what a vision is opened by this belief!

"They have overcome, have risen, are crowned, glorified; but still they remain to us, our assistants, our comforters, and in every hour of darkness their voice speaks to us: 'So we grieved, so we struggled, so we doubted; but we have overcome, we have obtained, we have seen, we have found; and in our victory behold the certainty of thy own.'"

In a poem clipped from the New York *Independent*, she writes her clairaudient experiences in Spiritualism, in lines thus sweet and tender:

> "Those halting tones that sound to you
> Are not the tones I hear;
> But voices of the loved and lost
> Now greet my longing ear.
>
> I hear my angel mother's voice;
> Those were the words she sung;
> I hear my brother's ringing tones,
> As once on earth they rung.
>
> And friends that walk in white above
> Come 'round me like a cloud,
> And far above those earthly notes
> Their singing sounds aloud."

REV. WM. E. CHANNING'S testimony:

"I live, as did Simeon, in the hope of seeing a brighter day. I do see gleams of dawn, and that ought to cheer me. I hope nothing from increased zeal in urging an imperfect, decaying form of Christianity. One higher, clearer view of religion rising on a single mind, encourages me more than the organization of millions to repeat what has been repeated for ages with little effect. The individual here is mightier than the world; and I have the satisfaction of seeing aspirations after this purer truth. * * * * We need not doubt the fact, that angels whose home is heaven, visit our earth, and bear a part in our transactions; and we have good reason to believe that if we obtain admission into heaven, we shall still have opportunity, not only to return to earth, but to view the operation of God in distant spheres, and be his ministers in other worlds."

BAYARD TAYLOR's testimony:

Referring, in the New York *Mercury*, to "mysterious incidents," happening upon the Pacific coast, and in other countries, as singular personal experiences of his own, Mr. Taylor writes:

"Let skeptical, hard, matter-of-fact men talk as they may, there is a lingering belief in the possibility of occasional communication between the natural and the supernatural—the *visible* and the *invisible* world—inherent in human nature. There are a few persons whose lives do not contain at least some few occurrences, which are incapable of being satisfactorily explained by any known laws—remarkable presentiments, coincidences, and sometimes apparitions, even, which seem to be beyond the reach of accident or chance, and overcome us with a special wonder."

"It was, perhaps, an hour past midnight, along the foot-hills of the Nevadas, when, as I lay with open eyes gazing into the eternal beauty of Night, I became conscious of a deep, murmuring sound, like that of a rising wind. I looked at the trees; every branch was unmoved—yet the sound was increased, until the air of the lonely dell seemed to vibrate with its burden. A strange feeling of awe and expectancy took possession of me. Not a dead leaf stirred on the boughs; while the mighty sound—a choral hymn, sung by ten thousand voices—swept down over the hills, and rolled away like retreating thunder over the plain. It was no longer the roar of the wind. As in the wandering prelude of an organ melody, note trod upon note with slow, majestic footsteps, until they gathered to a theme, and then came in the words, simultaneously chanted by an immeasurable host: '*Vivant terrestriæ!*' The air was filled with the tremendous sound, which seemed to sweep near the surface of the earth, in powerful waves, without echo or reverberation.

"Suddenly, far overhead, in the depths of the sky, rang a single, clear, piercing voice of unnatural sweetness. Beyond the reach of human organs, or any human instrument, its keen *alto* pierced the firmament like a straight white line of electric fire. As it shot downward, gathering in force, the vast terrestrial chorus gradually dispersed into silence, and only that one unearthly sound remained. It vibrated slowly into the fragment of a melody, unlike any which had ever reached my ears—a long undulating cry of victory and of joy; while the words '*Vivat Cœlum!*' were repeated more and more faintly, as the voice slowly withdrew, like a fading beam of sunset, into the abysses of the stars. Then all was silent. I was undeniably awake at the time, and could recall neither fact, reflection, nor fancy of a nature to suggest the sounds. * * * How does one faculty of the brain act, so far beyond our conscious knowledge, as to astound us with the most unexpected images? Why should it speak in the Latin tongue? How did it compose music—which would be as impossible for me as to write a Sanscrit poem?"

Rev. G. H. Hepworth's testimony:

As a representative of liberal Unitarianism, this clergyman has few superiors. His sainted mother, a medium, lived and passed to the better-land a confirmed Spiritualist. In a funeral sermon, after Mr. Hepworth had cited sundry cases of mediumship in the Scriptures, the case of Joan of Arc, Socrates, Luther, Swedenborg and Indian medicine men, he remarked:

"I have been greatly interested in the new sect, or denomination, that has come into existence in the last few years. Its members call themselves Spiritualists. Fifteen years ago they were laughed at; *now, who laughs at them?* Then, few had ever heard of such a system of doctrines; now, they number their converts by millions—they tell me that there are six millions of believers, so-called, in the United States alone—and these converts belong to all classes of society, from the poorest to the richest and most learned. They have thirty journals devoted to the propagation of their faith. They have a library of five hundred volumes advocating their sectarianism. The moment your eye glances over these figures, you ask, Why is this? The answer is plain; first, because the doctrine of communion has put off its oppressive robes of selfishness and personal aggrandizement, and put on the *white garments of good news to the world;* and second, because nothing is more evident to my mind than that the world *longs to believe, and needs to believe, something of this sort.* It is essential to our religious well-being. The very minute that terrible desolation enters a house and robs the family of a loved member, leaving as a sacred memento of the past only the 'vacant chair,' the holiest part of our human natures looks up to heaven with a dim, vague expectation, with a belief that has never taken a definite shape, perhaps, that though we cannot see them, they do see and know us. * * * I have the very firmest faith in that kernel of inspiration which has given to the sect all its value, the assertion that heaven is close to us, and that its inhabitants walk the earth both when we wake and when we sleep. It seems to me that this truth is at the centre of all true religion; and when I bid the sect God-speed, it is with the grateful feeling that it is reviving the forgotten truth which the prophets and the Christ himself have taught us. Yes, I do believe in this possible communion with all my heart."

Rev. A. D. Mayo's testimony:

When pastor of the Unitarian Church, in Albany, N. Y., Mr. Mayo, in an excellent article on "Transcendentalism and Spiritualism," expressed his convictions thus definitely:

"Transcendentalism has been confined to the circles of the cultivated, though in many ways it is helping to form the national theology. This habit of thinking on religion, which has been ridiculed in every Evangelical pulpit and newspaper as the essence of absurdity and infidelity, is simply the American cultivated rendering of the words of Jesus— 'The kingdom of God is within you.' It is a protest against the banishment of God from nature and the soul; an assertion that the Deity lives in America as he did in Palestine, and underlies our consciousness as surely as that of Moses and Isaiah. To it we are indebted for the substitution of the simple doctrine of Jesus concerning Universal Inspiration, in place of the worn-out machinery of the orthodox Holy Spirit. * * * But it is not as a body of people interested in mesmeric media, that this large religious denomination, now numbering 4,000,000 of disciples, chiefly concerns the observer of American theology, but as an exhibition of the popular tendencies of thought on religion. *Spiritualism* is a *natural awakening of the American masses to the doctrine of the Immortal Life taught by Jesus.* This movement is mightily shaking the American church; severing great ecclesiastical bodies, rending churches, depopulating fashionably furnished temples, and every year coming up with increased assurance to demand of the popular theology an account of its stewardship. A portion of the churches have welcomed it, and we will be *saved* by their *wisdom;* but woe to the sect or church that sets its face against it. It is not to be stayed by criticism from a theological or æsthetical point of view. We shall learn out of it *what it means in the 19th century to believe in the immortality of the soul;* and it will be found that this doctrine will come to us fraught with vaster relations, suggesting larger duties, and elevating with nobler aspirations, than to the darkened masses of the early ages of Heathenism or middle ages of Christianity. * * * Invisible hands leave upon our tables gifts of faith and deathless love and immortal hope, of which our fairest Christmas flowers and our greenest wreaths are but withered and vanished types. The pavement is thronged with a mighty host that crowds no hasty passenger, and speaks in no audible voice, but all the time holds sweet converse with the hearts of them that go to and fro. The school and the senate, and the places where men congregate for the serious work of life, have their empty chairs; empty to our mortal vision, yet to the eye of the soul filled with forms of unearthly wisdom and dignity and grace. I preach not to-day to this congregation alone; but this church is thronged and overflowed, yea, the whole air is populous with an audience you cannot see; for every beloved spirit that has left its mark on mine, and every weary and stricken soul that I have tried in feebleness to help, and every countenance that only for once has gleamed out in spiritual recognition from the strangest crowd; all who have heard my words on earth will hear them no more; all whose words I have heard for the last time in this valley of mortality, all are here to-day."

When a few more of the "Rulers of the Pharisees have believed"—when a few more esteemed great, gifted and reputable, as guaged by the world's standard, openly avow their knowledge of a future existence through modern spiritual phenomena, certain clergy will re-affirm their once brave utterances breathed in moments of inspiration, and stoutly aver that early in the resurrection morning of American Spiritualism, they were present and among the first to proclaim it as a "natural awakening of the masses to the doctrine of immortality!" Spiritualists must keep their chain of historic records bright against that prophetic day, when the "priests of my people shall be brought into judgment."

Rev. G. W. Skinner's testimony:

"No matter what explanation we may give thereof, the facts of what is called modern Spiritualism have ever been in existence. To deny them is idle; to ignore them is trifling; to ridicule them is to exhibit our own weakness.

"What shall we do with the facts? The records of all times mention them; the Bible is full of them; they are said to be happening all about us to-day. The movement of modern Spiritualism, by some, is supposed to rest solely on these phenomena. This question of Spiritualism will yet be a greater disturbing element in the religious world than it is at present. These wonderful facts will interest the curious and engage the attention of the candid; and from them much light may be shed on obscure natural laws. The intelligent masses of America want more rational ideas of God, of the soul, and of our future life."

Rev. G. S. Gowdy's testimony:

"I have no means of determining definitely what portion of our Universalist preachers are Spiritualists. * * * * For one, I believe that *spirits communicate with mortals.* I have not changed my mind upon this subject since my controversy with Bro. Hunt."

Rev. Dr. Eli Ballou's testimony:

"We believe it as probable that all angels in the spirit-world, or in the spheres above us, were once men in the flesh; and that when necessary, and under favorable circumstances, angels from the world of spirits *have* and *do* communicate with the spirits in the flesh."

Rev. Adin Ballou's testimony:

On page 38, of a volume published by this clergyman, several years since, is found this clear statement—

"So, then, there is an exquisitely subtle element * * * * communicable from one soul to another, under appropriate conditions, and thereby the two souls come into *rapport*, as the French call it, or soul-communication. The process whereby this is effected is called mesmerising, magnetizing or psychologizing. Its results are mesmeric and psychological phenomena of every grade and variety, from the lowest somnambulism, to the highest clairvoyance. Again, I ask, does the objector believe in *all this* as demonstrable between human spirits in the flesh? Yes. Very well; so do I. * * * I have laid down, as a part of my doctrine, that these mesmeric, clairvoyant, and psychological phenomena sometimes proceed from spirits in the flesh, and sometimes from departed spirits; always, however, in accordance with spiritual laws, common, more or less to the whole universe of souls. I have also taken the position that phenomena caused by souls *in the body* sometimes mix with those caused by *departed souls*, and that thus the *lower* are liable to be mistaken for the higher. Here I am but one step ahead of the objector in my credulity. *He* believes in marvels, utterly incredible to himself a few years ago, caused by mesmerism, clairvoyance, and psychological influence, exerted by soul on soul in the flesh. Having been strained up by irresistible evidence to this height of faith, he now obstinately denies that departed spirits ever mesmerise, magnetize, or spiritize susceptible persons in the body; that they ever exert psychologic influences over them to render them media; that they ever cause *any* of the phenomena purporting to be spirit manifestations. Why? Because mesmerism, clairvoyance, and psychological influence take place between soul and soul in the body, and these *may possibly* account for all higher phenomena of the same nature. Most lame and impotent conclusions! Some of the phenomena in question may be thus accounted for, but not the more important and peculiarly distinctive manifestations. * * * Departed spirits have a higher mesmeric, magnetic, or psychologic power than have mortals of a corresponding grade. Facts have proved this in many remarkable cases. It will yet be demonstrated to the conviction of all candid investigators."

Rev. J. P. Sanford's testimony:

Those reading the "*Monthly Clarion*," received this information from the Rev. Moses Hull—

"The last time we saw Mr. Sanford, (a Universalist clergyman) of Iowa, he told a large audience in our tent that he was a Spiritualist. Said he: 'Persons may, by the aid of their index finger, succeed in turning up their noses at Spiritualists, but it is too late in the day to think of hooting four millions of people down.'"

Rev. H. A. Reid's testimony:

"The real and living verity of the future life and the spirit-world is a doctrine which can appeal confidently to the Bible, to history, and. to science, for its substantial proof and reasonable confirmation.

"That the inhabitants of the spirit-realm, both good and bad, can and do, under some circumstances, manifest themselves to persons still in the flesh, is a doctrine of nature, taught most distinctly in the Bible, and proven by the concurrent testimony of every race of mankind, in all ages of the world.

"In the spirit world, those having similar tastes, loves and desires, good or bad, associate together by spontaneous mutual attraction or affinity. And each spirit is known by all the rest precisely AS IT IS, with all its goodness or all its badness unmistakeably discerned by every one."

Rev. Dr. Fisk's testimony:

"God, he said, has use or employment for all the creatures he had made: for every saint on earth, for every angel in heaven. He would that none be idle. He has a mission for every one. Angels and archangels, cherubims and seraphims, patriarchs and prophets, apostles and reformers, and all the holy hosts of heaven, are his ministering spirits, frequently dispatched to minister unto the strangers and sojourners of earth. He sends forth these spirits to guide and guard his contrite children through the wilderness world to their promised place at his right hand.

"Oh, consoling doctrine! Angels are around us. The spirits of the departed good encamp about our pathway. Who knows how many times the sainted spirit of Paul has been our guardian-angel, protecting and defending us. Who can tell how often Marah's humble spirit has surrounded our thorny pathway, strewing it with heavenly flowers and the golden fruits of the tree of life, and perfuming the atmosphere we breathe with celestial fragrance.

"Who knows how frequently the sainted spirits of Benson and Watson and Clarke have hovered over our minds, directing them to the sound doctrines of the Gospel of Truth; and how often has the fervent spirit of Wesley inspired us with zeal, and the spirit of Luther with holy boldness to contend earnestly for the faith once delivered to the saints. And how often has Bunyan's blessed spirit lingered around our path, to lead us on to God. And who knows, brethren, but it is the inspiring spirit of the flaming Whitefield, or Hall, or Chalmers, that sometimes sets on fire our stammering tongues with heavenly eloquence."

Rev. H. Elkin's testimony:

"The Bible is full of these revelations, sights and manifestations, and if we believe the Bible, why is it not as easy to believe that spirits can communicate with men now as anciently? If spirits ever could appear unto men, they can to-day. If man ever had intercourse with spirits he may to-day; but no doubt certain physiological and psychial conditions are necessary, else all men could hold intercourse. Not all men anciently could commune with spirits. Not all men at the present time can commune with spirits. But the same faculty which aided them to see and commune with spirits anciently, can, if rightly developed, aid them to-day; and modern manifestations are as real as ancient ones.

"Spiritualism comes to the aid of the church and they reject it. It supplies to atheists and infidels the lacking evidence of immortality, and they receive it. It thus resembles Christianity in its first movements, which was rejected by professedly religious men. The doctrine of immortality must ultimately rest upon proof, or be rejected. And if all the phenomena attending the modern movement be accounted for on physiological grounds, without the intervention of spirits, ancient phenomena will have to pass the same ordeal and receive the same sentence. Whatever physiological law will account for involuntary polyglot speaking and writing modernly, will account for the speaking in unknown tongues anciently. Whatever physiological law will account for the modern prophecies, gifts of healing, revelations, poems, hymns and doctrines, will account for the ecstacies, prophecies, gifts of healing, &c., in ancient times. Whatever physiological law will account for the apparitions, or the seeing of spirits, lights, hearing of music, &c., modernly, will account for the visions and voices heard anciently. Whatever physiological law will account for the lifting and moving of tables, pianos, &c. by invisible power, modernly, will account for the unbarring of the doors of Paul's prison anciently. Whatever physiological law will account for John Hocknel's seeing Ann Lee's spirit when it left the body, wafted upward in a golden chariot drawn by white horses, and scores of similar cases, when spirits have been seen to leave their earthly bodies, wafted upward by a convoy of angels, modernly, will account for the translation of Enoch, and Elijah, and the ascension of Christ, anciently. Whatever physiological law will account for Henry Gordon's being carried through the air, by invisible power from a sofa, across the room, and put upon a bed, modernly, will account for Jesus' walking upon the sea, anciently."

Rev. J. H. Tuttle's testimony:

This Universalist clergyman, reviewing a camp-meeting discourse of the Rev. Mr. Mattison, says, inquiringly:

"How do you KNOW that the soul, when it leaves the body, departs far away? and does not return? Solomon says the · Spirit shall return unto God who gave it—IS GOD SO FAR AWAY? One would think so from the screaming effort your brethren on the camp-ground made to enable him to hear their prayers! In the Bible, we can point out numerous instances where spiritual beings talked and communed with mortals; where, too, they assumed a form and were visible. If spirits cannot return, how did Moses and Elijah appear to Peter, James and John on the Mount? If you reply that this, and other instances of the kind mentioned in the Bible, were special interpositions of Providence, exceptions to a general law, we ask again, How do you *know* this? An angel appeared to John the revelator. (See Rev. 22, 8th.) If you reply that this was not a spirit which had once been in the flesh, then we ask you to read the following and learn your mistake: 'And I John saw these things, and heard them; and when I had heard and seen, I fell down, to worship before the feet of the angel, which showed me these things. Then saith he unto me, see thou do it not: *for I am thy fellow servant, and of thy brethren the Prophets, and of them which keep the sayings of this book:*' Paul, in Heb. 1st, 14th, says: 'Are they not all, (i. e. angels,) ministering spirits, sent forth to minister unto them who shall be heirs of salvation?' From these, and other passages, it is plain that spirits *do* come and minister unto us; and therefore, we have little regard for the speculations of man to the contrary."

Rev. W. Ker's testimony:

The gentleman criticising this clergyman's recently published work, pens the following meaning paragraph:

"The writer of these pages has, for a length of time, bestowed great attention upon the subject, and is in a position to affirm with all confidence, from his own experience and repeated trials, that the alleged phenomena of Spiritualism are, by far the most part, the products neither of imposture nor delusion. They are true, and that to the fullest extent. Nay, the marvels which he himself has witnessed in the *private retirement* of his *own home*, with only a few select friends, and without having even so much as ever seen a public medium, are in many respects fully equal to any of the startling narratives which have appeared in print. He has found that there is an intelligence behind, or under, those varied manifestations, which can read our inmost thoughts; can in many cases truly predict coming events; can tell what may be at the moment passing in distant places; can answer mental questions; and which, in his experience, has not only replied correctly to those queries, but even to the secret thoughts and unspoken desires which gave rise to them."

WASHINGTON IRVING'S testimony:

"What could be more consoling than the idea, that the souls of those we once loved were permitted to return and watch over our welfare?—that affectionate and guardian spirits sat by our pillows when we slept, keeping a vigil over our most helpless hours?—that beauty and innocence which had languished into the tomb, yet smiled unseen around us, revealing themselves in those blessed dreams and visions wherein we live over again the hours of past endearments? A belief of this kind would, I think, be a new incentive to virtue, rendering us circumspect, even in our most secret moments, from the idea that those we once loved and honored were invisible witnesses of all our actions.

"I see nothing in it (Spiritualism) that is incompatible with the tender and merciful nature of our religion, or revolting to the wishes and affections of the heart.

* * * * * * *

"My mind has been crowded by fancies concerning these beings. Are there indeed such beings? Is this space between us and the Deity filled up by innumerable orders of spiritual beings, forming the same gradations between the human soul and divine perfection that we see prevailing from humanity down to the merest insect? It is a sublime and beautiful doctrine of the early fathers, that there are guardian angels appointed to watch over cities and nations, to take care of good men, and to guard and guide the steps of helpless infancy. Even the doctrine of departed spirits returning to visit the scenes and beings which were dear to them during the body's existence, though it has been debased by the absurd superstitions of the vulgar, in itself is awfully solemn and sublime."

CHARLOTTE BRONTÉ's testimony:

The biographer of this talented writer, Mrs. Gaskell, speaking of her mode of composition in "Jane Eyre," says:

"I remember, however, many little particulars, which Miss Brontë gave me, in answer to my inquiries respecting her mode of composition, &c. She said that it was not every day that she could write. Sometimes weeks, or even months, elapsed, before she felt that she had anything to add to that portion of her story, which was already written. Then, some morning she would waken up, and the progress of her tale lay clear and bright before her in distinct vision."

These extracts, selected almost at random, reveal her mediumship and Spiritualism:

"Presentiments are strange things! and so are sympathies; and so are signs. I never laughed at presentiments in my life; because *I have had strange ones of my own.* * * *

"Besides this earth, and besides the race of men, there is an invisible world and a kingdom of spirits: that world is around us, for it is everywhere; and those spirits watch us, for they are commissioned to guard us; and if we were dying under pain and shame, if scorn smote us on all sides, and hatred crushed us, angels see our tortures, recognize our innocence, (if innocent we be,) and God waits only the separation of spirit from flesh to crown us with a full reward. Why, then, should we ever sink overwhelmed with distress, when life is so soon over, and death is so certain an entrance to happiness—to glory?"

Her biographer makes the further record:

"Some one conversing with her once objected, in my presence, to that part of *Jane Eyre*, in which she hears Rochester's voice crying out to her in a great crisis of her life, he being many, many miles distant at the time. I do not know what incident was in Miss Brontë's recollection, when she replied, in a low voice, drawing in her breath, 'BUT IT IS A TRUE THING; IT REALLY HAPPENED.'"

HORACE GREELEY'S testimony:

Noting the "Recollections of a busy Life," this politician and conservative moralist, in reference to attending spiritual *seances* with N. P. Willis, M'lle Jenny Lind, and others honored in the literary and musical world, writes:

"I never saw a 'spirit hand,' though persons in whose veracity I have full confidence assure me that they have done so, But I have sat with three others around a small table, with every one of our eight hands lying plainly, palpably, on that table, and heard rapid writing with a pencil on paper, which, perfectly white, we had just previously placed under that table; and have, the next minute, picked up that paper with a sensible, straight-forward message of twenty to fifty words fairly written thereon. I do not say by whom, or by what said message was written; yet I am quite confident that none of the persons present, who were visible to mortal eyes, wrote it. * *

"The 'mediums' are often children of tender years, who had no such training, have no special dexterity, and some of whom are known to be awkward and clumsy in their movements. The jugglery hypothesis utterly fails to account for occurrences which I have personally witnessed, to say nothing of others.

"The failures of the 'mediums' were more convincing to my mind than their successes. A juggler can do nearly as well at one time as another; but I have known the most eminent 'mediums' spend a long evening in trying to evoke the 'spiritual phenomena,' without a gleam of success. I have known this to occur when they were particularly anxious—and for obviously good reasons—to astound and convince those who were present and expectant; yet not even the faintest 'rap' could they scare up. Had they been jugglers they could not have failed so utterly, ignominiously. * * * All that we have learned of them (the spirits) has added little or nothing to our knowledge, unless it be enabling us to answer with more confidence, that old, momentous question, If a man die, shall he live again? The only certain conclusion to which my mind has been led in the premises, is forcibly set forth by Shakespeare in the words of the Danish prince:

> 'There are more things in heaven and earth, Horatio,
> Than are dreamt of in your philosophy.'"

MARGARET FULLER'S testimony:

"As to the power of holding intercourse with spirits emancipated from our present sphere, we see no reason why it should not exist, and do some reason why it should rarely be developed, but none why it should not sometimes. These spirits are, we all believe, existent somehow; and there seems to be no good reason why a person in spiritual nearness to them, whom such intercourse cannot agitate or engross so that he cannot walk steadily in his present path, should not enjoy it when of use to him."

GERRITT SMITH'S testimony:

No mortal—brave, free and generous as this life-long reformer—could be a sectarist. Referring to his "Sermons and Speeches"—p. 39-40—we find this statement:

"We are charged with being Spiritualists. Some of us are, and some of us are not Spiritualists. But what if we all were—still might we not all be Christians? To be a Spiritualist—that is, to believe that spirits can communicate with us—is no proof that a man is, or is not, a Christian. His cordial reception, as evidenced in his life, of the great essential moral truths which come to him, whether in communications from spirits or from any other source—this, and this alone, proves that he is a Christian. If Spiritualism has been the occasion of harm to some, nevertheless there are others in whom it has wrought good. We have neighbors, whose religious life has been greatly improved by their interest in Spiritualism. * * * A favorite, and certainly a very winning doctrine of the Spiritualists, is that a wicked man attracts wicked spirits, and a good man good ones. *How protective, purifying, and every* way happy, must be its influence on him who truly believes it! How efficient the motive it furnishes to avoid a bad and pursue a good life! * * I must not fail to add, in this connection, that the Spiritualists I met in my tours through the State, last fall, were nearly all reformers. They had broken off from both political and ecclesiastical parties, and were earnestly and openly devoting themselves to the abolition of sectarianism, slavery, intemperance, and other wrongs. I have no doubt that, in proportion to their numbers, Spiritualists cast tenfold as many votes for the abolition and temperance ticket as did others. Surely such a fact is highly commendatory of the influence of Spiritualism.

Mrs. STANTON, of the *Revolution*, writing of a visit to Mrs. Gerritt Smith and her sanctuary sacred to angel converse, says:

"This is Ann Fitzhugh, the wife of Gerritt Smith, and this is the place where she communes with the invisible world, with the spirits of just men and women made perfect through suffering. Here she reads Davis and Harris, and discusses the doctrines of modern Spiritualism in which she is a firm believer."

WILLIAM LLOYD GARRISON's testimony:

"As the manifestations have spread from house to house, from city to city, from one part of the country to the other, across the Atlantic into Europe, till now the civilized world is compelled to acknowledge their reality, however diverse in accounting for them—as these manifestations continue to increase in variety and power, so that all suspicion of trick or imposture becomes simply absurd and preposterous—and as every attempt to find a solution for them in some physical theory relating to electricity, the odic force, clairvoyance, and the like, has thus far proved abortive—it becomes every intelligent mind to enter into an investigation of them with candor and fairness, as opportunity may offer, and to bear such testimony in regard to them as the facts may warrant, no matter what ridicule it may excite on the part of the uninformed or skeptical. As for ourselves, we have been in no haste to jump to a conclusion in regard to phenomena so universally diffused and of so extraordinary a character. For the last three years we have kept pace with nearly all that has been published on the subject; and we have witnessed, at various times, many surprising 'manifestations;' and our conviction is, that they cannot be accounted for on any other theory than that of spiritual agency."

REV. DR. G. TOWNSEND's testimony:

"So completely has the skeptical philosophy of the day pervaded society, that even among *professed Christians*, he would now be esteemed a visionary who should venture to declare his belief in this most favorite tenet of the ancient Church. The early fathers regarded the *ministry of angels* as a consoling and beautiful doctrine, and so much at that time was it held in veneration, that the founders of Christianity cautioned their early converts against permitting their reverence to degenerate into adoration. We now go to the opposite extreme, and seldom think of their existence; yet what is to be *found in this belief, even if the Scriptures had not revealed it, which is contrary to reason?*"

Rev. Dr. A. Barne's testimony:

"In this doctrine, the ministry of spirits, there is nothing absurd. It is no more impossible that angels should be employed to aid men, than that one man should aid another; certainly not as impossible as that the Son of God should come down not to be ministered unto, but to minister. Angelic ministration 'constitutes the beauty of the moral arrangements on earth.' '*Is there any impropriety in supposing that they do now what the Bible says they ever have done?*'"

The London *Times* reported the Bishop as using the following language, in a Sunday sermon, at Westminster Abbey:

"There were many important lessons to be gathered from Jacob's dream. The especial lesson taught was that God constantly controlled our thoughts, *and that we are constantly in connection with the world of spirits*, whilst we think we are far away amid earthly things He entreated those whose thoughts turned heavenward not to check them, for they might be certain that they are enlightened by the same glorious presences which cheered Jacob in the wilderness."

Victor Hugo's testimony:

The exiled, yet loved! Hugo's life has been a strange one—so gentle, so rich and radiant. All nature seems to have poured into him her tributary streams of imagery, sympathy, beauty and poetry. Thus organized, it is impossible for him to be other than a Spiritualist. In his "Toilers of the Sea," he writes:

"There is a time when the unknown reveals itself in a mysterious way to the spirit of man. A sudden rent in the veil of darkness will make manifest things hitherto unseen, and then close again upon the mysteries within. Such *visions* have occasionally the power to effect a transfiguration in those whom they visit. They convert a poor cameldriver into a Mahomet; a peasant girl tending her goats into a Joan of Arc. Solitude generates a certain amount of sublime exaltation. * * * A mysterious lucidity of mind results, which converts the student into a seer, and the poet into a prophet; herein we find a key to the mysteries of Horeb, and Elron, and Ombos; to the intoxication of Castalian laurels, the revelations of the mouth Busion. Hence, too, we have Peleia at Dodona; Phemonæ at Delphos; Trophonius in Zebadea; Ezekiel on the Chebar; and Jerome in the Thepais * * * Luther holding converse with devils in his garret at Wittenburgh; Pascal shutting out the view of the infernal regions with the screen of his cabinet; the African Obi conversing with the white-faced God, Bossum, are each and all the *same phenomena*, diversely interpreted by the minds in which they manifest themselves, according to their capacity and power. Luther and Pascal were grand, and are grand still."

In a funeral address delivered at the interment of Emily De Putren, this French author said most feelingly:

" Death is the greatest of liberties; it is also the furthest progress. Death is a higher step for all who have lived upon its height. Dazzling and holy every one receives his increase, everything is transfigured in the light and by the light. He who has been no more than virtuous on earth becomes beauteous; he who has only been beauteous becomes sublime, and he who has only been sublime becomes good. * * * The soul, the marvel of this great celestial departure which we *call* death, is here. Those who that depart still remain near us—they are in a world of light, but they as tender witnesses hover about our world of darkness. * * * The dead are invisible, but they are not absent."

WILLIAM HOWITT'S testimony:

This eminent man and distinguished author, so scholarly in attainment and affluent in classical allusion, continually testifies—a living apostle—to a present communion with the spirit-world. He wrote thus vigorously last season to the English *Dunfermline Press:*

* * * * "SIR—Who are the men who have in every country embraced Spiritualism? The rabble? the ignorant? the fanatic? By no means. But the most intelligent and able men of all classes. When such is the case, surely it becomes the 'majority of reflecting men,' to use the words of your editor, to reflect on these facts. Let numbers go for nothing; but, when the numbers add also first rate position, pre-eminent abilities, largest experience of men and their doings, weight of moral, religious, scientific, and political character, then the man who does not look into what these declare to be truth, is not a reflecting, but a very foolish and prejudiced man. Now, it is very remarkable that, when we proceed to enumerate the leading men who have embraced modern Spiritualism, we begin also to enumerate the pre-eminent intellects and characters of the age. In America you justly say that the shrewd and honest

Abraham Lincoln was a Spiritualist. He was a devoted one. So also were, and are, the Hon. Robert Dale Owen and Judge Edmonds; so was Professor Hare. You are right in all these particulars. In fact, almost every eminent man in the American Government is a Spiritualist. Garrison, whom the anti-Spiritualists were so lately and enthusiastically fêteing in England, for his zealous services in the extinction of negro slavery, is an avowed Spiritualist. Horace Greeley, the editor of the New York *Tribune*, a man whose masterly, political reasoning has done more than any man to direct the course of American politics, is a Spiritualist. Longfellow, the poet, now in England, and just treated with the highest honors by the University of Cambridge, and about to be fêted by the whole literary world of England, is, and has long and openly been, a Spiritualist. But I might run over the majority of the great names of America. Turn to France. The shrewd Emperor, the illustrious Victor Hugo, the sage and able statesman Guizot, one of the most powerful champions of Christianity, are Spiritualists. So is Garibaldi, in Italy. In England, you might name a very long and distinguished list of men and women, of all classes, Spiritualists. If you had the authority you might mention names which would startle no little those who affect to sneer at Spiritualism. It is confidently said that a Spiritualist sits on the throne of these realms, as we know that such do sit on those of the greatest nations of Europe. We know that the members of some of the chief ducal houses of Scotland, and of the noble houses of Ireland and England, are Spiritualists. Are all these people likely to plunge their heads and their reputations into an unpopular cause without first looking well into it? But then, say the opponents, the scientific don't affect it. They must greatly qualify this assertion, for many and eminent scientific men have had the sense and the courage to look into it, and have found it a great truth. The editor of the *Dunfermline Press* remarks on your observations regarding Robert Chambers, that *Chambers' Journal* of the 13th of May last, has a certain article not flattering to Spiritualism. True, but not the less is Robert Chambers an avowed *Spiritualist*, and boldly came forward on the Home and Lyon trial, to express his faith in Mr. Home. The editor might quote articles in the *Times*, the *Standard*, the *Star*, and the *Daily Telegraph*, against Spiritualism, yet it is a well-known fact that on all these journals some of their ablest writers are Spiritualists; but is it not always prudent for a man to say what he is. This is not an age in love with martyrdom.

* * * * *

" Numbers of scientific men have embraced Spiritualism. Dr. Hare, mentioned by you, was a great electrician, rated by the Americans little, if any. inferior to Faraday. He did exactly what people now want scientific men to do. He thought Spiritualism a humbug, and went regularly into an inquiry in order to expose it. But it did—as it has done in every case that I have heard of, where scientific men have gone candidly and fairly into the examination—after two years of testing and proving, convince him of its truth. Dr. Elliotson, a very scientific man, and for years violently opposed to Spiritualism, so soon as he was willing to inquire, became convinced, and now blesses God for the knowledge of it. Dr. Ashburner, his fellow editor of the *Zoist*, has also long been an avowed Spiritualist. Mr. Alfred Wallace, a scientific man and excellent naturalist, who was on the Amazon with Mr. Bates, has published his conviction of its truth. Sir Charles Wheatstone, some time ago, on seeing some remarkable phenomena in his own house, declared them real. And just now, on the Home and Lyon trial, the public have seen Mr. Varley, a man of first rate science, the electrician to the Electric and International and the Atlantic Telegraph Companies, come forward and make affidavit of his having investigated the facts of Spiritualism, and found them real. Now, after such cases, why this continual cry out for examination by scientific men? Scientific men of the first stamp *have* examined and reported that it is a great fact. Scientific men by the hundred and the thousand have done it, and yet the crowd go on crying for a scientific man. Why? Simply because it is much easier to open their mouths and bleat as sheep do in a flock than exert their minds and their senses. It is time that all this folly had an end. There are now more Spiritualists than would populate Scotland seven times over at its present scale of population; and surely the testimony of such a multitude, including statesmen, philosophers, historians, and scientific men, too, is as absolutely decisive as any mortal matter can be. And pray, my good friend, don't trouble yourself that your neighbors call you mad. You are mad in most excellent company. All the great men of all ages who have introduced or accepted new ideas were mad in the eyes of their cotemporaries. As I have said, Socrates and Christ and St. Paul were mad; Galileo was mad; De Caus was mad; Thomas Gray, who first advocated railways, was declared by the *Edinburgh Review* mad as a march hare. They are the illustrious tribe of madmen by whom the world is propelled, widened as by Columbus, and enlightened as by Bacon, Newton, Des Cartes, and the rest of them, who were all declared mad in their turn. And don't be anxious about Spiritualism. From the first moment of its appearance to this, it has moved on totally unconcerned and unharmed amidst every species of opposition, misrepresentation, lying, and obstruction, and yet has daily and hourly grown, and spread, and strengthened, as if no such evil influences were assailing it. Like the sun, it has traveled on its course unconscious of the clouds beneath it. Like the ocean, it has rolled in billows over the slimy creatures at its bottom, and dashed its majestic waves over every proud man who dared to tread within its limits. And whence comes this? Obviously, from the hand which is behind it—the hand of the Great Ruler of the Universe. For my part, having long perceived this great fact, I have ceased to care what people say or do against Spiritualism; to care who believes or does not believe; who comes into it or stays out; certain that it is as much a part of God's economy of the universe as the light of the sun, and will, therefore, go on and do its work."

Robert Bell's testimony:

This distinguished dramatist, novelist and Spiritualist, of England, wrote one of the most graphic notices ever penned upon the subject of spiritual phenomena, describing the incidents occurring in a *seance* of Mr. Home:

"This Mr. Thackeray, then editor of the *Cornhill Magazine*, ventured to publish in the eighth number of that journal (August, 1860), an article entitled *Stranger than Fiction*.

"Mr. Thackeray, in a note, spoke of the writer 'as a friend of twenty-five years standing, for whose good faith and honorable character he would vouch.' Thackeray was himself a believer in *Spiritualism*, and with *good reason*. He had, I am told, evidence of its reality in his own family which made belief irresistible. Mr. Bell's narrative created great commotion in the literary world.

"It is true that the writer was a man of good faith and honorable character, who simply described what he and several others who were present had *seen* in a lady's drawing-room. His assailants, however, knew that it was a 'great imposture.' Mr. Thackeray and Mr. Bell thereafter kept their knowledge of spiritual subjects to themselves; but Mr. Bell had become too firm a convert to be indifferent to the spread of the great truth, and it was he who quietly got together the committee which met in Mr. Boucicault's drawing-room to investigate the claims of the Davenports; and that committee, composed of twenty-four leading men in science and literature, it will be recollected, declared upon the suggestion of Lord Bury, that 'there was no trickery in any form, no confederates nor machinery, and certainly the phenomena which had taken place in their presence were not the product of legerdemain.'"—*London Spiritual Magazine.*

Rev. E. C. Towne's testimony:

Preaching the funeral sermon of the great and good John Pierpont, poet reformer, and Spiritualist, Mr. Towne said:

"Other men might speak of peace; he loved it not less than they, but so long as there was defiant wrong on every hand, he wished to be able to say, 'I have fought the good fight—I have kept the faith.' He can say this now, as few that lived with him can. The crown of the faithful confessor is his. Higher than poet, scholar, or orator, stands the honest man, with his valiant confession of holy truth. When his eloquence is forgotten, when his verses are no more read, the undefiled integrity of John Pierpont will shine like a star in the memory of men.

"Comparing our friend's position as a Spiritualist with that of a crowd of most able men throughout Christendom who adhere to Romish or Protestant orthodoxy, this confessor of faith, somewhat despised, stands high above them all. It is necessary here to put by the common and more imperfect manifestations of Spiritualism, and also to concede to a man of able mind a large liberty of judgment. The common utterances of any faith would discredit it with one who had no sympathy with it. If a man of mind and character adopts a faith which is supposed baseless, it is necessary to assume that there may be some mistake in this supposition. He would be singularly at fault who should think it necessary to explain in the way of apology Mr. Pierpont's adherence to Spiritualism. The fact does not at all abate from his credit, but on the contrary to his honor.

"It is too early to vindicate, without extended explanation, the providential significance of the movement known as Spiritualism. I am not myself competent to adequately criticise this movement. But I have no doubt whatever that it is to become the most living and most valuable development of modern Christianity. It is working up from the people, from those to whom no Church penetrated, and in the day of its full power it will be a force in religious progress such as no Church has been. It will bring to all the Churches new life, in faith, hope and love. The day will come when the devotion of our friend to this movement will mark him as one on whom a prophetic spirit rested. It was in the high courage of a noble confessor that he took this step, as all the other great steps of his life."

ABRAHAM LINCOLN, generally considered an infidel by evangelical denominations, was a member of no church, and made no profession of religion. His tendencies were all towards Spiritualism and German Rationalism, as his real heart-friends unhesitatingly testify. That he invited media into his presence, attended *seances,* and devoted not a little time to the investigation of Spiritualism, none of even ordinary information upon the subject deny. Judge Edmonds delivering an oration in Hope Chapel upon the life of the martyred President, spoke of his close sympathy with him in that divine philosophy—the ministry of spirits. Mr. Lincoln's frequent presentiments were to himself authoritative prophecies:

"In Judge Pierpont's address to the jury at the Surratt trial, he said he now came to a strange act in this dark drama—strange, though not new—so wonderful that it seems to come from beyond the veil that separates us from death. It is not new, but it is strange. All governments are of God, and for some wise purpose the Great Ruler of all, by presentiments, portents, bodings, and by dreams, sends some shadowy warning of a coming dawn when a great disaster is to befall a nation.

So was it in the days of Saul—when Cæsar was killed—when Brutus died at Phillippi—so was it when Christ was crucified—so was it when Harold fell at the battle of Hastings—so was it when the Czar was assassinated—so was it before the bloody death of Abraham Lincoln, President of the United States. In the life of Cæsar, by De Quincy, in the life of Pompey, by Plutarch, is given the portents that came to warn Pompey. Here it is we find how Cæsar was warned. We find it true in all cases, and never in the whole history of the world has there been a single instance when the assassins of the head of the movement have not been brought to punishment. The assassin of a ruler never has escaped, though he has taken 'the wings of the morning and fled to the uttermost parts of the earth.' On the morning of April 14th, Mr. Lincoln called his cabinet together. He had reason to be joyful, but he was anxious to hear from Sherman. Grant was here, and he said 'Sherman was all right;' but Mr. Lincoln feared, and related a dream which he had the night before—a dream which he had previous to Chancellorsville and Stone River, and whenever a disaster had happened. The members of the Cabinet who heard that relation will never forget it. A few hours afterward Sherman was not heard from—but the dream was fulfilled. A disaster had befallen the government, and Mr. Lincoln's spirit returned to the God who gave it."

Incontrovertible evidences in confirmation of spiritual presences in our midst to impress, inspire and communicate—testimonies from clerical and literary gentlemen—from poets, authors, priests, judges and honored senators—are nearly as numberless as stars in the firmament. Put the inquiry directly, however, to some of the clergymen—Do you believe in Spiritualism?—believe that departed spirits communicate with friends on earth?—and piously declaring against "physical manifestations" by way of sprinkling a few grains of incense upon the altar of a church-begging respectability, they will answer—"We believe in the *Bible* ministry of angels." Down on this slimy policy—this consummate cowardice! Stirringly writes the English poet, Gerald Massey:

> "Out of the light, ye Priests, nor fling
> Your dark, cold shadows on us longer!
> Aside! thou world-wide curse, call'd king!
> The people's step is quicker, stronger.
> There's a Divinity within
> That makes men *great*, whene'er they will it!

> God works with *all* who dare to win,
> And the time has come—to reveal it—
> The People's Advent's coming!"

Spiritualism has incarnated itself into our literature, art, music, philosophy and legislation; and it gathers strength and courtly symmetry as it sweeps through the land, destined to become the universal religion of the enlightened world.

> "They builded wiser than they knew;
> The conscious stone to beauty grew."

Lecture VIII.

Exegetical Spiritualism.

CHAPTER XXIV.

POETIC TESTIMONY.

"Sounding through the dreamy dimness
Where I faint and weary lay,
Spake a poet: 'I will lead thee
To the land of songs to-day.'"

Sweet and heavenly sings the Poet Laureate of England:

"How pure at heart and sound in head,
With what divine affections bold
Should be the man whose thought would hold
An hour's communion with the dead.

In vain shalt thou, or any, call
The spirits from their golden day,
Except, like them, thou too canst say
My spirit is at peace with all."

Exalted minds dwell in the element of the spiritual. The spiritual is the real. Poets are the soul's prophets. Unlike metaphysicians, they give us the product of their spiritual life and intuitive insight, and appeal to the consciousness and deep sympathies of humanity for the verification. Poets are divinity-appointed interpreters, employing the shadows of the outer world to reveal the substance of the world within. From the Vedic hymns of the Hindoos their glory gleams all along the pages of thought and culture. Brain, sunned from heaven, pen afire with truth, their lines ever tender, glow with the fadeless radiance of immortal love. Divest God of the attribute of love—disrobe literature of its ideal—strip poetry of its Spiritualism, and the residuum is shells—nothing but shells. The nature-poet of Galilee, Jesus, walked under Syrian skies a Spiritualist, guarded by a legion of angels.

Want of space warrants but a few quotations from the rich poesy fields of Spiritualism. Grand this apostrophe of Coleridge:

> "Contemplant Spirits! ye that hover o'er
> With untried gaze the immeasurable fount
> Ebullient with creative Deity!
> And ye of plastic power, that interfused
> Roll through the grosser and material mass
> In organizing surge! Holies of God!"

LONGFELLOW'S testimony:

> "Some men there are, I have known such, who think
> That the two worlds—the seen and the unseen,
> The world of matter and the world of spirit—
> Are like the hemispheres upon our maps,
> And touch each other only at a point.
> But these two worlds are not divided thus,
> Save for the purpose of common speech.
> They form one globe, in which the parted seas
> All flow together and are intermingled,
> While the great continents remain distinct."
>
> * * * * * * *
>
> "The spiritual world
> Lies all about us, and its avenues
> Are open to the unseen feet of phantoms
> That come and go, and we perceive them not
> Save by their influence, or when at times
> A most mysterious Providence permits them
> *To manifest themselves to mortal eyes.*"
>
> * * * * * *
>
> "A drowsiness is stealing over me
> Which is not sleep; for, though I close mine eyes,
> *I am awake, and in another world.*
> Dim faces of the dead and of the absent
> Come floating up before me."
>
> * * * * *
>
> "When the hours of day are numbered,
>   And the voices of the night

> Wake the better soul that slumber'd,
>   To a holy, calm delight;
> Ere the evening lamps are lighted,
>   And like phantoms grim and tall,
> Shadows from the fitful fire-light,
>   Dance upon the parlor wall—
>
> Then the forms of the departed
>   Enter at the open door;
> The beloved ones, the true hearted,
>   Come to visit me once more;
> And with them the Being Beauteous,
>   Who unto my youth was given
> More than all things else to love me,
>   And is now a saint in heaven.
>
> With a slow and noiseless footstep
>   Comes that messenger divine,
> Takes the vacant chair beside me,
>   Lays her gentle hand in mine,
> And she sits and gazes at me,
>   With those deep and tender eyes,
> Like the stars, so still and saint-like,
>   Looking downward from the skies."
>
> * * * * *
>
> — "As the moon from some dark gate or cloud
>   Throws o'er the sea a floating bridge of light
> Across whose trembling planks our mem'ries crowd
>   Into the realm of mystery and light—
>
> So from the *world of spirits* there descends
>   A bridge of light, connecting it with this,
> O'er whose unsteady floor, that sways and bends,
>   Wander our thoughts above the dark abyss."

PHŒBE CARY's testimony:

That influential weekly, the New York *Independent*, relating the spiritual experiences of Cowper, subjoins some lines from Miss Cary's pen, at once poetic and appropriate:

"The most important events of Cowper's latter years were *audibly announced* to him before *they occurred*. We find him writing of Mrs. Urwin's 'approaching death,' when her health, although feeble, was not such as to occasion alarm. His lucid intervals, and the return of his disorder, were announced to him in the same remarkable manner.

"The pillow by his tear-drops wet,
　　The stoniest couch that heard his cries,
Had near a golden ladder set
　　That touched the skies.

And at the morning on his bed,
　　And in sweet visions of the night,
Angels, descending, comforted
　　His soul with light.
　　* 　* 　* 　* 　* 　*
And, as the glory thus discerned
　　His heart desired, with strong desire;
By seraphs touched, his lips have burned
　　With sacred fire.

As ravens to Elijah bare,
　　At morn and eve, the promised bread;
So by the *spirits* of the air
　　His soul was fed."

Mrs. M. A. Livermore's testimony:

The glory of genuine poets trails all along the eras of art and culture. Their inspirations are comparable to dewdrops dripping from the leaves of the "Tree of Life." The gifted Mrs. Livermore, wife of Rev. D. P. Livermore, and assistant editor of the *New Covenant*, sings the principles of Spiritualism in these lines:

"List thee, father: 'twas last evening as I lay upon my bed,
Thinking of my sainted mother, whom they hid among the dead,
Till my tears bedewed the pillow, as though wet with dropping rain,
And I prayed aloud in anguish that she might come back again—

'Twas just then, as I lay weeping, that the beautiful angel came,
And her voice was fraught with music as she called me by my name;
And her robe seemed woven sunbeams, 'twas so soft and clear and bright,
And her fair, high brow was circled by a diadem of light."

Describing the brightness of the shining angel mother, the imprinted kiss and her own calm, happy sensations, she thus continues:

"And she spoke—I cannot tell thee all the blessed angel said
As she bent above my pillow and kept watch beside my bed;
But of heavenly things she told me—of a light and lovely land,
Where there dwelleth angel-children many a fair and spotless band.

And she said such flowers bloom there as we never see below,
Rosier than the hues of sunset, brighter than the rain's fair brow;
And such gushing strains of music swell along the fragrant air,
As will soothe the ransomed spirit when released from earthly care."

MILTON's testimony:

"Millions of spiritual beings walk the earth unseen,
Both when we wake and when we sleep."

TENNYSON's testimony:

In that spiritual biography, "*In Memoriam*," is mirrored the various changes of a poet's love and tenderness upon the earthly loss of a friend. Death he considers an upward flight—the leaving of a mortal garment, a ruined chrysalis, a shattered temple.

The poems of this gifted son of song present a type of Spiritualism, as beautiful as philosophical:

"God's finger touch'd him, and he slept!

The great Intelligences fair
    That range above our mortal state,
    In circle round the blessed gate,
Received and gave him welcome there;

And led him through the blissful climes,
    And show'd him in the fountain fresh
    All knowledge that the sons of flesh
Shall gather in the cycled times.

* * * * * *

    And he the much-beloved again,
    A lord of large experience, train
To riper growth the mind and will:

And what delights can equal those
    That stir the spirit's inner deeps,
    When one that loves but knows not, reaps
A truth from one that loves and knows?

If such a dreamy touch should fall,
    Oh, turn thee round, resolve the doubt,
    My guardian angel will speak out
In that high place, and tell thee all.

If any vision should reveal
    Thy likeness, I might count it vain
    As but the canker of the brain;
Yea, though it spake and made appeal

To chances where our lots were cast
    Together in the days behind,
    I might but say, I hear a wind
Of memory murmuring the past.

Yea, though it spake and bared to view
    A fact within the coming year;
    And though the months, revolving near,
Should prove the phantom-warning true,

They might not seem thy prophecies,
    But spiritual presentiments!

*   *   *   *   *   *   *

Descend, and touch, and enter; hear
    The wish too strong for words to name;
    That in this blindness of the frame
My ghost may feel that time is near.

Come—not in watches of the night,
    But where the sunbeam broodeth warm
    Come, beauteous in thine after form,
And like a finer light in light.

Be near us when we climb or fall:
    Ye watch, like God, the rolling hours
    With larger other eyes than ours,
To make allowance for us all.

*   *   *   *   *   *

    And all at once it seem'd at last
His living soul was flashed on mine,

And mine in his was wound, and whirl'd
    About empyreal heights of thought,
    And came on that which is, and caught
The deep pulsations of the world."

WHITTIER's testimony:

    "With silence only as their benediction
        God's angels come,
    Where, in the shadow of a great affliction,
        The soul sits dumb"

*   *   *   *   *

"Where cool and long the shadows grow,
　　I walk to meet the night that soon
Shall shape and shadow overflow;
　　I cannot feel that thou art far,
　　Since near at need the angels are;
And when the sunset gates unbar,
　　Shall I not see thee waiting stand,
　　And, white against the evening star,
The welcome of thy beckoning hand?"

　　　　*　　*　　*　　*　　*

"There are, who, like the seers of old
　　Can *see* the helpers, God has sent,
And how life's rugged mountain side
　　Is white with many an angel tent."

LOWELL's testimony:

"One day, as Ambrose was seeking the truth
In his lonely walk, he saw a youth
Resting himself in the shade of a tree;
It had never been given him to see
So *shining* a *face*, and the good man thought
'Twere a pity he should not believe as he ought.
　　*　　*　　*　　*　　*　　*
Now there bubbled beside them where they stood,
A fountain of waters sweet and good:
The youth to the streamlet's brink drew near,
Saying, 'Ambrose, thou maker of creeds, look here!'
Six vases of crystal then he took
And set them along the edge of the brook."

Discoursing of the figure of the vases, and the water assuming different forms, the poet continues—

"When Ambrose looked up, he stood all alone—
The youth, and the stream, and the vases were gone;
But he knew by a sense of humbled grace,
He had *talked* with an ANGEL, *face* to *face*,
And felt his heart change inwardly,
As he fell on his knees beneath a tree."

CHAPTER XXV.

EXISTENCE OF GOD.

"The people were astonished at his doctrine."—*Matthew.*

"My doctrine shall drop as the rain ;
My speech shall distil as the dew ;
As the small rain upon the tender herb,
And as the showers upon the grass."—*Jehokah.*

"As other men have creeds, so I have mine ;
I keep the holy faith in God, in man,
And in the angels ministrant between."—*Tilton.*

"I hold a faith more dear to me
Than earth's rich mines, or fame's proud treasure,—
* * * * * *
A faith that plucks from death its sting ;
Communes with angels every day,
Sees God, the good in everything,
Where *Truth Eternal* holds her sway."—*Powell.*

Reason pertains to God; reasonings, with their inductive and deductive methods, to progressive man. Moral freedom is liberty of action, achieved in accordance with the divine forces of our being and the laws of the Infinite. The sphere of freedom is the relative. It stands related to the absolute, something as the varying eddy to the deep, clear, rolling river, destined to sweep onward to the ocean.

Belief is an assent of the mind to certain propositions. It is based principally upon testimony. Sufficient evidences compel it; a lack of demonstration precludes any rational belief. The reasonableness of evidence is the *soul* of evidence, and the highest authority that any individual can possibly have, is the voiced command of God in his own soul.

Spiritualists have no authoritative book-oracles, nor petrified Apostles' creeds to be interpreted by cowled priests or mitered pontiffs. They bow to no kingly master — Chrishna, Jesus nor John. They trust in no external signs, ceremonies or institutional law-logic, scriptural or secular, for salvation. They rely upon no wafers, sacramental altars red with the crimsoned currents of slain goats, kids or Christs, to remove the legitimate consequences that result from infringements of natural law. They acknowledge no ecclesiastical authority, nor lean upon clergymen or popes, Romish or American, for their knowledge of those spiritual matters that relate to immortality and eternity.

In giving general doctrinal statements, then, we define not for such Spiritualists as the King of Bavaria or Napoleon of France, or Garabaldi of Italy; not for the Howitts and Wilkinsons of England; not for Senator Wade and other honorable members of Congress; not for Robert Dale Owen, Prof. Upham or Col. Higginson; not for numbers of the most celebrated judges, jurists, poets and writers of the age; not for Theodore Tilton's "*many* honored members in evangelical churches who are Spiritualists;" neither for Judge Edmond's estimated "eleven millions of believers" in this country; but for *ourself* only, with an eye to the usually accepted opinions of the main body, and are therefore alone responsible for these doctrines and definitions.

Ignoring the fetich gods of Africa—the repenting, jealous god of Judaism—the changing, angry-getting god of Catholicism, the partial, malicious god of Calvanism—the masculine, miracle-working god of Universalism—we find infinitely higher conceptions of Deity in the definitions of Plato, Proclus, Jesus, John, Mahomet, Parker and Davis:

"Of *good* there is one eternal, definite and universal Cause—the Infinite Soul."

"God is spirit, and spirit is causation underlying all things."

"God is a spirit, and they that worship him must worship him in spirit and in truth."

"God is love."

"There is one God."

"To God—our Father, and our Mother, too—will we ascribe all praise."

"The great positive mind of the universe—Father God and Mother Nature."

Those accepting the Spiritual Philosophy believe in the Divine Existence, the Infinite *Esse*, embodying and enzoning all principles of mind and properties of matter; all wisdom and love; life and motion; God manifest in everything from sands to solar systems. This is the spontaneous concession of the world's consciousness. Egypt's Osiris, India's Brahma, Judea's Jehovah, the Grecian's Jupiter, the Mussulman's Allah, the Platonist's All-Good, the Theist's Deity, the Christian's Our Father, the Northman's Odin, the Indian's Great Spirit, express more than glimmerings of universal beliefs in that God whose altars are mountains and oceans, and whose pulpits are fields, earths, orbs and circling systems, perfect in order, musical in their marches, and flaming with holiest praises.

Rejecting the human-shaped, prayer-idolized, personal God of evangelical theologians,—because personality logically implies locality, and whatever becomes localized in space is necessarily limited and imperfect—to *us*, God is the *Infinite Spirit;* Soul of all things; the incarnate Life-Principle of the universe; impersonal, incomprehensible, undefinable, and yet immanent in dewdrops that glitter and shells that shine —in stars that sail through silver seas, and angels that delight to do the immutable will. When we designate God as the Infinite spirit-presence and substance of universal Nature, from whose eternally-flowing life wondrous systems of worlds have been evolved, we mean to imply, in the affirmation, all divine principles, attributes, qualities and forces, positive and negative—*Spirit*, as spirit-substance, and *matter* as physical substance, or a solidified form of force, the former depending upon the latter, for its manifestations. The masculine alone cannot create. There was never a higher formation without the two forces—positive and negative.

The progress of matter is through motion, organization, segregation, accretion, disintegration, and re-combinations reaching continually towards higher structural formations. The law is from angles to circles. Progress, so far as legitimately referable to Spirit, relates to the manifestational rather than the absolute. God as the Infinite Soul or the Life-Principle is *not* progressive. Progress, as applicable to the consciousness and ratiocination of mortals, implies, not only a low condition of imperfection to progress from, but investigation, experiment, defeats and victories.

Matter, or physical substance, does not become essential spirit—does not, as certain French philosophers have taught, "go up into consciousness." If an aggregation of unthinking monads may become thought—if one particle of matter may become *spirit*—two, ten thousand, all worlds, all matter, may become pure spirit! a method comparable to feet "going up" into limbs—limbs into body—body into brain—and brain into divine mind! This reasoning, carried logically into the actual, would finally ultimate in the transfer of "Mother Nature" into "Father God;" or the consummation contemplated by the Brahminical doctrine of the absorption of individualities, and all else, into the "Oceanic vortex of absolute Spirit." The position is untenable, and destructive to conscious individuality. Spirit must eternally depend upon matter for manifestation and the molding of sensuous forms. Spirit and matter, as substances, are not utterly discreted, as Swedenborg taught; but blended and correlated as the spiritual and physical body—duality in unity. Reduced to the last metaphysical analysis, we have this problem for solution:

Given physical substance, spirit substance, and the Divine Energy, to account for the origin and destiny of cells, worlds, systems and conscious spirits.

The existence of God is not only the logic of intuition; but one of the primary recognitions of human consciousness, which consciousness, therefore, is absolutely *inseparable* from the Infinite Consciousness.

Napoleon, while upon the ocean, pointed starward, and said—" Talk, talk much as you please, gentlemen; but who —what made and governs those unnumbered worlds that pasture in the illimitable fields of heaven ? "

Only apprehending and comprehending that which is inferior to ourselves, we cannot comprehend God, nor can we *fully* fathom the measureless possibilities connected with the Divine within ourselves; much less can we reach the perfections of the Infinite through any lengthened series of finite progressions. Until parallel lines meet and circles are squared, never can any continuous number of multiplied finites amount to the sum of an infinite. All human progress is upon the finite plane. All true unfoldment is from the center outward. The ratio of the moral being mathematical, it is clear that man may progress endlessly without reaching God. Progress is not attributable of God, and no methodical thinker connects progression with the infinite energizing Life-Principle of the universe.

In conic sections there is what is termed the mathematical paradox, where the asymptote continually approaches the curve, but never meets it; otherwise expressed, we have the formula of two mathematical lines, eternally approaching and *never meeting;* so finite man may forever progress; eternally nearing the infinite fountain of causation without reaching God. If matter, as certain theorists have taught, becomes essential spirit, then progress is ultimately defeated, for man necessarily loses his individuality and consciousness by assimilation with and absorption into, the infinite ocean of Pure Spirit!

Demosthenes is represented to have said through a modern medium :

"Had you asked me concerning God, a thousand years ago, I could have told you all about him ; but now, after I have walked the highway of celestial worlds for more than two thousand years, I am so far lost and overpowered amid the splendors of Infinitude, I can say nothing. Height on height beyond the penetration of finite vision, I see the dim outlines of a deific universe; I feel the flood-tides of Divinity flowing down through all the avenues of my immortal being. I hear peal after peal of archangel eloquence ringing through the endless archways of the empyrean, evermore sounding into my ears the name of God, God, God! I am silent, dumb!"

Philo, asserted in the most positive manner the masculinity and femininity of God and the sexual order of creation. He repeatedly represented Wisdom as "spouse of God and *mother* of all things;" and he further says, "We may rightly call God the Father and Wisdom the Mother of the universe." Also according to Michelange Lanci, the Egyptian Hieroglyphs, interpreted in the light of Egyptian theosophy, taught that both the male and female principles inhered in Deity, *spirit* and *matter*, as father and mother. Indian Gymnosophists also admitted, in the most ancient periods, the duality of the Divine Existence. Abraham, a dissatisfied, ambitious Brahmin, inaugurated the worship of a unitive *masculine god*. Moses built upon the same rock; hence his masculine, blood-thirsty, retaliatory laws, founded upon "Thus saith the Lord." And the popular Pauline Christianity of the past eighteen centuries, is Judaism, only sparingly galvanized.

The paternity and maternity of the Divine Nature, the fraternity of human souls, originating from the same primal fountain, and the progressive evolutions of all the races, are truths that will bloom into wider acceptance as the ages ripen.

The manifestational order of the past demonstrates that God—the Divine Energy—*was*. The fixedness of law and the uniformity of Nature's processes, prove that God now *is*. Yea, " of him, and through him, and to him, are all things, to whom be the glory forever." Looking from the mount of vision, we behold Deity enthroned everywhere in majesty and splendor—a *holy presence*, which is the innermost light and life of all lives. Springing from the paternal and maternal Source, and divinely allied therewith, upon the loving bosom of God we recline and rest, with a trust so beautiful and a confidence so deep, that nothing can disturb the calm.

CHAPTER XXVI.

THE DIVINE IMAGE.

> "In me God dwelleth;
> I in Him and He in me!
> And my yearning soul he filleth,
> Here, and through eternity."

Divine and unitive in purpose are manhood and womanhood! In the "divine image made he *them*." The expression is oriental. Hillel and other scholarly Hebraists may have seen the substance under the symbol.

Man, the crown-flower of Nature's formative forces, stands erect a polished shaft upon the summit of earth's granitic-paved pyramid. In him are focalized the refined and sublimated ultimates pertaining to the whole. Stars may waltz and whirl through space; but they cannot think. Planets, to the music of immutable law, may polka across tesselated floors in the temple of the eternal; but they can neither reason nor love. Man and woman alone, essential equals of a perfect circle, walk forth in the divine image; but this image does not consist in physical formation, for God is not, as we have previously shown, a shaped personality outside the visible universe, rolling and guiding astral worlds mechanically as school-boys roll their hoops; but is *Infinite Spirit*, containing the elements of all forms, the principles of all forces, and the attributes of all intelligence, acting by unchanging methods for the highest good.

The divine image in which man is made consists in those original constituents and principles that constitute him an eternal individuality. At the inner basis he is essential *spirit*, clothed secondarily with a spiritual or soul body, and rimmed with a grosser physical organism. Trinal in constitution, with crowning brain-organs inviting angel guests, man is a perfect structure. The spiritual nature—" Keystone" to the moral arch—seals with eternity's seal both his divinity and immortality.

The basis of man's immortality is deific substance. As a conscious *spirit* in the innermost, he is incompounded and therefore indissoluble. Having in spirit neither a beginning nor ending, he is eternally past and eternally future—ever living in eternal life. Neither burial in the placenta walls of maternity, nor burial in the human organism, nor burial from sight, can effect the essential *real*.

The animal having only a portion of the primary elements of life, having a less number of brain-faculties, and unconscious of its relations to the original fountain of being, is comparably an imperfect structure. Logic cannot legitimately affirm of a part what it does of a whole; neither will philosophical minds, conversant with the results of analysis and critical exegesis, claim—for entities and individualities—destinies to which they never aspired. These statements admitted, animals, as such, are not immortal. There is, however, no annihilation; no absolute loss in the universe. When the grazing animal dies, earth crumbles to its native earth, and the spiritual substances, disintegrated, pass into the great vortex of spirit, to be elementarily re-incarnated for use in higher forms.

That human beings dwell in distant countries or islands, with no conceptions of God, or of worship germinal or expressed, is not merely doubted, but denied. If such people exist, not only their location, but their deplorable position, is susceptible of proof. When those Spanish conquerors reached Mexico and Peru, the historian, Prescott, says they found there an "abiding faith in God and immortality."

Roman Catholic Jesuits, fired with a missionary enthusiasm, visiting China, Thibet, and the distant islands of the ocean, found everywhere the religious idea firmly rooted. The North American Indians, when first discovered by European explorers, had their religious ideas of God, worship and heavenly hunting-grounds. Dr. Livingstone, the English traveler, penetrating into the interior of Africa, brought home this report: "There is no necessity for beginning to tell even the most degraded of these people of the existence of God, or of a future state, these facts being universally admitted. * * * *

On questioning intelligent men among the Bakwains as to their former knowledge of good and evil, of God, and of a future state, they have scouted the idea of their ever having been without a tolerably clear conception on all these subjects. They fully believe in the soul's continued existence apart from the body, and visit the graves of relatives with offerings."

Unfolding humanity in every country and condition—worshipful, aspirational and conscious of vast capabilities for progress—has within itself the prophecy of a future as endless as golden.

Admitting true the old legend of man's creation, or rather hurried improvisation from the "dust of the ground," and woman's from "Adam's rib," when in deep sleep, the position would afford no logical basis for the affirmation, that man was made in the "divine image." Philosophy, older than traditions, goes beneath symbols. Listen to its divine voice!

All known substances are composed of some sixty-five simples called *primaries*, because first found in the rocks. These rocks, from pulverization and the attritions of ages, result in soils. From these soils—spirit the motive force—vegetables are evolved, which still lift and more thoroughly refine the primates, aiding them to become sufficiently attenuated and potentialized to sustain animal organizations. Man's physical constitution is the grand reservoir of all the ultimates of rocks, soils, vegetables, forests, fruits and animals. He does not appropriate the primates as such. There's no affinity. These basic elements, taken up by the lower order of plants, and progressing upward through all the ascending grades, ultimate in man. As a physical being, then, he is related to all orders of existence below him, and, as a spiritual being, composed of original *spirit substances* and *principles*, he is connected not only with all the higher intelligences of the heavens, but with the Infinite himself, as a ray from a central sun, or stream proceeding from and sustained by an Infinite Fountain. A chemist, analyzing a drop of water from a thermal sulphur or sodium spring, will show by critical, chemical analysis that each drop not only partakes of, but contains, the identical elements and properties of the whole fountain. Well, man is the drop, and God the Eternal Fountain! And the divine chemistry of logical analysis— intuition, reason and science—demonstrates that every essence attribute and principle of God exists finitely in man, and thus is he truly made in the *divine image* — a perfect structure — a god "manifest in the flesh," imaging the eternal principles and properties of Father and Mother.

Chapter XXVII.

MORAL STATUS OF JESUS.

* * * * * Ecce Homo !
"But whom say ye that I am?"

The divine out-pushing impulse to ask, implies intelligence somewhere to answer every natural inquiry. Denying the existence of the Asian Nazarene, is simply assertive negation and valueless to the thinker, besides exhibiting little scholarly attainment, and less historic research. If poesy needed a Homer—Sculptor a Phidias—jurisprudence a Lycurgus—morals a Confucius—philosophy a Plato—and oratory a Demosthenes—the Israelitish nations, given to religious contemplation, required just such an intuitive, loving, self-sacrificing character, as Jesus of Nazareth—the central personage of the gospels. His advent, heralded by angels, his mission was one of mercy, and "Peace on earth, good will to men."

It is difficult to disconnect countries from nations and nations from their inspired leaders, who tower up, as lofty columns, the glory of future eras. Gœthe says:

"It is with nations as with families. When a family has lived a long time, it finally produces an individual who gathers up into himself the attributes of all his ancestors; rallies their scattered or half-developed qualities, and presents them incarnate in their full perfection. So the felicity of Providence will occasionally sum up in an individual the virtue of a nation."

The ascended John Pierpoint, reflecting upon oriental lands and their illumined seers, gives expression to his admiration for Syrian scenery in these rhythmic lines—"The airs of Palestine."

> ——"Let a lonelier, lovelier path be mine,
> Greece and her charms I'd leave for Palestine.
> These purer streams thro' happier valleys flow,
> And sweeter flowers on holier mountains blow.
> I should love to breathe where Gilead sheds her balm,
> I should love to walk on Jordan's banks of palm,
> I should love to rest my feet in Hermon's dews;
> I should love the promptings of Isaiah's muse;
> In Carmel's holy grots I'd court repose,
> And deck my mossy couch with Sharon's blooming rose."

Abraham went west and founded Israel; Cadmus went west and founded the second Thebes; Æneas went west and founded Rome; leaving Jerusalem, Jesus went west to seek and save "his people from their sins." It was not Israel, Judea, Carmel, nor Sharon, but representative men — the men of ideas gracing those ancient countries, who live in history so fadeless, and continue precious along the memories of many generations. Human nature in its best estate, rising above family, social relations, country, nation, is ever regardful of the great, and loyal to the good, whenever and wherever found.

Admitting the general tendency of the Asiatic mind to the dreamy exercise of a vivid imagination, coupled at times with exaggeration, still it is very clear to those read in the philosophy of history, that the more ancient parables and myths were not the empty fictions of an idle fancy; but rather the utterances of an immortal and ubiquitous intuition, whose substratum is truth.

To assume the absolute creation of such a personage from nonentity as Jesus of Nazareth, entitles the one thus affirming to the charity of imbecility. He was the child of the heavens, of prophecy, and of harmony. The wisdom of the angels threw him into an age of conservatism and stupid bigotry. The Mosaic law had degenerated into cold formalisms; brotherly kindness into caste and currency, and principle into policy. Judaism, large mingling with the currents of history, had become divided into two branches—Palestine and that called the "*dispersion.*" Such sectarists were they in their own Asian country, bordering Africa and Europe, that, pressing around one temple and one altar, the Rabbins cursed all Israelites who proved so recreant to the law of Moses, as to teach their children *Greek.*

The Sadducees were a sort of Epicureans; materialistic in tendency, denying the immortality of the soul and the existence of angels. The Pharisees were *Separatists*, clinging to the letter of the law, and the traditional injunctions of Jehovah. The Essenians were the Shakers of that period. Jesus was in full sympathy with them.

War, commerce, the Assyrian captivity and nomadic tendencies, had scattered many of the Israelites throughout the world. These spoke the Greek tongue. This language, derived largely from the Sanscrit, had become, what Latin was at a much later period, the court language and medium of communication among all the more enlightened nations. In those prominent eastern cities, especially Alexandria and Antioch, flourishing capitals of Egypt and Syria, these scattered Jews formed numerous societies, placing at the head some rich, influential families. Their Palestinean brothers called them *Hellenists.* They were not considered soundly Orthodox, even though they had succeeded in getting the Jewish Bible translated into Greek, under the Ptolemies.

At this initial point in the religious cycle of that era, we get a correct clue to those moral forces constituting the peculiarities of John — the disciple that "Jesus loved." Zebedee, his father, a wealthy Israelite, was a profound thinker of the school of Hillel, and exceedingly liberal in doctrinal tendencies. John, a natural genius, rich in the gift of a warm, sensitive love-nature, endowed with a fine delicate organization, highly mediumstic, a thorough-trained scholar for that age of the world, and wonderfully gifted with a capacity for acquiring a knowledge of the languages, was just adapted for the constant companionship of Jesus. Literally, John was a Hellenistic Jew, thoroughly initiated into the civilization, literature, and philosophy of the Greeks. This accounts for the continually cropping out of Pythagoric doctrines in his gospel. John, our patron saint, is, in many respects, the ideal man of the New Testament. Holy and heavenly was the perpetual friendship existing between Jesus, John, and his brother James. Superior scholarship, coupled with a sweet-tender heart-fellowship, entitled John to the privilege of ever accompanying Jesus as lingual interpreter and counselor, which enabled him more fully to comprehend the scope and moral grandeur of Jesus mediatorial work; for, medium-like, "he came not to do his own will, but the will of him that sent him."

Dying a martyred death, Jesus committed to the care of John, his sainted Mother. Love and tenderness grow from the same stem. Budding on earth they unfold and bloom forever in the heavens. Enwrapt and emblazoned in the glory of fraternal affection, Jesus and the disciple he "loved," now together, traverse the celestial heavens, doing the will of the Eternal, by teaching in supernal spheres, and inspiring God's dear humanity.

Though the Church-Fathers may have manipulated the primative manuscripts—gospels and epistles—one giving to the Nazarene a certain attitude; another some peculiar expression of form or forehead; and others still, crowning him with plumes originally worn by Chrishna, Confucius, Plato, and Hillel—our belief in Jesus remains unshaken. We believe in him, not as the Infinite God, not as a supernatural being, not as a miracle-begotten specialty to patch up an inefficient "plan of salvation" and ward off divine wrath; but as a *man*—a mortal brother of the immortal gods and goddesses, who temperamentally helped fashion him, that, inspired by them and a "legion of angels," he might aid in uplifting and molding the future ages. He called himself the "Son of man." The Apostle termed him "our elder brother." He ate, drank, slept, hungered, thirsted, and, weary from journeyings, rested by Samaria's well. He was tempted; endured pain; impetuously cursed a fig-tree; "learned obedience by the things he suffered;" was "made perfect" by draining bitter life-cups of experience, and finally, with soul aglow to the logic of love and intuition, and prayer-words of forgiveness dropping from fevered lips like gems from a crown, he died a martyr!

The German Zschokke says: "If Jesus were to come to-day among Christians, they would nail him to the cross, as did the Jews."

Appearing, as of old, in some of our commercial cities, he would not "go on 'Change at 12 o'clock;" would not visit an 8 o'clock prayer-meeting to make an oration to the Lord; would not swing a censer in a Catholic Cathedral, muttering Latin; would not swell in the Episcopal robes of Ritualism; would not conjure up a creedal interpretation, to a Universalist confession of faith; but, with a toleration wide as human wants, he would say as of old—"By this shall all men know that ye are my disciples, if ye have love one for another." Then, going about blessing children, seeking vagrants, eating with sinners to reform them, healing the sick and teaching by the wayside, till weary, he would retire for rest to some Shaker community, Essenian-like, where love was pure, free and fraternal. Sincerely do we believe in this Jesus of the gospels—the *man* that *was*—the Christ-*spirit*, that *is*.

No star continually courses the same orbit. No man bathes in the same stream twice. The Bryant of Thanatopsis is not the Bryant of to-day. Longfellow's "Psalm of Life" reveals less strength and culture than his "New England Tragedies." Individualities do not vary; but their expressions do. The Jesus who scourged the "money-changers," compared errorists to "swine"—to "thieves and robbers"—and threatened his conservative fellow-countrymen with the "damnation of hell," is not the gentle Jesus who breathed the beatitudes; who said to the woman, neither do I condemn thee, go and sin no more," and prayed upon Calvary, "Father, forgive them." When uttering these tender sentiments, feeling a quickening of the divine nature,— and literally "born again,"—born into the celestial degree of the Christ-life—coming into close magnetic fellowship and oneness with his "My Father" or Spirit guide, truthfully he said, "I and my Father are one"—that is, I and my controlling spirit intelligence are one in desire, purpose and the great work of human elevation. Referring to the Infinite Presence, he exclaimed: "God (*Theos*, not *Pater*) is a Spirit, and they that worship him, must worship him in spirit and in truth."

Harmonial, prayerful, divinely overshadowed, he grasped and appropriated the good, the pure, and the true, found in the older systems, and lived them in his daily life. Though walking with man, he talked with angels. He had bread to eat, that the Jewish external world "knew not of." He went forth, especially towards the close of his mission, a practical impersonation of the principles he taught— UNIVERSAL LOVE—UNIVERSAL PURITY—UNIVERSAL CHARITY. These being the three pillars in his soul-temple, his kingdom was not of this world. His heavens and hells were conditions higher or lower; his salvation self-growth. Caring little for outward purity, nothing for the cowardly "what will the people say," and desiring only to establish the inner reign of truth, love and self-denial, he left no writings, no creed, no code, no rule of life, no church organizations, no plan for State constitutions, no clerical investitures, no baptismal ceremonies, nor fossil forms of worship. His trust in God was absolutely sublime. His hopefulness of man was unbounded. His love for women was angelic; and purity, the only guarantee for seeing God.

Jesus, then, stands in relation to the past the best embodiment of Spiritualism, the richest Judean outgrowth of the spiritual idea, and looking lovingly down from the Summer Land, sweetly says, "Come up hither." By the exercise of sympathy and aspiration, by effort and consecration to the truth, by daily holy living, he came into the highest heavenly relations. Quickened, intensified from the celestial heavens, his original pre-existent home, (for before the mortal Abraham was, he had a "glory with the Father,") his inmost yielded an elemental flow of pure spiritual life. The finest textured type, the most harmonial brain organism perhaps of this planet, in that era, he virtually lived in two worlds—the Christ of tenderness and love, experiencing sweetest union with God. A thorough intuitionist by nature, he was a *practical* SPIRITUALIST in word and deed. He worshiped in spirit and in truth. His kingdom was a spiritual kingdom, with the center in humanity's great throbbing heart, and *Love* the king. His church was a spiritual church, built up in the souls of men and extensive as the races. His second coming was spiritual—coming, as a *spirit*, in spirit and power. That "second coming" in the "clouds of heaven," with holy angels and ministering spirits freighted with exalted truths and the enunciation of eternal principles, is in process now. Multitudes of the more mediumistic feel this divine down-flowing influx as the breath of an eternal spring.

Beautiful is this faith, this belief, in Jesus, the ascended Son of Nazereth. All those who thus believe—that is, come into harmonial relations with the Christ-principle, living the same time spiritual life that he lived—may do similar, and, perhaps, "greater works than these." True, he did not give all the "tests," all the signs, nor do all the works that Jewish skeptics, plodding in cold externalisms, expected. He did not transform "stones to bread," by command; did not "save himself by coming down from the cross." He *could* not thus save himself; for he could transcend no established law of Nature. At certain times, owing to "conditions," unbelief, lack of harmony or passivity, he could do comparatively nothing. Hence in Matthew (xiii: 58) we read, "Jesus did not many mighty works there, because of their unbelief." And the Evangelist Mark says distinctly, "*And he could there do no* MIGHTY *work,* * * * *and he marveled because of their unbelief.*" Before departing, however, for that many-mansioned house in the upper kingdoms of the Infinite, he assured his disciples in all ages—"These signs shall follow them that believe: In my name shall they cast out devils; they shall lay hands on the sick and they shall recover; and if they eat any deadly thing it shall not hurt them: Go ye therefore into all the world and preach the gospel to every creature"

While sincerely believing in Jesus, infinitely deeper is our trust in God, the incarnate life and light of eternity. In holiest fellowship with Jesus, angels and loved spirits in the bosom of the Infinite, then, is our rest forever.

Chapter XXVIII.

THE HOLY SPIRIT.

> "Lie open, Soul! lo, angels wait
> To enter thine abode!
> Messiahs linger at thy gate;
> Let in the truth of God."

The Spirit, the Paraklete, the Comforter, is frequently referred to in the gospels. In John's record we read: "But the Conforter, which is the Holy Ghost, whom the Father will send in my name, he shall teach you all things, and bring to your remembrance whatever I have said unto you."

Ghost is a most barbarous translation of the Greek, *pneuma*—the Latin, *spiritus*. *Pneuma*, naturally of the neuter gender, should have been translated—spirit. "He shall baptize you with the holy spirit (*en pneumati agio*) and with fire;" that is, shall surround and infill you with a most exalting and spiritualizing influence, the purifying effects of which are comparable to fire. As scripturally used, the phrase sometimes signifies influence or agency, and at other times individualized, immortalized spirits.

"The disciples * * * were terrified and affrighted, and supposed they had seen a *spirit*."

"Well spake the Holy Spirit by Esaias the prophet unto our fathers."

"Whatsoever shall be given unto you in that hour *that* speak ye; for it is *not* YE *that speak;* but the *Holy Spirit*."

"Then said Jesus to them again, peace be unto you. * * * And when he had said this, he breathed on them, and said, Receive ye the Holy Spirit."

"After they were come to Mysia, they assayed to go into Bithynia; but the *spirit* permitted them not."

"While Peter thought on the vision, the spirit said unto him, Behold, three men seek thee."

"Then the spirit said unto Philip, Go near and join thyself to this chariot."

"And when Paul laid his hands on them, the Holy Spirit came on them and they spake with tongues and prophesied."

"Then Peter and John * * * laid their hands on them, and they received the Holy Spirit."

These apostles, as well as Paul, being powerful developing mediums, so intensified the spiritual atmosphere, that, by laying their hands upon those susceptible persons, thus increasing the magnetic battery, they were surcharged and thrilled with the electric influx. So at the Pentecostal scene described in Acts, "when they were *all* with one accord in one place, suddenly there came a sound from heaven, as of a rushing mighty wind, and it filled all the house where they were sitting. And there appeared cloven tongues like as of fire. * * * And they were all filled with the Holy Spirit, and began to speak with other tongues, as the spirit gave them utterance."

The spiritual manifestations upon present pentecostal occasions, when our media are in harmony, corroborate those of the past; and the past, to historic inclined minds, confirm the present. Thus the old and the new, as witnesses in a common cause, clasp hands.

One of the demonstrations of spiritual clairvoyance, establishes the fact that each individual is enveloped in a spiritual sphere or emanation. This is often seen by the exceedingly sensitive, and sometimes absolutely felt even by those of dull and deadened sensibilities. The discovery of the spectrum analysis, which now occupies so important a position in the investigation of the physical sciences, is already helping Spiritualism, by demonstrating similar auroral spheres and emanations around physical substances. Spiritualists have taught this for years. It was a clairvoyant discovery. Science follows Spiritualism—a great way off.

Mr. Ruskin, writing a friend in the north of England, says:

"You most probably have heard of the marvelous power which chemical analysis has received in recent discoveries respecting the laws of light. My friend showed me the rainbow of the rose, and the rainbow of the violet, and the rainbow of the hyacinth, and the rainbow of the forest leaves being born, and the rainbow of forest leaves dying. And, last, he showed me the rainbow of blood. It was but the three-hundreth part of a grain, dissolved in a drop of water; and it cast its measured bars, for ever recognisable now to human sight, on the chord of the seven colors. And no drop of that red rain can now be shed, so small as that the stain of it cannot be known, and the voice of it heard out of the ground."

If there is a spheral emanation around the crystal, the plant, the rose, and a drop of blood, how natural that there should be electro-odylic spheres around physical and more etherealized spiritual bodies. The earthly is but the analogue of the spiritual.

Sensitive persons, with organisms like iodized plates, sympathetically sense these spheres. Clairvoyants see, and read therefrom the true character.

This age has few secrets. Seers see the innermost of things, and conscious souls know kindred souls. When rapt in this holy soul-blending sympathy, law is useless, labor a pleasure, and duty a word obsolete. Such souls converse across oceans when no sounds pass. Oblivious to the outward, to time and space, they live the inner life. Those positive impart to the negative—impart what they have, the quality of the efflux corresponding to the interior state. If good and pure-minded, they impart the "*Holy Spirit;*" that is, a most uplifting and spiritualizing influence. This rationally explains why Jesus "took little children in his arms and blessed them." The blessing did not consist in the uttered words, but in the celestializing influence of the divine magnetism he imparted.

It explains also why he "breathed upon his disciples," and how it was that he "felt virtue go out of him" when the negative woman touched the hem of his garment.

To feel the breath of the pure—to come into soul-fellowship with the true and noble, is equivalent to a baptism of the "Holy Spirit;" a crown of joy and a moral transfiguration.

CHAPTER XXIX.

BAPTISM.

> "Teach me Thy Truth to know,
> That this new light which now I see
> May both the work and workman show;
> Then by baptismal love, I'll climb to Thee."

In tropical countries of the East, ablutions were common. Since water was efficacious in removing effete substances from the body, it became, in time, an accepted emblem of moral purification. Immersion was doubtless the outward method. The Christian church has contended that Jesus dictated a fixed formula of baptism, when he charged the apostles to "Teach all nations, baptising them in the name of the Father, and of the Son, and of the Holy Ghost;" but the apostles themselves thought differently, and baptized simply in the name of Jesus. Spiritually interpreted and applied, the Father may signify the absolute religion; the Son, the religion of humanity; and the Holy Spirit the religion of the conscience and affectional nature, kindled into holy aspiration by the magnetisms of angels.

The Greek word *baptisma*, rendered baptism from the verb *baptizo*, implies rite or ceremony. Relative to this matter of baptism we accept the following Pauline teaching:

"One Lord, one faith, *one* baptism.
"One God and Father of all, who is above all, and through all, and in you all."—*Eph.* iv: 5–6.

This one *genuine* baptism, however, is not, never *was*, water baptism. All outward baptisms are Mosaic. After every act of defilement, the Israelites were commanded to bathe and wash themselves clean with water.

John the Baptist, seemingly disorderly and fanatical, a partially developed medium, controlled by Elias to cry in Judean forests, never embraced Christianity as taught by the Nazarene; neither did he spiritually enter in fulness the Messiah's " Kingdom of Heaven." Hence, said Jesus, " He that is *least* in the kingdom of heaven is greater than *he*." John came under the law dispensation. Immersion in some flowing stream was his manner of initiating converts. Many of his more aspirational disciples soon left him, however, and followed the man of Nazareth. John, by the aid of his mediumship, caught a glimpse of this superior teacher and testifier: "I indeed baptized you with water unto repentance; but he that cometh after me, whose shoes I am not worthy to bear, shall baptize you with the Holy Ghost and with fire." "But Jesus himself baptized *not*" with water.

His disciples in a few instances baptized by immersion; so, not having attained unto the higher and more spiritual, they also, in the earlier years of their mediumship, occasionally circumcised and practiced other Jewish ceremonies. None of them, save John the Evangelist, understood Jesus, or the import of his spiritual kingdom. They received the Nazarenean baptism of fire, of love, of consecration and holy spirit influx, only in part, and hence their doubts, fears and tergiversations. Honoring John the Baptist for his zeal, admiring his immersion rites because of their cleanly and invigorating effects in that dusty tropical country, and believing also in the necessity of present physical ablutions, we recommend *daily* baptisms in summer-time, and their frequency in winter.

There is, however, an efficacy of water baptism, under spiritual control, not yet understood or appreciated by the church—a baptism which the spirits were able to induce through John, in one of his exalted mediumistic states, whilst baptising Jesus in Jordan. It is well known that water can be magnetically spiritualized by repeatedly touching and agitating it; and that water being a conductor of electric action, can thus be made a powerful agency in curing diseases and spiritualizing body and mind. It is said that an angel, at certain times, stirred the pool of Bethesda, and whosoever *then* stepped into it, was healed of any disease. No doubt the angel magnetized it—charged it with spiritual vitality. A baptism therein was efficacious to the well and the sick. The water that closed over Jesus in baptism, was spiritualized by spirits through the mediumship of John, and therefore was more than a *sign* of purity. Spirits have been known of late to sprinkle a whole circle of inquirers with spiritualized water, the influence of which was most beneficent to harmonize the mediumistic conditions. We do not dissent from such uses of water, but recommend them. We, however, would have no special formality. Let all elements be spiritualized, even the food we eat, as an every-day eucharist. When we are intromitted into the *real* spiritual life, and all our being is thus harmonized to the music-ripples of "the water of life"—the divine inflowings—not only are we in person, but all things around us, are truly baptized and consecrated to holiness. There is, then, but one true Christ-baptism—the baptism of the "Holy Spirit,"—the descending, divine afflatus, lifting the soul into that sweeter, calmer fellowship of the more heavenly intelligences. In this divine baptism, whether from good men or women, or angels, we believe, and unto it continually seek.

CHAPTER XXX.

INSPIRATION.

"There is a spirit in man, and the inspiration of the Almighty giveth it understanding."

* * * * * "Inspiration clothes creation in a robe of day."

Inspiration—God's outflowing breath—is man's inbreathed life—a constant power. The universe is a many-toned harp with strings swept by the forces of the Infinite. Aspirations are the vibrations. All souls feel them. Uplifted, they measure the divine light poured into receptive spirits.

Spiritual illuminations,—exalted and original thoughts—evidently emanate from an over-arching world of subtile principles and invisible powers. The heavens vivify the earth.

"Every soul is aflame with God."

From the Latin, *inspiro*, comes the word *inspiration;* implying inbreathings, impregnating and opening the avenues of perception, the infusion of feeling, influence, ideas from the All-perfect and the angelic—from the immortalized, and from mortals—from forests, fields, flowers, and the beautiful in nature everywhere. As God is infinite, filling immensity, inspiration is necessarily universal and perpetual as the river of life. Not creating within us new faculties, it arouses and kindles into keener activities all the hidden forces of our conscious beings. Pertaining more to souls than books or traditionary legends, it oversweeps the epochs of all the dust-buried ages, and is even more perfect now than in those earlier mornings of time.

As water, crystal or clouded, assumes the shape of its vases, so inspiration is graded in quantity and quality. Who has not, in the higher moments of thought or aspiration, felt a sweet, hallowed inbreathing from the great pulsing soul of nature? Who has stood upon some emerald-carpeted mountains in the hush of evening, and not felt the soul expand as it caught glimpses of immortal truths? Who, walking among the lilies of the field, has not been startled and thrilled with the consciousness of those eternal principles that stream in liquid pearls through universal being?

Rising liking shafts of flame from the abysmal past, we see in Hesiod a poet, Jeremiah a weeper, Pythagoras a thinker, Socrates a philosopher, Pericles a constructor, Appeles an artist, Jesus a Spiritualist, John a mystic, Perasee a scientist, Mozart a musician, Bacon a logician, Ballou a theologian. These, with others, yielding to what Emerson facetiously terms "the broodings of the oversoul," enriching their receptive minds by the study of the spiritual laws that map the universe, and mentally appropriating the living sermons preached daily in the great Temple of Nature, with birds for singers and oceans for organs — *these*, we repeat, speaking words that burned, or breathing music that charmed—touched the world's heart and left their psychological imprint thereon—*touched* it, because divinely inspired.

Not the sacred books of India or China—not the many-versioned Bibles in use by Jews or Christians, are inspired; but rather the *truths* they mirror.

All *truth*, in Bibles or out of them—all truth, scientific philosophic or religious—is inspired. Truth is a unity. It is only in the seeming that truths clash. Octave notes do not jar. The unripe peaches of July do not contradict the blushing and mellowed ones of October. They only manifest the different stages consequent upon the law of growth. Our media, like the seers of Egypt, Greece and Rome,—like the prophets of Hebrew history, — like the apostles and martyrs of the better dispensations, are—in their hours of abstraction or loftiest contemplation, beautifully inspired. As one among these, "doomed to-day," we take a manly pride in acknowledging our helps from the world of spirits.

There is a general and a special inspiration—both natural. Our spirit guides inspire us, either by willing a magnetic current to touch, as with regenerating fire, our brain faculties; or—the conditions previously prepared—by approaching and breathing the inmost feelings of their own heaven-illumined souls into ours. God, being infinite and impartial, all humanities, constituting a fraternal unity in diversity of individualities, are inspired from higher or lower planes of conscious existence. The truer the aim, the diviner the purpose, sweeter the nature and holier the aspiration, the more exalting and ecstatic is the inspiration. Plato, mantled in Grecian grandeur, gathered his highest inspirations while summering upon the cloud-piercing Hymettus; Mahomet, from Arabian summits; Confucius, from Asian mountains, and Jesus, tearful and prayerful, from Kedron's valley, and Olive's mountain.

Inspiration comes obedient to the law of attraction; it is as natural to the mental affections as air to the lungs. It is ever ratioed to the plane of our moral status of character. Only the active, thinking, loving, aspiring mind is *truly* inspired. We get here what we seek. There are spiritual strata of inspiration as there are natural strata in our material atmospheres for each grade of sentient being. We may, therefore, be inspired in the department of passion, of reflection, of invention, of music, of poetry, of patriotism, of philanthropy, of the loves of childhood, of moral justice, of divine recognition, just as we adjust and habituate these functional organs and faculties. The lower the plane the grosser is the qualitative inspiration; the higher the plane the purer is the inspiration. Our status of love-life determines the degree of our heaven or spiritual sphere of use. If we would be ushered into holy light, the holiest purpose must animate the will to corresponding activities. Thus, and thus only, do we drink of the immortal fountains of undimmed and celestial goodness. Under such an inspiration, we are able to discover defects in our forces of character, creating a keen, sharp pain in a tender conscience that rouses up to focalize those dormant faculties to higher points of mind and heart, that then loom up in visions as an attainable glory. The holiest spirits have the deepest pain when any taint is found upon their inner life. When admitted to inspirations and consociations of such spirits, our unstrung or untouched chords of love are attuned to heavenly order, when our whole being is at length spiritually musicalized, heard and felt in raptured gratitude to the "white-vestured" come to lead us into their Edens of Innocence and Beauty.

Believing in inspiration, then, we would go up day by day on to the Mount of Transfiguration; would open the windows of our souls to the constant reception of higher truths; would be charitable to all fresh thoughts, from whatever source, to all newly conceived ideas, for they may have traveled as blessings down from sunnier zones. Behind even the faintest coruscation of some wierd, half-expressed truth, there may gleam a star silver-shrouded, or a celestial sun awaiting earthly recognition.

God is in the present. The books of inspiration are not closed and sealed. Ideas, principles, the laws of pure intelligence, require no crutches. Americans can stand erect without spinal stiffenings from Asian monuments. Prayer need not float to heaven on the breath of ancient memories; nor assume oriental attitudes to secure a hearing.

> "Where'er there's a life to be kindled by love,
>   Wherever a soul to inspire,
> Strike this key-note of God that trembles above,
>   Night's silver-tongued voices of fire."

Our granite-hills and highlands, are sacred as Israel's mountains; our rivers holy as the Jordans of Asia, and our forests beautiful as the olives and cedars that shaded Lebanon. God did not speak his first word to Moses in the Old Testament; nor pronounce his last to John on Patmos. The aspirations of true men cannot be held in slavish subjection to the letter of past revelations. Souls must have living bread. They must bathe in living streams, branching from the "River of Life." They must be free as God's winds—free as the loves of the angels.

Inspirations can never know a finality, being manifest in all forms of life; in the progressive movements of the ages; in religion, art and science; in the moral heroism of reformers; in the tender affections of woman; in the ministry of spirits; in the sincere devotions of the prayerful, and in the sweet trust of a pure and holy life.

Chapter XXXI.

BEAUTY OF FAITH.

> "The soul's vague longing—
> The aching void which nothing earthly fills—
> Oh, what desires upon my heart are thronging,
> As I look upward to the heavenly hills!"

The acceptance of the sciences is based more upon the investigations of others than personal research. Christendom, rejecting the inspirations and spiritual manifestations of the present, rests its bony head upon the old grayed monuments of antiquity, and strives to fill its leanness upon histories and doubtful facts connected with ancient Jewish feasts. It piously prefers dipping from the "Dead Sea," than drinking from America's gushing fountains. This is an abuse of faith. Spiritualists understand the import of these teachings—"Give us this day our daily bread"—"a well of water within you springing up into everlasting life"—"Lo! I am with you alway, even unto the end of the world!"

Faith is perpetual. When its "substance of things hoped for" is swallowed up in fruition, like the bud blossoming into the flower, it unfolds a yet higher life—*ever higher*—preluding immortal progress.

Faith often used in a subjective sense for personal belief, is elemental in the human soul, and may be defined an assent of the mind to propositions based upon the testimony of others, or an acceptance of such truths as seem legitimately deducible from the investigations of physical and moral science. Faith, differing essentially from mere belief, is graded upward from the more external to the divine, corresponding relationally to the outer and inner consciousness. The latter is closely allied to intuition. It is a glimmering from the star of destiny. Faith is essential to successful communication with ministering spirits. The adjustment of the spirit batteries, under this law, is most delicate and beautiful. The spirit has to employ our magnetic sphere—enters into *rapport* with us sympathetically—and if we are any ways deceptive and tricky, gloomy and unbelieving, our very mental and moral condition defeats the object; for then a pure and truthful spirit, who *would* communicate, finds it very difficult to reach our sphere, it being so magnetically repellant. *Honest* doubt does not imply *un*-faith; in fact, it *is* faith in embryo. The candid inquirer always gets light; for such a sphere attracts the angel who comes to bless "the poor in spirit." Faith, then, is rooted in innocency. "Thy *faith* hath made thee whole." How beautiful it is under the effulgence of this spiritual light! When our purpose is sincere, Faith-angels come, administering "good tidings of good" to those who "seek immortality—eternal life!"

Louis Napoleon landed upon the French coast with a few adherents, shouting—"Long live Napoleon." The thoughtless called him a madman; but to-day he guides the destinies of an empire. Garibaldi put his foot down firmly in Sicily, raised the cry of revolution, drove out a ruling tyrant, and offered a kingdom to Victor Emanuel—a kingdom that shall yet call Rome its capital, and send sunshine into every Italian heart. Joan D'Arc, fired with enthusiasm and inspired by avenging angels, led the French army against the English to victory—a sample of faith and will-force. Columbus, dreamy and visionary, conceived of continents and islands in the West. We see him drafting his course; now a weary pilgrim at the king's gate, and now at royal courts pleading for ships. At length, the wish attained, the sails are hoisted and the prows turned; he puts out into the great deep, under the loftiest inspiration of faith. The needle trembling, turned from its accustomed position; strange sea-birds whirled by; storms danced their demon-dances in the rigging; but a divine current, seemingly, swept them on, till a new world gladdened their vision. Such a *faith* is the fountain-head, the mighty, propelling force we see manifest in the field, the shop, the academy, the commercial mart, the studio of the artist, the observatory of the astronomer, and the literary altitudes attained in American and English universities.

Beautiful, truly, is a calm, abiding faith—faith in the measureless possibilities of humanity—faith in the governing guidance of the spiritual heavens—faith in the unchangeability of the divine laws, and faith in the ceaseless, outflowing love of the Infinite. This kind of faith has more to do with the moral nature than the intellect. Science, if touching the intellect only, is cold and chilling, though clear as crystal. And philosophy alone, without the warming religious influences of love and sympathy, faith and trust, is comparable to a glistening iceberg, hugging the human soul into a resurrectionless death.

How sweet and perfect the little child's faith in the parent; and how firm should be ours in the innate goodness of every human being! Under the ice the water runs; above the clouds the sun shines; upon the moldering piles of India and the marbled ruins of Greece, mosses are green; and wild vines, clinging, climb sunward. So, nestling under the roughest exterior, and growing out from every conscious soul, there is something fair and heavenly. Aye, an angel is hidden there, awaiting the better, higher conditions to produce the Eden-blooms of good works. In every fainting, struggling Magdalen are all the divine elements of a Virgin Mary; and in every denying, weeping Peter are all the soul-prophecies of angelic life—a structural pillar in the present to be hewn, polished and fitted into the living church of humanity.

Cherishing this deep faith in the divinity of humanity, in the good, the beautiful and the true, Spiritualists should cultivate the tenderest charities, encourage the widest sympathies, and, despising none, despairing of none, should strive everywhere to bring out and build up the pure and the holy.

> "Where'er we go in weal or woe, whatever fate befall,
> In sunny glade or forest shade, a *Heaven* is over *all*."

Thinkers, ignoring the forms of faith and theologic dogmas of churchmen, consider the *creeds* fashioned in the last century hardly fitted for spittoons in the present. Asserting a true manhood, they stamp them under their feet, and clasping the hands of the immortalized, walk up daily on to some mount of ascension, to commune with nature and talk with the gods. But *faith* in man and woman, in law and God, and faith in an endless progressive existence, involving its demonstration ever approximating the divine perfections, are necessities of the soul and beautiful as holy.

> "Thither our weak and weary steps are tending;—
> Loved angel friends! with each frail child abide!
> Guide us towards Home, where, all our wanderings ending,
> We shall see *ye*, and, 'shall be satisfied!'"—

Chapter XXXII.

REPENTANCE.

"Repent ye; for the kingdom of heaven is at hand."

"Oh, for those humble, contrite tears,
Which from repentance flow."

"How oft in still communion known,
Those spirits have been sent
To share the travail of the soul,
And show it what they meant."

Repentance implies genuine reformation. The Greek word is *Metanoia*, and literally denotes the soul's recollections of its own actions, in such a way, as to produce both sorrow and the purpose of amendment. The word occurs about sixty times in the New Testament.

John, the precursor of the Nazarenean Spiritualist, preaching in the mountains and wildernesses of Syria, under the psychologic control and inspiration of Esaias—*Isaiah*—cried, "*Repent ye;*" that is, reform, for the kingdom of heaven—a more spiritual dispensation—is ripening for acceptance, destined to kindle into a richer, rapturous glow our national life.

Repentance in no way indicates security from punishment; nor is it logically allied to any system that promises escape from the legitimate consequences attending the violations of natural law. Nature, though rigid, is a righteous master. Poised, she holds the golden scales of justice—obey and enjoy—transgress and suffer.

Vicarious atonements, cradled in ignorance, belong originally to the lower social strata of Egyptian life, Jewish ceremonies and Christian superstitions—all mere devices to evade just penalties. Pythagoras, Plato, Jesus, and other intuitive thinkers of the oldest ages, avoided introducing atoning substitutions into their religious instructions. Not from Jesus, but from the policy-inspired Pauline writings of the New Testament, do churchmen gather their dogmas of atonement and imputed righteousness.

The soul keenly alive to justice—a justice that would punish the *guilty* only—repudiates such popular church doctrines as these, expressed in verse:

> "Just as I am, without one plea,
> But that thy *blood* was shed for me.
> * * * * * *
> Just as I am and waiting not
> To rid my soul of one dark blot,
> To thee, whose blood can cleanse each spot,
> O Lamb of God, I come, I come!"

No crimson sacrifices of slain goats and kids, no sacred waters of Gunga, in India, no Grecian draughts of hemlock, nor streaming blood from Calvaries, can avail anything, even judicially, in saving from the consequences of those just penalties, threading Nature's laws, as cause and effect.

The inebriate's repentance does not save him from the past shame, debility, degradation and torment, resulting from years of physical transgression. The poisoned libations daily consumed, impregnating every bone, muscle, sinew, nerve, deadening the finer emotions and benumbing the mind, leave their stings and scars upon the vital organism; while memory—the "undying worm"—lives to torture the mental with humiliation and remorse. These cannot be forgiven in the sense of blotting them into a forgetless oblivion. The universe knows no loss. But repentance in the sense of reformation, lifting the drunkard from the condition and further practice of the habit, will, by destroying the cause, save him from further disciplinary punishment.

Effects, however, linger long after the operating causes have ceased to act, as rills continue to flow after the storm-clouds have settled away in the distance.

While accepting repentance upon a philosophical basis, Spiritualism has no forgiveness in the sense of negating justice—none in the sense of warding off just and deserved punishment. The original Greek word for forgiveness is *Aphiemi* in the verbal, and *Aphesis* in the substantive form, literally implying "putting or sending away, removal, or deliverance from." It is sometimes translated by the English words (Luke iv: 18), "deliverance" and "liberty"—thus: "to preach deliverance to the captives, and to set at liberty them that are bound." Punishment, repentance and forgiveness, are all clearly illustrated in the wanderings, sufferings and return to a father's embrace of the Prodigal Son.

Repentance, implying sorrow and reformation, Jesus taught that there was "joy in heaven over one sinner that repenteth." This work continues in the future life. The republic of the angels spans all worlds. According to the "Apostles' creed," Jesus, "crucified, dead and buried, *descended into hell*"—the invisible state—the under-world of departed spirits. Speaking of this descent into hell, the celebrated Dr. Campbell confesses that "Jesus' descriptions of the abodes of departed souls, were not drawn from the writings of the Old Testament, but have a remarkable affinity to the descriptions which the Grecian poets have given of them." Enriched by the scholarship and companionship of the evangelist John, and conversant with the Indian, Egyptian and Grecian philosophies, this would be perfectly natural in Jesus' parabolic descriptions of the future existence.

Admitting, as the "Apostles' creed" affirms—the descent into hell—what the purpose? That prominent disciple, Peter, answers: "Jesus put to death in the flesh, but quickened by the spirit by which he also went and preached unto the *spirits* in prison, which were sometimes disobedient * * * in the days of Noah. * * * For this cause also was the gospel preached to them that are *dead*, that they might be judged according to men in the flesh, but live according to God in the spirit."—(1 Peter iii: 18, and iv: 6.) Beautiful this mission of Jesus preaching to the "dead"—preaching the gospel to darkened "spirits in prison." The fact of such preaching implies that those listening, could, and would, be benefited and permanently reformed by practically actualizing the divine teachings. Jesus' sermon on the mount was not his last. Reformers continue their redemptive efforts in the world of spirits. This is natural. Teaching and being taught is to be the work of eternity. That "cloud of witnesses," summering in the magnetic strata that envelope the earth in concentric circles, thus testify.

Marked individualities, nationalities and conditions pertain to all lower realms of progressive life. "In my Father's house," said Jesus, "are *many mansions.*" There are palatial homes for the angelic, and prison-houses for "prisoners of hope." These prison-spheres are the temporary residences of ignorant and angular spirits. Their psychological control is not to be courted. It produces disorder. The Apostles had power to cast out, or dispossess such. By their "fruits ye shall know them." Their emanations, rising like vapory flames, correspond to their moral states. To angel eyes these aural clouds appear dull, hazy, dark. Light from the celestial heavens streams in divine radiance all through these aromal stratifications. The divine Presence—the heavenly arabula—is everywhere manifest. Love encircles all. God and heaven triumph. Preceded, therefore, by repentance and reconciliation, holiness and happiness will be the certain destiny of a universe of conscious and reasoning intelligences. All will find this heaven—this paradise of bliss—when they are spiritually imparadised in God.

CHAPTER XXXIII.

LAW OF JUDGMENT.

"Justice is a theorem; punishment is as exact as Euclid; crime has its angles of incidence, and its angles of reflection; and we men tremble when we perceive in the obscurity of human destiny the lines and figures of that enormous geometry which the dunce calls chance, and the thinking man Providence."

> "Richer for the storms and trials,
> Finer for the searching fire;
> Let each flame that scathes thy spirit
> Draw thee to the angels higher."

Egyptian Judges, occupying official seats of honor, wore, as insignia, breast-plates of judgment. Jewish high-priests, copying after Egypt, put on the breast-plates, ephod, robe and girdle, adding to the breast-plate of judgment the Urim and Thummim. Christianity, modified by Buddhism and Hellenism, is grafted upon Judaism; hence the phrases *judgment-seat* and *judgment*.

The literal import of the Greek term—*Krisis*—judgment, implies *rule, government*. As a scriptural doctrine, rightly interpreted, it has no reference to a "future *general* judgment" in the spirit world. These are among the biblical expressions:

"Sampson *judged* Israel twenty years."—1 *Sam.* viii.

"According to their ways and doings I *judged* them"—past time.—*Ez.* xxxvi.: 19.

"Verily he is a God that *judgeth* in the earth."—*Jer.* 9.

"I am the Lord which exerciseth loving kindness, *judgment*, and righteousness in the earth."—*Ps.* 96: 10–13.

"The Father judgeth no man; but hath committed all judgment to the Son."—*John* v.: 22.

"For *judgment* I am come into this world."—*John* ix.: 39.

"As I hear—(clairaudiantly)—I judge; and my judgment is just; because I seek not mine own will—(medium-like)—but the will of the Father."—*John* v.: 30.

Judgment and justice are requisites in all moral governments. Especially is this true during the growth of souls through experiences into high spiritual states of being. Divine penalties, as effects, are neither postponed, nor evaded by atonements.

When the immoral and oppressive Felix swayed a sceptre of power over a Judean province, the inspired Paul "reasoned with him of righteousness, temperance and judgment to come," till he trembled. It was not, however, suffering to be endured in an eternity to which he was hastening that caused the trembling, but rather of a judgment to *come*—to come to *him*, to *all*, as the natural consequences of plunging into false relations with divine laws. Man, a moral actor, is a subject of law, a responsible being, reaping anguish from vice, and enjoyment from virtue.

Originally the dogma of a future general judgment was an Egyptian myth. It has traveled down to us through a Judaized Christianity. Where volcanic fires concentrate, there they burst; where storms gather, there they spend their fury; where and what men sow, there and *that* they reap. Jesus said expressly, "*Now* is the judgment of this world." Whoever did a base deed, whoever defrauded his brother, and slept sweetly through the shades of night? Every man has a judgment-seat in his own soul. The recording angel is there also. Conscience is judge; reason is judge; truth is judge. Before this august tribunal mortals stand each day, each hour, approved or condemned.

Memory is the undying worm. Thoughts, affections, plans, accompany souls into the future world. Each there gravitates to his own plane. This life determines the commencement of the next stage of existence.

The divine law by which individuals are judged is not penned in Vedas or Upanishads, in Old or New Testaments, but, mapping the universe, is written in ineffaceble lines of light by the breath of the Eternal upon man's mental and moral constitution. The highest, the *only* supreme authority, is the voice of God in the soul. All are not equally amenable to even human laws. If anything has been demonstrated in mental science, it is that hereditary taint may so penetrate the substance of an individual's being, as to weaken his will-force and put his tendencies into the pathway of perverted relations toward that which tends to the highest good. The incompatibility of social relationships, ante-natal conditions, early education and physical comforts, exercise such an influence over individuals as in many respects to absolutely control their motives. Such are more the subjects of pity and compassion than objects of blame. Instead of penitentiaries, hospitals and houses of correction should be erected, and reform-schools opened for these unfortunates, with wise and loving teachers and pleasant surroundings. Said the gentle Jesus, "I come not to condemn, but save the world."

All being divine in the innermost, the lowest have a dim consciousness of the good, the just, the right. In the infinite administration, the scales of justice balance. Vice and emendatory penalties shoot up from the same soil. The thief sees, after a time, he has stolen from himself. The deceiver that he has deceived himself—not nature, angels, God. The slanderer discovers that his poisoned javelins all return to pierce his own heart. All learn that what they throw out returns with increase, and that it is impossible to hide away from one's conscious selfhood, or escape the legitimate result of voluntary acts. Feelings, thoughts, deeds are from the inner life, and, changing the relation of things, are, in one sense, eternal in their effect. Each sweet hope cherished is an immortal flower. Every ill-purpose conceived is a poisonous breath that lives to blight. Our thoughts, aims, plans are carved upon our spiritual natures. As the woven web here, so the garment over there. What responsibilities! Heaven help us to weave life's web well!

Rocks, trees, flowers, men have radiating emanations—atmospheres peculiarly their own. The nature of this electric sphere surrounding mortals corresponds to the soul's unfoldment. Jesus, ever seeing this magnetic effluence through his clairvoyance, "knew what was in man." This electric envelope around the gross and depraved is hazy and murky. Around the merely intellectual it appears clear, cold and positive, with bluish shadings. Around the genial, spiritual and harmonial, it is bright and silvery, mellowing into the golden. This idea is elaborated in the Scriptures with reference to spirit-clothing. Matthew writes, "The angel of the Lord descended from heaven, rolled back the stone from the door, * * * and his raiment was *white* as snow." Luke says, "They found the stone rolled away, * * * and two men stood by them in *shining garments.*" It is said that on the mount, "Jesus's face did shine as the sun, * * * and his raiment was white as the light." When Cornelius was praying, he says, "A man stood before him in bright clothing." The light that shone round about Paul was "above the brightness of the sun;" and John, entranced upon the Isle of Patmos, perceived that those who had "*overcome were clothed in white robes.*" Overcome what? Their perversions, passions and earthly appetites. As the flower imbibes the dew or sunlight, so, revealed before the heavens, are our spheres both seen and felt by ministering angels by whom we are thus weighed as in a balance and credited exactly for what we are worth in the "Book of Life"—even our own soul. Appropriately Paul affirmed, "The saints shall judge the world." The chancery angel—judgment and justice—is a daily attendant of each through the vicissitudes of our eternal pilgrimage. What an incentive to live a pure, divine life.

CHAPTER XXXIV.

EVIL SPIRITS.

> "What men call evil, only is
> The germinating seed,
> Fromwhence, by sure development,
> Shall spring good fruit indeed.
> And man all evil shall outgrow,
> In spite of doubts and fears;
> In faith and hope shall plume his wing,
> And soar to brighter spheres."

Illumined thinkers can never force themselves to believe that evil, *as an end*, essential and absolute, can exist under the moral government of an infinite God whose nature is goodness, whose essence is love. But, from the stand-point of observation, there are conditions and diverse actions, resultant of human conduct, designated by moral philosophers as evil. Comparison is elemental in human nature. Contrasts there must be. Can better terms be found to express certain qualities, certain properties and relations in the physical world, than straight lines and curves, heat and cold, light and darkness—better terms to express certain moral conditions in the conscious reasoning world than wisdom and folly, truth and error, good and evil? All these are relative in significance, of course, and consequently the more applicable to men and spirits, as finite existences.

All counsels, exhortations, commands—all rewards and punishments—all praise and reproof in learned bodies—all jurisprudence and orderly society, are based upon the ground that men are moral actors and capable of good and evil. The reason why moral precepts are addressed to men and women rather than to the lower orders of creation, is because they have a rational and spiritual nature; because they can understand moral obligation, and are conscious of a divine consciousness within them. Moral ability measures the extent of moral responsibility. According to the original gift, so is the expected measure of the talent.

That there are educated and ignorant, good and bad men on earth, are not debatable propositions. Death, being more chemical than psychical, a mere musical ripple upon the ocean of life, and neither a spasmodic educator or savior, there necessarily must be educated and uneducated, good and evil spirits, of higher or lower conditions in the summer and winter lands of the future, so constantly peopled from this earth. And yet, as on earth, they all constitute a banded brotherhood and sisterhood of interests, and are the subjects of eternal progression.

Prof. Wm. Denton, in a lecture delivered in Music Hall, Boston, entitled, "Spiritualism Superior to Christianity," said: "No wonder that those who believe in this Orthodox religion, believe also, that we shall be miraculously changed at death. But Spiritualism teaches us that spirits when they pass from the body to the future life, take with them everything which is necessary for their individuality. Take out of any one the good or bad tendencies that distinguish him, and he will become somebody else immediately."

Admitting an intercommunion between this and the spirit-world—a conscious presence of spiritual beings, and of minds influencing minds, as among the facts connected with the Spiritual Philosophy, it is as natural as evident that all classes of spirits may, under conditions adapted to their magnetic and spiritual states, impress, inspire, entrance, and at times partially, and then again completely, control mortals. The higher operating influences are usually denominated entrancements and inspirations; the lower, possessions and obsessions.

Threading the historic testimony of India, Egypt, China, Persia, Syria, Greece, Rome, the medieval ages, down to American Indians, we have the same chain of general statements—by willing or unwilling witnesses—of the existence and power of demoniacal spirits.

We have previously shown by valid authors that the term *demon* is used indiscriminately without reference to the moral status of the spirit. In further confirmation, as evidence in point, we subjoin the following:

Demon, in the Greek, is *daimon*, to *know*, *a god*, used like Theos and Thea of individual *gods* It is defined and used by scholars, lexicographers and classical writers thus:

Jones—*Demon*, "the spirit of a dead man."

Cudworth—*Demon*, "a spirit, either angel or fiend."

Grote, the celebrated Grecian historian, declares that "demons and gods were considered the same in Greece."

Lucianus, a Greek writer, born at Samosata, in Syria, used *demon* in the sense of "departed souls."

Archbishop Whateley says: "The heathen authors allude to possession by a demon (or by a god, for they employ the two words with little or no distinction) as a thing of no uncommon occurrence."

The Psalmist David speaks of the "operation of evil angels.'"

Plato, speaking of a certain class of demons, says:

"They are demons because prudent and learned. * * * Hence, poets say when a good man shall have reached his end, he receives a mighty destiny and honor, and becomes a demon according to the appellation of prudence."

Worcester, in his synonyms, says:

"Demon is sometimes used in a good sense; as, 'The demon of Socrates, or the demon of Tasso'—and then, to illustrate, quotes from that fine author, Addison: My good *demon*, who sat at my right hand during the course of this whole vision,' " &c.

That learned *savant*, Cardan, honored with the friendship of Gregory XIII, says:

"No man was ever great in any art or action, that did not have a demon to aid him."

RALPH WALDO EMERSON writes:

"Close, close above our heads
The potent plain of *demons* spreads;
Stands to each human soul his own,
For watch, and ward, and furtherance."

DR. LARDNER writes:

"The notion of demons, or the souls of the dead, having power over living men, was *universally* prevalent among the heathen of those times, and believed by many Christians.

"The demons of Paganism, Judaism and Christianity were spirits of dead men."

EURIPIDES, Hipp. v, 141) makes the chorus address Phedra:

"O young girl, a *god* (demon) possesses thee; it is either Pan, or Hecate, or the venerable Corybantes, or Cybele, that agitates thee."

DR. CAMPBELL says;

"All Pagan antiquity affirms that from Titan and Saturn, the poetic progeny of Cœlus and Terra, down to Æsculapius, Proteus, and Minos, all their *divinities* were *ghosts of dead men*, and were so regarded by the most erudite of the Pagans themselves."

BISHOP WHATELY ably argues for the "reality of demoniac possession," as related in the New Testament, against those rationalizing critics who would explain away the narratives and the language of Christ himself as simply an "accommodation" to a vulgar superstition. He shows that the belief in spiritual possession was held, not only by the Jews and primitive Christians, but generally by heathen antiquity; that "the heathen authors allude to possession by a *demon* (or by a *god*, for they used the two words with little or no distinction), as a thing of no uncommon occurrence." He tells us that they represent the priests and priestesses of their celebrated oracles as possessed of a spirit of divination similar to that of the damsel of Philippi mentioned in the Acts of the Apostles. He considers that the agency attributed to *demons* in the New Testament, " was *not* a mere fanciful description in figurative language of natural diseases, but literally and undoubtedly a fact."

Certain churchites consider all demons " evil spirits"—that is, irredeemable, fallen angels. On the other hand, a few German Rationalists and many Universalists, theorizing outside of facts, and recently well established principles of psychological science, regard " demons," *all* the spiritual beings of the spirit-world, as perfect and holy. The truth lies between these extremes. Demons are simply the immortalized men of the other life — *spirits* occupying various planes or mansions in that " house not made with hands"—the temple of the Eternal.

The Vedas, Puranas and Upanishads, abound in references to the *Devatas* and *Soors*—good angels and subordinate celestial beings; and to the *Dews, Asoors* and *Danoos* — evil spirits, and the method of destroying their influences. Upham says this " doctrine of demons, in full force to-day in the island of Ceylon, is older than Buddhism. Gotama found it when he there made his appearance, 540 B. C. (Ast. Res. viii, 531.)

The Chaldean philosophy, with whom at Babylon the Jews had so much to do, contains an elaborately constructed system relative to the obsessional powers of demons. Speaking of the devices they employ to carry out their arts and selfish schemes, Psallus, quoting from Marcus, of Mesopotamia, says:

"They effect these things not as having dominion over us, and carrying us as their slaves withersoever they please, but by *suggestion;* for applying themselves to the spirit which is within us, they themselves being spirits also, they instil discourses of affections and pleasures, not by voice verberating the air,. but by whisper insinuating their discourse. * * * * * * *

If the insinuating demon be one of the subterraneous kind, he distorteth the possessed person, and speaking by him, maketh use of his lingual organs to convey his ideas. * * * Others stop the voice, and make the possessed person in all respects like one that *is dead*."

No one can fail to see the resemblance between these paragraphs and statements, and certain disorderly " spirit manifestations" of the New Testament. Take an instance from the gospels :

"And one of the multitude said: Master, I have brought unto thee my son, which hath a *dumb spirit* ; and wheresoever he taketh him he teareth him, and he foameth and gnasheth with his teeth, and pineth away. * * * And the spirit cried and rent him sore and came out of him; and he was as one dead; insomuch that many said, He is dead."

The learned Marcus, writing of another kind of demon—undeveloped spirit—says :

"And because it is irrational, void of all intellectual contemplation, and is guided by irrational phantasy, it stands not in awe of menaces, and for that reason most persons aptly call it *dumb and deaf*, nor can they who are possessed with it by any other means be freed from it, but by the divine favor obtained by fasting and prayer."

See a similar account in the ninth chapter of Mark, where a Jew brought his son to Jesus, possessed with a dumb spirit:

And Jesus asked his father, How long is it since this came unto him? And he said, Of a child. * * * If thou canst do anything, have compassion on us and help us.

Jesus said unto him, If thou canst believe; *all* things are possible to him that believeth.

And straightway the father of the child cried out and said with tears, Lord, I believe; help thou mine unbelief.

When Jesus saw the people come running together, he rebuked the foul spirit, saying unto him, Thou deaf and dumb spirit, I charge thee come out of him and enter no more into him. And the spirit cried and rent him sore and came out of him, and he was as one dead.

But Jesus took him by the hand and lifted him up, and he arose.

Then Jesus said to the disciples, This kind can come forth by nothing but by prayer and fasting."

Aware that these demoniacal possessions of the New Testament have been the subject of much discussion for centuries by the learned, we present certain logical facts for candid consideration. The Christian Fathers, several Neo-Platonic writers of eminence, and the most distinguished biblical commentators, with great unanimity agree that these obsessions literally occurred. The position of "Rationalists" and "Universalists" that these demons were nothing more than lunacy, epilepsy and sundry diseases, must seem to every sound thinker exceedingly weak and illogical.

I. The demoniacs of the gospel records and cotemporary literature are represented as differing widely from more insane and epileptic individuals. In Matt. iv : 24, the Greek terms show this contrast in a marked manner. See also Luke iv : 33–36. And verse 41, as compared with the 40th, presents the contrast still more direct. Dr. Clarke, commenting upon the 24th verse of the 4th of Matt., says, "Possessed with devils—*demoniacs*. Persons possessed by evil spirits. This is certainly the plain, obvious meaning of *demoniac* in the Gospels." (Com., Vol. V, p. 62.)

II. If *demons* were simply natural, physical diseases, was it not a matter of the highest importance that Jesus should have undeceived his cotemporaries, Jews and Greeks, upon this vital point, thus correcting the erroneous and pernicious philosophy of the age? But he did not in a single instance. To say, as some have, he accommodated himself to the prevailing notions of the times, is simply to say, in the language of another, "He who came to bear witness to the truth, accommodated himself to a *lie*." Suppose we were to substitute diseases for *demons*, in the scriptural accounts. Take, as an illustration, Mark xvi : 9, reading, "Now when Jesus was risen, * * * he appeared first to Mary Magdalen, out of whom he had cast seven devils"—*daimonia*, demons. Who, with any scholarly reputation at stake, would assume the responsibility of giving us such a rendering and exegesis as the following : "Out of whom he had cast seven devils"— that is, seven diseases, lunacy lumbago, dyspepsia, rheumatism, colic, pneumonia and the measles!

III. These obsessing *demons* could not have been diseases and lunatics alone, because they conversed intelligently with

Jesus, uttering propositions undeniably correct, and such as were happily adapted to the occasion. On the other hand, Jesus addressed these *demons*—spirits—as thinking, conscious individualities, and commanded them, as beings distinct from the obsessed or psychologized parties, to leave. The Rev. Dr. Wolff, who labored so long as a missionary in Asia, informs us, in his "Life and Travels," that obsession is common to this day in the East.

In the writings of the early Church Fathers,—Ignatius, Clemens, Origen, Basil, Gregory of Nyssa, Chrysostom, Ambrose, Augustine, &c.,—are frequent references to demoniacal obsessions.

Judge Edmonds in his "Spiritualism as Demonstrated from Ancient and Modern History," says: Jesus of Nazareth, the founder of the Christian religion, found this belief in devils (*demons*) fast rooted in the Jewish faith at his advent to earth! It had not its origin with him. He found it there, and recognized it as a *truth*."

Porphyry, dwelling largely "upon the folly of invoking the gods in making bargains, marriages and such like trifles," strenuously condemned the lower phases of soothsaying and divination, as tending to obsession. Jamblichus, the Cœlo-Syrian who passed to spirit-life in the reign of Constantine the Great, wrote largely of the power of demons to influence and obsess mortals. *

In Copeland's Medical Dictionary it is stated that Phœnecians and Chaldees considered insanity a species of "obsession produced by demons or evil spirits."

It will be remembered that the famous physicist, and English physician, Dr. Grath Wilkinson, published an able pamphlet a few years since upon this subject, asking such of the medical fraternity especially as were connected with

---

* A. E. Carpenter, the energetic agent of the Massachusetts State Missionary Society, of Spiritualists, and gifted with a clear discrimination, published an able paper based upon facts, (in the *Banner of Light*, July 25, 1868,) relating to obsessions and remarkable spiritual manifestations.

Lunatic Asylums to recognize in Spiritualism—in magnetism and spiritualistic treatment—the surest remedies for restoring the insane and the obsessed, (so-called insane) to sanity and a healthy, organic balance.

Strauss, the celebrated German writer, in one of his friendly papers, when making the *amende honorable* to Kerner for his severe criticism upon the "Seeress of Prevorst," gives the following agreeable description of life beneath Kerner's roof:

"A more beautiful or refined hospitality it would be difficult to encounter in any dwelling. Amongst the numerous strangers who each year visit Kerner's home, there is not one whose peculiarities are not recognized and to whom especial attention is not paid. * * * No wonder is it that here persons tormented by *evil spirits* seek for aid and healing! The good spirits must infallibly drive away the *evil demons*. An Angel of Peace appears to brood over this household. A sense of order, of quiet gayety and benevolence, is seen to beam from all countenances, is felt in all that is beheld and heard."

Why are evil—undeveloped spirits—allowed to return? Why does God unbar the gate immortal to all conditions of spirit life for every quality of control, knowing that mischief will be wrought and misery produced? As well ask, why did God constitute man a moral actor? Why is suffering permitted in this world? Why does might prevail over right? Why is confidence betrayed, virtue outraged, the honest robbed, and peace-men murdered? We must accept facts as they are, and build thereon true philosophies. What if through such hells humanity must necessarily pass to heaven, shall we therefore complain of the divinity that educes order from discord? The rainbow from the cloud, the lily from the mud, the crystal spring from the sand, the sweet summer from the frozen winter, the immortal from the mortal, life from seeming death—is not this development? "It must needs be that offences come." Nothing so sanctifies the soul as moral victory over temptations; must not therefore temptations be, as all pictures have shadings for expressive sympathy? The right is not in the wrong;

but the triumph over wrong. Virtue is not vice, but the destruction of vice by the supremacy of virtue. To drive away darkness from a room, introduce light. Good is primal, eternal—evil is incidental. All endings are like beginnings. In spite of evil God governs.

Like attracts like. Every door must have a hinge to swing upon. No evil spirit can approach us unless—morally weak—we possess a magnet within, attracting corresponding influences. This, so painful to endure, is the lesson of our frailty, teaching the moral necessity of fostering better conditions for more heavenly relations.

Sensitiveness to psychological influx, susceptibility to mediumistic control, implies higher and lower use, and abuse. Will not the tender flower be touched by the frost as well as by the sunbeam? The greater the capacity to rise involves a similar capacity to fall. The charm of a darkened demon is as potent as an angel's, where a point of ingress is possible. Then, according to the apostolic injunction of John, trust not—"believe not every spirit, but *try* the spirits!"

If spirits uncultured and evil, impress, and, at times, completely obsess mortals, is not the practical of phenomenal Spiritualism dangerous? Yes, dangerous as the sunshine, that, falling alike on flowers and thorns, the just and the unjust, produces an occasional sun-stroke; dangerous as the spring rains that, sweeping away old rickety bridges, carries rich alluvial to the valley below; dangerous as steamers, that now and then send bodies down to find graves under green sea-weeds, whilst on their beneficent missions of international commerce; dangerous as mining, railroading, telegraphing, which develop the hidden wealth of a nation. Shall we therefore dispense with them? Shall none pursue geological pursuits because Hugh Miller committed suicide? Briars abound where berries grow. It is one of the offices of guardian angels to protect their mediums from the inharmonious magnetisms of unwise, perverse spirits, and the psychological attractions of depraved mortals.

Obsessions being adverse, inauspicious, psychological influences, cast upon the organism—being the thoughts and feelings of individuals controlled by such spirits as are necessitated in accordance with the immutable laws of compensation to range for a season the lower plains of life—the preventive lies in good health, good nature and a good life; in the cultivation of broad, loving, aspirational aims—a firmness of moral principle—a determined purpose to do, dare, live the right—a calm trust in the overshadowing presence of the Infinite, and the holy watch-care of those beautiful angels that delight to do the will of heaven. Ill-health, nervous affections, dejection, despair, suspicion, jealousies, expose the subject to obsessions, or they offer suitable conditions for demons inclined to fun, mischief or base schemings, to carry out their selfish plans. Truth attracts the true, wisdom the wise, love the lovely, charity the charitable, and purity the pure of all worlds.

Kindness and firmness, aspiration and self-reliance,— pleasant, physical, social and mental surroundings, with gentle, harmonizing, magnetic influences from circles of spirit-electricians through noble, pure-minded media—these are the remedies. Speak to the obsessing powers as men, brothers, friends—reason with them as members of a common Father's family, and, at the same time, demagnetizing the subject, bring a healthier, purer magnetism, and calmer, higher and more elevating influences to the patient's relief. Jesus' wonderful power consisted in this: He was the child of love—sweet in his nature—harmonial in organization—intuitive and inspirational—consecrated and attended by a "legion of angels"; all of which peculiarly fitted him to "cast out demons"—that is, to dissever by will-power, voice and touch, aided by his angels, the magnetic relations woven by low spirits around the unfortunate media of his time. He "cast seven demons" out of Mary Magdalen— that is, he cut the electric chains, or demagnetizing, dissipated the aural emanations thrown about this woman, thus destroying the sympathetic relations and psychological influences thrust upon and into the very tissues of her being by those seven *demons*—spirits.

Those who lack in organic balance and symmetry of mental expression, being negative, and hence sensitive and psychologically mediumistic, are the more often subjects of disorderly control, during the changes incident to development. Such excite our sympathy. We would brush away every tear—relieve them of every thorn-thrust; but in no possible way would we convey the *thought* of their non-responsibility. All mortals, as conscious reasoning beings, are the subjects of individual responsibility. Of those most gifted, the more is required. It is enough to make good men sad and angels weep to see the efforts in given directions, to fasten *all* the shortcomings of media upon the spirits; thus virtually making the spirit-world a scape-goat for all the ills of this! Influence is not absolute control.

Socrates and Jesus put forth every possible power to perfect themselves in the highest knowledge and freshest mental philosophy of their time. The millions of American Spiritualists, when more critically studying the principles of life, the necessity of temperamental adaptation, the potency of psychologic force, the attractive and repellant relations of mind to mind, (whether in or out of human bodies), and the special conditions as well as the general laws connected with and governing mediumship, will see the indispensability of investigating and comprehending *science*, the importance of system, order, purity of purpose, religious association, consecration to the best work of the age, and of living lives so beautiful and heavenly, that angels will delight to daily put our hands into the shining palms of theirs, and lead us up to mountains of hourly beatitude.

CHAPTER XXXV.

HELL.

"And death and hell delivered up the dead which were in them."—*Bible.*

> "What Hell may be I know not; this I know—
> I cannot lose the presence of the Lord;
> One arm, Humility, takes hold upon
> His dear Humanity; the other, Love,
> Clasps his Divinity. So where I go
> He goes, and better fire-walled Hell with him
> Than golden-gated Paradise without."—*Tauler.*

Evangelical denominations originally preached the doctrine of literal hell-torments. Rev. Mr. Benson, Methodist commentator, says:

"Infinite justice arrests their guilty souls, and confines them in the dark prison of hell, till they have satisfied all its demands by their personal sufferings, which, alas! they can never do. * * He will exert *all* his divine attributes to make them as wretched as the capacity of their nature will admit. * * Number the stars in the firmament, the drops of rain, sand on the seashore; and when thou hast finished the calculation, sit down and number up the ages of woe. Let every star, every drop, every grain of sand, represent *one million of tormenting ages*. And know that as many more millions still remain behind, and yet as many more behind these, and so on without end."

The Rev. Mr. Ambrose, in a discourse entitled "Doomsday," pictures the torments of lost souls thus:

"When the damned have drunken down whole draughts of brimstone one day, they must do the same another day. The eye shall be tormented with the sight of devils, the ears with the hideous yellings and outcries of the *damned* in *flames*, the nostrils shall be smothered, as it were, with *brimstone;* the tongue, the hand, the foot, and every part, shall *fry* in *flames.*"

Rev. Mr. Emmons wrote in his series of sermons:

"The happiness of the elect in heaven will, in part, consist in witnessing the torments of the damned in hell. And among these it may be their own children, parents, husbands, wives, and friends on earth. One part of the business of the blessed is to celebrate the doctrine of reprobation. While the decree of reprobation is eternally executing on the vessels of wrath, the smoke of their torment will be eternally ascending in view of the vessels of mercy, who, instead of taking the part of those miserable objects, will say, 'Amen, hallelujah, praise the Lord!'"—*Emmons's Sermons*, xvi.

"When they (the saints) shall see how great the misery is from which God hath saved them, and how great a difference he hath made between their state and the state of others who were by nature, and perhaps by practice, no more sinful and ill-deserving than they, it will give them more a sense of the wonderfulness of God's grace to them. Every time they look upon the damned, it will excite in them a lively and admiring sense of the grace of God in making them so to differ. The sight of hell torments will exalt the happiness of the saints forever."—*Ib.*, *Sermon* xi.

Rev. Mr. Edwards penned these sentiments in his "Practical Sermons:"

"The saints in glory will be far more sensible how dreadful the wrath of God is, and will better understand how terrible the sufferings of the damned are, yet this will be no occasion of grief to them, but rejoicing. They will not be sorry for the damned; it will cause no uneasiness or dissatisfaction to them, but on the contrary, when they see this sight, it will occasion rejoicing, and excite them to joyful praises."

Rev. Thomas Boston, in his "Four-fold State," informs us that—

"The godly wife shall applaud the justice of the judge in the condemnation of her *ungodly husband*. The godly husband shall say *amen!* to the damnation of her who lay in his bosom! The godly parent shall say *halleluiah!* at the passing of the sentence of their ungodly child. And the godly child shall from the heart approve the *damnation* of his wicked parents who begot him, and the mother who bore him."—p. 336.

Rev. Thomas Vincent, a Calvinistic clergyman of the past, indulges in the following strain:

"This will fill them (the saints) with astonishing *admiration* and wondering joy, when they see some of their near relatives going to hell; their fathers, their mothers, their children, their husbands, their wives, their intimate friends and companions, while they themselves are saved! * * * Those affections they now have for relatives *out* of Christ will *cease;* and they will not have the *least trouble* to see them sentenced to *hell,* and thrust into the *fiery furnace!"*

Rev. James Smith, of the American Tract Society, Cincinnati, published the following:

"The fire of hell is such that multitudes of tears will not quench it, and length of time will not burn it out. 'The wrath of God abideth; on the rejecter of Christ.—*John* iii : 36.

"Oh, eternity! eternity! Who can fathom it? Mariners have their plummet to measure the depths of the sea; but what line or plummet shall we use to fathom the depth of eternity? The breath of the Lord kindles the flames of the pit, (Isa. xxx : 33,) and where shall we find waters to quench those flames? OH, ETERNITY! If all the body of the earth and the sea were turned to sand, and all the space up to the starry heaven were nothing but sand, and if a little bird should come once every thousand years and take away in her bill but a single grain from all that heap of sand, what numberless years and ages must be spent before the whole of that vast quantity would be carried away. Yet if even at the end of all that time the sinner might come out of hell, there would be some hope. But that word FOREVER breaks the heart. 'The smoke of their torment ascendeth up for ever and ever.'"

The Rev. Mr. Walworth, son of the formerly distinguished Chancellor Walworth, of New York, in a discourse describing the locality and intensity of hell, said:

"The Scriptures had invariably spoken of hell as beneath us, not above or far removed. As heaven was above, and the souls of the righteous were said to ascend to heaven, so the damned descended— went down into hell.

"The rich man, tormented in hell, 'lifted up his eyes' and saw Lazarus in Abraham's bosom, and to his entreaties for succor and intercession, Abraham had replied, 'between us and you there is a great gulf fixed.' So, too, Christ, in the parable of the marriage feast, said, 'Take him and bind him hand and foot, and cast him into outer darkness.'

"He cited many other texts from Scripture to fix this locality, and deduced, as a conclusion therefrom, that hell must necessarily be in the centre of this earth, as in no other way could our conceptions of its position beneath us, as defined in the Scriptures, be adequately realized; our ideas of what is above us might be infinite as space itself, but there could be but one 'beneath,' and that was subterranean.

"He then inquired into the degree of intensity of this heat, which almost passed the bounds of human conception. As a means of approximating to a result, however, he referred to experiments which had been made with a thermometer in Artesian wells and deep mines. Here it had been observed that with every fifty feet of depth one degree of Fahrenheit had been gained; consequently, at this ratio of increase, it would only be necessary to penetrate the crust of the earth twenty-one miles, in order to reach a state of heat, in which the granite would be molten. Water boils at two hundred and twelve degrees Fahrenheit, but it requires two thousand and six hundred degrees to melt rocks. This, therefore, was the *minimum* of the heat of hell, whose *frontiers*, therefore, lie twenty-one miles below the *surface* of the *earth*.

"What would be the duration of the punishment and of these terrible fires? Here there was no room left for doubt! The Church, in concurrence with the awful testimony of the Scriptures, had pronounced them eternal; Christ himself had said, 'It is better for thee to enter life maimed than, having two hands, to go into hell, into the fire that shall never be quenched.' It would be vain to attempt to conceive the duration of that eternity; the boldest intellects shrank appalled on the very threshold of their inquiry. To illustrate the futility of any such attempt, he begged his hearers to picture to themselves one of those infinitely small animals, of which millions dwell in a single drop of water, and which only the most powerful microscope can reveal to our gaze.

"Let them suppose one of these infinitesimal creatures to consume the whole earth, to eat all the leaves of the trees, the fruits of the ground, and sand of the seashore, the mountains and the plains, to drink up the oceans, lakes and rivers, taking one mouthful in a thousand years, and then to devour in turn the sun and the planets and all the visible creatures of the universe, and, after the incalculable lapse of time, consider how much nearer they would be to the solution of this great mystery? Not one step; eternity would be as far beyond their contemplation as ever.

"In these eternal fires every limb and member of our bodies, every nerve and muscle and tendon, every part of us, in fire, over which the sense of feeling predominated, would be forever racked and tortured and yet never consumed. And to these exquisite torments of the body would be added the pangs of remorse and stings of conscience."

This is locating and preaching *hell* to some purpose. It is admirable! Such square sermonizing is in no way allied to this delectable, dodging indefiniteness that characterizes the evangelical discourses of the present. Perhaps the mitigation, softening and bridging over of that liquid stream of fire, form no exception to the general improvement of the age. These Orthodox clergy—"fat, oily men, with a roguish twinkle in their eyes"—if believing their creeds, certainly take the matter of endless hell torments very easy. They smile, enjoy good digestion, walk daily over this "twenty-one miles" crust of hell, crack jokes, drive good bargains, loan money, and do other things quite human.

The old is passing away. It is effete, barren, dead! Art, science, commerce, poetry, painting, music, telegraphic communications, in connection with the phenomena and philosophy of Spiritualism, have all exerted their liberalizing tendencies upon the theologies of the times.

Spiritualists, though utterly rejecting the commonly received orthodox doctrines of hell, as a place of future endless punishment, firmly believe in hell—believe in good and evil, heaven and hell, as subjective relations and conditions.

There are four words in the Old and New Testaments translated hell: *Sheol, Hades, Tartarus* and *Gehenna.* The first two—the former Hebrew, and the latter, Greek—are synonymous. It is difficult to find English words that precisely correspond with them.

The Orthodox commentator, Dr. Campbell, writes thus of Hades:

"In my judgment, it ought never in the Scriptures to be rendered hell, at least in the sense wherein that word is now universally understood by Christians. In the Old Testament the corresponding word is Sheol, which signifies the state of the dead in general, without regard to the goodness or badness of the persons, their happiness or misery."

Dr. Chapman, in his "Critical Notes," assures us that—

"Neither Sheol nor Hades, in themselves considered, have any connection with future punishment, as will be evident to any man who will examine the Hebrew Bible and the Septuagint translation."

The late Professor Stuart left recorded these words:

"There can be no reasonable doubt that *Sheol* does most generally mean the *grave, sepulchre, the world of the dead,* in the Old Testament scriptures."

Here are several passages from the Old Testament, where Sheol —hell—is rendered grave. Gen. xxxvii. : 35 :

"I will go down into the *grave* (*Sheol* or *hell*) unto my son mourning." "Oh, that thou wouldst hide me in the grave" (*Sheol* or *hell*). Hosea xiii : 14 : "I will ransom them from the power of the grave ; I will redeem them from death ; O death, I will be thy plagues ; O *grave* (*Sheol* or *hell*) I will BE THY DESTRUCTION."

These passages show that Jacob expected to go to Sheol—*hell*—to meet his son, and that Job actually prayed to be hid in hell.

Sheol is found in the Old Testament sixty-four times. It is translated three times *pit*, twenty-nine times *grave*, thirty-two times *hell*. Hades occurs eleven times in the New Testament, translated once grave, ten times hell. The learned Parkhurst says :

"Our English, or rather *Saxon* word *hell*, in its original signification, exactly answers to the Greek word *Hades*, and denotes a *concealed* or *unseen place*; and this sense of the word is still retained in the eastern, and especially in the western counties of England. To *hele* over a thing is to cover it."

Mr. Sabine says :

"It appears to me that in the time of this translation, hell, pit and grave, were synonymous."

Tartarus, frequently used by the Grecian poets, is described in the Iliad as a place far below Hades. It occurs in the Bible but once, and is used in the participle form— *Tartarosas*. It literally implies a portion of Hades—hidden regions.

There is but one opinion among the erudite concerning *Gehenna*, found twelve times in the Bible. Dr. Campbell says :

"It is originally a compound of two Hebrew words, *ge hinnom*, the valley of Hinnom, *a place near Jerusalem*, of which we hear first in the book of Joshua, xv : 8."

Rosenmuller says :

"Gehenna is a Hebrew word, denoting *a place near Jerusalem*."

Clark says, respecting the passage of Matt. v : 23 :

"Our Lord here alludes to the valley of the son of Hinnom. This place *was near Jerusalem*," etc.

These Orthodox scholars were correct is saying Gehenna—hell—was a place near Jerusalem, and not in the "centre of the earth," nor the future immortal world. The Roman Catholics, seemingly more honest, and certainly more profound in research than Protestants, translate *Shoel* and *Hades* candidly in giving to the English word *hell* its original and proper meaning, viz : secret, covered—the state of the dead without reference to their condition. In the Douay Bible, first published in Douay in 1609, among others we find this text and sensible note thereon :

"1 Sam. ii : 6 : 'The Lord bringeth down to *hell* (sheol) and bringeth back again.' Job xiv : 13 : 'That thou mayest protect me in *hell* (sheol) and hide me till thy wrath pass.'' Note.—'Protect me in *hell*, that is, in the state of the dead, and in the place where the souls are kept waiting for their Redeemer.'"

Rev. B. H. Wilson, in an essay relating to the "National English Church," alluding to the *Limbus Infantum* of the Catholic Church, says :

"There may be mansions hereafter for those who are infants in spiritual development—nurseries ; or seed grounds, where the undeveloped may grow up under new conditions, the stunted become strong, and the perverted restored."

Liberal sentiments of this character indicate the benevolence of the heart and the rapidity of religious progress. That judicious author of the "Serious Call," Wm. Law, in one of his best inspirational moments, writes :

"No hell in any remote place ; no devil that is separate from you ; no darkness or pain that is not within you ; no anti-Christ, either at Rome or England ; no furious beast ; no fiery dragon, without or apart from yourself, can do you any hurt. It is your own hell, your own devil, your own beast, your own anti-Christ, your own dragon that lives in your own heart's blood, that alone can hurt you."

Heaven is harmony; hell is discord. Heaven is love and purity; hell is hate. "The kingdom of heaven is within you," said the Galilean teacher. If heaven is within the good and pure, hell is within the impure and depraved. It implies sorrow, darkness, trouble, regret and remorse. The Psalmist, David, because of transgressions, was forced to exclaim—"I found sorrow and trouble; the pains of *hell* got hold of me." This is the experience of all wrong-doers. The universe is vocal with warnings. In the sense of an escape from just punishment, there is no forgiveness. Compensation is certain. The "uttermost farthing" must be paid. As reaping to sowing, so is misery to vice, or happiness to virtue. They are as indissolubly connected as the pillars that support the universe.

The comparative darkness attending certain spirits for a long period in the land of souls, is only the reflex action of their own spiritual states. They generate the mist that dims their vision. Life is one lengthened chain. Voluntary acts are the links. As to-day is related to to-morrow, and as the conduct of youth affects manhood; so this life's thoughts, purposes, deeds, determine the immediate condition and position of those entering the immortal world. No death-miracle transforms sordid, scheming, wicked men in the "twinkling of an eye" to angels. True growth is a stranger to abrupt leaps. All progress is gradual. The malicious and depraved of this, carrying their hells with them, enter the hells or lower spheres of the spirit-life. They are in prisons of moral darkness. They lived base, and selfish lives. Their affections centered upon earth and earthly things, and by an inexorable law of their being they are mentally and psychologically imprisoned for a time near the surface of this planet. As fish to water, bird to air, so the earthly-minded to the grosser strata and aural circles belting the earth, till through aspiration, unfoldment, and refinement, they become prepared to traverse the starry spaces of the higher heavens.

The New Testament scriptures inform us that Jesus, after being put to "death in the flesh, but quickened by the spirit, preached to the *spirits* in prison." Peter further speaks of the "gospel being preached to them that are *dead*." The fact of such preaching implies a moral benefit derived therefrom. The divine, uplifting law of progress spans all souls, all worlds. Jesus and angels, prophets, martyrs and the sainted of all ages, delight in descending to teach in the darker spheres of ignorance, as reformers of earth find supreme joy in rescuing and redeeming the erring.

"*I can but trust that* GOOD SHALL FALL
*At last—far off—*at last to all,
And every *winter* change to *spring*."

———"Not one *life* shall be destroyed,
Or cast as rubbish to the void,
When God hath made the *pile complete*."

CHAPTER XXXVI.

HEAVEN.

"I saw a new heaven and a new earth. * * * He that overcometh shall inherit all things."

"Sweet land! I have dreamed of thee."

"There, all being is eternal; things that cease have ceased to be;
All corruption there has perished, there they flourish, strong and free;
This mortality is swallowed up of life eternally."

Brimming with hallowed associations is the delightful thought of Heaven. All have friends there whose memories are sacred. Trustingly they await our arrival for holy re-union.

"Paradise," writes Dr. Hales, "is the region appropriated to good souls."

Some of the Church Fathers considered paradise one division of the under-world; others thought it high in the atmosphere, but below the dwelling-place of God. Christians generally consider it a located place—a city celestial, in distant, undefined regions. All fail to discern the obvious difference between paradise and heaven. "To him that overcometh," declared the ascended Jesus to the medium St. John, "I will give to eat of the tree of life that groweth in the midst of the paradise of God."

The terms *paradise, heaven, spirit-world, spiritual world, spirit-land, summer-land, &c.*, used interchangeably, constitute, literally, a "confusion of tongues." Unlike in the original, and having different shades of meaning, they should be employed with the nicest discrimination. Angry discussions would often be avoided, if words and terms symbolizing ideas, were rightly understood and applied.

Spirit-world, in the best acceptation of the phrase, signifies, all space. Each individual is in the spirit world now, though encoffined in a mortal body. Vast multitudes people the world of unfleshed spirits, who are not in the spiritual world. Those only are in the spiritual world, who, through discipline and progress, have outgrown the depressing conditions of organization with all earthly passions and tendencies. The harmonial and blissful graduate from the spiritual world into the celestial heavens. Here dwell the pure and holy. Clothed in white, and wearing golden girdles, they rush with the melodies of star-orbits to other planets and systems, the teachers of love and holiness.

The spirit, or summer-land, is real and substantial—more substantial to spirits than this earth to mortals. It is beautifully described by A. J. Davis, in his "Stellar Key." The spiritual is the real. As John, entranced on Patmos, saw throngs of "angels," "harpers," "thrones," "rainbows," "crowns," "lamps of fire," "seas of glass," "chariots," "vials of odors," "golden harps," "trumpets"—as Stephen and Paul "looked up into heaven," beholding "spirits and angels," and hearing "unspeakable words;" so the entranced and clairvoyant of this age behold delightful fields, landscapes, gardens, flowers, fruits, rivers, lakes, fountains, vast assemblages of spirits, musical bands, lyceum gatherings, sportive children, schools of design, art galleries, magnificent mansions, and architectural abodes of beauty, where loving hearts beat and throb as one.

All spirits were once mortals. All angels were once spirits. The child, the man, the spirit, the angel, the arch-angel, is the divine order, corresponding with the musical scale of the overarching spirit spheres. Those in the celestial heavens are termed angels, because they have advanced beyond the taints and selfish loves of their mortal existence.

It is difficult to entirely disconnect heaven from surrounding, substantial scenery. It is self-evident that whatever exists in the realms of the relative, must exist somewhere. All substance has form. If there are organized spiritual beings—spirits—there must be extent and limit, bearing upon them relationally, and whatever is in extent, must be in space, and have some kind of location. Nature knows no vacuum. If there is anything not in space, it can have neither form nor figure, for figure is defined by logicians to be "the limit of extent;" and the human mind cannot conceive of form without limit, of limit without extent, or extent without space.

Spiritual beings, then, have location, and, in a subordinate sense, heaven may be connected with locality; that is, there must be a harmony between the objective and subjective—a correspondence, or divine adaptation between spheral strata, scenery, surroundings, and those heavenly societies.

Exalted spirits often speak of their beautiful homes, where life is love,—and love is law; of music, and fountains casting their silvery spray; of ever-green gardens, isles of entrancing loveliness, flowing streams with jeweled banks, harmonial congresses of angels and heavenly universities of wisdom.

When passive and prayerful, our spirit-guide descending and describing to us, in voice lute-like and loving, the magnificence of his celestial residence, ever closes in these thrillingly searching words—"*All these shall be thine, child, when thou art worthy.*" "*To him that overcometh is the promise of the blessed inheritance.*"

> "Is this the way, sweet angel? 'Tis, my child!
> Thou must pass through the tangled, dreary wild,
> If thou wouldst reach the city undefiled,—
>   Thy peaceful home above.
>
> Angel, I'm weary! Child, then lean thy head
> Upon my breast; it was my love that spread
> Thy rugged path; hope on, till I have said,
>   'Rest, rest for aye, above!'"

"In my Father's House," said Jesus, "are many mansions. I go to prepare a *place* for you."

Poets, in their sacred lyrics, frequently sing of heaven as a place.

> "There is a *land* of pure delight,
> Where saints immortal reign."
> * * * * * *
>
> "Mortals! we travel through a darksome cave;
> But still, as nearer to the light we draw,
> Fresh gales will meet us from the upper air,
> And wholesome dews of heaven our foreheads lave."
>
> "Up above, the host no man can number,
> In white robes, a palm in every hand,
> Each some work sublime forever working
> In the spacious tracts of that great *land.*"

Cultured and spiritually enlightened, the more advanced consider heaven not so much a world in the starry firmament as the interior state of the soul. If this is in conscious communion with God, if at peace with itself, and moving onward through the everlasting sweep of being in harmony with the unalterable laws of the Infinite, it is in the *constant* enjoyment of heaven.

The primal purpose of the spiritual dispensation, with its ministering angels, is the building up of the Republic of God on earth; and while its continued prayer is "Thy republic come," it seeks to establish the truth of universal laws, the fruit of good works, the purity of undefiled consciences, the sweet experience of sympathy, charity and forgiveness, the innocency of little children, and humility of sincere souls, consecrated to the good of humanity.

Heaven, remember, is a condition of self-balance, harmony and happiness, and is attained in all worlds through aspiration and obedience to divine laws. The spirit land constituted of the particles, emanations and etherealized essences from this and other earths in the universe—all bathed in the sunlight of an eternal morning—is no shadow-realm; but real and permanent—a "city that hath *foundation*, whose builder and maker is God." Its inhabitants are earnest and untiring in their activities. Apostles, martyrs, reformers, continue their holy missions. Newton pursues his investigations. Fulton's inventive genius finds broader scope for action. Mozart sweeps golden harp-strings, toning to harmony the discords of the spheres. Philosophers pursue their studies. Gardeners continue their pleasing vocations. Geologists probe newly-formed earths, and astronomers become enthusiastic in measuring the mighty orbs of space. Spirit life, then, is an active life, a social life, a retributive life, a constructive life, a progressive life. Reason, affection, conscience and memory, go with us into that world of conscious souls. Individualities are eternalities.

A change of clothing, or a change of place, does not change character. Entrance into the future world of spirits, will no more affect the moral tendencies of the soul, or miraculously give it new directions, desires and aims, than a voyage across the Pacific to California, would transform a thief into a saint. All grow to be angels by degrees. The process of death, with the improved surroundings and conditions incident thereto, will better each and all only in the sense of helping them to more clearly see the true relation of things.

In an inspirational discourse, H. W. Beecher said—

"We shall enter upon another life divested of many of the hindrances and incumbrances of this.   *   *   *   *

"If you take a seed that has ripened in Nova Zembla, and bring it into the tropics, and plant it, it will not be what it would have been in Nova Zembla, with a short growing season, and the scantiest supply of food. It will have, with a long summer, and an abundant supply, a growth to which no one would suspect that it could attain, who had only seen it grow in the frigid zones. Many things that are shrubs in the frigid zones, are high, waving century oaks in the tropics. And so men in this life are in conditions which, though fitted to develop the earlier stages of human growth, are not fitted to develop the full estate of that idea which God has expressed in the creation of man. And we may hope that when we bid adieu to our mortal life, we shall leave behind some things which are necessary to the exigencies of our condition here, but which will not be necessary to our state there. Our imagination, our reason, our affections, and our moral sentiments, we shall doubtless carry with us; but the conditions of our life will be so different that we shall be like men taken from poverty into abundance; from winter into summer; from a cold climate and a frozen soil, into a soil never locked by ice, and skies that never know frost. Our life there shall be ampler, fuller, nobler than it is here."

A man cannot become scientific and holy as a garment is cleansed by washing. Volition and effort are involved in moral purity. Salvation is the result of soul-growth, not physical chemistry.

When a drowning mortal heavily encumbered with thick garments, succeeds in throwing them off, he is not saved, nor do his tremulous feet press the shore; but he is in a far better condition for reaching it. So the circumstance termed *death*, "one step up higher," puts all the conscious humanity of God into better conditions to attain knowledge, wisdom, purity, heaven. Salvation then is not mechanical, chemical nor cataclysmic; but a gradual interior unfoldment—a coming into harmony with divine law—a blissful sequence achieved through the exercise of the will, wisdom and love of a moral actor.

There is no such law in the universe as absolute retrogradation. Spirit is never less than essential spirit. Downward tendencies are more in seeming than the real. The prodigal son departing for that "far-off country," was spiritually approaching the Father. He required the terrible experience. Arresting him in his course, the punishment was disciplinary. It brought him to himself. It helped the Christ triumph over the Adam.

The primary meaning of the Greek word, *Kolásis*—punishment—is pruning or trimming, as of a tree; severing diseased limbs, and cutting away distorted branches to restore it to a healthy condition and symmetry of form.

The growth of plants is intensified and hastened by rich soil, clear light and an increased supply of electricity. All this may be done in harmony with natural law. Such stimulants are adapted to the structure of the plants. So the influences, incentives, spiritual light and presence of angel-guides extending their shining hands, will exert a mighty moral influence in turning spirits, disenthralled from their fleshly bodies, towards the more pure and heavenly altitudes of perfection.

> "God is a worker. He has thickly strewn
> Infinity with grandeur. God is love.
> He yet shall wipe away Creation's tears,
> And all the worlds shall *summer* in his smile."

> "One God, one law, one element,
> And *one far-off, divine event*,
> *To which the whole creation moves.*"

"Thus heavenward all things tend. For all were once perfect, and *all must be at length restored.*"

"Each is born for a higher destiny than that of earth; there is a realm where rainbows never fade; where the stars will be out before us like islets that slumber on the ocean; and where the loved beings that pass before us like shadows, now will stay in our presence forever!"

CHAPTER XXXVII.

HISTORIC IMMORTALITY

"Deep love, the god like in us, still believes
Its objects are immortal as itself."

"The form is in the archetype before it appears in the work; in the divine mind before it exists in the creature."

The immortality of the soul is a doctrine ancient as the remotest records. Jesus may have brought it to "light," in the estimation of Paul—originally Saul of Tarsus, then a bigoted self-willed Jew, wedded to the dim twilight shadows of the Old Testament dogmas. But Paul should not have presumed upon weighing other men's, and other nations' knowledge of "life and immortality" in his personal scales of ignorance. India's Vedas, Egypt's Hieroglyphs, and Assyria's scrolls, as well as the philosophies of Greece, were all aflame with the golden light of "life and immortality," thousands of years before the arrest and crucifixion of Jesus.

Doubtless the oldest distinctive statements of man's knowledge of a future existence are found in Egypt's sacred "*Book of the Dead.*" [These books treat upon the divine attributes of the Deity and the destinies of human souls after death, who, passing the gates of darkness, were introduced into *Amenthe*, place of departed spirits, to be judged. After this trial, they ascended, or descended to higher or lower spheres, according to the "deeds done in the body."

Those sublime, old Hindoo Hymns, the Vedas, richly abound in the doctrines of "life and immortality."

"The wise man, to whom pain and pleasure are the same, is formed for immortality. * * * The spirit is not a thing of which a man may say, it hath been, it is about to be, or is to be hereafter; for it is without birth, ancient, constant and eternal, and is not to be destroyed in this its mortal frame. As a man throweth away old garments and putteth on new, even so the soul, having quitted its old mortal frames, entereth into others which are new."—*Bhagavat Geeta.*

"May I arrive at that abode of Vishnu (God) where dwell in bliss the men who have been devoted to Him. He who has honored Vishnu with libations, becomes his friend in the world above." "Go, give to the waters and to the plants thy body which belongs to them: but there is an immortal portion; O Djatavedas, transport it to the world of the holy."—*Rig Veda.*

"Generation is not a creation of life, but a production of things to sense and making them manifest. Neither is change death, but a hiding of that which was."—*Hermes Trismegistus.*

"He who speaks wisely, moderately, kindly goes (after death) to those worlds which are the inexhaustible sources of happiness. He who is intelligent, modest, devout, who reverences wisdom, and respects his superiors and the aged, goes to the highest heaven. Sinless among the sinful, speaking friendly words to all men, his whole soul melting with benevolence, final happiness is within his grasp."—*Vishnu Purana.*

"There is another invisible, eternal existence superior to this visible one, which does not perish when all things perish. Those who attain this never return. This is my supreme abode."—*Bhagavat Geeta.*

"The soul is immortal; again, it is incorruptible, it never dieth. * * * But when a man who has lived justly dieth, his soul ascendeth to the pure heaven, and lives in the happy œvum with the blessed."—*Pythagoras.*

One of this Grecian's golden verses is this:

> "When thou shall have laid aside thy body,
> Thou shall rise freed from mortality,
> And become a *god* (angel) of the kindly skies."

"Dying, * * * she shall be welcomed by her father, her mother, and her brother in that other world."—*Sophocles.*

"An honorable and virtuous man, may rest assured as to his future fate. The souls of the lawless departing this life suffer punishment. But the good lead a life without a tear, among those honored by the gods for having always delighted in virtue."—*Pindar.*

"As they who run a race are not crowned till they have conquered, so good men believe that the reward of virtue is not given till after death. * * * * Not by lamentations and mournful chants ought we to celebrate the funerals of the good, but by hymns; for in ceasing to be numbered with mortals, they enter upon the heritage of a diviner life."—*Plutarch.*

"If my body be overpressed, it must descend to the destined place; nevertheless, my soul shall not descend, but, being a thing immortal, shall fly up to high heaven."—*Heraclitus.*

"When, therefore, death approaches a man, the mortal part of him dies; but the immortal departs safe and uncorruptible, having withdrawn itself from death. The soul, therefore, is most certainly immortal and imperishable, and our souls really exist in the world of spirits. Those who shall have sufficiently purified themselves by philosophy [religion], shall live without their bodies received into more beautiful mansions. * * * * For the sake of these things, we should use every endeavor to acquire virtue and wisdom in this life; for the reward is noble and the hope is great. A man ought then to have confidence about his soul, if during this life he has made it beautiful with temperance, justice, fortitude, freedom, and truth; he waits for his entrance into the world of spirits, is one who is ready to depart when destiny calls. I shall not remain, I shall depart. Do not say then that *Socrates* is buried; say that you bury my *body.*"—*Socrates.*

"This was the end of the best, the wisest, and most just of men,—a story which Cicero professed he never read without tears."—*Plato.*

"The origin of souls cannot be found upon earth, for there is nothing earthly in them. They have faculties which claim to be called divine, and which can never be shown to have come to man from any source but God. That nature in us which thinks, which knows, which lives, is celestial, and for that reason necessarily eternal. God himself can be represented only as a free Spirit separate from matter, seeing all things, and moving all things, himself ceaselessly working. Of this kind, from this nature, is the human soul. * * It cannot be destroyed." He represents the aged Cato as exclaiming, "O happy day when I shall remove from this crowd of mortals, to go and join the divine assembly of great souls. Not only shall I meet again there the men who have lived godlike on earth; I shall find again my son, to whom these aged hands have performed the duties which in the order of nature he should have rendered to me. His spirit has never quitted me. He departed, turning his eyes upon me and calling on me, for that place where he knew I should soon come. If I have borne his loss with courage, it is not that my heart was unfeeling, but I consoled myself with the thought that our separation would not be long."—*Cicero.*

These citations, taken as selected pebbles from an immeasurable ocean of evidence, prove that the doctrine of future, immortal existence is as natural to the soul as a heart-beat in its casement; that, like sunlight, it has flowed into and bubbled from the spiritual affections of all seers in all ages, and become there a prophecy, yea, a positive knowledge. Even the ruder tribes of earth, less favored with the supports of civilization, instinctively entertain this truth. The poor Indian of America's wilds, child of fate falling before the *more* savage monopoly of his pale brother, is nature's diorama of immortal lights and shades from the spirit hunting-grounds. When a brave chief dies, the survivors, bending down a sapling pine till the roots jut out, place under it the tenantless form, letting the tree spring back to its original position, where, spiring up a symbol of towering spirituality, it is nourished with the rich "dust to dust" and becomes greener and stronger, rising higher towards the wierd lands of the hereafter.

Death strikes no class of persons with such terror as professed Christians. Their sighs, groanings, moanings and mourning apparel—black fitting their condition—a church-menagerie of sable show and brooding despair—absolutely shock the seers and sages of India, Greece, Rome, the millions of present Spiritualists, and even the North American Indians.

What consummate bigotry, then, or learned malignity—culpable in that they know no better — for clergymen, sneering at the manifestations of angel presence, to insist, as they do, that the only reliable evidence of immortality is revealed in the Bible, or "brought to light" in the historic resurrection of Jesus! Even the Hindoo Menu can teach them; "Universal instinct is transcendent law." The human soul will burst all fetters, and, child-like, find \[fu\]ture a perpetual paradise of immortal fore-gleams, and its own inner springs of love the future "river of life" flowing into the estuary of eternity.

"Upon the frontier of this bright summer-land,
We, pilgrims of cankering sorrow, stand :—
What realm lies forward, with its happier store
   Of forests green and deep,
   Of valleys hushed in sleep,
And lakes most peaceful! 'Tis the land
   Of evermore."

CHAPTER XXXVIII.

RESURRECTION.

> "The grave itself is but a covered bridge,
> Leading from light to light, through a brief darkness."

> "The eye that shuts in a dying hour
>   Will open next in bliss;
> The welcome will sound in the heavenly world
>   Ere the farewell is hushed in this."

> "There shall be no more death, neither sorrow nor crying, neither shall there be any more pain; for the former things are passed away."

Death, the shade-side of conscious life, is comparable to a star, that, fading from telescopic vision, sets to illumine others in the siderial heavens; to a rose that, on a morning in June, climbs up the garden wall to bloom the other side.

The Greek, *anastasis*, generally translated by the English word, *resurrection*, does not necessarily signify, that those to whom it refers should be physically dead. In the scriptures and the classics, it is often applied to the living. Its best definition implies a *rising*, an *exaltation*, a being *lifted up higher* in regard to condition or circumstance. The learned Dr. Campbell says: "It denotes simply being raised from inactivity to action, or from obscurity to eminence." *Anisterni*, the verb form, has a signification equally wide, as used by Grecian writers, both before and after the Christian era. Therefore, in the original, rising from a seat, awakening out of sleep, or being promoted to a higher condition, may be legitimately, termed an *anastasis*—a resurrection.

Persians, Mahommedans, Jews, and Christians, with very few exceptions, believe in the literal resurrection of these physical bodies—*somata*—while the great army of Spiritualists, in constant converse with the spirit-world, utterly repudiates the theory.

Mineral matter to matter in accordance with gravitation and adaptation—dust with its primitive dust—and spirit heavenward towards the perfections of Infinite spirit—is the immutable law as seen from the spiritual side of this question.

In that Christian writer's work—Dr. Young's—entitled "The Last Day," the dogma of the resurrection of the mortal body is carried to the ultimate Augustine, hard pressed upon the point, of cannibalism, said, "The flesh shall be restored to the man in whom it first became human flesh, regardless of the changes it may have passed through; for it is to be considered as borrowed, and, like borrowed money, must be returned to the one from whom it was taken."

Among the most important words of the Episcopal creed, are these: "I believe in * * * the resurrection of the body and the life everlasting."

Brigham Young, the Mormon leader, preaching the funeral discourse of elder Heber C. Kimball, said:

"He has fallen asleep for a certain purpose. to be prepared for a glorious resurrection; and the same Heber C. Kimball, every component particle of his body, from the crown of his head to the soles of his feet, will be resurrected, and he, in the flesh, will see God and converse with Him; and see his brethren and associate with them, and they will enjoy a happy eternity together."

The bodies that once walked the New Atlantis Isle—the mummied forms of Egypt's cemeteries transferred to fuel, or to medicines upon apothecaries shelves—the crumbling scattered remains that once peopled those old catacombs, in the Via Appia—the organized particles passing into invisible gases, freed by the process of combustion, incident to *cremation*, as practiced by some of the orientals—where are they?—are they to be raised, and reconstructed to constitute the future temples of souls? If so, "flesh and blood *will* inherit the kingdom of God;" though Paul, in one of his more highly illuminated moments taught the contrary; and further, we sow—*bury* the veritable body which shall be; though this same apostle said: "We sow *not* that body that shall be." "There is a natural body, and there *is* a spiritual body." These natural, earthly bodies correspond to the chaff of the wheat—the husks of the corn. Harvest-time separates them forever; because the end for which they were united has been subserved. So with the earthly and spiritual bodies. The death-angel divides them forever.

And just as well expect the blade of wheat to return and re-enter the kernel; the oak, the acorn, the butterfly, the chrysalis—or, as reasonably expect songful birds to seek their dilapidated nests, taking on, and re-living in their old shells, as immortal spirits to return grave-ward in some future period, to seek and re-inhabit their earthly bodies. Nature knows no retrogression. Our mortal bodies are raised only in grasses and grains, forests and fruits; but our conscious souls move on in the line of progress towards the great infinite Soul of all things.

Roger Williams, too liberal for the Puritanic Christianity of his time, was banished by Christians afar off among the heathen Indians—the *Narraghansetts*, who, in the gentle tolerance of Jesus, received him into their weird, wigwam homes. The Rev. J. H. McCarty, writing recently relative to the importance of erecting a suitable monument over the place where his body was interred, says:

"On digging down into the 'charnel house' it was found that everything had passed into oblivion. The shapes of the coffins could only be traced by a black line of carbonaceous matter the thickness of the edges of the sides of the coffins, with their ends distinctly defined. The rusted remains of the hinges and nails, with a few fragments of wood and a single round knot, was all that could be gathered from his grave. In the grave of his wife there was not a trace of anything save a single lock of braided hair which had survived the lapse of more than 180 years. Near the grave stood a venerable apple tree, when and by whom planted is not known. This tree had sent two of its main roots into the graves of Mr. and Mrs. Williams. The larger root had pushed its way through the earth till it reached the precise spot occupied by the skull of Roger Williams. There making a turn as if going round the skull, it followed the direction of the back bone to the hips. Here it divided into two branches, sending one along each leg to the heel, where they both turned upward to the toes. One of these roots formed a slight crook at the knee which makes the whole bear a very close resemblance to a human form. This singular root is preserved with great care, not only as an illustration of an important principle in vegetation, but for its historic association. There were the graves, emptied of every particle of human dust! Not a trace of anything was left!"

The grave emptied of every particle of human dust!—where gone? Those apple-tree roots, thrusting out their hungry feelers, absorbed it, to feed a yearly fruitage. Man partaking of this fruit, and appropriating it by a law of assimilation, it formed a part of their own bodies. The inquiry is, who will legitimately claim these elements, providing human bodies are to be raised?

Motion inheres in all things. Particles in human bodies change from seven to twenty-seven years, depending upon condition and occupation. Admitting the record, Methusaleh living over nine hundred years, must have had some sixty or seventy different bodies—*which* is to be anastasized! In certain islands of the ocean, savages, termed *cannibals,* killing their enemies, devour their flesh and drink their blood; so that the same earthly materials form the component parts of two or more individualized beings. Who is to own them in the resurrection? Where Bonaparte fought his most sanguine battles, waved the next season golden grain. These harvests were unusually luxuriant, because blood and muscle, had enriched the soil — a *soil* yielding in turn grains and grazing herds for the sustenance of man. To whom will these life-materials belong when anastasized and re-constructed? Children, passing as withered buds to summer-land spheres of innocence, grow in those angel gardens to spiritual manhood and womanhood. Must their beautiful well-rounded forms return at the sounding of a resurrection trumpet and, re-entering, be compelled to dwell in their infantile bodies? *All* these physical and moral impossibilities are legitimately connected with the resurrection of the body.

It is often asked, Was not Jesus's physical body raised? These passages give the answer:

"And their eyes were opened, and they knew him; and *he* VANISHED *out of their sight*."

"Then the same day at evening, when the *doors* were *shut*, where the disciples were assembled, * * * came Jesus and stood in the midst, and saith, Peace be unto you." "After that, he appeared *in another form* unto two of them, as they walked, and went into the country."

These passages affirming that he "stood in their midst, the doors being shut;" that after his crucifixion he drew near and went with them towards Emmaus, their "*eyes* being holden," that "they knew him not," that he appeared in "another form," that he "*vanished* out of their sight," &c., clearly show that it was the *spiritual* Jesus, clothed with the spiritual body that pertains to the resurrection state of immortality. The disciples saw him, because clairvoyant. The conditions destroyed, "he vanished from their sight." *They* "vanished," not *he*. In the "twinkling of an eye" a clairvoyant of normal mediumship can pass from the internal to the external. In this sense the disciple withdrew from Jesus.

Again it is asked, If the physical body of Jesus was not raised, what became of it?" We can easily conceive that the friends might have removed it before the "watch" was set, or that the same angel, who rolled the stone from the door of the tomb, might have transported away "the body of their Lord." The disposition of that *body* is of no more interest to us than that of Zeno, Plato, or Confucius. The important question is—Did the man of Nazareth *live?* did he walk again in their company clothed with his glorified body? This we believe, as his reputed biography demonstrates.

Death is the disengagement of the spiritual from the fleshly—the severance of the sympathetic copartnership between the spiritual and earthly bodies. The thinker will note the distinction between the soul and spirit. The old philosophers clearly perceived this distinction. Plato considered the soul to be "the image of the spirit." Paul prayed God to "preserve body, soul and spirit." Professor Bush, of the New York University, said:

"As it is through the gross material body that the soul manifests itself in the present world, so are we warranted in believing that it is through the soul that the spirit manifests itself in the other world; in other words, it performs for the spirit the office of a body, and is consequently so termed."

Soul and spiritual body, often confounded with spirit, are synonymous. We employ the terms, soul and spiritual body reciprocally; and, as constituting the man, use this formula —Physical body, Spiritual body, Spirit; or, body, soul and spirit.

As the butterfly's folded wing, in its rudimentary state, can be traced under the shell of the chrysalis, so the whole future, resurrectional body is contained, or wrapped up, in the material form, during mortal life. Its release, termed death, is really birth. A modern seeress, writing upon the "Philosophy of Life," well says, "As the physical birth of the fœtus is death to its placenta envelope, so a spiritual birth is death to its physical casket, the body; or, as the destruction of the casket in which the child is developed, implies the birth of the physical system, so the destruction or death of the physical body implies the birth of its spiritual system." Death, as a divine appointment in harmony with natural law, and in its time beautiful, is equivalent to spiritual birth, giving enlarged freedom to the soul, and increased facilities to the spirit for manifestation and perfection. The buds swell into flowers wooed by the sunlight; the birdlings burst from their shells for flight on joyous wing; the child, maternally developed, gains its individual freedom in outer life through pain, effort and crying; so the spasms, throes and pantings, sometimes beheld with sympathizing sorrow, are but the strugglings of the soul to release itself from the coffined walls of its earthly tabernacle. What seems agony to us may be pleasure to the emancipated.

The process of death does not involve the disorganization of the spiritual body. If it is thus absolutely disintegrated into scattered particles, by what law is it reorganized? May not more positive individualities, sustained by such elements, selfishly appropriate what belongs to another, thus virtually involving the destruction of individual identity? In no department of nature does structural disorganization precede birth. *Here*, disorganization is retrogression to the individuality thus subjected to the unnatural process of *unmaking!* The grain does not resolve itself into its original elements when ready to be ripened; the bird does not return to its indefinable diffuseness in its shell when plumed for an exit; the animal does not cease to be, for a moment, when nature casts it forth for a higher being.

The spiritual *body*, composed of the ultimates of all the primates, constitutes a symmetrical wholeness of structure, and is unitively unfolded from its earthly casket as the rose from the rose-bud. The God-principle, pivotal and central in man, continually acts, as a divine magnet, by the law of necessity, holding the spiritual body to itself in a continuous organized unity. The law of attraction, as in a magnet to steel, is an *infinite* law, and as such is equally active during physical life, during the process of death, and forever thereafter.

That unformed, cloud-shapen, magnetic mass, seen by clairvoyants, hovering over the corpse, is not the scattered fragmentary substances of the spiritual body thrown around loosely, but the electric emanations and radiations enveloping it as aural atmospheres around the earth. Clairvoyants, subject to the law of conditions, and, consequently, not always authoritative, may mistake this magnetic envelope for the real substance whence it is evolved.

During the process of death, consciousness, in the seeming, is sometimes suspended, as with those who are suddenly ushered into the spirit world by capital punishment, suicide or accident, and with those especially whose habits of life, given to pernicious gratification, have materialized their senses, as if locked in "chains of darkness." Those who have lived pure and exalted lives, aglow with truth and charity, do not lose their consciousness for a moment, but cognize the transition from a darker to a more illumined room in the mansions of the Father.

There are no idiots to the spiritual vision. Imbecility is caused by malformation of the physical organization. Entering the spirit world, released from ante-natal and social perversions, they immediately commence their upward march of knowledge and wisdom.

Infants are immortal from the sacred moment of embryonic existence. Uniting the alkali and acid, instantly you have the third and higher compound—the salt. So when the positive and negative relational forces blend, then and there is the divine incarnation. Nature never takes a retrogressive step. If purposely blasted, during the gestative life, the spiritual principle remaining undisturbed, and the individuality *in tact*, the tender riven bud is borne by matronly angels to the nursery gardens of innocence to be trained in the virtues of the spheres. Designed abortion is murder! Multitudes will meet those offended little ones that ought to have had a natural, physical birth and the experiences of an earthly life, preparatory to a ripened entrance into the world of spirits. Prematurely ushered there, the spiritual objective being based upon the material, they are necessitated by a law of their being, to return under heavenly guidance to the mediumistic spheres of sympathizing friends to gather glimpses of, and participate in, earthly struggles and victories.

Identity is cognate with existence itself. It is the natural attribute of spirit—its very impressibility. It depends not on form for recognition, but the form on it. Every part of the grain we sow is represented in the harvest. Essential spirit being inseparable substance, and ever reporting itself magnetically, we recognize it by sympathy, the same as a child in the darkness knows its mother without the aid of sight or hearing. Our spheres are ourselves extended—our very loves and thoughts in telegraphic communication. When, therefore, spirits from the mortal lands meet the gone before, instantly, by sympathy, they recognize each other, and the past, with all its checkered pilgrimages, indellibly engraved on the tablet of memory, rolls in upon the consciousness with light and shadow, all in order of relations and events, in sweet, unspeakable joy and full of glory.

The king will know his subjects there—they the more kingly now; the Indian chief will know his tribe there; the teacher, the pupil; the parent, the cherub child; congenial souls will blend in sweetest fellowship; harmonial spirits will mingle in holiest tenderness; and weary, thorn-crowned pilgrims of earth, finding rest, will meet their redeemers, face to face. "Blessed are the dead that die in the Lord;" that is, die in the sphere of the Christ-life—"they rest from their labors, and their works do follow them." The works of the good both follow and precede them into the heavenly courts of blessedness. Courage, sister! Every pure thought breathed, every generous word uttered, every charitable deed wrought, every heart-beat for virtue and peace, will live forever!

> "Beside the toilsome way,
> Lonely and dark, by fruits and flowers unblest,
> Which thy worn feet tread sadly, day by day,
> Longing in vain for rest,
> An angel softly walks,
> With pale, sweet face, and eyes cast meekly down,
> The while from withered leaves and flowerless stalks
> She weaves thy fitting crown."

Courage, brother! Martyrs have trodden the paths of peril—saints have paced the cold cells—hearts have ached—souls have hungered—fires have burned around the forms of the faithful—storms and adversities have pelted the prophets—eyes have wept tears of blood, and brows platted with coronals of persecution, ere the world knew them, or they reaped the harvests of their diligent sowing. Courage, sister, brother, speaker, medium, worker—courage!

A beautiful, guardian angel once said to her mate on earth: "Mind echoes to mind; heart throbs with heart. Together we will read beauties—together sing one melody of love—together twine garlands to deck the brow of sorrow—together tread eternal pathways, and bathe in life's fountain of light. Yes, together we will sing the song of life—together and forever. We shall be there together; no partings ever there; the hands once joined at greeting, shall never be unloosed; two buds blossom in one flower. I am ever near thee. Ask me not to come. Shall the rose say, I wait for fragrance? Does it invite sweetness? Thus are we united!"

"I shall know her there! I shall know her there,
By the shining folds of her wavy hair,
By her faultless form with its airy grace
That an angel's pen might fail to trace—
By the holy smile her lips will wear,
When we meet above, I shall know her there!

I shall know her there, and her calm, dark eyes
Will look in mine with glad surprise,
When my bark, wild-tost o'er life's rough main,
The far-off port of heaven shall gain;
Though an angel's robe and a crown she wear,
By the song she sings I shall know her there."

Existence is unitive—eternal. This life is a hotel in which mortals tarry but a little season for rudimental experiences. Earthly furniture is not transferable. Ripening through toil and suffering, the soul emerges from this chrysalis state, through a sweet death-trance, to form new connections and go up one step higher in the graduated ascent of creation.

Not the drooping willow, nor dark cypress; but myrtle, laurel, rose-buds and immortelles are fitting funeral emblems. Mourning apparel belongs to the superstitions of the past. Pleasant words—cheerful music, should be voiced in the calm hour of burial, and cemeteries should be made as beautiful as the groves of tropical climes.

> "No gloomy vault, no charnel cell,
>   No emblem of decay,
> No solemn sound of passing-bell,
>   To echo—'gone away;'
> But angels whisper soft and clear—
> 'The loved, now risen, is standing near.'"

CHAPTER XXXIX.

PRAYER.

> "If truth the inmost soul and being share,
> The universe becomes a book of prayer."

> ———— ———— "Prayer pushes prayer
> Up into heaven's sublime air."

> — "He gathers the prayers as he stands,
>   And they change into flowers in his hands,
> Into garlands of purple and red;
>   And beneath the great arch of the portal,
>   Through the streets of the city immortal,
> Is wafted the fragrance they shed."

Not pre-arranged words or the utterance of measured phrases, after the custom of the ancient Pharasee and modern hypocrite, but aspiration is prayer, the up-welling of the soul's holiest desires and struggles to attain the moral altitudes of perfection, the language of the innermost panting for the actual, the rising flame, the incense of pure thought, the prophecy of a better life, the chariot of love bearing us into the realm of the divine.

Prayer, uttered or repressed, affects no deific law or principle. Dews freshen the evening; sunlight bathes the morning; fruits fall in the autumn-time; meteors descend to the earth; stars move in nightly battalions over the radiant plains of heaven, all in accordance with infinite causation, reckless of prayers or intercessions.

The immutable and unalterable I AM is in no way affected by the instabilities of men. Neither smiles nor tears—vices nor virtues, nor prayers, change that divine Energy, who is "the same yesterday and forever." Prayer expands the soul that breathes it, and opens to clearer vision the portals of the spirit-world, in which all have the right of citizenship. It intromits the petitioner into closer fellowship with heavenly hosts, and, imparting a holier baptism, raises him above the worthless things of earth. The soul in self-communion feels its immensity, its relation to the universe, and its illimitable future. And through prayer and meditation, the external universe partially reveals its inmost self, and another universe within—the subjective—opens in grandeur, seemingly limitless before the spirit vision.

One of our most philosophical writers on Spiritualism, purely appreciating the law of prayer, says:

"When man comes into that department of being where all that is evil and false ceases, when every impure and unjust desire and impulse is banished, and when the soul, in its yearnings after the divine, puts forth all its life and power in humble, submissive prayer—then is such soul elevated to the summit of its being, and there is infilled with the living presence of Divinity, which makes the whole being radiant with spiritual light. Such a degree of elevation is coming into the 'Mount of Transfiguration,' and all who have really been there, have felt its blessedness and desired to establish his tabernacle thereon."

Jesus, speaking from the inner life, said—

"When thou prayest, thou shalt not be as the hypocrites are; for they love to pray standing in the synagogue and at the corners of the streets to be seen of men. * * * But when thou prayest, enter into thy closet, and when thou hast shut thy door, pray to thy Father which is in secret, and thy Father which seeth in secret shall reward thee openly."

James the apostle, in an inspired moment, asked—

"Is any sick among you? let him call for the elders of the church; and let them pray over him, anointing him with oil, * * * and the prayer of faith shall save the sick."

To plead with God for this or that, "for Christ's sake," is churchal, but not philosophical. Prayer moves us, and all in sympathy with us, as one chord in a musical instrument tones another, bringing us more and more into harmony with heavenly order. It is devoid of all virtue without practice. The sectarist prays God to send rain in the dry season, while the philosopher prays by irrigating his fields and gardens. The bigot prays God to feed the poor, whilst the philanthropist prays by carrying supplies to their very doors. The churchman, partaking of a rich repast, prays God to clothe and comfort the widow and the fatherless, and expects by these soulless ceremonies to win the special favor of heaven. Up from your knees, O Ritualist! and bestow the blessings which you ask God to confer. Golden the age when men will *do*, rather than *say* their prayers. The Grecian drayman received no help from Hercules, though calling in prayer, until he put his shoulder to the wheel.

Invocations to spirits, angels, God—"Jehovah, Jove, or Lord"—when bubbling up spontaneously from the inner depths, are vitalizing and strengthening to the divine forces of the soul. Whether most efficacious, voiced, or breathed in calm silence, each must determine. No mortal is independent. Sympathies and destinies blend like the tremulous branches of forest trees. Man, dependent as stream upon fountain, is fed from the ever-flowing rivers of inspiration. Is it not expressive of gratitude, as well as wisdom, then, for man to look to God, as drop, rill, stream, lake, all, to the immeasurable oceanic fountain of waters? Thus, aspiring to the good and lofty, to angels and arch-angels, we approximate their states of recipient love, and become illumined with the Promethean fires of God's eternal sunshine, our souls invited up and standing upon high mountains of holiness, under the arching rainbows of Infinite Mercy.

Aspiration knows no bounds; ideally it measures all spaces over which the soul treads; it is the highest form of prayer. The immediate object of prayer, then, is to incite calmness of spirit. It puts us into an inspirational condition, enabling us to come into rapport with heavenly presences, association with whom transforms us into their own moral likeness. Companionship with poets makes us poetical; with musicians, musical; with objects of beauty, beautiful in character; with the good, divinely spiritual. Folded under the wing of immortal hope, embosomed on the heart of the Infinite, thrilled with the pulsations of angel faith, we thus ascend higher, higher in thought and purpose—the children of God gathered home in the heaven of Love.

CHAPTER XL.

FREEDOM AND FUNCTION OF LOVE.

"Love is the fulfilling of the law."

"Come angel! for I need thy love
 More than the flower the dew, or grass the rain.
Come angel! like the mystic dove,
 And let me in thy smiles rejoice and live again!"

"Love communes in gentle glances,
Feet responsive glide in dances,
 Over there;
Orange-buds and pure white flowers,
Lattice the hymenial bowers,
 Over there."

Jesus loved Martha, and her sister Mary, and Lazarus. Love is not merely a white lily undulating upon embosomed waters, not an æolean harp murmuring music in the window, not the cooing of the turtle doves, but an active principle, a divine soul-emotion, the central magnet of our conscious existence. Just in the ratio of the soul's unfoldment, love becomes subjective, philosophic, idealistic and universal. Platonic love, blending with the fraternal, and enzoned by the infinite, is exalting beyond all heights of mortal perception; and yet as well talk metaphysics to mummied gorillas, as such love, disenthralled of passion and earthliness, to those who swelter in the lower brain department of their cranial organisms.

The inimitable Emerson, determined to preserve his wholeness, and recognizing no one being as absolutely necessary to his happiness, says of those early selfish loves:

"I know how delicious is this cup of love—I existing for you, you existing for me; but it is a child clinging to his toy, an attempt to eternize the fireside and nuptial chamber; to keep the picture alphabet through which our first lessons were prettily conveyed. * * * Once abroad, we pity those who can forego the magnificence of Nature's Eden for candle light and cards. * * * This early dream of love, though beautiful, is only one scene in our life-play. In the procession of the soul from within outward, it enlarges its circles, like light proceeding from an orb. It passes from loving one to loving all; and so, this one beautiful soul opens the divine door through which he enters to the society of all true and pure souls. Thus in our first years are we put in training for a love which knows neither *sex*, *person*, nor *partiality*; but which seeks virtue and wisdom everywhere, to the end of increasing virtue and wisdom."

Say not that Emerson's nature is cold and icy, reflecting only the crystalline side of life. To those sufficiently exalted rightly to translate him, he is warm, fresh, and golden. His soul feeds ours. Abiding in such love, we drink at his living fount of ideas, thrive upon his inspirational truths, bathe in his dreamy mysticisms, and feel the influx of eternal youth.

Souls require no introduction. The recognition is intuitional. Meeting a noble soul that knows our soul, we indulge the pleasing truth to us, that we knew the loved one in a pre-existent state, and delicious were those delicate experiences in the sweet realms of blessedness. Too etherial were the workings of that inner consciousness, *then*, to be now projected into the external memory of earth's sordid masses, cloyed with the cares of this material life.

"'Tis somewhere told in Eastern story,
That those who loved once bloomed as flowers
On the same stem, amid the glory
Of Eden's green and fragrant bowers;
And that, though parted oft by fate,
Yet when the glow of life is ended,
Each soul again shall find its mate,
And in one bloom again be blended."

While Thomas Carlyle worships force—a king being to him the man that *can* and *does*—while John Stuart Mill continues to scatter incense upon the altar of original ideas, be it ours to do homage at the sacred shrine of *love*—a love pure, Platonian and universal. Such germinating from the soul's center, summering eternal in the brain's crystal dome, and looking tenderly towards the Infinite, incarnated in all humanity, is not passional, selfish, nor exacting. It does not demand attention, talks not of duty, lusts not after virtue, but trusts in principle—law—liberty—God!

Beautiful in effect is the medicine of love to the morally diseased. It works by an infinitude of methods, but always to redemptive ends. When fires, faggots, clanking chains, and gloomy penitentiaries had all failed to reform, "the still small voice" of love touched the heart-strings, opened a new fountain and redeemed the erring. This principle wielded by William Penn, tamed the Indian soul and toned it to throb in kindness. Wielded by the benignant Howard, it made dingy prisons, in Europe, schools of reform. Breathed by the great-hearted Oberlin, it transformed many by-corners of pollution, in the old world, into blooming gardens. Whispered by the womanly Elizabeth Fry, it filled those dungeoned in houses of refuge and asylums of outcasts with higher thoughts and purer ideals—as sure to produce high, elevating influences, as are shivering lightnings to do their missioned work. Moral power is the only force ever employed by God, or angels, in the divine order of subjugation. It is the deepest and mightiest principle in the universe—the silvery sea over which mortals sail to the heaven they seek. Oh, it is sweet—it is life evermore to breathe the beauty of love!

> "For love is the theme that the seraph choirs
> Are now hymning through the stars,
> And we catch the strain from their golden lyres,
> When our souls let down their bars."

Love bears no more relation to lust, than Christ to the Adam, than heaven to the hells. Lust is perversity, and is no more love than light is darkness, or good is evil. How important clearly to comprehend the occult forces of life, to distinguish between use and abuse! The legitimate purpose of Combativeness is not pugilism, but a force-power acting in conjunction with benevolence and justice. So the primal purpose of Amativeness is not gratification, nor pleasurable intoxication, but "the replenishing of the earth." All more than this is wasted expenditure, and nature hurls terrible penalties at those who thus destroy their vital forces. The legitimacy of the generative plane, under the guidance of the wisdom principle, is admissible.

On the earthly planes of life, reproductions are earthly; in the spirit realms, spiritual; in the celestial, celestial. Angels generate thoughts, ideas, redemptive reforms. It is beautiful to become angelic on earth. There should be a mount of ascension, a spiritual birth to each brain organ, a heavenly polarity, before physical death. Said Jesus, "Ye must be born again!" Each faculty should be developed on the ascending line of divine use. Desire should be gratified only when pure, normal and subjected to the highest reason.

Through ante-natal perversions and individual excesses, humanity stands arraigned to-day, degenerate and incomplete. The remedy is not in multiplying the causes. God's laws are not to be trifled with. Perverted passions that blotch the face and cloud the moral nature, are not to be permitted to run their course, but to be curbed, controlled, directed and lifted to higher fields of action. Nothing could be more dangerous than railroad-riding, with the steam-forces neither managed nor guided by the engineer.

To let the "*passions* flow as rivers from lands to seas," is equivalent to saying—let the drunkard drink—drinking deeper draughts of liquid poison, will cure inebriation and usher in the millenium morn of temperance! Intensifying the darkness of a dark apartment, would be considered by a scientist a very singular method for producing light. True, the passions are not to be utterly eradicated; but to be subordinated to holy uses. They are not, as a loose, slipshod optimism affirms, to have full sway, producing physical haggardness and spiritual imbecility. Checked, trained, educated, as nature-forces, by resurrectional processes, they are to rise through the strata of organic being to the arching brain faculties, clarified and purified to blend and act in harmony with the moral and reasoning brain-regions of man's spiritual nature. Mrs. Willard, in her "Sexology," makes this pointed statement:

> "It is excessive sexual abuse that produces so much nervous debility in men and women. We have inherited it from our ancestors, and we transmit it to our children. * * * Houses of infamy and their pollutions are not the worst results of sexual abuses, because they are confined to them; they are diffused into families and transmitted to children. * * * Sexual commerce is just as bad as self-abuse, when carried to the same excess. In a certain sense it is worse."

In "Memoranda of Persons and Events," A. J. Davis testifies that—

> "That misery-promoting abuse of the conjugal relation, called free-passionism, is an 'incident' to the development of mankind out of blood into spirit—out of materialism into spirituality—out of prostitution, into the divine order of society, when moral women will be but little lower than the angels. * * * There is but one *true* marriage; namely, *the marriage of the right man with the right woman, forever.*"

The apocalyptic John saw, in vision, "an hundred and forty and four thousand," having his Father's name written in their foreheads. And he heard the voice of these harpers harping with their harps. They sung, as it were, a new song, and none could learn the song but the redeemed. * * * And the voice said—"These are they which were not defiled with women. * * * They enter through the gates into the city"—city of the "New Jerusalem"—the angelic dispensation that "cometh down from God out of heaven."

"Starving souls" cannot find supplies on the animal plane. Physical commerce cannot satisfy *soul*-wants. "That which is born of the flesh is flesh." As the beautiful vine in the filthy cellar, pale and sickly, needs solar light; so the soul, satiated on the poisons of sensuality, is emaciated and dying

—dying for love—for heart-love—for divine love—the solar love of angels.

Hidden deep under soils and sloughs are the nuclei, the types and buds of unblown flowers, struggling to rise from their sedimental graves into the free, fresh light of heaven. So are there mortals who, from pre-natal conditions and debasing associations, live and seemingly luxuriate down in the lower, back-brain department of their being. Their condition is deplorable; their suffering must be intense—their struggles long and tearful. Far be it from us to condemn them. Jesus did not "condemn the woman caught in sin;" but he *did* say, "GO AND SIN NO MORE!" White-robed angels, standing upon the mountains of the pure and beautiful, are saying to those—to all—"Come up higher!"

All the germinal forces of the soul are divine; the wrong comes from their misdirections through material forms; the transgression from the ignorant or the wilful abuse of the good. Amativeness disrobed of earthliness, turned into higher channels, resurrected and actualized, as in angelic life, may not only originate, but may be considered the synonym of emotional love—a love pure, free and divine, working with and inspiring the moral excellence of the immortalized in heaven. This love, so spontaneous and holy, flowing out in gushing fountains of purity from regenerate souls to all humanity, should be cramped by no chains, crushed by no "law-corpse," appropriated by no selfish parasite, nor hedged about by the cage-wires and conventionalities of custom.

* * * * * * * *

"One night I watched the shapeless clouds
  That o'er my mind were rolling,
Till the clock's slow and measured tones
  The hour of twelve were tolling."

Then o'er the loved disciples' page
  Was I my vigil keeping:
I read and mused and read again,
  While all the world was sleeping:

And as I mused, I felt a fire
  Within me gently glowing;
Passion sunk low, as drooping gales
  At hush of eve stop blowing.

The clouds that o'er my spirit hung
  Gave sweet and gentle warning;
They changed to white and purpling flakes
  As at the dawn of morning;
And then looked through the countenance,
  Clothed in its sun-bright splendor,
The 'loved' who with the saints of old
  Kept holy watch, and tender.

His robe was white as flakes of snow
  When through the air descending;
I saw the clouds beneath him melt,
  And rainbows o'er him bending;—
And then a voice,—no, not a voice,—
  A deep and calm revealing
Came to me like a vesper-strain
  O'er tranquil waters stealing.

And ever since, that countenance
  Is on my pathway shining;
A sun from out a higher sky
  Whose light knows no declining.
All day it falls upon my road,
  And keeps my feet from straying;
And when at night I lay me down
  I fall asleep while praying."

The tendency of the spiritually minded is from grossness to refinement—from promiscuity to chastity—from chastity to holiness—from holiness to divinity. The higher the moral ambition, the more complete and victorious the virtue! This Adamic battle ground cleared, the kingdom of God has come with its newness of life—"Not according to the flesh, but according to the spirit." The Apostle John declared that he had passed from death unto life; because he loved the brethren. *This* love can never degenerate into license, nor its liberty into anarchy; for it is a principle, disrobed of earthly passion—a holy resurrection.

All men are my brothers; all women, my sisters; all children, my children; and I am every mortal's child. Deep is our interest in every infant born into earth-life. Its destiny is linked with ours, and our love flows to it free, to *all* humanity free as God's sunlight.

Let, then, our country be the universe; our home the world; our religion to do good; our rest wherever a human heart beats in harmony with ours; and our desire be to enkindle in the breasts of earth's millions the fires of aspiration, aiding them in their progress up the acclivities of life, even to the very gate of heaven. Let all the love that can be attracted from our inmost being, be appropriated by the poor, and the crushed, and the needy, and the fallen—by you, the world, the angels. Then will be actualized the words of Jesus—" All mine are thine, and thine are mine."

During that precious pentecostal hour, when the divine afflatus streamed down in rivers of light from angelic abodes, not only " many believed," but they were so baptized into those unselfish loves of the spiritual world, that they resolved to " have all things in common." When these universal love-principles are made practical, the soil will be as free to all to cultivate as the air they breathe; gardens will blossom and bear fruitage for the poor, and orphans find homes in all houses, there drawn by the music of tenderest sympathy; the brows of toiling millions be wreathed with white roses—symbols of perpetual peace.

CHAPTER XLI.

GENIUS OF SPIRITUALISM.

> "And God will make divinely real
> The highest forms of their ideal."—*Chapin.*

> "Now concerning spiritual gifts, brethren, I would not have you ignorant. For to one is given by the Spirit, the word of wisdom; to another the word of knowledge by the same Spirit; to another the gifts of healing by the same Spirit; to another the working of miracles; to another prophecy; to another discerning of spirits."—*Apostle Paul.*

> "Upspringing from the buried Old
> I see the New."—*Whittier.*

The rapid diffusion of the divine principles involved in modern Spiritualism, startling to conservative Protestants, is unprecedented in the historic annals of any religious movement. An accredited church historian estimates that when Jesus suffered crucifixion, he had, aside from his apostles and a few angular, uneducated disciples, less than three hundred believers. It is certain that when the Nicean Council assembled early in the third century, there were hardly thirty thousand Christians on the face of the earth. Now, at the expiration of twenty years, numbering millions, Spiritualism has entered the domain of science, art, religion and the most acceptable literature of the country. Roman Catholicism, seeing Protestantism crumbling into sectarian fragments, fears only the rapid march of Spiritualism.

Waging a war of ideas, the new against the old—knowledge against creedal faith—science against sectarianism—freedom against dogmatic formulas, and the broadest liberality against an effete theology—denying an arrogant priesthood and a catering public press—reckless of popish bulls and judicial decisions—heedless of the long-established authorities of Church and State—facing fashion with the religious responsibility commonly ascribed to the popular worship—Spiritualism, heaven-born and angel-guarded, has moved forward to a prominent and enviable position, and now shouts in trumpet tones—

> "Sects must unmask to man's diviner needs,
> Kings from their mocking thrones must topple down;
> God! in thy name, Humanity yet bleeds,
> But Truth hath risen, and marcheth to renown."

Spiritualism, a divine eclecticism, is based upon present tangible facts, upon past historic testimonies and the soul's highest intuitions. In addition to a national organization, denominated, "*The American Association of Spiritualists*," Spiritualism has already several energetic State Conventions; thousands of local societies and circles, sustaining lecturers and media; a large number of flourishing Children's Progressive Lyceums; State Missionary organizations, sending out efficient workers thoroughly imbued with the elements of reform and the heavenly inspirations of the age; and not mentioning those known to fame, it has tens of thousands of media in private families, who purposely hide themselves from the wanton glare of public life. It publishes nine periodicals in the United States—weeklies and monthlies—and its publishing and yearly book-trade is rapidly increasing.

Notwithstanding the gathered lore and historic records of the ages, demonstrating the ministry of spirits, in connection with the phenomena of the present, the groping, unthinking multitudes reject Spiritualism—reject it precisely as did men, in high reputed places, the telegraphic discovery of Prof.

Morse. At a banquet in his honor, recently given in New York, Prof. Morse said:

"A brief narrative of certain events in the early history of the invention, when it was a suppliant for aid in the halls of Congress, will give the answer to many questions. I must not detain you with too much detail, but the contrast of then and now cannot fail at least to amuse you. As the narrative is very short, allow me to quote it:

'HOUSE OF REPRESENTATIVES,
'February 21, 1843.

'ELECTRO AND ANIMAL MAGNETISM.

'On motion of Mr. Kennedy, of Maryland, the committee took up the bill to authorize a series of experiments to be made in order to test the merits of Morse's electro magnetic telegraph. The bill appropriates $30,000, to be expended under the direction of the Postmaster General.

'Mr. Cave Johnson wished to have a word to say upon the bill. As the present Congress had done much to encourage science, he did not wish to see the science of mesmerism neglected and overlooked. He therefore proposed that one-half of the appropriation be given to Mr. Fisk (a gentleman at that time lecturing in Washington on mesmerism), to enable him to carry on experiments as well as Professor Morse.

'Mr. Houston thought that Millerism should also be included in the benefits of the appropriation.

'Mr. Stanley said he should have no objections to the appropriation for mesmeric experiments, provided the gentleman from Tennessee (Mr. Johnson) was the subject. (A laugh.)

'Mr. Cave Johnson said he should have no objections, provided the gentleman from North Carolina (Mr. Stanley) was the operator. (Great laughter.)

'Several gentlemen called for the reading of the amendment, and it was read by the clerk, as follows:

'Provided that one-half of the said sum shall be appropriated for trying mesmeric experiments under the direction of the Secretary of the Treasury.'

'Mr. Mason (of Ohio) rose to a question of order. He maintained that the amendment was not *bona fide*, and that such amendments were calculated to injure the character of the House. He appealed to the chair to rule the amendment out of order.

'The Chairman said it was not for him to judge of the motives of members in offering amendments, and he could not therefore undertake to pronounce the amendment *bona fide*. Objections might be raised to it on the ground that it was not sufficiently analogous in character to the bill under consideration; but, in the opinion of the chair, it would require a scientific analysis to determine how far the magnetism of mesmerism was analogous to that to be employed in telegraphs (laughter); he therefore ruled the amendment in order. On taking the vote the amendment was rejected—ayes 22, noes not counted. The bill was then laid aside to be reported.'

"The temper of the House," says Prof. Morse, "is easily inferred from this narrative. To those who thus ridiculed the telegraph it was a chimera, a visionary dream like mesmerism, rather to be a matter of merriment than seriously entertained. Men of character, men of erudition, men who, in ordinary affairs, had foresight, were wholly unable to forecast the future of the telegraph."

Sectarists and political partisans, at their Belshazzar feasts, make merry over modern Spiritualism in much the same style that those clergy and senators in Congress spit their venom, in the form of dead jokes and witticisms, upon mesmerism and Prof. Morse's telegraphic discoveries. These now stand upon the Congressional records, living and "swift witnesses" against the short-sightedness of their perpetrators. Starved, hunted, persecuted of one generation, to be banqueted and honored with hero-worship in the succeeding, is the world's method of expressing gratitude.

"To-day abhorred; to-morrow adored,
So round and round we run."

When this youth of twenty years—Spiritualism—puts on the full strength of sterling manhood—when it expands into the proportions of a moral giant—when its theories and prophecies have become established facts—when its visions have taken the forms of tangible realities—when, as in the Nazarene's time, the "Rulers of the Pharisees" openly confess the gospel of spirit communication, then will the weak, mimicking masses begin to "banquet" those whom to-day it denominates dreamers and enthusiasts.

As a general definition of Spiritualism, the following is submitted:

Its fundamental idea is, God, the infinite spirit-presence, immanent in all things.

Its fundamental thought is, joyous communion with spirits and angels, and the practical demonstrations of the same through the instrumentality of media.

Its fundamental purpose is, to rightly generate, educate and spiritualize all the races and nations of the earth.

Its worship is aspiration; its symbols, circles; its prayers, good deeds; its incense, gentle words; its sacrament, the wine of holy affections; its baptisms, the fervent pressure of warm hands and the sweet breathings of guardian angels; its mission, human redemption, and its temple, the universe.

Spiritualism, considered from its philosophical side, is rationalism, from its scientific side naturalism, and from its religious side the embodiment of love to God and man, a present inspiration and a heavenly ministry. In the year nineteen hundred it will be the religion of the enlightened world!

It underlies all genuine reform movements, physiological, temperamental, educational, parental, social, philanthropic and religious; and spanning all human interests with holy aim, it seeks to re-construct society upon the principles of a universal brotherhood—the strict equality of the sexes.

Desirous of greater knowledge touching the relations of spirit with matter, and of men with God and the intelligences of the surrounding world of spirits, Spiritualists study and reverently interrogate the laws and principles that govern the phenomena and occult forces of the universe; the histories of the past, and the experiences of the present, anxious to rightly solve those psychologic and spiritual problems of the ages—man's origin, capacity, duty and final destiny.

Interrelated with spirit and matter in their varied evolutions, and with the highest interests consciously connecting all worlds, Spiritualism is neither supernatural in philosophy, nor sectarian in tendency; but broad, catholic and progressive—the voiced truth of God through nature to the rational soul—a science, philosophy and religion.

Seen from this mount of vision, it is the "second coming of Christ;" not in person, but in principle—the divine principle—the indwelling God—the Christ-principles, of wisdom, love, truth. Since the physical coming in Bethlehem, the revolution of a religious cycle has been completed. The "New Jerusalem" is descending; the "hope of Israel," and the promised "kingdom of heaven," that must be preached to all nations.

The prophecy is now fulfilling. It is waking to higher life the inhabitants of India and China; shedding its kindling glories upon the hills of Hindostan; beaming in splendor along the vine-clad foot-hills of South America; crossing blue oceans, it is unfurling standards of progress in the peopled isles of the deep, and looking down in its might from the thrones of England, France and Russia.

Positive science consists in the discovery, co-ordination and practical application of natural laws. All phenomena subject to the natural laws are for the same reason susceptible of becoming the subjects of real science. When once admitted that all phenomena, including those of human existence, physical, mental, spiritual, are the subjects of unchanging natural laws, the circle of scientific research and religious aspiration is complete, whether geometrized by the inductive or deductive method of reasoning. Spiritualism, tolerant as divine, clasps and consecrates to human good the true and the beautiful in both science and religion. Seeing more to love in the Jove of the Greek than the grim Jehovah of the Jew—more to admire in the smiling Olympus than thundering Sinai—more truth in the teachings of the old Platonists than the creeds of "liberal" Christians, and more true worshipers, after the pattern of the meditative Nazarene, in the living Temple of Nature opening as the Pantheon of truth for all races, than in the rented pews of bigoted sectarists, it comes to the thinking millions of the nineteeth century, joyous with *immortality demonstrated*, jubilant with proofs of the future identity and recognition of the "loved gone before," and brilliant with precious prophecies of the ceaseless march of all conscious intelligences toward the higher and purer, even the *Infinite*.

"If a man die, shall he live again?" was the question of old. With the masses it has been the problem of all the centuries. The mourner, blinded by tears, propounds it to the preacher still. In sepulchral tones he breathes only the word "Hope," and that tremblingly. But Spiritualism, born of heaven and pouring its celestial tides of divine life into human souls till they become clear as the crystal waters of Paradise, answers the inquiry in the affirmative, and sustains it by tangible demonstrations and the testimony of living witnesses.

On the grave of Orthodoxy it is the green couch, arched with flowers, for the weary pilgrim. In the worshiping temples of "Liberal Christians," wherever an automatic Rationalism is brilliantly cold and clammy in heart, or a fierce iconoclasm destroys but builds not, it prophesies "change, speedy change!" and invites the bewildered devotees to listen to what "The Spirit saith unto the churches"—what the angel with the seven seals of destiny in hand, saith : "I would that thou wert cold or hot, but because thou art lukewarm, I will spue thee out of my mouth."

Spiritualism, the blossom now of all religions, the *soul* of the body which the past has developed, is adapted to the genius of the age and the entire human constitution. It addresses his reason and his aspirations. It enlarges the understanding, and gives vigorous activity to the intellect. Its benefits are not exclusively for the rich or poor, virtuous or vicious, happy or unhappy, civilized or savage, but for the race of humanity in all its variety of endowments, culture, character, needs and circumstances.

Authoritative, so far as it expresses *truth* to individual consciousness, it stimulates all instinctive aspirations, awakens the divinest emotions, enkindles the most magnificent aims, and, purifying the imagination, strives to perfect the whole being. Showing the naturalness of the converse with the spirit-world by sympathy, vision, trance, clairaudience, impression and inspiration, its tendencies are to elevate and spiritualize the affections. Bearing the olive-branch of peace, it comes with manifestations and inspirations from heavenly worlds, and strives to maintain the republic of God in every heart. It is not destructive alone, but constructive. It brings from the chrysalis of old forms, risen men and women "clothed in their right minds." It invites the children of earth to daily walk the mount of Beatitude, and commune with the transfigured who softly glide along the summer land-slopes of eternal progress. It extends the shining hands of angels who talk of love and sing of the high birth. It wipes the tears of sorrow from weeping eyes, breathes the sweet breath of tenderness into starving souls, and, sweeping away the lingering clouds of death, bids all God's dear humanity tread the pearl-paved paths traversed by the triumphal armies of heaven. Oh, how resfreshing, burdened with cares and crosses, to catch occasional breezes from Eden-lands, and songs of encouragement from immortalized hosts of reformers, martyrs, apostles, prophets! Lifting the glass of memory and reverting backward, it reveals the eternal purpose of good from seeming evil—of sorrow blossoming into joys, of thorns transformed into roses, and tears crystalizing into pearls of matchless brilliancy. Musical with the love-ministries of angels, it is a perpetual baptism from on high, a continual regeneration, a succession of higher births and endless privileges, a gentle dispensation of divine love guided by wisdom, the strength of the weary, the balm of healing for the sick, the consolation of the dying, the comfort of the mourner, and the sweetest answer to prayer! As a moral power in the world, its influence is exalting, its purpose uplifting, its work apostolic, its inspiration continuous, and, with improved implements suitable for all redemptive purposes, its great design is to lift humanity, through angel ministry, into higher physical, mental and spiritual conditions, preparatory to that future, progressive existence that stretches in increasing love-lines along the measureless eras of eternity.

Spiritualism, the desire of all nations, symbolized by "light," beautifully expresses the out-flowing love of God—

the divine principle of holiness—the indwelling Christ-principle of love and salvation—the Arabula—the comforter—the divine guest—the Savior of the world.

Incidentally, Spiritualism incites unflinching action on the plane of moral principle; renders one tenderly sympathetic; reasonable and rational, and, subjecting the passions to wisdom and virtue, it awakens holy, emotional affections, rooted in God. It induces fidelity to promise, and abounds with charity.

> "There is a grandeur in the Soul that dares
> Live out all the life God lit within;
> That battles with the passions hand to hand,
> And wears no mail and hides behind no shield!
> That plucks its joy in the shadow of Death's wing—
> That drains with one deep draught the wine of Life,
> And that with fearless foot and heaven-turned eyes,
> May stand upon a dizzy precipice,
> High o'er the abyss of ruin, and *not fall!*"

Facing the frowning Alps, the impassioned Napoleon said: "Officers! soldiers! the eyes of all Europe are upon you—conduct yourselves accordingly!"

Spiritualist! the eyes of the church, of the world, of the angels, are upon *thee;* conduct thyself accordingly! Quit thyself like a man. So guide thy bark, that though it flounder in tempestuous seas, it may right itself again for a safer voyage. Live to-day for to-morrow, for eternity. Be above the commission of an unworthy act. Tread not on the threshold of thy neighbor only with the purest and loftiest intentions. Filch no entrusted secrets from others. Indulge in no ignoble insinuations. Take no selfish advantage of another's weakness. Be candid and sincere. Affirm thyself. Celebrate thyself in goodness. Testify of thyself in integrity. Be a *practical* reformer. Seek no praise, nor fulsome flattery. Intrigue for no office. Fail of thy purpose rather than secure it by dishonorable policy. Partake of the bread of honest labor. Administer reproof in gentleness and love. Forgive as thou wouldst be forgiven. Kind to the poor, the unfortunate, the sick, the dying—live to lift up others, to brighten the chain of friendship, to educate mind and heart for a heaven on earth. Enflower the pathway of humanity with the beautiful in life; plant gardens of love in unhappy bosoms; welcome the angels to angelize the shades of our pilgrimage, and be welcomed into light, the sweet light, the music light of Immortality!

Contents.

General Divisions.

PREFATORY.

	Page.
1.—Greeting to Aaron Nite	3– 4
2.—The Horoscope	5– 10

I. SPIRIT OF THE PRESENT AGE.

Chap. I.—Spirit of the Age	13– 19
II.—Spiritual Ratios	20– 22

II. ANCIENT HISTORIC SPIRITUALISM.

Chap. III.—Indian	25– 30
IV.—Egyptian	31– 35
V.—Chinese	36– 40
VI.—Persian	41– 43
VII.—Hebraic	44– 52
VIII.—Grecian	53– 67
IX.—Roman	68– 74

III. CHRISTIAN SPIRITUALISM.

Chap. X.—The Foreshadowing	77– 79
XI.—Mythic	80– 88
XII.—Theologic	89– 93
XIII.—The Nazarene	94–110

IV. MEDIÆVAL SPIRITUALISM.

Chap. XIV.—Transitional	113–117
XV.—Apostolic	118–120
XVI.—Post-Apostolic	121–128
XVII.—Neo-Platonic	129–135
XVIII.—Churchianic	139–187

V. MODERN SPIRITUALISM.

Chap. XIX.—The Prelude 191–194
 XX.—Spirit Phenomena...197–202
 XXI.—Mediumship...203–206
 XXII.—Witnesses..207–215
 XXIII.—Clerical and Literary 216–246
 XXIV.—Poetic Testimony..247–253

VI. EXEGETICAL SPIRITUALISM.

Chap. XXV.—Existence of God...254–260
 XXVI.—The Divine Image..261–264
 XXVII.—Moral Status of Jesus 265–272
 XXVIII.—The Holy Spirit...273–276
 XXIX.—Baptism 277–279
 XXX.—Inspiration..280–284
 XXXI.—Beauty of Faith..285–288
 XXXII.—Repentance 289–292
 XXXIII.—Law of Judgment 293–296
 XXXIV.—Evil Spirits 297–308
 XXXV.—Hell..309–317
 XXXVI.—Heaven...318–324
 XXXVII.—Historic Immortality 325–329
 XXXVIII.—Resurrection 330–340
 XXXIX.—Prayer..341–344
 XL.—Freedom amd Function of Love............................345–352
 XLI.—Genius of Spiritualism 353–362

INDEX.

AND

ALPHABETICAL CLASSIFICATION.

	PAGE.		PAGE.		PAGE.
ABRAHAM—		BAPTISM—		BRUNO, GIORDANO—	
Brahminic	28	Spiritual	277	Testimony	157
AGRIPPA	149	Water baptism	278	BROWN, SIR THOMAS—	
ALEXANDRIA		Spiritualized water	279	Testimony	160
Eclectic School	129	BALLOU, ADIN—		BUDDHA	97
AMBROSE	127	Testimony	229	BUTLER, BISHOP—	
ANGELS—		BALLOU, DR. ELI—		Testimony	155
National superintendence	122, 125	Testimony	229	CARY, PHEBE—	
Incarnation	125	BABEL	48	Testimony	249
Reverence for	143	BACON, LORD—		CARDAMUS, JEROME	157
Higher than spirits	319	Testimony	160	CERENTHUS—	
Ministers of God	49	BACON, ROGER	143	Testimony	116
Names of	27, 39 49, 114	BEVEREDGE, BISHOP—		CHURCH—	
Congresses	192, 193	Testimony	155	Anglican	156
Guardians	115	BEETHOVEN	171	Private circles	156
ANGLES—		BEECHER, H. W.—		Divorced from reason	166
Symbolic	10	Testimony	217	For the age	18
ANTE-NATAL—		BEAUTY OF FAITH	285	Protestant	147
Perversities	348	BELL, ROBERT—		English	152
Of Jesus	79, 94	Testimony	241	Catholic fidelity	146
APPOLLINARIS	119	BHAGAVAT GITA	81	Uninspirational	152
APOLONUS—		Antiquity of	84, 85	"Slough of Despond"	153
Guarded by spirits	114	BIBLE—		Sectarian uses	15
APOSTOLIC FATHERS	118	Canonical voting	95	Decaying tendencies	17
APPARITIONS	72	Translators of	96	Greek	142
ARISTIDES—		Inner sense	159	CHURCH FATHERS—	
On healing	61	BLAKE, WILLIAM—		Immoral teachings	88
ATONEMENT	290	Testimony	166	Evil spirits	115
AUGUSTINE	127	BODIN	149	Spiritual gifts	121
Beautiful testimony	141	BŒHMEN, JACOB—		Miracles	125
AUBREY, JOHN—		Testimony	158	CHURCHIANIC	139
Exorcisms	163	BREAD OF LIFE	15	CHAPIN, REV. E. H.—	
BARNE, REV. DR. A.—		For spirits	43	Testimony	219
Testimony	237	BRAHMINS—		CHANNING, REV. W. E.—	
BAXTER, RICHARD—		Sacred Books	27	Testimony	224
Testimony	162	Deific ideas	27		
		BRONTE, CHARLOTTE—			
		Testimony	233-4		

INDEX.

CHINESE—
 Measure of time... 26
 Chronology of....... 26
 Bible of............... 36
CHINA—
 Mental structure... 36
 By Burlingame...... 38
CHRIST—
 Theologic 89
CHALDA in India 28
CHRISTIANITY—
 Primitive............. 105
CHRISHNA—
 Identical with
  Christ......81, 83, 85
 Incarnation.......... 82
 Education of......... 82
 Miracles 83
 Birth 83
 Descent to Hades... 83
 Antiquity of......... 84
 Worship of........... 85
CIRCLES—
 Spiritual.............. 205
 When needless...... 206
 Law of................ 191
 Pentecostal...........274
 Symbol of India... 8
 Waves of............. 22
 Ethereal............... 32
CIVILIZATION—
 Western movements
266
CICERO 148
CLARKE, ADAM—
 Testimony 181
CLAIRVOYANCE 151
 Highlanders..........164
 Animals................164
 Thomas Say 175
 John Murray........184
 In Asia................141
CLAIRVOYANTS—
 Mistakes of............336
CLERGYMEN—
 Refusing light......200
 Cowardice of.........243
 Inconsistency of....313
 Injustice of... 61
 Deceptions 81, 85
COLERIDGE—
 Testimony 248
CONIC SECTIONS........258
CONGRESSIONAL BIG-
 OTRY 355
CONSTANTINIAN ERA..139

CONFUSION OF TONGUES
 48
CONFUCIUS—
 Spiritual character 39
CRANMER................153
CREATION—
 Duality of............. 13
CREEDS—
 Athanasian 90
 Plan of salvation... 91
CROSS—
 Spiritual sign........140
CYPRIAN 125
DANNECKER.............159
DAVENPORT BROTHERS
209
DEBES—
 Angel healing.......162
DEMONS—
 Classical and scrip-
  tural 299
 Worshiped............. 34
 Good and bad........ 50
 Mission of............ 56
 Miracles...............153
DEMON—
 Of Socrates..........58–9
DEATH—
 Not redemptive...322–3
 Professed Chris-
  tians 328
 Birth 335
 Dissolves not spirit336
 When conscious....337
 Ascension 67
 Incarnation.......... 66
DELUGE 46
DIVINE IMAGE..........261
 Unity of...............264
DIVINATION............. 69
EDMUNDS, JUDGE—
 Testimony 207
EGYPT—
 Psychological char-
  acteristics.......... 9
 Wisdom of........... 31
 Colonized by India. 45
EGYPTIAN JURISPRU-
 DENCE.... 32
ELKIN, REV. H.—
 Testimony. ..231
EPIMENIDES—
 France................. 61
 Poetical............... 61
ESSENIANS—
 Mystic science 97

ESSENIANS—
 Physicians...........98–9
 Pythagoric........... 98
 Lineage............... 98
 Morality 100
 Social system........100
 Diffusive..............100
EVIL.......................297
 Relative........297, 306
 In spirit life.........298
 Uses of................305
EVIL SPIRITS—
 Ministrants...........298
EXORCISM—
 Law of..........128, 163
 Method of Fathers.125
 By Apollinaris......119
 By Jesus..............302
FAITH 297
 Defined................285
 Spiritual correla-
  tion..................286
 Practical..........286–7
 Funeral emblems...340
FISK, REV. DR.—
 Testimony 230
FLETCHER, REV.—
 Testimony 180
FOX, GEORGE 161
FREEDOM AND FUNC-
 TION OF LOVE.........345
FRIENDS OF GOD......145
GARRISON, WM. L.—
 Testimony 236
GASSNER, DR.—
 Prophecy..............168
GHOST—
 Translation of.......273
GENIUS OF SPIRITUAL-
 ISM 353
GNOSTICISM—
 Origin of.............. 81
 Inductional..........130
GNOSTICS—
 Concerning Jeho-
  veh.................. 28
 Spirits ascended ... 62
 Representatives.....130
GOWDY, REV. G. S.—
 Testimony............228
GOLDEN RULE........ ..104
GOD—
 Absolute and rela-
  tive..................254
 Inner soul............255
 Defined......... 256

INDEX. 367

God—
  Consciousness of....256
  Unprogressive 257
  Father and Mother.259
  Order of manifesta-
    tion..................259
  Voice of the pres-
    ent 15
  Pythagoric............102
  Testimony of an-
    cients................102
  Duality of............114
  Revealed by angels.122
Greely, Horace—
  Testimony 234
Greece—
  Psychological
    structure........... 53
  Oracular religion... 54
  Mythology and the-
    ology 62
Gregory................127
Gregory VII............143
Grossetete, Bishop..145
Guizot....................140
Gymnosophists—
  Wisdom of........... 98
Haunted Houses—
  Obsessed..............163
  Baxter's statement.163
  Homes of spirits ...142
Hades—
  Of the Greeks 66
Hall, Bishop............154
Hepworth, Rev. G. H.—
  Testimony 226
Hellenists..............267
  Knowledge of gods 56
Hell—
  Description of.309–312
  Biblical Exegesis ..313
  Spiritual view 316
Heaven—
  Names of.. 318
  Local 320
  Promise of...320, 338–9
  On earth..............321
  Conditional..........321
  Employments 322
Hebrewism—
  From India........... 28
  Origin of Scrip-
    tures................ 44
  Theology............. 45
  Civilization Egyp-
    tian.................. 54

Heathen—
  Scholarship of......103
Hermas...................124
Historic Immortal-
  ity 325
Hierombalus—
  Priest of Iao......... 28
History—
  Psychological........ 6
Hindoos—
  Originally not idol-
    ators................. 28
Howitt, Wm.—
  Testimony 238
Horoscope 5
Homer—
  Guardians of......... 55
  Iliad and Ramaya-
    na.................... 55
Hooker, Judicious—
  Testimony 154
Human Brotherhood—
 103
Hugo, Victor—
  Testimony 237–8
Hume—
  Seances 209
Ignatius..................119
Immortality—
  Basis of.........262, 264
  Platonian............. 57
  Socrates' view of.. 59
  Animals...............262
  Universal belief.....263
  Ancient testimony..326
  N. A. Indians........328
Imagination—
  Effects of.............157
  Founded in facts...266
Indians—
  Infant seership......164
  Abuse of...........186–7
India—
  Historic greatness.. 25
  Philosophy 27
  Mother of tribes... 29
Insanity—
  Obsessions............304
  Cure for..............305
Infidels—
  Honesty of 200
Infanticide 337
Inscriptions—
  Hindoo............... 84
  Golden ages.........198
Inspiration 280

Inspiration—
  Signs of............... 35
  Poetical............... 61
  Varied to condi-
    tions.................281
  General and special 282
  Perpetual 283
  Sacred everywhere 284
Irenæus..................121
Irving, Washington—
  Testimony 233
Island—
  Ancient, now ex-
    tinct................. 26
Israel—
  Mental structure... 44
Jamblichus..............133
Jesus—
  Moral status.. 265
  National culmina-
    tion..................265
  Real personage 266
  Brother man.........268
  Faithful 269
  Progress of..........269
  Exorcising 307
  Scholarship.......... 60
  Prophecy of......... 78
  Ante-natal 79, 94
  Associations 95
  In Egypt..........96, 97
  Essenian............97, 99
  Interior life..........101
  Doctrines derived 103
  Precepts of..........106
  Character of........107
  Mediumship 107
  Cotemporaries 113
Jehovah—
  Priestly origin...... 34
  Jeud.................. 46
  An angel...49, 115, 117
Jews—
  Inferior to Classics 46
Jerome 127
Joan d'Arc...............157
Josephine 169
John.......................268
  Scholarship of...... 81
Jones, Sir William.. 26
Justin, Martyr.......122
Judaism Paganized...139
Julian, the Apostate
 141
Judgment—
  Biblical..............294

JUDGMENT—
  Inward law....294, 295
  Spiritual..............296
KABBALA............... 41
KER, REV. W.—
  Testimony............232
KERNER..................305
KNOX, JOHN..............164
  Secret Spiritualist.165
LANGUAGE—
  Hebrew.............. 26
  Sanscrit 26, 38
  Shemitic............. 27
LAO-TSE................. 39
LATIMER 153
LEE, ANN...............182
LE CAN................. 36
LINCOLN, ABRAHAM...242
LIVERMORE, MRS. M. A.
  Testimony............250
LITERATURE—
  Homeric.............. 80
  Hindoo.............. 80
LOUIS XVI..............168
LONDON TIMES—
  Testimony............237
LONGFELLOW—
  Testimony..........249-9
LOWELL—
  Testimony............253
LOVE—
  Selfish 346
  Not lust 348
  Purely free..........350
  Progressive..........350
  Universal............352
LUTHER, MARTIN......145
  Roaring Devil 146
  Healing power......147
MAN AND WOMAN......261
MARRIAGE...............349
MAGNETIC TELEGRAPH
 355
MATHER, COTTON 165
MARIA ANTOINETTE...168
MADAME ELIZABETH...169
MAYO, REV. A. D.......227
MATTER AND SPIRIT...257
MAGIC STAFF........... 33
MAGICIANS—
  Persian 41
MAGIC 43
  Rivalship............ 50
  "Wisdom" 50
MANETHO—
  On Hebrews 45

MAGNETISM............. 99
MATERIALISM...........140
MEDIUMSHIP—
  Disorderly...........173
  Orderly 174
  Universal............203
  General phases......205
  Children 234
  Truth in failures...235
  Pythian.............. 70
METHODISTS 180
MELANCTHON,..........147
  Saved by spirits.....147
MIRACLES—
  Faith-principle 271
MILTON—
  Testimony............251
MORAL RESPONSIBILITY................298, 308
MOZART 170
  Beautiful death 171
MOSES—
  Seeing God.......... 51
  Egyptian medium.. 34
  Persian rites....... 45
MONTANUS..............124
MOURAVIEFF—
  Testimony............142
MURRAY, JOHN..........184
MUMMIES—
  Hebraic heads 45
MUSIC—
  Philosophy of....... 64
MYTHS—
  Brahminic 27
MYTHIC JESUS 80
NEO-PLATONIC............129
NITRE, AARON—
  Greeting to.......... 3
NICENE COUNCIL......353
OBSESSIONS—
  By curiosity.........160
  By influence.........301
  By neglect of reason................122
  Deaf and dumb 302
  Tutelary 126
  General belief in 303-4
  Supposed diseases..303
  Law of ingress 306
  Cures for............307
ORACLES—
  Tower of Belus 29
  Golden ship 35
  Inarticulate 60
  Delphian, etc 70

ORACLES—
  Christ and Christna 85
ORIGIN..................125
ORTHODOXY 16
PARKER, THEO.—
  Testimony............221
  Grave of.............220
PARACELSUS............156
  Law of healing......156
PASSIONS..................348
PASTOPHORA 8
PALESTINE—
  Psychological........ 9
  Jewish character... 9
PAST—
  Religious uses 14
  Representatives..... 15
  Virtues of.......... 21
PERSECUTIONS—
  Of church...142, 144-5
  Of Catholics 149
  Against Tasso.......151
  Of inquisition......157
  Of Puritans 165
  Of English 158
  For heresy 159
  Of Methodists 180
PETER D'APONO........144
PERSIA—
  Psychological
    structure........... 41
  Commerce............ 41
  Mythology 42
PENTATEUCH—
  Brahminical 45
PHARISEES 267
PHILO JUDÆUS—
  Cosmogony ...113, 114
PHŒNECIANS—
  History of.......... 28
  Commerce............ 28
  In America.......... 29
  Cosmogony........... 46
PICTURES—
  Of Grecian saints ..142
PLATO—
  Dialogue 57
PLANCHETTE 208
  Scientific American 214
PLINY—
  Oracular 72
PLOTINUS—
  Theology of 131
POST-APOSTOLIC........121
POTTER, JOHN—
  Building church....185

INDEX.

PORPHYRY 132
  Learning of 132
  Works burned 132
  Teachings 133
POETIC TESTIMONY 247
  Soul prophets 247
POETS—
  Interpreters of gods 57
POLYCARP
  Vision of............. 118
  Moral courage...... 119
PRAYER 341
  Virtue of........342–344
  Healing 342
  Hypocritical 343
  Receptive 134
PRE-EXISTENCE—
  Of Jesus 116, 271
  Of all................. 125
  Philo Judæus........ 114
PRESCOTT, ELDER J. S—
  Testimony 183
PROGRESS—
  Circles............... 191
  Scientific 199
  Relatively finite.... 258
  Causal 13
  Spiral 25
PROCLUS................. 135
  Divine demon 135
PROPHECY—
  By fasting 133
  Of inventions 144
  Of discoveries 148
  Laws of............... 144
  Of schisms 145
  Blazing star 153
  Spirit guided 158
  Of mutations 165
  Of death 169
  Of Shakers........... 183
  Queen of France ... 170
  Of books 193
  Of Miller 193
  Of A. J. Davis 194
  Of Nineveh........... 48
  Of "Rappings" ... 193
PSYCHOLOGY—
  Fantastic forms..... 116
  Sign of cross......... 140
  Ante-natal 87, 114
  Return of Jesus..... 108
  By Moses 51
PYTHAGORAS—
  Incarnation 86

PYTHAGORAS—
  Scientific travels... 86
  Identical with Jesus 86
  Characteristics 87
  Angelic child........ 87
  Mediumship 87
  Gymnosophic 98
RACES—
  Shemite............. 27
RASHEES 98
RAPHAEL 159
RELIGION—
  Consecutive 105
  Modified 105
  Psychological 106
  Biblically threefold 124
REID, REV. H. A.—
  Testimony. 230
REPENTANCE—
  Law of. 289, 290
  In future life 291
REFORMATION—
  Spiritual mistake .. 146
RESURRECTION 330
  Of the body 331
  What to be raised.. 333
  Body of Roger Williams.................. 332
  Jesus' body........... 334
  Of nature 335–6
  Idiots and infants.. 337
  Identity 338
  Progressive 339
ROME—
  Psychological structure........... 68
ROMULUS—
  Spiritual address... 71
SAY, THOMAS 175
SANCHONIATHAN—
  Pupilage 28
  Before Moses........ 46
SANSCRIT—
  On emigration...... 29
  Key of Buddhism .. 38
SARDONAPOLUS—
  Faith in the gods .. 48
SALLUST—
  Law of correspondence............... 68
SALVATION—
  Inner merit 92
  Universal 292
SADDUCEES 267

SANFORD, REV. J. P.—
  Testimony 230
SCHILLER—
  Inspirational 161
SCOTCH—
  Seership 164
  Infants 164
  Animals.............. 164
SCIENCE—
  Occult 34
SCANDINAVIA—
  Buddhistic descent 29
SEXUAL ABUSES 349
SECTS—
  Decline of........... 18
SHAKERS—
  Spirit gifts 183
  Social system........ 184
SHERLOCK, BISHOP—
  Gifts of spirit 155
SIMON MAGUS—
  Teachings............ 115
  Mediumship 116
SKINNER, REV. G. W.—
  Testimony........... 228
SMITH, GERRITT—
  Testimony........... 236
SOLAR SPECTRUM—
  Analogous with spirit 274
  Of fragrance, blood, etc 275
SOUL—
  Distinct from spirit 335
  Germinal forces.... 350
  Of things 125
SOCIAL SCIENCE—
  Prospective 352
SOCRATES—
  Testimony 58
  Death of............. 59
  Death by evil spirits.................. 122
SOZOMEN—
  Church historian... 140
SPIRIT—
  Infinite substance.. 20
  In man................ 20
  Creation developed 21
SPIRITS—
  In prison.......292, 317
  Classification 301
  Vanishing........... 334
  Author's band 6
  Egyptian gods...... 34
  Sustenance of. 108

24

INDEX.

SPIRITS—
Return of..32, 110, 212
Of Jesus' disciples.. 50
Host of 51
Abodes of 61
Bands of 204
SPIRIT OF THE AGE ... 13
SPIRIT WORLD—
Causation 192
Described ....
...319, 175, 176, 178
Ratios of life 322
Progressive 324
Degrees of 319
SPIRITUAL BODY—
A unit 336
Sphere of............336
Identity 338
SPIRITUAL DREAMS—
Of Caracalla......... 72
Attila's bow 72
For Sculpture 159
SPIRITUAL DELIVERANCE
From drowning.....180
From prison...141, 149
From fire.............134
Waldenses...........149
From robbers.......154
SPIRITUAL FORMS—
Opinion of Beveredge 155
Tully thro' Agrippa149
Appear as men...... 46
Seen by Tasso 151
Old Testament...... 52
SPIRITUAL FORCE (Moving bodies)—
Removing stones...142
Brahmins in air..... 30
Ancient media in air 35
By hair of head.... 48
Simon Magus in air 116
Clash of arms...... 66
Commotions of things..................151
Jamblichus lifted up 133
Guiding a ship......185
Spiritual dancing..182
SPIRITUAL GALLERIES—
For paintings........ 61
SPIRITUAL GIFTS—
Transmissible 107
Post-Apostolic 123
Christian proof of..155

SPIRITUAL GIFTS—
Decline of............128
Of 3d century......125
Of early Christians 127
SPIRITUAL HEALING—
Healing temples..... 61
Restoring life.......121
Vespasian's miracles................... 73
Wesley's laying on of hands,..........179
Secret by angels ...155
By St. Bernard ...143
Direct by angels...
...................154, 162
By Luther............147
By vision.............154
By sign of cross.....120
By Thomas Say.....176
Egyptian method... 34
Of the 5th century.127
SPIRITUAL INVENTIONS—
By Roger Bacon....144
SPIRITUAL INFLUX—
Conditions of 175
SPIRITUAL LEADERSHIP—
Of Joshua............149
House of worship..185
Constantine's cross 140
Jerome Cardanus..157
SPIRITUAL MUSIC—
By angel choirs.....119
For Mozart....170, 171
At death of Bœhmen 159
In the sky............225
Inspirational...61, 167
In rocks............... 33
By staves.............201
By bells..........63–65
For Beethoven......171
Producing trance...135
For Mahomet....... 65
Elegant sounds..... 35
SPIRITUAL PAINTING—
Spirits seen by artist 166
SPIRITUAL POETRY—
Inspiring Tasso.....150
Improvised, Schiller.....................161
Modern 247–253
SPIRITUAL RAPPINGS—
Sweetness of........198
March, 1848.........201
In 1849................211

SPIRITUAL RAPPINGS—
Through Bodin......150
In Wesley family...179
For warning.........163
SPIRITUAL SECTS...97, 98
SPIRITUAL SPEAKING—
From heaven........119
To Columbus.........148
Spirit of Tully......149
By ancient media... 35
SPIRITUAL SCULPTURE—
Impressed by dreams..............159
SPIRITUAL SEERSHIP—
By Faith..............155
Of Gregory VII.....143
Of Plotinus..........131
SPIRITUAL TABLE TIPPING—
Chinese............... 37
SPIRITUAL VISIONS—
By Louis XVI.......168
By Sylla............... 72
By Hermas..........124
By Ambrose........127
Mother of Hall.....154
SPIRITUAL WARRIORS—
Joan d'Arc 158
SPIRITUAL WRITING—
In 1849........211, 213
Alphabet 201
Spirit Pendulum ...201
SPIRITUALISM—
Universal 207
English believers208–9
Catholic idea 208
Success of...........210
In Peru...............210
Permanency.........215
Grandeur of........222
Aggressive 355
Future of.............356
Synopsis of..........357
Propagative 358
Religion of the world 359
Beauties of..........360
Heavenly influence 184
Perils of its forces.306
Virtues of............276
Effects of infidelity 167
Of the 5th century.127
SPIRITUALISTS—
Charge to 361
Illustrations....239, 240
Independent.........255

SPHERES—
  Electric 204
  Emanation 274
  Of plants, blood etc 275
STOICISM—
  Brotherly 103
STOWE, H. B.—
  Testimony 223
SWEDENBORGIANS—
  Estimate of Spirit-
    ualists 174
SYMPATHY—
  Between the two
    worlds 198
  Harmonial... 204
  Musical 64, 163
SYMBOLS—
  Of Trinity 8
  Of India 8
  Of Egypt 9
  Of Palestine 10
TAYLOR, BAYARD—
  "Mysterious inci-
    dents" 225
TASSO—
  Spiritual poems, etc 150
TEMPLES—
  Of Jove 29
  Of Serapis 32
  Of Memnon 33
  For manifestations. 34
TERTULLIAN. 123
  On exorcisms 122
  Character of 123

TENNYSON—
  Angel guardians.... 251
THACKERAY—
  Testimony 241
THEURGY—
  Conditions of 134
THERAPUTES—
  Of Egypt 99
TILLOTSON 155
TIME—
  Spiritual impres-
    sions 20
TITUS—
  Address to soldiers. 51
TIBERIUS—
  Warned by spirits.. 71
TOWNSEND, REV. DR...
    G.—
  Testimony 236
TOWNE, REV. E. C.—
  At Pierpont's fu-
    neral 241
TOWER OF BELUS—
  For oracles 29
TRANSFIGURATION—
  Of brain organs 348
TRANCE—
  Of Methodists 180
  Quaker, Say 176
  Early Christians.... 123
  Of boys 126
  "Sacred Sleep" 33
TRIANGLE—
  Horoscopic 9

TRINITY—
  Hindoo 81
TRITHEMIUS—
  Mental telegraph-
    ing 150
TUTTLE, REV. J. H.—
  Testimony 232
UNIVERSALISM—
  Crystalizing 186
VESPASIAN 72
VICE—
  Spiritual injury 69
VISHNU—
  Incarnation 81
WALTON 163
WALDENSES—
  Spirit guided 148
WESLEY, JOHN 178
WHITTIER—
  Testimony 232
WITCHCRAFT—
  Of New England 165
WOMEN—
  Spiritual.. 202
WORSHIP—
  Heavenly 19
  Angelic liturgy 119
YONGE—
  On the gods 49
ZEND AVESTA—
  Angelic origin 42
ZOROASTER—
  Spiritualistic 42

NAMES OF THE PRINCIPAL AUTHORS CONSULTED,

WITH A CLUE TO THEIR MORE PROMINENT WORKS.

Higgins, Godfrey...Anacalypsis.
Pythagoras, by...Jamblichus.
Behme, Jacob...Concerning the Soul.
Jenner, Thomas...What the Soul Is
Baxter, Richard...Nature of Spirits.
Priestly, Joseph...Matter and Spirit.
Hittell, John S...Pantheism.
Fitche, J. H...Phil. Confession.
Ennemoser, Joseph...Historic Psychology.
Glanvill, Joseph...Pre-existence of Souls.
Parker, Samuel, Bp...Platonic Philosophy.
Reynaud, Jean...Philosophy of Religion.
Cardano, Girolamo...De Im. Animorum
More, Henry...Philosph. Poems
Lavater, David...Human Mind.
Hume, David...Essays.
Eckermann, J. C...Immortality.
Strauss, D. F...The Future Life.
Parker, Theodore...Sermons, Lectures.
Bunsen, C. C. J...Egypt-History of Religion.
Rawlinson, George...Christ. vs. Heathenism.
Schoolcraft, H. R...Indian Tribes.
Mallet, P. H...Northern Antiquities.
Rosellini, J...Egyptian Monuments.
Champollion-Figeac...Ancient Egypt.
Wilkinson, Sir J. G...Manners and Customs, Egypt.
Klenker, J. F...Zend-Avesta.
Pope, J. A...Ardai Viraf.

Wilson's	Rig Veda
Haughton, Sir. J. G	Institutes of Manu.
Wilkins, Charles	Bhagavat Gita.
Roer, Dr. E	Brihad Aranyaka.
Colebrook, H. T	Is. Vara Chrishna.
Wilson, H. H	Vishnu Purana.
Ward, William	Mythology of India.
Muller, Max	Languages.
Gutzlaff, Chas	Buddhism in China.
Guignes, M. de	Confucius.
Collie, David	Chinese-Sse-shu.
Legge, James	Chinese Classics
Jortin, John	Dissertations.
Whewell, DD. Wm	Plato.
Fincke, C. E.	Olympiodorus.
Taylor, Thomas	Plotinus.
Bellows, J. N	Cicero's Immortality.
Warburton, William	Legation of Moses.
Tillard, John	Beliefs of the Ancients.
Butler, W. A	Lect. on Ancient Philosophy.
Dennis, J	Hist. of Theories and Morals.
Kenrick, J	Rom. Sep. Inscriptions.
Hampden, R. D	Fathers of Greek Philosophy.
Calmet, Augustus	Dissertations.
Priestly. Joseph	Knowledge of Ancient Hebrews.
Wette, W. M. L. de	Bib. Doctrines.
Chubb, Thomas	Dis. on Miracles.
Philo, Judæus	De Infernis.
Josephus, Flavius	Hist. of Jews.
Taylor, W. C	Hist. Mohammedanism.
Renan, J. Ernest	Life of Jesus.
Tholuck, F. A. G	Theos. Per. Pantheism.
Olshansen, H	Ant. of Immortality.
Friedlieb, Leipz	Sibylline Oracles.
Child, L. Maria	Prog. Rel. Ideas.
Lactantius, by J. B. Le. Brun	Immortality of the Soul.
Savonarola, Girolamo	Dialogues—Future Life.
Ambrose, I. U	The Last Things.
Clarke, Samuel	Lec. and Discussions.
Benson, Joseph	Scrip. Essay

NAMES OF THE PRINCIPAL AUTHORS CONSULTED. 375

Newton, Thomas	Diss. Int. State.
Dick, Thomas	Phil. Future State.
Taylor, Isaac	N. Hist. of Enthusiasm.
Alger, W. R.	Hist. of Future Life.
Stuart, Moses	Doub. Sense of Scripture.
Bush, George	Script. Psychology.
Ballou, Hosea	Atonement.
Dewey, Orville	Views of Death.
Davis, A. J.	Nature's Divine Revelations.
Campbell, Archibald	Death and Resurrection.
Robinson, W.	Invisible World.
Miles, J. Browning	Spirits in Prison.
Luther, Martin	Doc. Sermons.
Usher, James Abp	Prayers for the Dead.
Cudworth, Ralph	Intellectual System.
Locke, John	Immortality of the Soul.
Mosheim, John L. Von	Eccl. History.
Wigglesworth, Michael	Des. of Last Judgment.
Neander, Michael	Heaven and Hell.
Boston, Thomas	Fourfold State.
Swedenborg, Emanuel	Heaven and Hell.
Balfour, Walter	Int. State of the Dead.
Baxter, Richard	Saints Rest.
Chalmers, Thomas	New Heavens and Earth.
Newton, Andrews	Future Life of the Good.
Channing, W. E.	The Future Life.
Horne, Robert	Sermons.
Campbell, Geo.	Dissertations.
Brownson, O. A.	Pun. of Reprobates.
Tillotson, John Abp	Eternity of Hell Torments.
Whiston, Wm.	Sermons and Essays.
Law, William	Address to the Clergy.
Emmons, Nathanial	General Judgment.
Winchester, Elhanan	Universal Restoration.
Edwards, Jonathan	Theo. Controversy.
Foster, John	Letter on Future Punishment.
Maurice, J. F. D.	Theo. Essays.
Crowe, Mrs. C. (Stevens)	Night Side of Nature.
Owen, R. D.	Footfalls—Bound. of Another World.
Howitt, William	Hist. of the Supernatural.

Atkinson, J. C..Reason and Instinct.
Zschokke, Joh. D............................Med. on Death and Eternity.
Dubois, B...Doc. of N. Testament.
Denon, M..Hist. Anct. Religions.
Maurice, Rev. Mr...Ind. Antiquities.
Jones, Sir Wm..Asiat. Researches.

BANNER OF LIGHT
SPIRITUAL AND REFORM BOOKS,

ALSO

LIBERAL AND PHILOSOPHICAL WORKS,

ETC., ETC., ETC.,

PUBLISHED AND FOR SALE BY

WILLIAM WHITE & COMPANY,

158 WASHINGTON STREET, BOSTON, MASS.

Letter Postage required on books sent by mail to the following Territories: Colorada, Idaho, Montana, Nevada, Utah.

SPIRITUAL AND PROGRESSIVE WORKS.

Arabula; or, The Divine Guest. Containing a New Collection of Gospels. By A. J. Davis, author of several volumes on the Harmonial Philosophy. $1,50, postage 20 cents.

A Stellar Key to the Summer-Land. Illustrated with Diagrams and Engravings of Celestial Scenery. By A. J. Davis. $1,00, postage 16 cents.

A B C of Life. By A. B. Child, M. D. 25 cents.

Arcana of Nature; or, The History and Laws of Creation. By Hudson Tuttle. 1st Vol. $1,25, postage 18 cents.

Arcana of Nature; or, The Philosophy of Spiritual Existence and of the Spirit-World. By Hudson Tuttle. 2d Vol. $1,25, postage 18 cents.

Arnold, and Other Poems. By J. R. Orton. 75 cents, postage 12 cents.

A Letter to the Chestnut-street Congregational Church, Chelsea, Mass., in Reply to its Charges of having become a Reproach to the Cause of Truth, in consequence of a Change of Religious Belief. By John S. Adams. 20 cents, postage 2 cents.

Answers to Ever-Recurring Questions from the People. A Sequel to the "Penetralia." By A. J. Davis. $1,50, postage 20 cents.

Approaching Crisis. By A. J. Davis. Being a Review of Dr. Bushnell's Lectures on Supernaturalism. $1,00, postage 12 cents.

Apostles. By Ernest Renan, author of "The Life of Jesus," being part second of "The Origin of Christianity." Translated from the French. $1,75, postage free.

A Guide of Wisdom and Knowledge to the Spirit-World. 20 cents, postage 2 cents.

After Death; or, Disembodied Man. The Location, Topography and Scenery of the Supernal Universe; Its Inhabitants, their Customs, Habits, Modes of Existence; Sex after Death; Marriage in the World of Souls; The Sin against the Holy Ghost; Its fearful Penalties, etc. Being the Sequel to "Dealings with the Dead." $1,00, postage 8 cents.

SPIRITUAL AND REFORM BOOKS.

Brittan and Richmond's Discussion. 400 pages, octavo. This work contains twenty-four letters from each of the parties above-named, embodying a great number of facts and arguments, pro and con., designed to illustrate the spiritual phenomena of all ages, but especially the modern manifestations. $2,50, postage 23 cents.

Brittan's Review of Beecher's Report of Spiritualism; wherein the conclusions of the latter are carefully examined and tested by a comparison with his premises, with reason and with the facts. Cloth bound, 75 cents, postage 8 cents.

Brittan's Review of Rev. C. M. Butler, D. D. This is a brief refutation of the principal objections urged by the clergy against Spiritualism, and is, therefore, a good thing for general circulation. 60 cents, postage 4 cents.

Bible Dissolved; or, Divine Illumination. 20 cents, postage 2 cents.

Blossoms of Our Spring. A Poetic Work. By Hudson and Emma Tuttle. $1,00, postage 20 cents.

Bible Convention at Hartford. $1,00, postage 16 cents.

Be Thyself. A Discourse by Prof. William Denton. 10 cents, postage 2 cents.

Branches of Palm. By Mrs. J. S. Adams. A book for every Spiritualist and Friend of Truth and Progress. Gilt $2,00, plain $1,25, postage 16 cents.

Celestial Telegraph. $1,50, postage 20 cents.

Clairvoyant Family Physician. By Mrs. Tuttle. Muslin $1,00, postage 12 cents.

Courtney's Review of Dod's Involuntary Theory of the Spiritual Manifestations. A most triumphant refutation of the only material theory that deserves a respectful notice. 50 cents, postage 4 cents.

Christ and the People. By A. B. Child. $1,25, postage 16 cents.

Children's Progressive Lyceum. A New Manual, with full directions for the Organization and Management of Sunday Schools. By A. J. Davis. 80 cents, postage 8 cents, $63,00 per hundred. Abridged Edition, 45 cents, postage 4 cents, $15,00 per hundred.

Dissertation on the Evidences of Divine Inspiration. By Datus Kelley. 25 cents, postage 4 cents.

Day of Doom; or, A Poetical Description of the Great and Last Judgment, with other Poems. By Rev. Michael Wigglesworth, A. M. From the sixth edition of 1715. $1,00, postage 12 cents.

Dealings with the Dead: The Human Soul—its Migrations and its Transmigrations. By P. B. Randolph. 75 cents, postage 12 cents.

Death and the After-Life. Three Lectures. By A. J. Davis. Cloth 60 cents, postage 8 cents; paper 35 cents, postage 4 cents.

Extracts from Unpublished Volumes. No. 1. Divine Attributes and the Creations; The Sun; The Moon; Homer; Hesiod; Socrates. $1,00, postage 8 cents.

Errors Corrected: An Address by the Spirit of Stephen Treadwell. 10 cents, postage 2 cents.

Fugitive Wife. By Warren Chase. Paper 35 cents, postage 4 cents; cloth 50 cents, postage 8 cents.

Faith, Hope and Love. A Discourse by Cora L. V. Daniels. 20 cents, postage 2 cents.

Familiar Spirits, and Spiritual Manifestations: Being a Series of Articles by Dr. Enoch Pond, Professor in the Bangor Theological Seminary, with a Reply by A. Bingham, Esq., of Boston. 20 cents, postage 4 cents.

Further Communications from the World of Spirits, on subjects highly important to the Human Family. By Joshua, Solomon, and others. Paper 50 cents, postage 8 cents; cloth 75 cents, postage 12 cents.

Footfalls on the Boundary of Another World, with Narrative Illustrations. By Robert Dale Owen. $1,75, postage 25 cents.

SPIRITUAL AND REFORM BOOKS. 3

Gist of Spiritualism: Being a Course of Five Lectures delivered by Warren Chase in Washington. 50 cents, postage 4 cents.

Great Harmonia, in Five Volumes. By A. J. Davis. Vol. 1—The Physician; Vol. 2—The Teacher; Vol. 3—The Seer; Vol. 4—The Reformer; Vol. 5—The Thinker. $1,50 each, postage 20 cents each.

Gospel of Harmony. By Mrs. E. O. Goodrich Willard. 30 cents, postage 4 cents.

Harmonial Man; or, Thoughts for the Age. By A. J. Davis. Paper 50 cents, postage 6 cents; cloth 75 cents, postage 12 cents.

Harbinger of Health. By A. J. Davis. $1,50, postage 20 cents.

Healing of the Nations. By Charles Linton, with an Appendix by Nathaniel P. Tallmadge. Fourth edition. 537 pp. $3,00, postage 36 cents.

Healing of the Nations. Second Series. By Charles Linton. 363 pp. $2,50, postage 30 cents.

History and Philosophy of Evil. By A. J. Davis. Paper 50 cents, postage 6 cents; cloth $1,00, postage 20 cents,

History of the Supernatural. By William Howitt. Two Volumes. $3,00, postage 40 cents.

History of the Davenport Brothers. 25 cents, postage 2 cents.

Hymns of Progress: Being a Compilation, original and selected, of Hymns, Songs and Readings, designed to meet a part of the progressive wants of the age, in Church, Grove, Hall, Lyceum and School. By L. K. Coonley. 75 cents, postage 12 cents.

Hierophant; or, Gleanings from the Past. By G. C. Stewart. $1,00, postage 12 cents.

Improvisations from the Spirit. By J. J. Garth Wilkinson. 75 cents, postage 12 cents.

Immutable Decrees of God. A Discourse by Cora L. V. Daniels. 20 cents, postage 2 cents.

Intellectual Freedom; or, Emancipation from Mental and Physical Bondage. By Charles S. Woodruff, M. D., author of "Legalized Prostitution," etc. 50 cents, postage 4 cents.

Incidents in My Life. By D. D. Home, with an Introduction by Judge Edmonds. $1,25, postage 16 cents.

Judge Edmonds's Tracts. 25 cents, postage 2 cents.

Judge Edmonds's Letters. 30 cents, postage 2 cents.

Joan D'Arc. A Biography. Translated from the French, by Sarah M. Grimké. With Portrait. $1,00, postage 12 cents.

Jesus of Nazareth; or, A True History of the Man called Jesus Christ: Embracing his Parentage, his Youth, his Original Doctrines and Works, his career as a Public Teacher and Physician of the People, &c. New Edition. $1,75, postage 24 cents.

Koran: Commonly called the Alcoran of Mohammed. Translated into English immediately from the original Arabic, by George Sale, Gent. New Edition. 472 pp. $1,50, postage 30 cents.

Kingdom of Heaven; or, The Golden Age. By E. W. Loveland. 75 cents, postage 12 cents.

Lady Lillian, and Other Poems. By E. Young. $1,00, postage 12 cents.

Lectures on Geology, on the Past and Future of our Planet. By Prof. William Denton. $1,50, postage 20 cents.

Life-Line of the Lone One. By Warren Chase. New Edition. $1,00, postage 16 cents.

Lily Wreath of Spiritual Communications. Received chiefly through the mediumship of Mrs. J. S. Adams. $1,25, postage 16 cents.

Legalized Prostitution; or, Marriage as it Is, and Marriage as it Should Be, Philosophically Considered. By Charles S. Woodruff, M. D. $1,00, postage 16 cents.

SPIRITUAL AND REFORM BOOKS.

Life Incidents and Poetic Pictures. By J. H. Powell. $1,25, postage 12 cents.

Lyric of the Golden Age. By Thomas L. Harris. $2,00, postage 20 cents.

Light from the Spirit-World. By Rev. Charles Hammond. $1,25, postage 12 cents.

Lecture on Spiritualism. By Prof. Hare. 20 cents, postage 2 cents.

Morning Lectures. Twenty Discourses delivered before the Friends of Progress in New York. By A. J. Davis. $1,50, postage 20 cents.

Magic Staff: An Autobiography of Andrew Jackson Davis. $1,75, postage 20 cents.

Memoranda of Persons, Places and Events: Embracing Authentic Facts, Visions, Impressions, Discoveries in Magnetism, Clairvoyance, Spiritualism. Also Quotations from the Opposition. By A. J. Davis. 488 pp. $1,50, postage 20 cents.

Mediumship: Its Laws and Conditions. With brief instructions for the formation of spirit-circles. By J. H. Powell. New and Revised Edition. 25 cents, postage 2 cents.

Man and His Relations. By Prof. S. B. Brittan. One elegant volume, 8vo., tinted laid paper, extra vellum cloth, bev. boards, with steel engraved Portrait. $4,00 postage 40 cents.

Man of Faith. By Henry Lacroix. 25 cents, postage 2 cents.

Messages from the Superior State. Communicated by John Murray, through J. M. Spear. 75 cents, postage 12 cents.

Nature's Divine Revelations. The profoundest production of spirits through the mediative qualities of Andrew Jackson Davis. 786 pp. $3,50, postage 40 cents.

New Testament Miracles, and Modern Miracles. The comparative amount of evidence for each; the nature of both; testimony of a hundred witnesses. An Essay read before the Divinity School, Cambridge. By J. H. Fowler. 40 cents, postage 4 cents.

Night-Side of Nature; or, Ghosts and Ghost-Seers. By Catherine Crowe. $1,25, postage 20 cents.

Penetralia: Being Harmonial Answers to Important Questions. By A. J. Davis. $1,75, postage 24 cents.

Philosophy of Special Providences: A Vision. By A. J. Davis. 20 cents, postage 2 cents.

Philosophy of Spiritual Intercourse: Being an Explanation of Modern Mysteries. By A. J. Davis. Paper 60 cents, postage 6 cents; cloth $1,00, postage 12 cents.

Plain Guide to Spiritualism. A Spiritual Handbook. By Uriah Clark Full gilt $1,75; plain $1,25, postage 16 cents.

Poems from the Inner Life. By Lizzie Doten. Sixth Edition. Full gilt $2,00, postage free; plain $1,25, postage 16 cents.

Peep Into Sacred Tradition. By Rev. Orrin Abbott. 50 cents, postage 4 cents.

Philosophy of Mesmerism and Clairvoyance. Six Lectures, with instructions. 50 cents, postage 4 cents.

Philosophy of Electrical Psychology. In Twelve Lectures. By Dr. Dods. $1,25, postage 16 cents.

Principles of Social Science. By H. C. Carey. Three Volumes. $2,50 per volume, postage 30 cents per volume.

Present Age and Inner Life. By A. J. Davis. Being a Sequel to Spiritual Intercourse. This is an elegant book of near 300 pages, octavo, illustrated. $1,50, postage 24 cents.

Physical Man, Scientifically Considered. By Hudson Tuttle. $1,50, postage free.

SPIRITUAL AND REFORM BOOKS.

Principles of Nature, as discovered in the Development and Structure of the Universe. Given inspirationally, through Mrs. J. King. 327 pages. $2.00, postage 24 cents.

Physical Perfection: Showing how to acquire and retain bodily symmetry, health and vigor, secure long life, and avoid the infirmities and deformities of age. By D. H. Jacques. Beautifully illustrated. $1.75, postage 16 cents.

Poems. By Achsa W. Sprague. $1.50, postage 20 cents.

Poems by Cousin Benja, with Steel Portrait. $1.50, postage free.

Reichenbach's Dynamics of Magnetism, Electricity, Heat, Light, Crystallization and Chemism, in their relations to vital force. Complete from the German second edition; with the addition of a Preface and Critical Notes, by John Ashburner, M. D. Third American Edition. $1.50, postage 20 cents.

Road to Spiritualism. By Dr. R. T. Hallock. 50 cents, postage 4 cents.

Spiritual Harp: A collection of Vocal Music for the Choir, Congregation, and Social Circles. By J. M. Peebles and J. O. Barrett. E. H. Bailey, Musical Editor. $2.00, postage 20 cents.

Self-Contradictions of the Bible. 144 Propositions, without comment, embodying most of the palpable and striking self-contradictions of the Bible. 25 cents, postage 2 cents.

Spiritual Reasoner. By Dr. E. W. Lewis. $1.00, postage 16 cents.

Spirit Manifestations: Being an Exposition of Views respecting the Principal Facts, Causes and Peculiarities involved, together with interesting Phenomenal Statements and Communications. By Adin Ballou. Paper 50 cents, postage 6 cents; cloth 75 cents, postage 12 cents.

Soul Affinity. By A. B. Child, M. D. 20 cents, postage 2 cents.

Soul of Things; or, Psychometric Researches and Discoveries. By Prof. William and Elizabeth M. F. Denton. $1.50, postage 20 cents.

Spirit Minstrel. A Collection of Hymns and Music for the use of Spiritualists in their Circles and Public Meetings. Sixth Edition, enlarged. By J. B. Packard and J. S. Loveland. Boards 50 cents, paper 35 cents, postage free.

Spiritual Invention; or, Autobiographic Scenes and Sketches. 20 cents, postage 2 cents.

Spiritualism. Vol. 1. By Judge Edmonds and Dr. Dexter. $2.50, postage 32 cents.

Spiritualism. Vol. 2. By Judge Edmonds and Dr. Dexter. $2.50, postage 32 cents.

Seeress of Prevorst. By Justinus Kerner. A book of facts and revelations concerning the inner life of man, and a world of spirits. New Edition. 60 cents, postage 4 cents.

Six Lectures on Theology and Nature. By Emma Hardinge. Steel plate Portrait of Author. Cloth $1.00, postage 12 cents; paper 75 cents, postage 8 cents.

Scenes in the Spirit-Land; or, Life in the Spheres. By Hudson Tuttle. 75 cents, postage 4 cents.

Sabbath of Life. By R. D. Addington. $1.50, postage 20 cents.

Spirit Communion. By J. B. Ferguson. $1.50, postage 20 cents.

Shekinah. Vols. I, II and III. By S. B. Brittan. $2.50 per volume, postage 30 cents per volume.

Spiritual Teacher: Comprising a series of Twelve Lectures on the Nature and Development of the Spirit. Through R. P. Ambler. 75 cents, postage 12 cents.

Spirit Works, Real but not Miraculous. A Lecture, read at the City Hall, in Roxbury, Mass., by Allen Putnam. 30 cents, postage 6 cents.

Three Voices: A Poem in Three Parts. By Warren S. Barlow. $1.25, postage 16 cents.

Truth for the Times, gathered at a Spiritual Thought Concert. 15 cents, postage 2 cents.

SPIRITUAL AND REFORM BOOKS.

Theodore Parker in Spirit-Life: A Narration of Personal Experiences. Inspirationally given to Fred. L. H. Willis, M. D. 25 cents single copy; 50 copies $8.00; 100 copies $15.00.

The Worker and His Work: A Discourse. By Dr. R. T. Hallock. 15 cents, postage 2 cents.

Twelve Messages from the Spirit of John Quincy Adams, through Joseph D. Stiles, medium, to Josiah Brigham. Gilt $3.00, postage 32 cents; plain $2.00, postage 32 cents.

The Bible: Is it of Divine Origin, Authority and Influence? By S. J. Finney. Cloth 60 cents, postage 8 cents; paper 35 cents, postage 4 cents.

The Living Present and Dead Past; or, God made Manifest and Useful in Living Men and Women as he was in Jesus. By Henry C. Wright. New and Revised Edition. Cloth 75 cents, postage 8 cents; paper 50 cents, postage 4 cents.

Tracts on Spiritualism. Lectures delivered by A. J. Davis, at Dodworth's Hall, New York. "Defeats and Victories—Their Benefits and Penalties." "Death and the After Life." "Appetites and Passions—Their Origin, and How to Cast Them Out." 5 cents each.

The Harvester: For Gathering the Ripened Crops on every Homestead, leaving the Unripe to Mature. By a Merchant. $1.00, postage 12 cents.

Thomas Paine in Spirit-World. 75 cents, postage 8 cents.

Underhill on Mesmerism, with Criticisms on its Opposers. By Samuel Underhill, M. D., L.L. D., late Professor of Chemistry, etc. $1.38, postage 12 cents.

Voices from Spirit-Land. By Nathan Francis White, medium. 75 cents, postage 16 cents.

What is Spiritualism? An Address delivered by Thomas Gales Forster, in Music Hall, Boston, Mass., Sunday afternoon, Oct. 27, 1867. 25 cents single copy; 50 copies $8.00; 100 copies $15.00.

Wildfire Club. By Emma Hardinge. $1.25, postage 20 cents.

Whatever Is, is Right. By A. B. Child, M. D. $1.00, postage 16 cents.

Whatever Is, is Right Vindicated: Being a Letter to Cynthia Temple, briefly reviewing her Theory of "It isn't all Right." By A. P. McCombs. 10 cents, postage 2 cents.

Woman and Her Era. By Mrs. Eliza W. Farnham. Two Volumes, 12mo., nearly 800 pages. Plain muslin $3.00, postage free.

What's O'Clock? 25 cents, postage 2 cents.

ENGLISH WORKS.

Animal Magnetism. By Dr. Lee. $3.75, postage 16 cents.

From Matter to Spirit. $4.50, postage 24 cents.

"Primeval Man." The Origin, Declension and Restoration of the Race. Spiritual Revealings. $2.50, postage 20 cents.

Supramundane Facts in the Life of Rev. Jesse Babcock Ferguson, A. M., L.L. D., including Twenty Years' Observation of Preternatural Phenomena. Edited by T. L. Nichols, M. D. $1.75, postage free.

Spiritualism. By J. H. Powell. $1.00.

WORKS IN THE GERMAN LANGUAGE.

Arcana of Nature. Vol. I. By Hudson Tuttle. Paper. $2.50, postage 8 cents.

Magic Staff. By A. J. Davis. With Steel Portrait of Author. $3.50, postage 32 cents.

Reformer. By A. J. Davis. Illustrated. $2.75, postage 28 cents.

SPIRITUAL AND REFORM BOOKS.

MISCELLANEOUS AND REFORM WORKS.

Age of Reason: Being an Investigation of True and Fabulous Theology. Cloth. 50 cents, postage 8 cents.

Art of Conversation, with Directions for Self-Education. $1.50, postage 20 cents.

American Crisis; or, The Trial and Triumph of Democracy. By Warren Chase. 25 cents, postage 2 cents.

Apocryphal New Testament. $1.25, postage 16 cents.

A Child's Book of Religion, for Sunday Schools and Homes. Compiled by O. B. Frothingham. $1.00, postage 12 cents.

Astro-Theological Lectures. By Rev. Robert Taylor. $2.00, postage 24 cents.

Art of Amusing: A Collection of Graceful Arts, Merry Games, Odd Tricks, Curious Puzzles and New Charades; with suggestions for private theatricals, tableaux, all sorts of parlor and family amusements, etc. By Frank Bellew. $2.00, postage 20 cents.

A Trip to the Azores, or Western Islands. By M. Borges D. F. Henriques. $1.50.

Atlantis, and Other Poems. By Amanda T. Jones. $1.25, postage free.

Adventures of Elder Tubb. 65 cents, postage 8 cents.

Biography of Satan; or, A Historical Exposition of the Devil and his Fiery Dominions, disclosing the Oriental origin of the belief in a Devil and future endless punishment. By K. Graves. 35 cents. postage free.

Book of Religions: Comprising the Views, Creeds, Sentiments or Opinions of all the principal Religious Sects in the World. By John Hayward. $1.75, postage free.

Book of Notions. By John Hayward. 75 cents, postage 12 cents.

Companion Poets for the People. Illustrated. Vol. 1—Household Poems, by H. W. Longfellow; Vol. 2—Songs for all Seasons, by Alfred Tennyson; Vol. 3—National Lyrics, by John G. Whittier; Vol. 4—Lyrics of Life, by Robert Browning. Each volume complete in itself. 50 cents each, postage 2 cents each.

Complete Works of Thomas Paine, Secretary to the Committee of Foreign Affairs in the American Revolution. Three Volumes. Consisting of his Political, Theological and Miscellaneous Writings. To which is added a brief sketch of his Life. $6.00, postage 90 cents.

Combe's Constitution of Man. Twenty-Eighth American Edition. One Volume, 16mo. $1.75, postage 16 cents.

Dissertations and Discussions. By John Stuart Mill. Three Volumes, 12mo., cloth. $6.75.

Diegesis: Being a Discovery of the Origin, Evidences and Early History of Christianity, never yet before or elsewhere so fully and faithfully set forth. By Rev. Robert Taylor. $2.00, postage 24 cents.

Dawn. A New Work of Exciting Interest. $2.00, postage 24 cents.

Eliza Woodson; or, The Early Days of One of the World's Workers. A Story of American Life. $1.50, postage free.

Effect of Slavery on the American People. By Theodore Parker. 10 cents, postage 2 cents.

Empire of the Mother over the Character and Destiny of the Race. By Henry C. Wright. Paper 50 cents, postage 4 cents; cloth 75 cents, postage 12 cents.

Errors of the Bible, Demonstrated by the Truths of Nature; or, Man's only Infallible Rule of Faith and Practice. By Henry C. Wright. Cloth 60 cents, postage 8 cents.

Examination of the Philosophy of Sir William Hamilton. By John Stuart Mill. Two Volumes, 12mo., cloth. $2.25 per volume, postage 20 cents each.

SPIRITUAL AND REFORM BOOKS.

First Years in Europe. By G. H. Calvert, author of "Scenes and Thoughts in Europe," "The Gentleman," &c. $1,75, postage 20 cents.

Gazelle. A Tale of the Great Rebellion. The Great Lyrical Epic of the War. By Emma Tuttle. $1,25, postage free.

Habits of Good Society. A Hand-Book of Etiquette for Ladies and Gentlemen. Large 12mo., elegant cloth binding. $1,75, postage 20 cents.

Is it I? A Book for Every Man. A companion to "Why Not?" By Prof. H. R. Storer, M. D. Paper 50 cents, postage 4 cents; cloth $1,00, postage 8 cents.

Is there a Devil? An Argument *pro* and *con.*, with an Inquiry into the origin of Evil, and a Review of the popular notion of Hell and Heaven, or the state of the dead. By John Baldwin. 20 cents, postage 2 cents.

Infidel's Text-Book: Being the substance of Thirteen Lectures on the Bible. By Robert Cooper, author of "The Holy Scriptures Analyzed," &c. First American republished from the London Edition. $1,00, postage 12 cents.

Life of Jesus. By Ernest Renan. Translated from the original French, by Charles Edwin Wilbour. $1,75, postage free.

Life of Thomas Paine, author of "Common Sense," "Rights of Man," "Age of Reason," &c., with Critical and Explanatory Observations of his Writings. By G Vale. $1,00, postage 18 cents.

Little Brother, and Other Stories. By Fitz Hugh Ludlow. $1,50, postage 20 cents.

Marriage and Parentage; or, The Reproductive Element in Man, as a Means to his Elevation and Happiness. By Henry C. Wright. $1,25, postage 20 cents; extra gilt $2,00, postage 20 cents.

"Ministry of Angels" Realized. A Letter to the Edwards Congregational Church, Boston. By A. E. Newton. 20 cents, postage 2 cents.

Mistake of Christendom; or, Jesus and his Gospel, before Paul and Christianity. By George Stearns. $1,50, postage 16 cents.

Martyria; or, Andersonville Prison. By Lieut.-Col. A. C. Hamlin, late Medical Inspector in the Army. Illustrated with maps and cuts. $2,00, postage 20 cents.

Natty, a Spirit; His Portrait and Life. By Allen Putnam. Cloth 75 cents, postage 8 cents; paper 50 cents, postage 4 cents.

New Republic. By L. U. Reavis. 50 cents, postage 4 cents.

Optimism, the Lesson of Ages. By Benjamin Blood. 75 cents, postage 12 cents.

On the Border. By Edmund Kirk. $1,75, postage 20 cents.

Poems of David Gray, with Memoirs of his Life. Elegant cloth binding, tinted laid paper, with gilt top. $1,50. postage 20 cents.

Poems and Ballads. By A. P. McCoombs. Cloth bound. $1,00, postage 12 cents.

Peterson's New Cook Book: Containing Eight Hundred and Fifty-Eight New and Original Receipts for Cooking and Preparing Food. $1,50, postage free.

Political Works of Thomas Paine, to which is prefixed a brief sketch of the Author's Life. Bound in calf. $4,00, postage 60 cents.

Philosophical Dictionary of Voltaire. Fifth American Edition. Two Volumes in one, sheep, containing 876 large octavo pages, with two elegant steel engravings. $5,00, postage 65 cents.

Positive Philosophy of Auguste Comte. By John Stuart Mill. $1,25, postage 16 cents.

Plato's Works. Translated by the Rev. H. Cary and others. Six Volumes, with general Index. $2,25 per volume, postage 20 cents per volume.

Poems of Jean Ingelow. Elegantly bound, tinted paper, gilt top, &c. $1,75, postage 20 cents.

Queen Mab, with Notes. By Percy B. Shelley. 75 cents, postage 12 cents.

www.ingramcontent.com/pod-product-compliance
Lightning Source LLC
Chambersburg PA
CBHW030347230426
43664CB00007BB/556